Lineages of the Feminine

For Marc and Sophie

Lineages of the Feminine

An outline of a history of women

Emmanuel Todd

With the collaboration of Baptiste Touverey

Translated by Andrew Brown

polity

First published in French as *Où en sont-elles ? Une esquisse de l'histoire des femmes* © Éditions du Seuil, 2022.
Figures 4.1, 4.2, 17.1 and maps 12.1, 12.2, 12.3, 12.4, 12.5 by Légendes Cartographie.

This English edition © Polity Press, 2023

Polity Press
65 Bridge Street
Cambridge CB2 1UR, UK

Polity Press
111 River Street
Hoboken, NJ 07030, USA

ISBN-13: 978-1-5095-5508-6 – hardback

A catalogue record for this book is available from the British Library.

Library of Congress Control Number: 2022948023

Typeset in 10.5pt on 12pt Sabon
by Cheshire Typesetting Ltd, Cuddington, Cheshire
Printed and bound in Great Britain by CPI Group (UK) Ltd, Croydon

The publisher has used its best endeavours to ensure that the URLs for external websites referred to in this book are correct and active at the time of going to press. However, the publisher has no responsibility for the websites and can make no guarantee that a site will remain live or that the content is or will remain appropriate.

Every effort has been made to trace all copyright holders, but if any have been overlooked the publisher will be pleased to include any necessary credits in any subsequent reprint or edition.

For further information on Polity, visit our website: politybooks.com

CONTENTS

Figures, maps and tables   vii
Preface   x

Introduction: The future is now   1

Part I. The contribution of historical anthropology

 1 Patriarchy, gender and intersectionality   25

 2 Degendering anthropology   48

 3 The tools of historical anthropology   61

 4 In search of the original family   71

 5 The confinement of women: history comes to a halt   88

 6 A detour by way of Australia   107

 7 The sexual division of labour   118

 8 Christianity, Protestantism and women   132

Part II. Our revolution

 9 Liberation: 1950–2020   143

10 Men resist but the collective collapses   165

11 Gender: a petty-bourgeois ideology   178

12 Women and authority   196

13 The mystery of Sweden   213

14 Homophobia: a male business   223

15 Women, between Christianity and bisexuality 237

16 The social construction of transgender 248

17 Economic globalization and the deviation of
   anthropological trajectories 268

Conclusion: Has humanity come of age? 279

Notes 285
Index 309

FIGURES, MAPS AND TABLES

Figures

0.1. Female homicide rate in Europe and Japan 4
1.1. The terms 'patriarchy' (English) and *'patriarcat'* (French)
since 1950 26
1.2. Evolution of the frequency of use of the terms 'gender' and
'genre' 37
1.3. Evolution of the frequency of use of the terms 'gendered'
and *'genré'* 38
1.4. Evolution of the frequency of use of the English term
'vibrant' 39
1.5. Evolution of the frequency of use of the terms
'déconstruction' and 'deconstruction' 40
1.6. Evolution of the frequency of use of the English term
'intersectionality' and the French term *'intersectionnalité'* 43
4.1. The conservatism of peripheral zones: typical diagram 75
4.2. The stages of patrilineality in history 77
9.1. Female suicide rate 159
9.2. Male suicide rate 160
9.3. Sex ratio of suicide rates 161
9.4. Gap between male and female life expectancies 162
11.1. The sex ratio of French theses 187
11.2. 'Gendered' sociology theses by sex since 1985 189
11.3. 'Sexed' sociology theses by sex since 1985 190
14.1. Evolution of the frequency of use of the terms
'homosexuel' ('homosexual') and *'pilule'* ('pill') 225
14.2. Evolution of the frequency of use of the term 'gay' in
English and in French 226
14.3. Evolution of the frequency of use of the terms *'lesbienne'*
and 'lesbian' 227

14.4. Evolution of the frequency of use of the terms *'bisexuel'*
and 'bisexual'   228
16.1. Evolution of the frequency of use of the terms
'transgender' and *'transgenre'*   261
17.1. East/West dialectic of relocation/denunciation–reaffirmation   275

Maps

1.1. Kinship systems before urbanization   28
1.2. The sex ratio in 2020   31
1.3. The status of women today   33
1.4. The rate of patrilineality by state   35
4.1. Residence of spouses: after their marriage   81
4.2. Residence of spouses: neolocality and ambilocality   82
4.3. The nuclear or independent family   84
4.4. Exogamy and endogamy   85
5.1. The original hubs of agriculture   89
5.2. The role of women in agriculture   94
5.3. Residence of spouses in intensive agriculture   96
5.4. Residence of spouses in extensive agriculture   97
5.5. Residence of spouses among pastoralists   99
6.1. Polygyny among hunter-gatherers according to Binford
(in %)   110
6.2. Differences in age at marriage among hunter-gatherers
according to Binford   111
6.3. Australian Aborigines in 1788   113
6.4. Kinship systems in Australia and New Guinea   114
6.5. Residence of spouses in Australia and New Guinea   114
6.6. Kinship systems in the Americas   116
6.7. Residence of spouses on the American continent   117
7.1. Role of men and women in hunting   120
7.2. Role of men and women in gathering   121
7.3. Role of men and women in fishing   122
7.4. Role of men and women in boat building   123
7.5. Role of men and women in pottery   124
7.6. Role of men and women in house building   125
7.7. Role of men and women in leather work   126
12.1. The three major Swedish regions   203
12.2. Nuclear and stem hubs in Sweden around 1900   203
12.3. Agricultural employees in Sweden in 1960   204
12.4. Workers in Sweden in 1970   204
12.5. Social democracy in Sweden in 1968   205
12.6. Exceptional women   207

14.1. Homophobia   234
16.1. Berdaches in North America   252
17.1. Proportion of industrial jobs in 2019   271

Tables

0.1. Top stratum of organizations in the West by sex   2
1.1. Voting in the 2020 US presidential election   45
4.1. Survival of original traits   87
8.1. The religiosity of men and women in the mid-1990s   135
11.1. Class structure according to sex: a first approach   183
11.2. Class structure according to sex: ideal-types   183
11.3. Theses: proportion of women by university discipline and
      year of thesis defence   186
11.4. INED researchers by sex and age around 2019   192
12.1. Parent–child communication around the age of 15   209
12.2. Proportion of women in the judiciary, 2016   211
16.1. The berdache phenomenon in North America   254
C.1. The National Front vote by sex   281

PREFACE

If I had been asked to choose a concept to characterize the West, fifty years ago, when I was starting to do research, I would probably have given the banal answer: *progress*. The physical and human sciences were advancing, the standard of living was rising, decolonization was coming to an end, the emancipation of women was beginning. My first book, *La chute finale* (*The Final Fall*), published in 1976,[1] expressed this optimism since it predicted (within ten, twenty or thirty years – it actually took fifteen) the collapse of the Soviet system, undermined not simply by the inefficiency of its economy but above all by educational progress and the change in mentality which accompanied it. The declining birth rate in the Muslim world today shows that the latter is modernizing despite the persistence of many despotic regimes within it. But even those who are not enamoured of Islam have to accept that, at present, the birth rate is 2.0 children per woman in Turkey, 2.1 in Iran, 2.4 in Morocco and 2.2 in Saudi Arabia. Even if people cannot vote there, or only in an imperfect way, the term 'progress' therefore still applies to the Muslim world. And to India, too, where the birth rate is 2.2. With a birth rate of 1.3, China is already, in spite of its low standard of living, demonstrating problems of post-modernity which make the use of the term 'progress' problematic for it. The inability to produce enough children to sustain the population prevents us from using the word 'progress', a word which presupposes the certainty of a future. The number of children per woman is 1.9 in France, 1.7 in Sweden, 1.7 in the United States, 1.65 in the United Kingdom, 1.5 in Germany, 1.5 in Russia, 1.4 in Japan, 1.2 in Taiwan and 0.9 in Korea. The two countries which dominate the production of the semiconductors necessary for current technologies are, demographically, in the process of disappearing.

If I were asked this same question today – what concept can be seen as characteristic of the West? – I would answer without hesitation: *false consciousness*. And I would place the status and emancipation of women at the centre of our false consciousness.

We have allowed our industries and our working classes to be destroyed. Inequalities are soaring and our standard of living is falling. In the United States, mortality is increasing, life expectancy is decreasing. The power of finance capital and the individualistic pulverization of ideologies have transformed our political systems. The new educational stratification into college-educated and the rest has led to the emergence of separate mental worlds for the former, on the one hand, and for the semi-citizens who leave education after high school, on the other. If economic and cultural transformations have allowed the *institutions* of democracy to subsist, they have destroyed the *mores* that animated these institutions. The populace no longer decides. Communities no longer act. A democracy is as much a group as it is a sum of citizens with the right to vote; and without the ability of individuals to feel that they are also a group, democracy dies.

Western democracies have mutated, they have become, without realizing it, 'something else', different from democracies. A Western nation without a *false consciousness* should define itself (without value judgement) as a *liberal oligarchy* rather than as a *liberal democracy*. But we still believe, for the most part, that we are liberal and democratic, and continue to affirm our superiority and the universality of our values.

The Trump phenomenon, Brexit, the reversal of the *Roe v. Wade* decision on the freedom of abortion and the paralysis of the French political system, however, all suggest that our political false consciousness is crumbling. It is recognized that a crisis of democracy is looming. The successive waves of Covid have, for their part, shaken our false economic consciousness by exposing our industrial deficiencies. The economic sanctions imposed on Russia following the invasion of Ukraine, added to Covid, and against a background of industrial underproduction, have tipped the West into inflation. This should bring us to a better economic consciousness of ourselves. But the heart of our false consciousness lies elsewhere, and it is intact. It lurks in the anthropological foundations of our societies: family life with, at the very heart of this core factor, the status of women and the dramatic changes it has seen in the last seventy years. I am here defining Western women as our primary false consciousness (this 'our' includes women). We do not realize that the status of Western women has always been specific, and that the emancipatory revolution that we have been experiencing for seventy years is taking us a little further away from the rest of the world (75% of the total) whose anthropological trajectory has been different for millennia, since this trajectory has granted women a lower status, a historical movement associated with the rise (as the anthropological term puts it) of the patrilineal principle. We therefore underestimate the socio-historical importance of the emancipation of these Western women whose status had not been all that low. It is in this anthropological unconscious that the cause of our paralysis, of our inability to think and act collectively, must be sought. Putting women at the centre of recent history is the purpose of this book.

I have spent most of my life as a researcher constructing a model that links the diversity of family structures with the diversity of the historical development of nations. In my *Lineages of Modernity*, I presented the condensed results of this lifetime of research.[2] But it dawned on me during the #MeToo crisis that I had remained blind to one of the most important elements of the story. While I had placed the family structure at the heart of the economic, political, educational and religious life of peoples, I had not been able to fully grasp the specific role of women in the great transformation that we are experiencing. *Lineages of the Feminine: An Outline of the History of Women* describes this feminine side of history, over the same long-term period (*longue durée*), ever since the emergence on earth of the species *Homo sapiens*. We can only understand the extent of the feminist transformation of Western societies if we situate it correctly in history, i.e. as a direct transformation of the system of mores of the first society of *Homo sapiens*, one that was certainly patridominated but in which women enjoyed a relatively high status. Never in the past have English (and therefore American), French or Swedish societies resembled today's patrilineal Russia, China, India, Arab-Persian world or Africa, within which the status of women is the outcome of ten thousand years of history, ever since the emergence of agriculture. Only a historical study over the long term, and taking in the surface of our entire planet, will allow us to escape our false family and sexual consciousness.

Our family lifestyle is obvious to us, it defines our existence as human beings – it is *indisputable*, in exactly the same way that our relationship with women (I am a man, but I would write 'our relationship with men' if I were a woman) defines our existence (and I would write the same if I were gay or transgender). All this is even truer and even more significant for us because our system of mores is undergoing a radical change, indeed a revolution. It is even more immediate, close to the centre of our life and, as such, even more difficult to perceive correctly. We cannot see what defines us the most. We have to gaze into a mirror to see what we look like. We need to look at the rest of the world to understand who we are, to escape narcissism. This is an intellectual but also a psychological exercise. It is characteristic that for the first time in my life, in *Lineages of the Feminine*, certainly the most scholarly of all my books (and this is rather to be expected after half a century of research), I have allowed a few ironic remarks about myself and my own family of origin to find their way into the text. Historical anthropology, however, allows us to move away from ourselves by contemplating the whole of human history in all its geographical scope and by dealing with the French, the English, the

Americans and the Swedes in the same way that classical anthropology dealt with the peoples of colonized countries, each one being provided with a system of mores – an irrational, non-universal and indisputable system – invented to give meaning to life. Analytical philosophy helps us to admit that these values are in no way 'provable'. This difficult exercise of distancing ourselves from ourselves requires an enormous work of empirical accumulation of objective data. But it allows us to escape from our false consciousness. Basically, long-term history (the *longue durée*) and planetary exhaustiveness make it possible for us to develop a kind of psychoanalysis of our own society.

The feminist revolution is a great thing (I'm an ordinary Westerner on the point) but we are not yet able to see how much the emancipation of women has radically altered the whole of our social life. Because we always see women as minors, as victims, we do not place them, for better or for worse (i.e., like men) at the centre of our history: they are the protagonists, for example, in the rejection of racism and homophobia, but they are also the unconscious protagonists of our neoliberalism, our deindustrialization and our inability to act collectively. Substantial and no doubt crucial inequalities persist between men and women. I will study them at length in this book; but we must accept that the inequalities between human beings in general, in the West, have increased at the same rate as the decrease in inequalities between men and women. I will therefore present in this book a critical analysis of antagonistic feminism, because this, despite its goodwill (it is essential to fight against inequalities between the sexes, against sexual harassment and femicide), basically erases women, and abolishes them as protagonists in history.

Antagonistic feminism distorts present history and past history, and cannot serve as a guide for future history. It is typically a phenomenon of false consciousness. It prevents us from seeing in particular that the advances have been of such a kind that the category 'woman' is now becoming divided, more and more clearly, according to a class criterion (where class is increasingly defined by education).

In fact, women themselves, *independently of* men, are increasingly defining the class structure of society. I have long believed that the petty bourgeoisie, rather than the proletariat, is the potentially destabilizing class for any society: in France in 1789, in Russia in 1917, in Germany in 1933.[3] I had always rightly thought of this petty bourgeoisie as male. In this book, I identify a whole new female petty bourgeoisie, the source and site of the flourishing of antagonistic feminism. The working classes themselves cannot be defined today as matridominated, but in the United States, as in France, the dissidence of the working classes reveals a specific role for women, in the anti-tax movement of the Yellow Vests as much as in the pro-life, anti-abortion movement. However feminized it may be, history remains diverse!

I would like to end this preface with an apology for some of the shortcomings of this book. In particular, you will not find in it a nuanced description of current neo-feminist debates, which would in fact deserve a whole book to themselves: I content myself with an evocation of the antagonistic atmosphere which now characterizes the ideological debate on the relationship between men and women. I am simplifying here, admittedly. But everything in this book is a simplification. To describe the history of women (and therefore of men) by defining five fields – the familial, the religious, the educational, the economic and the political – in order to grasp their interaction, throughout the whole of history and across all of the earth's inhabited spaces, presupposes a simplification, to say the least. It is a rich but sketchy story that I offer and I know from experience that such an exercise can give the impression that the author is arrogant and unfair. I can well understand that perceiving the current world as being organized into two blocs, one patrilineal and the other feminist (quite simply!), may create a feeling of annoyance in the reader. But one has to simplify in order to understand. This is even one of the basic principles of the scientific method. Here lies the ultimate flaw: I admit that putting forward the concept of simplicity to understand the relationships between women and men brings us dangerously close to an absolute oxymoron. I want to point out, however, by way of conclusion, and to defend myself against the accusation of arrogance, that the starting point of this book was, after all, admitting to an error, to the existence of a blind spot in *Lineages of Modernity*: the fact that I had not understood the importance of women in the upheaval of Western societies in the last seventy years. This book is an atonement.

2022

INTRODUCTION:
THE FUTURE IS NOW

It's clear that we're living through an anthropological revolution. Here at the beginning of the third millennium we have seen the emergence of the #MeToo phenomenon, which was given global momentum by the Harvey Weinstein affair in 2017. In its (less elegant) French version, this wave turned into #BalanceTonPorc.[1] On the walls of Paris and provincial towns, denunciations of what has been called 'femicide' have flourished. The paradox of this renewed protest against men, a protest violent in its expression and evocative of a structural antagonism between the two sexes, lies in the fact that it began just as the women's liberation movement seemed on the point of achieving its goals.

I am not claiming here, which would be absurd, that all the goals of feminism have been achieved. Far from it. Women have certainly gained massive access to the labour market, but significant wage inequalities remain. Their share in low-paid temporary work is still much higher than that of men in Western countries, where a thin layer of male domination in the highest positions remains. The top stratum of organizations is still mostly occupied by men: in politics, in public administration and in the private capitalist sector of the economy (see table 0.1). But the general trend is clear: these remnants of domination are being rapidly eroded.

The positive acceleration between 2000 and 2022 is impressive. The number of women entering elected assemblies in the West is increasing according to a curve that seems exponential. Since the publication of the French edition of this book, the war in Ukraine has mobilized a multitude of women actors at the highest level in the Western camp: prime ministers in Scandinavia, directors of intelligence and Ukrainian affairs in the United States, heads of foreign affairs in the United Kingdom and Germany, a minister of defence in France, a top representative of the European Union in Brussels. I am only mentioning a few examples but here, for the first time in history, is a global conflict in which men are

1

Table 0.1 Top stratum of organizations in the West by sex

2019	France	United Kingdom	United States	Sweden
MANAGEMENT				
Proportion of female managers	34.5%	36.8%	40.7%	40.3%
PART-TIME WORK				
Proportion of women in part-time jobs (W)	20.4%	36.2%	16.8 %	17.3%
Proportion of men in part-time jobs (M)	6.9%	11.8%	8.3%	10.5%
Women's disadvantage: (W)/(M)	3	3	2	1.7

not the only actors. Some sectors, such as private capitalism, are resisting the rise of women, but others, such as the cultural sector, are already showing a predominance of women right up to the top of the ladder. I will explain this resistance by new contradictions in the female condition, brought about by emancipation, rather than by a masculinist plot.

It is true that in the United States, the Supreme Court's reversal of the *Roe v. Wade* ruling on freedom of abortion, which has made it possible for some American states (a minority among states and an even smaller minority in terms of population) to actually ban abortion, is a serious attack on women's right to control their own bodies. But I'll give a detailed, and tragic, interpretation of the pro-life regression, in terms of social class and increased mortality rather than of a lowering of the status of women in the states concerned. This book will suggest that we give the north–south divide or the influence of the religious right too much importance in our interpretation of the conflict over abortion. Educational stratification and class conflict have emerged as the dominant factors in the recent aggravation of the conflict.

The fact remains that in the global context of an accelerating emancipation of women, the antagonistic feminist revival, a new revolutionary upsurge at heart, is not logical, even if it must be admitted that the development of concrete history is rarely 'logical'. To better understand the problem, let's go back to the history of a previous revolution, the rise of socialism, and to the opening of the revisionist quarrel that divided Marxists from the end of the nineteenth century. Eduard Bernstein (1850–1932) pointed out, from an empirical perspective, that concrete capitalism, far from leading to an ever-increasing concentration of capital and impoverishment of the workers, as predicted by Marx, in fact led to an increase in the standard of living of the masses, allowed for a diversity of sizes of enterprises and did not prevent the development of the middle classes. Any revolutionary catastrophism could only lead, in his view, to the justification of an anti-popular and anti-democratic reaction. Current data on the status of women in the West should have led to the emergence of a feminist (and female) Bernstein, but what we are seeing is the rise of a new antagonism, a logical cousin to Leninist-style catastrophism, yet without any 1914–18 war-like catastrophe to explain the new antagonistic trajectory of feminism.

At the deepest and hardest level of antagonistic feminism, we find the theme of femicide, which evokes an evil essence of man in his relationship to woman, just as Leninism considered the bourgeois as inherently evil, incapable of accepting the humanity of the proletarian.

The existence of a specifically masculine violence is indubitable; it can be verified in all its atrocity back to the mists of time. But confusing random fluctuations with long-term trends often entails serious errors in analysis. Caution was needed, for example, when analysing the observed increase of 21% in the number of women killed in France by their part-ners or ex-partners between 2018 and 2019 (146 as against 121); this increase was not statistically significant. The number of women killed by their partners had been 148 in 2006, when measurements began, and 179 in 2007.[2] An article by Cédric Mathiot in *Libération*, written before the publication of the figures for 2019, quite rightly noted a drop in cases of femicide from 2006 onwards, and a stagnation over the last six years.[3] In 2020, 90 femicides were committed.

Let's extend the area studied to Europe and Japan. While it's true that at least half of the women who are victims of homicide are killed by their partners, a global demographic approach indicates that the trend, since 1985, has shown a significant decline (see figure 0.1).

Without wishing to minimize the horror of these crimes, there is evi-dently a considerable gap between the rising emotions stirred by this subject and the reality of its downward trend, and we must also note the ideological indifference that prevails vis-à-vis other much more socially and sexually significant phenomena of violence. Suicide rates, for example, are heavily biased against men: 1,985 female suicides and 6,450 male suicides took place in France in 2016. Yes, men are more violent (to deny this would be absurd), but most of their violence is turned against themselves, or against other men: let's look at wartime fatalities, which are very masculine in nature despite indiscriminate bombardments, or, in peacetime, all of the homicide data, where men account for 65% of victims in France. Still, while the emotion associated with femicide doesn't seem linked to any aggravation of the problem, it's a social fact that we can't ignore.

Let's take a step back. We must first consider the statistically more massive phenomena that demonstrate the considerable historical pro-gress in the situation of women. Of course, we can still measure, as I said, differences in salary, in the distribution of part-time jobs, and the remnants of male dominance in the economic and public spheres, but the empowerment of women through employment remains the fundamental

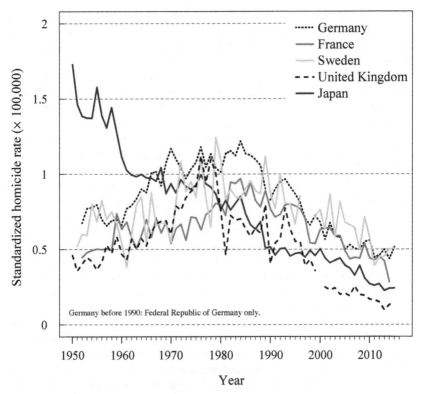

Figure 0.1 Female homicide rate in Europe and Japan

phenomenon. The most recent years have seen a decisive ascent of women in the political field in France, the Anglo-American world and Scandinavia, if we stick to the three main hubs of women's liberation in the developed world.

Above all, for the first time in human history, the educational relation between the sexes has shifted. All upsurges in literacy have involved men taking the lead. In Sweden, women caught up with and overtook men especially early, in the eighteenth century, but they had to catch up with them first, of course. Even Sweden, a country where feminism has become a matter of identity, and one that is proud of its leading position in women's liberation in terms of all the parameters of the *Gender Gap Global Report*, did not escape an initial male predominance. The only groups and societies where women have become literate faster than men are Black American, Brazilian, Colombian and West Indian, but this is because the family and the status of fathers had been deliberately destroyed in those cultures by slavers, who were White and male. I will

4

return to the particular family situation of Black women in the New World later in this book.

What are we now seeing in advanced countries? Women more often go into higher education, for shorter or longer courses, than men. The latest figures from the OECD tell us that in 2019, among 25–34-year-olds, in France, 52% of women had followed shorter or longer higher education courses, as compared to 44% of men.[4] In the United Kingdom, it was 55% of women as compared to 49% of men. In the United States, the figures were 55% women and 46% men. In Italy, there was a significant gap, but at lower levels: there were 34% higher educated women aged 25–34, and 22% men. In Japan, the difference was small but at high levels: 64% women and 59% men. Russia has a surprise up its sleeve for us: the figures were 69% for women and 55% for men, although it's not clear whether the definition of higher education there is directly comparable to that of the countries of the OECD. Germany deviates from the common law: the rates here were fairly low and not very different by sex: 34% for women, 32% for men. China, finally, had 18% men and 18% women with a higher education. But this is a less advanced country – one in which, as we will see, the status of women has been brought down particularly low by a very lengthy history, one that we will study. Although we can still find, everywhere, an over-representation of men in the very upper levels of higher education, something I'll discuss later in this book, we still have to admit that the uneducated masses are predominantly male today.

An individual's education largely prefigures his or her profession and these figures tell the crystal ball gazer that the basic problem of feminist demands will be solved in the not-too-distant future. This, at least, is what a feminist and female Bernstein would have deduced from present trends. It's true that all types of higher education are not professionally equal and that there are important areas of male resistance, particularly in France when it comes to the sciences and the highly selective *grandes écoles*. I will discuss the meaning of these resistances, their causes and their consequences, in due course. But we're now in a situation where friendly and reformist thinking should dominate, rather than any perception of men as murderers. Such progress could not have happened without the existence of fathers (and mothers, of course) concerned about the education of their daughters, or rather of fathers who did not view the education of their daughters as any less important than the education of their sons. Yet it is among these educated women that an antagonistic conception of the relations between the sexes is often born and flourishes.

The struggles of third-wave feminism may not be the crux of the problem. The success among the French middle classes of a book like Mona Chollet's *In Defence of Witches* points, rather, to a sense of disorientation.[5] How can so many modern women these days identify with the almost 40,000 women massacred by male fury in the sixteenth and seventeenth centuries? There's something strange here, a kind of glitch in the process of women's liberation.

Whenever there's a paradox, contradiction, or some strangeness in a social phenomenon, my instinct as a researcher is alerted – as here. It's often by observing anomalies and making them part and parcel of one's reflection in order to explain them that science progresses. The glitch we observe in women's liberation must be explained.

Hitherto, I have to admit, the question of feminism hadn't interested me. One might say that there's another – minor – paradox here, since my job is the analysis of family systems, the heart of which is precisely the relationship between men and women. Historical anthropology analyses the evolution of this relationship. It focuses on patrilineality (the priority given to the male lineage) and to matrilineality (the rarer equivalent for the female lineage – a phenomenon that does not imply any feminine power), patrilocality and matrilocality (when a young couple settle near the family of the husband or wife), etc. I have devoted several books to these problems, tracing in particular the long history of the family systems of Eurasia and resulting in the definition of an original form of the family of *Homo sapiens*.[6] I have identified correspondences between forms of the peasant family and the type of ideology emerging as a result of literacy and secularization.[7] I showed that some aspects of long-term cultural dynamism could be explained by a relatively high status afforded to women.[8] I ended up diagnosing, in my last book, the disappearance of the regional family systems that for centuries had organized the territory of France.[9] I had clearly perceived how women had overtaken men educationally in the majority of European countries, but I had not made much of this transformation, even though it is highly surprising – after all, in *Sapiens*, it abolished between 100,000 and 300,000 years of patridominance, to use the concept defined by American anthropology.

But precisely, women's liberation was well underway, and I didn't see what I could have contributed to something that wasn't actually a problem, even if I realized that a certain Western narcissism prevented us from perceiving the cause of the resistance that Chinese, Indian, Arabic, Afghan and even, to some extent, Japanese, German and Russian patrilineal societies evinced towards our 'values'. The emergence of internal contradictions, of a glitch in women's liberation in the Western world in the strict sense – mainly the Anglo-American world, France and Scandinavia – has made me change my mind. Historical anthropology can help us to understand our present and future difficulties.

The singularity of the original human couple

To understand the importance of the transformation we are undergoing, we will first need to track the status of women over the last 5,000 or even 10,000 years – ever since the appearance of writing or even agriculture. In this way, we will realize that the feminist evolution of the Western world has, since the 1920s, reversed a major historical trend towards giving women a lower status, a trend observable in its fullness at the centre of the Eurasian mass, just as in Africa and New Guinea. But because the most recent feminism includes a new antagonism between the sexes, we will need, if we are really to understand the importance of these issues for the future of the species, to go even further back in the history of the human couple.

As an animal species, human beings differ from their cousins, the chimpanzees, by their ability to establish long-term ties between the two sexes. Monogamy – a tempered monogamy – has statistically dominated the species *Homo sapiens* since its appearance between 200,000 and 300,000 years ago, in Africa.

This observation of a stable original link between men and women – of which I am here giving merely an outline, reserving a more detailed analysis for chapter 4 – is relatively recent. It was not the conclusion reached by late nineteenth-century anthropologists. The founding fathers of the discipline believed in a primitive sexual communism. These serious-minded middle-class men projected onto the savages of the past a sexual life contrary to their own morality – one that was a vaguely pornographic fantasy.

The breaking of the pansexualist consensus was brought about by a Swedish-speaking Finn, a teacher at the London School of Economics, Edward Westermarck (1862–1939), who, ethnographic data in hand, with his *The History of Human Marriage* (1891) destroyed the idea of a primitive sexual promiscuity.[10] We owe him not only one of the first formulations of the most commonly accepted thesis today, but also the explanation which remains the most convincing and the most fundamental: the idea of an original nuclear family that was naturally selected for its effectiveness in bringing up the young. This is the conclusion to which I myself came, after many other people and by a different methodological path, in *L'Origine des systèmes familiaux* (*The Origin of Family Systems*).

The nuclear family is simply a father and a mother with their children, and it is the basic unit of hunter-gatherer societies, heirs to the lifestyle of the original *Homo sapiens*, the surviving representatives of which we have been able to study, mainly in America and Australia but also in southern and eastern Africa and in Southeast Asia. Here, the single household is part of a group that contains several other nuclear families, most often related via the men or the women (it doesn't matter which). The young couple, once married, form their own household, but they can co-reside for a time with a related couple. They are quite capable of taking in the elderly, widowers and this or that isolated individual. Such a couple is most often monogamous, but marriage, in its customary sense, with two wives is possible (polygyny) though it doesn't involve more than 15% of cases – as is the case, as I am increasingly convinced, with the marriage of one woman with several men (polyandry). An examination of the Shoshone groups of the inner basin of the Rocky Mountains, which I will examine in detail, strongly points to an originally natural polyandry.

Westermarck sees the nuclear family as following a Darwinian-type evolutionary logic. Why do human beings, unlike chimpanzees, not live in sexual promiscuity where everyone sleeps with everyone else, even if a few dominant males breed more efficiently than others? What advantage is there for the species in a lasting bond between a man and a woman? The key is the long time it takes to bring up a human child. A baby comes out of its mother's womb in a remarkable state of unpreparedness (primary altriciality) and it takes about fifteen years to rear it (secondary altriciality). Collaboration between the two members of the couple is a condition for the possibility of this exceptional upbringing. Unlike the male chimpanzee, who doesn't know whose father he really is, a man can invest time in his children's upbringing because the bond he maintains with their mother allows him to be their father.

Two invariants characterize the original human family. First of all, there is an undeniable 'political' male predominance in the local group. It's not an overwhelming predominance, far from it, but it does exist. Then there is a sexual division of labour. When we examine all the examples of hunter-gatherer societies that have been ethnographed, we find that men hunt and women gather. In some cases, the men also gather, but the women almost never hunt. The men and women who these days are disturbed and exasperated by the way men monopolize hunting invariably cite the case of the few Agta women (the Negrito group in the Philippines) who sometimes go hunting. These marginal cases do not represent much statistically, when you look closely at the data. I will come back to this.

The original human family type is efficient and flexible, and it has ensured the success of the species. We therefore find at its heart a stable, economic and emotional bond between a man and a woman, a bond that can usually tolerate divorce, abortion, infanticide and a certain degree of polygyny or polyandry. The element of inequality in favour of the males that we have found cannot counterbalance the weight of collaboration and solidarity within the couple, necessary for survival in the environment specific to the hunter-gatherers.

Research versus ideology

The now dominant ideology of the Western world, third-wave feminism, has distorted the history of relations between the sexes. By no means all historical propositions put forward by this kind of feminism are absurd. Its vision of witchcraft trials as a war on women by power-hungry men seems to me essentially correct. It is verifiable that the berdache phenomenon – in which American Indian men are able to take on a woman's economic and sexual status – is primordial to human beings, as I will explain later. But third-wave feminism, with its central but uncertain concepts of 'gender' and 'patriarchy', flattens history out, mixing together all levels of masculine dominance without really understanding them.

The first part of this book is a reorganization of the concepts of the relations between men and women, and of the history of these relations. I have worked in a methodical way, producing a critical examination of the feminist contribution to my two basic disciplines, anthropology and history. My conclusion is simple: feminism has had a dynamic effect on history and has positively destroyed anthropology with the force of dynamite.

I then retrace the history of the status of women through the history of family systems, to place the West narrowly understood – the Anglo-American world, France and Scandinavia – within the general evolution of humanity. We will then be able to perceive Westerners as the direct legitimate descendants of the hunter-gatherers; here, women's status has never been lowered as it has in Japan, Germany and Russia (level 1), in China (level 2) and in northern India and the Arab world (level 3). The low status of women in Africa and New Guinea can be considered as intermediate between levels 2 and 3. To describe this historical pattern, I will be making a new cartographic use of the *Ethnographic Atlas* of George Peter Murdock (1897–1985) and the tabulations of Lewis R. Binford (1931–2011) on hunter-gatherers, two databases digitized and posted on the D-PLACE platform by a team from the Max-Planck Institute for the Science of Human History at Jena.[11] The reader will of course find our mapping of data from the *Atlas* throughout the pages of this book, but also in a form that he or she will be able to explore in detail thanks to an app that we have put online.[12]

Defining a starting point for the history of the human family is crucial. After ten years of reflection, I have chosen the North American model of the original family instead of the Australian Aboriginal model dear to Durkheim, Freud and, more recently, Alain Testart. I will explain why. The problem is not so much the economic and emotional association between men and women which is common to both models, but the status of women, a status that was high among the Indians of northwest

9

America but very low among the Australian Aborigines, where it combined very significant age differences between spouses and a very large degree of polygyny.

Without this in-depth historical examination, we could not understand the violence of the shift we are experiencing, or feel how disorienting it is in magnitude, even before we ponder the viability of the anthropological system which is now trying to establish itself. In seventy years, conceptions more than 100,000 years old have been reversed. But not everywhere on the planet. The patrilineal world, which after all still includes three-quarters of humanity, is still resisting.

This book integrates religion with historical anthropology. The co-evolution of religion and family seems more and more obvious to me. To understand the differences between the current feminisms of the three hubs of the West as narrowly understood, I will need to examine how Christianity, followed by the Protestant Reformation, changed family forms and impacted on the status of women in those areas. The United States, the United Kingdom and Scandinavia are, more than France, the dominant hubs of Western feminism. They are also countries with a Protestant tradition. This fact, so obvious and simple, nonetheless confronts us with a paradox. Protestantism, born in Germany in the sixteenth century, was clearly patricentric and included an anti-feminist nuance to which English-speaking and Scandinavian societies had to adapt, accepting it, attenuating it, rejecting it or all three at the same time.

I must here recognize an intellectual debt to feminism, a movement that is absolutely right to denounce history as a discipline which has long been blind to women. I have in mind not just the history of events, made up of wars and conquests, all the endless agitation of men in arms, but also the study of all the elements of social life. In my *Lineages of Modernity*,[13] I failed to fully realize the historical importance of Protestant patricentrism, and thus the problems that this patricentrism raised for the Anglo-American world. The present book can be considered as a rebalanced, even feminized, complement to my previous outline of human history. The experience is fascinating for me as I have realized how much my self-identity as an anthropologist involved paying attention to women, while my self-identity as a historian was masculine in the most banal sense of the word.

The power of women today

Now that we have set out the history of the *longue durée*, it will be quite easy to talk about our present. The glitch in women's liberation will make sense.

What we are experiencing is the accentuation of a rather high status given to women and not the overthrow of some fantasized 'patriarchal' order. I will show how liberation is possible and even natural once the technological conditions of safe and secure contraception and economic abundance have been met. The absence of a serious and solid male rejection of this liberation will have been a fundamental element in anthropological evolution. I would be tempted to say that the destruction of patriarchy was easy for us because it had never really existed. Some fathers (and mothers) were afraid that their daughters might fall pregnant, yes; men and women specialized economically to survive in harsh conditions, yes. But were men truly convinced of their intrinsic superiority? No. I'm fully aware that I'm exaggerating things a bit here to make my argument clear. Still, no blood-stained revolutionary confrontation was necessary to pave the way for the educational and sexual liberation of women, simply because men – husbands, fathers and brothers – benefited from it too. The first two waves of feminism certainly gave many men the opportunity to utter many silly generalities about women, but the speed of the shift shows how tenuous and fragile masculine dominance was, and how it hardly counted given the extent of the habits of cooperation between men and women. This collaboration is the basis of human nature when it has not been reoriented by the patrilineal principle.

I will here summarize the three feminist stages or waves, of which the first two aimed to correct the imbalance of the initial masculine domination, moderate in nature (as I have said), in bilateral kinship systems.

First, the citizenship phase. From the end of the nineteenth century, suffragettes claimed the right to vote. This first demand was satisfied in the United States in 1920 by universal female suffrage. In England, it took two steps: in 1918, suffrage was granted to women, but at a later age than that of men, 30 rather than 21; from 1928, the minimum age changed to 21 for both sexes. In Sweden, experiments in women's suffrage in municipal elections took place from the eighteenth century, with various extensions, going backward and forward until the end of the nineteenth century; women's suffrage in national elections to the Riksdag was granted in 1919, in time for the 1921 elections. France was particularly conservative here since French women had to wait until 1944 to have the right to vote. The French delay cannot, however, be interpreted as the expression of direct anti-feminism. The 'radical social-ist' (meaning extremely moderate) Left feared that the link between women and Catholicism might give the Right undue influence. If we accept that the Church had established a special bond with women, and, in a way, represented them, we can understand that anxiety. The connection between women and Christianity will be discussed in chapter 8.

The interplay between gaining the right to vote and the savage masculine violence of the two world wars is obvious. However, the entry of women into political life did not lead to any immediate upheavals.

The second phase was that of 'sexuality'. It opened with Pincus's invention of the contraceptive pill in the United States; this was put on the market on the American side of the Atlantic in 1961, and authorized by the Neuwirth law in France in 1967. When we worry today about the status of women, we don't always fully measure the risks of the sexual act for them before the pill. This opened up to them – but also to their masculine partners – the possibility of a different sexual life.[14] Parents no longer needed to fear for their daughters. This second phase culminated with the legalization of abortion. Here, Britain led, with the passing of the Abortion Act in 1967 (note that 'Britain' is the appropriate term, as Northern Ireland was left out). The United States followed, on a national scale, in 1973, with the Supreme Court passing its decision in *Roe v. Wade*. France quickly followed the Anglo-American world, with the Veil Law of 1975.[15] The main progress was made between the 1960s and the 1980s. This period was also that of a massive entry of women into the labour market.

In the mid-1980s, a third phase began, and the debate shifted from women's liberation to a questioning of what men and women actually are – a re-examination of their essential natures. Biological? Social? Antagonistic? Stable? Negotiable? This was the period of 'identity', which came to France later than in the United States.

Judith Butler's *Gender Trouble* should be seen as an important ideological step because it took to its most absurd consequences the use of the concept of gender, which became popular during feminism's phase II. This text, as fundamental as it was obscure, appeared in 1990.[16] It was an academic text inspired by French Theory (Derrida, Foucault, Wittig, Kristeva – a guarantee of opacity), and it had an unparalleled impact in the United States. It is still a marvellous illustration of the conceptual difficulties that arise, necessarily and without limits, if the binary opposition masculine–feminine – an opposition that has contributed, with many other conceptual pairs (top–bottom, left–right, day–night, past–future, hot–cold) to the structuring of human thought – is undermined.

The very obscurity of the text was programmatic, because it prefigured the confusion of the debates involving changes in sex, gender and sexual orientation. Thanks to it, we are prepared for the present-day world in which lesbians on noisy Gay Pride marches in San Francisco and London denounced transgender women as masculine 'submarines' who have infiltrated the feminist movement.

At this point, let me sincerely announce that I will be a conceptual conservative in this book, perhaps even a reactionary, since the term 'gender' has now supplanted that of 'sex' in the human sciences. In spite of this, I will stick to the opposition of two 'sexes', the one feminine, the other masculine, defined by the ability (except in cases of accidental sterility) or the inability to carry a child. But the concept of gender does exist socially, and I will study its meaning and spread in chapter 1. I will explain later in the book why, without a conservative conceptual definition of the two sexes, one cannot understand ongoing developments such as the transgender phenomenon. Thus, my decision is not ideological. It just dawned on me, after several months of sincere efforts to move away from a stable, biologically based view of men and women, that I could no longer carry out my research, because categories that are too shifting prohibit any understanding of social reality and its evolution. I can't be the only person who is looking for fixed marks in these days of conceptual turbulence: the term 'gender' is on the way not only to becoming hegemonic, but above all to assuming in a large majority of texts the exact meaning that the word 'sex' used to have. If the word 'gender' replaces the word 'sex', it becomes impossible to distinguish the social from the biological, while pretending to do so, and this loss of conceptual precision makes it impossible to analyse the current ideological transformation.

So, we have citizenship, sexuality and identity. And, in this last period, the rise in France (it happened much earlier in the United States) of the representation (I am not talking about reality here) of a relationship between the sexes no longer based on collaboration and solidarity, but on antagonism.

So our original question remains. Why have we witnessed this recent rise, in France and elsewhere, in cultural and ideological life, of an antagonistic conception of the relations between men and women? I will give my answer straightaway, in its most general form: the situation is explained by the fact that women's liberation has essentially already taken place, but it did not have all the positive effects that were expected – and led to some consequences or correlates that were indeed regrettable. Our belief in the excellence of women's liberation is such that the negativity of the present time prevents us from seeing that women are, in many domains, already in power.

I'd approached my research for this book as an effort to anticipate the future and glimpse a coming 'matriarchal' order of one kind or another. But what I found, after reviewing the educational, demographic and sexual parameters, was that, from the beginning of the 2000s, an already established situation of ideological matridominance (my terminology here again derives from American anthropology) was encountering a de facto economic resistance.[17] This resistance results from contradictions within feminine identity much more than from any desire for masculine domination. Women are now the actors of their own history. And they have access not just to freedom but, at the same time, to a direct encounter, independent of their partners, with economic anxiety, social conflicts, Durkheimian anomie, and a questioning as banal as it is tragic of the human condition. They are no longer social minors, and some of them, in certain socio-economic groups, are manifesting social pathologies that were formerly a male preserve: false consciousness, resentment, scapegoating. I sometimes think that this book, basically indifferent to any ideology, could serve to define a fourth-generation feminism because it treats women as social adults rather than victims.

Ideological matridominance did not take place in a happy world. No sunny utopia resulted from the massive entry of women into the labour market, from their material independence and their new political weight. Some positive effects are evident such as a drop in physical violence, as well as a decline in racism. I will show in this book that the fairly rapid overcoming of homophobia, leading to marriage for all, is one of the important effects of the new ideological power of women and that the LGBT complex itself has gone into matricentral mode since the beginning of the third millennium.

But the era of women is also one marked by a drop in economic dynamism and the standard of living, and by a collapse of the feeling of equality between human beings in general. It is characterized by the decay of the freedom of expression, a phenomenon most often referred to by the term 'politically correct', and an authoritarianism of a new kind, diffuse and widespread though not violent. Even more fundamental is the collapse in the sense of the collective which blocks any political or economic action (in France) or twists it into strange shapes (in the United Kingdom, the United States and Sweden). The era of women is also that of elitism and populism, censorship and conspiracy theories. Am I here trying to make women's liberation responsible for all the regressions we are witnessing? Of course not – that would be silly. The two halves of humanity are also collaboratively involved in the emergence of regrettable social phenomena.

But a researcher cannot be satisfied with a heterogeneous social world where nothing can be connected to anything else – worse, a world where we can put all the positives on one side and all the negatives on the other, without ever raising the question of an interaction between the two spheres. This would mean putting feminism, the empowerment of women, peace, homosexual marriage, ecology and the abolition of 'races', on the one side; and rising inequality, falling worker wages, deindustrialization, the rise of fierce tension between Democrats and Republicans in the United States, and the emergence of a French state that is running amok, on the other. This kind of depiction would bring us back to the Middle Ages, with its random universe and its disconnected processes, explicable solely in terms of the local interventions of a God without a plan or of a Devil hell-bent on thwarting his superior. Seeing the ideological power of women in the context of the present, or better, of the last twenty years, rather than placing it in some indefinitely postponed future, immediately eliminates the currently dominant interpretation that tacitly underlies so many assessments, and deems that what is good is feminine, while what is bad results from a persistence of masculine domination. A masculine domination whose negative effects increase at the same rate as women's liberation would be too reminiscent of the USSR, where the consequences of capitalism worsened with each step forward in communism. The clash with reality threatens all ideologies, whether predominantly economic or anthropological, and all ideologies react in the same way.

Economics and anthropology

The obligation to grasp simultaneously, in the present, the evolution of relations between men and women, the terminal collapse of religion, the economic crisis and the collapse of democracy have finally led me to revise my general interpretive model. Work on hunter-gatherers, in particular, made me give up a view of history that put anthropology above economics. The original human couple, in the context of their bilateral kinship group, collaborated in reproduction, childrearing and the acquisition of resources without it being possible to seriously hierarchize those functions which are all equally necessary for the survival of the species. The first division of labour was, as we have seen, sexual.

Since writing L'illusion économique in 1997, I had constructed a representation of social life and history in three layers: conscious, subconscious, unconscious.[18]

In the conscious, I place politics and economics, in all eras. Journalists tell us about it every day, differing little from the mediaeval chroniclers in their perception of these levels.

Education today is a matter of the subconscious: parents know its importance for the destiny of their children and the OECD measures its quantity and quality in its member countries to try to understand their economic performance. But there is nowadays a reluctance to see that education defines the movement of history itself better than the economy does. For Condorcet, Hegel and Durkheim, literacy was the very march of progress, of the human spirit or of social disarray. Their perception was the common and conscious opinion of their times, among the bourgeois elites as much as among the poorest of the people. Thus education oscillates, historically, between the conscious and the subconscious.

I situate religion today at the interface of the subconscious and the unconscious. In the Middle Ages, as in the time of the Reformation or the Counter-Reformation, the social importance of religion was fully accepted – conscious, to put it mildly. People were in communion

15

with one another or killed each other in its name. Today, using the concept of 'zombie Catholicism' to explain a low unemployment rate or a neo-republicanism that doesn't like Islam triggers a sense of surprise, oscillating between disbelief and fury, because our religious structuring has become unconscious. Yet we cannot understand our time without grasping the elements of social life that represent a survival of religious attitudes beyond the death of belief properly speaking. I will need to describe a zombie Protestantism to understand English, American and Swedish feminisms, and a zombie Christianity to understand gay identity and the transgender phenomenon.

I place in the *unconscious*, at all times, family structures – that is to say, in this book, the relations between men and women. Many authors, from Aristotle to Freud, have noted the existence of a relationship between the authority of the father and political authority. But Frédéric Le Play's work on the diversity of family structures, which alone makes it possible to explain the diversity of ideological temperaments, has not been heeded, and mainstream political science fails to perceive the anthropological structuring of today's world. Family values lie in the unconscious of societies.

I still believe in this representation which distinguishes between conscious, subconscious and unconscious layers. But I have realized that its effective simplicity led me to a logical mistake. I slipped, without thinking, from the image of superimposed layers to the idea that what is deepest, and most exciting to discover, is inherently more important than what lies on the surface. I (unconsciously!) followed psychoanalysis in its suggestion that the most buried and obscure was the essential thing, neglecting the force of consciousness and the will in what makes a human being. But a three-layered representation of history can work quite well without us hierarchizing the conscious, subconscious and unconscious elements. Historical processes involving family structures unfold over a very long period of time and without people seeing them. They are very important. But the economy, which people see clearly, and which can act violently in the shorter term, is just as important.

I will give a concrete example to illustrate my error. I have often used the crisis of 1929 to show the importance of the family and of religion in determining national historical trajectories. I said that the economic crisis led to the New Deal in the United States, to the Popular Front in France, to the Conservatives in England and to Nazism in Germany. Unconscious family structures (authoritarian and non-egalitarian in Germany, liberal and egalitarian in France, liberal and non-egalitarian in Anglo-Saxon countries) and sub- or unconscious religious transformations (faith collapsed in England and Germany between 1870 and 1930) explain the divergence between the advanced nations. This interpretation remains absolutely correct. But I have long seen in this example the proof of a

16

causal superiority of anthropology over the economy. This was a logical mistake which failed to note something equally obvious: without the economic crisis of 1929, we are equally unable to explain the German Chancellor Adolf Hitler, the US President Franklin D. Roosevelt, British Prime Minister Stanley Baldwin or French Prime Minister Léon Blum.

In the present work, I will begin to apply a unified problematic. Like the description of hunter-gatherer families that I proposed above, characterized by the sexual division of labour, this problematic will not separate the question of equality and inequality between men and women – in other words, anthropology – from economic life. We will see how the economy determines the family and the family the economy, according to a causal sequence of a new type where conscious and unconscious phenomena combine with and follow each other without being a priori placed in any hierarchical order. The subconscious, whether educational or religious, will also occupy a place of equal importance in the causal sequences.

In women's liberation, the link with socio-economic, technological and scientific evolution is obvious: we can simply note the invention of the pill, placed on the American market at the very beginning of the 1960s. There is no sexual revolution without endocrinology. There is also, within the general mishmash of cultural changes, and still in the 1960s, a rise in the standard of living and in the aspirations of those populations with full employment – an optimistic economic world without which it is difficult to imagine the relatively untroubled elevation in the status of women. Times of economic crisis have equally significant consequences for family organization, of which women are not the only victims. In her 1940 book, *The Unemployed Man and His Family*, the American sociologist Mirra Komarovsky (1905–99) showed the destructive effect of the Great Depression on the status of fathers.[19]

A study of how the link between men and women interacts with economic life leads naturally to an examination of how the relations between the sexes interact with the relations between social classes. There are notable differences in the place occupied by women within the couple according to their social position. In 1957, the classic by Michael Young (1915–2002) and Peter Willmott (1923–2000), *Family and Kinship in East London*, highlighted the matricentric character of working-class families, in contradiction with the vision often held by the educated petty bourgeoisie.[20] Olivier Schwartz (born in 1951) refined their analysis in *Le Monde privé des ouvriers* (*The Private World of the Working Classes*), which concerns working-class circles in northern France and dates from 1990.[21] In contrast, what was observed in the Western world as a whole was a rather masculine inflection of the world of the upper and petty bourgeoisie, with its well-known association between property and masculine domination. More recently, Hanna Rosin's 2012 book *The End of*

Men describes how men in the United States have often become useless in the working classes as well as in the middle classes, albeit not in higher strata.[22] Rosin notes the persistence of a slender upper layer of masculine domination in the highest strata of society. This last point intrigues anthropologists, since matrilineal systems in Kerala, and among the Na of China, were most often topped by a patrilineal keystone.[23] Are the last bastions of masculine domination just residues destined to be eliminated, or irreducible universals? I will try to answer this question.

The functionalism that I apply is not, however, that of those anthropologists who thought they were studying immobile societies in which the functional interactions between the various elements of the social structure were meant to ensure the stability or even the immutability of the whole. It is a moderate and dynamic functionalism which simply postulates that the modification of one important element of the social structure will most often lead to the modification of other important elements. It defines historical sequences in which anthropological, religious, economic and ideological traits interact in an endless succession that is history. Thus, it obliges us to ask the question of a possible relationship between the rise in equality between men and women and the decline of collective feelings.

Mankind has experimented widely in matters of mores. But our dynamic functionalism will not accept that any example can be decontextualized and used independently of the economic or religious dimensions of the social structure. Take the institution of the berdaches, mentioned above, which, among North American Indians, allowed men to take the roles of women or, less frequently, the reverse. The berdaches actually tell us that today's transgender people represent an original human possibility. But we must ask ourselves whether the institutionalization of the transgender phenomenon does or does not imply our return to an organization in human groups that do not exceed a few thousand individuals, practise gathering and hunting, lack any central coordination and practise shamanism. We will also need to understand that being berdache in a predominantly masculine society cannot be the same as being transgender in a society that has shifted into a matricentric ideological mode.

Women's liberation and the antagonism between (or abolition of) the sexes

The emergence of the transgender issue at the heart of ideological concerns must also be considered as a consequence of women's liberation, or rather of the new significance of women in the ideological orientation of our societies. It arises in the context of the growth of an antagonistic feminism, of struggle, but also, as I have said, more broadly of disorientation. Exaggerating somewhat, we could describe an ideological situation organized around two hubs. On the one hand, a radicalization of the belief in the existence of intangible essences of man and woman, now in antagonistic mode; on the other, the temptation to overcome this antagonism by bisexuality, the possibility of claiming another 'gender' than the sex fixed at conception, not to mention the rejection of binarity and yet other conceptions.

It seems pointless to me to seek consistency in these various ideological innovations. For example, it would be easy to point out that the transgender phenomenon, far from going beyond the opposition between men and women, dramatizes it. It seems to represent the quest by the individual for a sexually different, but strong, identity. However, we would then be faced with the latest variation of the transgender theme, a third sex capable of combining the potential of the other two. I won't get entangled in these debates and I will settle for the social diagnosis of a generalized identity disorder. I will need to situate this disorder and its ideological formulation on the socio-economic, demographic and temporal levels, as dynamic functionalism requires.

Today we face a quite incoherent ideological constellation that simultaneously presents the man, partner or father as a problem, and the opposition between the sexes as outdated.

The question is: can such conceptions found a sustainable society? And not simply viable in itself, but also competitive and able to survive in a world of conflict? For it's not enough to show that North American Indian societies, fully human, often very egalitarian as to the relationship between men and women – I will later show exactly how egalitarian they were – did not actually bother with strict monogamy or a rigid distinction between the sexes. One has to realize that the world of the berdaches was swept away by the English anthropological system which had gained a foothold in North America; this system was admittedly bilateral through kinship, nuclear by family structure, and egalitarian as regards the relations between men and women, but already strongly normalized by Christian monogamy, and nuanced by Protestantism with a rigorous separation between the sexes. The data on the Indians of California, Oregon and Nevada, wonderfully preserved and published at Berkeley by Driver, Steward and Kroeber – a huge and respectful work – form a tribute to the vanquished by representatives of the victorious Anglo-American society.[24]

We will therefore need to ask ourselves if the efficiency – demographic, economic, technological and military – of Western societies as they evolve will remain comparable to that of the more conservative societies in the heart of Eurasia that stick to the perpetuation of a more or less active patrilineal principle, rejecting the West's latest innovations in mores.

19

Thus, I have finally tried to evaluate, in chapter 17, the economic and demographic strengths and weaknesses of worlds that face each other without being fully aware of this – matricentric and patrilineal worlds, respectively. The West narrowly defined, as we shall see, has already paid a high economic price for women's liberation. From this point of view, the Covid-19 pandemic, in its first phase, will have been a rude awakening, since it affected the United Kingdom, the United States, Sweden and France much more severely than Germany and Japan, not to mention China. We will see, however, that economic globalization has shifted, symmetrically, the anthropological trajectory of the West towards feminism and that of the Eurasian heartland towards a conservatism of mores, to the disadvantage of both sides. This makes the question about the long-term viability of the Western model very difficult to answer.

* * *

I would like the reader to feel that my attitude is that of an old researcher who is not threatened by what the West will be like in fifty or a hundred years. Nor am I an ideologue who takes sides, who deplores trends, who is nostalgic for a world that no longer exists. Women's liberation is a fact, one which has consequences for the general functioning of the economy and society, a phenomenon so obvious and massive that 'judging' it would be as absurd as criticizing continental drift, just as it would be silly to judge homosexual liberation, or to denounce as contrary to good morals an identity crisis which is a self-evident sociological reality. Let's observe, measure and try to understand the phenomena that we have in front of us. Let's look for relationships between things, refusing to simply collect social facts independent of one another. In every society there are functional relationships between the economy, education, relations between men and women, and relations between the evolutions of these various elements.

But it must be admitted that the desire to understand can also be a passion. Ideology is admittedly necessary if societies are to project themselves into the future, but it can be infuriating when it denies reality, when it affirms the false. I beg the reader to accept the idea that, if he or she finds in this book an ironic remark, a joke (good or bad), or more generally something that seems to them a 'taking of sides' or prejudice, this will simply be a prejudice in favour of research as against ideology. My only prejudice, basically, is that I'm trying not to die stupid.

This book will travel down many paths – studying the differences between men and women, whether in education, occupation, longevity, suicide or homicide, voting behaviour or racism – and, beyond these differences, it will examine masculine and feminine homosexuality, single-parent families, and the transgender phenomenon. It will try to understand the meaning of our crisis, at its deepest, in its economic, educational and anthropological dimensions. Its conception was a complicated process. As with my *Les Luttes de classes en France au XXIe siècle* (*Class Struggles in the Twenty-First Century France*), I have been greatly helped by my partner in crime Baptiste Touverey, to whom I dictated a first text. The to-and-fro of intellectual speculation shifted the distribution of work a little. Baptiste has played a much more active part in the general shaping, including the clarification of the logical sequence and the division into chapters. More than for the previous book, I wrote certain chapters and passages directly. Nicolas Todd drew my attention to the D-PLACE project and helped us develop the cartographic app that accompanies this book.[25] I also thank Philippe Laforgue for his assistance in the demographic analysis of life expectancies as well as suicide and homicide rates by sex.

Part I

The contribution of historical anthropology

— 1 —

PATRIARCHY, GENDER AND INTERSECTIONALITY

Like an artisan who tidies up his or her work plan before getting down to the job, I will in this first chapter examine three concepts that feminism has given the human sciences: the concept of 'gender', of course, but before that the concepts of 'patriarchy' and, finally, 'intersectionality'. Can they be used by the anthropologist to analyse relations between the sexes? Let's say one thing right away: in the case of patriarchy, the answer will be a firm and clear 'no', because it spreads only confusion. In the case of gender, it will be another 'no', since after a hectic journey, the term has now been established as a Puritan duplicate of the word 'sex'. In the case of intersectionality, I will be more measured: the concept contributes something important – but not what was expected by its promoters.

In each case, I'll start by using the program Ngram Viewer from Google Books to follow the spread of the term in printed works, giving an idea of its social importance at a given moment.

The fog of patriarchy

The use of the term '*patriarcat*' ('patriarchy') goes back a long way in French. It formerly referred to a religious institution, for example the Orthodox Patriarchate of Alexandria.[1] The decline of the concept between 2005 and 2018 (figure 1.1), after a long, slow rise since 1950, perhaps owes more to dechristianization than to its new ideological use. The English term 'patriarchy' is arguably better at tracking its presence in feminist ideology because it has never had any other use than the anthropological use. The spread of this term to mean 'masculine domination' comes from the United States. In the case of '*genre*' ('gender') we will find the irruption of an Anglo-American meaning for a term already used in French to designate something else.[2] The frequency of the English term

25

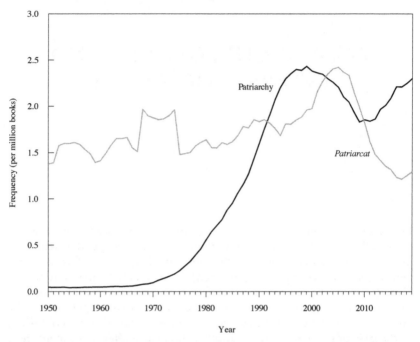

Figure 1.1   The terms 'patriarchy' (English) and *'patriarcat'* (French) since 1950
Source: Google Ngram Viewer

'patriarchy' steadily increased in the literature between 1970 and 2000 and then fluctuated. Most of its rise therefore occurred in the United States during the second wave of feminism. In America, it was already tinged by a strong anti-masculine resentment.

While the French term *'patriarcat'* declined in use at the beginning of the third millennium, it has revived in recent years and figure 1.1 shows this upturn, with a surge in 2020. In the press and the human sciences, the term *'patriarcat'* can now be found everywhere. Basically, it means masculine dominance – a dominance that is universal and intolerable. In this view of the world and of history, the relations between men and women display an uninterrupted violence ever since the appearance of the species. Note that, with regard to this brutal masculine *Sapiens*, the general cultural context evokes a nature which itself is good, with its wolves, bears and poisonous spiders. As I've said, to seek absolute coherence in ideology is a Mission Impossible. You sometimes find logical bits and pieces, but a harmonious system? Never.

Such a conception of patriarchy poses a fundamental problem for the anthropologist: it puts all kinship systems, all family structures, on

26

the same level. For instance, it places in the category 'patriarchy' the masculine predominance of the original hunter-gatherers and the vestiges of masculine power among the Americans and French of the twenty-first century. In these three cases, we are indeed dealing with equally bilateral kinship systems in which paternal and maternal forebears weigh the same in the definition of the child's social status. The family is independent or nuclear in each case. We can certainly speak of masculine pre-eminence, but this is too low-intensity for it to have anything in common with what we can observe and measure in other anthropological systems. The Indian or Chinese patrilineal and communitarian family, for example, as it presented itself on the eve of urbanization, crystallized a lowering of women's status that had taken several millennia. The Arab endogamous communitarian family showed the same fall in status, and also confined women to close kinship through preferential marriage between cousins. In the current ideological literature, the term 'patriarchy' is therefore applied to all systems – Indian, Chinese, Arabic, French, American, original. It abolishes any possibility of comparison between bilateral, patrilineal and matrilineal systems, in history as well as in the present. By flattening out the differences, it deprives the anthropologist of the results of more than a century and a half of research.

The word 'patriarchal' had been used in the earliest anthropology, that of Frédéric Le Play (1806–80), who applied it to the Russian or Middle Eastern patrilineal communitarian family. Nowadays, it spills over onto all family systems. The term 'patriarchal' indicated a strong domination over the group of women, sometimes, but not always, accompanied by a large age gap between the spouses (hypergamy of age). This had nothing to do with masculine predominance in the nuclear family, which was largely reined in by the centrality and solidarity of the couple, the sole structural element of the household; this predominance could not come with very wide age gaps. A single semantic shift could hardly sow more confusion in a debate.

We are going to look at four maps which would be rendered incomprehensible by the current notion of patriarchy. They will prepare us to handle the classic anthropological concepts that allow us to classify and understand societies.

Map 1.1 was created using data from the *Ethnographic Atlas*. Mainly developed between 1945 and 1965 by George Peter Murdock and his team, based at Yale, the *Atlas* was recently put online, as I said in the introduction, by linguists from the Max-Planck Institute in Jena, in an updated and corrected version containing 1,291 peoples. The *Atlas* is based on data collected mainly between 1880 and 1960, largely by Anglo-American ethnologists. Some female researchers from the University of Utrecht have confirmed its weakness in the case of Europe, a legacy of the times when anthropology was the science of primitive peoples rather

27

Map 1.1 Kinship systems before urbanization
Source: Ethnographic Atlas

than of humanity as a whole.[3] Only late in the day did the European peasantries attract the attention of anthropologists, who focused mainly on Ireland, Italy and Russia – admittedly somewhat primitive societies if seen from an American and Protestant point of view. The *Atlas* does not include data on the family collected by members of the Le Play school in the nineteenth and early twentieth centuries, nor the data amassed by the historical anthropology of the Cambridge School led by Peter Laslett (1915–2001) from the middle of the 1960s onwards.

Let's not forget, however, that Murdock's *Atlas* contains a lot more than family data, since it is interested in kinship in general, in the acquisition of resources, in construction techniques, in the size and political organization of groups, and in religious life. The detailed documentary records of the peoples are collected in the Human Relations Area Files (HRAF) of Yale University.[4] As regards mapping the variables – an exercise made easy by the D-PLACE platform – the *Atlas* is a magnificent working tool of which we will make great use in this book.[5] The planispheres presented will all put Eurasia and Africa on the left, and the Americas on the right – the latter were occupied by hunter-gatherers later, once they had crossed the newly emerged Bering 'Strait'.

On our first map we have therefore projected the systems of patrilineal, matrilineal and bilateral kinship described by Murdock. We speak of a patrilineal kinship system if the social status of the child, in terms of name, heritage or membership of a group specialized in a certain activity, depends on the father and the father's father. We speak of a matrilineal kinship system if the social status of the child depends on the mother and the mother's mother. We speak of a bilateral, undifferentiated or cognatic kinship system if the status of the child is optional and s/he can choose or even not choose between one side and the other. Finally, we refer to a bilineal system if certain elements come under paternal ancestry and others under maternal ancestry.

Note that the maps drawn from the *Atlas* describe anthropological systems before European modernity turned them upside down. For the American continent, for example, it is the pre-Columbian Indian systems that are represented, not the systems of the present. If you want to 'see' the current systems on the map, you just need to transfer the English system to North America, and the systems of Castile and central Portugal to Latin America, while giving Bolivia, Ecuador and Peru an Aymara or Quechua patrilineal nuance, and Mexico a Nahua patrilineal nuance – heritages of the Inca and Aztec traditions, respectively. We have not eliminated the few 'historical' peoples included in the *Atlas*, for which the data are unreliable, but which are few in number, such as the Romans, Babylonians, Hebrews, Aztecs and Incas.

What does this map tell us? We note the fundamental bilaterality of European kinship systems (we will be qualifying these data in chapter 5).

29

Among North American Indians, often hunter-gatherers, there is the same predominance of bilateral kinship systems, but with a small minority of pockets of patrilineality to the west of the Great Lakes, in southern California, Central America and the Amazon Basin. In Africa, patrilineal systems form a majority bloc but, to the south of the patrilineal area, we observe a matrilineal belt in which the status of women is higher. All of Southeast Asia and Oceania has bilateral kinship systems and is thus more similar to Europe. However, there is a patrilineal hub in New Guinea. Finally, patrilineality dominates the Middle East, India and China. We will explain this fundamental map in chapter 4. A major patrilineal space therefore occupies the centre of the Old World, between China and Africa. We have marked the Beijing–Baghdad–Ouagadougou (BBO) axis around which it is organized.

The next two maps show the present. The first one shows the sex ratio (number of men per 100 women), all ages combined (map 1.2).

The sex ratio reveals the differences in treatment between men and women throughout their lives. These differences between countries stem, essentially, from social organization: the presence or absence of the selective abortion of female foetuses, selective infanticide, a differential attention to the diet and health of little boys as opposed to little girls, and privileges enjoyed – or not – by men compared to women in adulthood, in diet as well as in interpersonal violence, not to mention differential suicide according to sex. Consider, for example, the dark patch that covers India and China and indicates a very unbalanced sex ratio in favour of men. It would once have resulted from the infanticide of little girls; these days, it is mainly the effect of sex-selective abortion of female foetuses, something made possible by technological modernity.

Though they are mainly determined by social factors, sex ratio differences cannot be considered as purely social. It should be borne in mind that if the natural sex ratio at birth, i.e. the ratio without selective foeticide, is generally of the order of 105 or 106 boys for every 100 girls, it is most often 103, sometimes 102, in Africa. This minor difference reminds us of the common origin of the Eurasian, Oceanian and Native American peoples, all derived from small human groups that left Africa less than 100,000 years ago. It also implies that our map somewhat underestimates the anti-feminism of African patrilineal systems, since the sex ratio for all ages combined obviously depends both on inequalities in the treatment of men and women over the course of life and on the natural sex ratio at birth. But as we can see, this modern map essentially reproduces map 1.1 of the kinship systems derived from Murdock's *Ethnographic Atlas*. This map too seems to be organized around the BBO axis. The overlay is possible because Anglo-American and Iberian bilateralism has replaced Native American bilateralism. A few specific, extreme or deviant cases deserve comment.

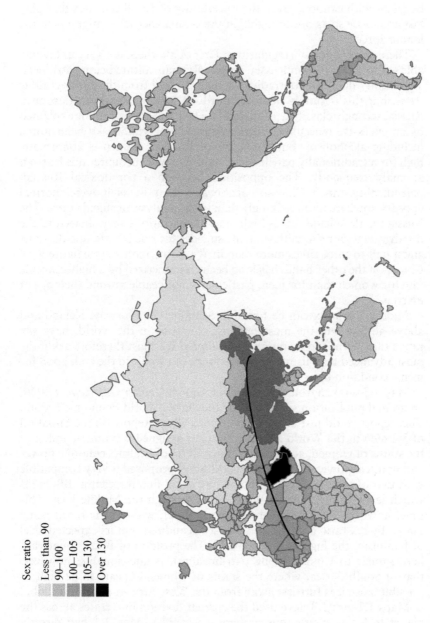

Map 1.2 The sex ratio in 2020

Source: 'Population prospects', United Nations Organization

Sex ratio

- Less than 90
- 90–100
- 100–105
- 105–130
- Over 130

In black, we find Saudi Arabia, where it is hardly surprising to find a very unfavourable sex ratio for women. This peak of imbalance should be taken with caution, given the uncertainty of Saudi censuses that play fast and loose so as not to highlight the significance of immigrants in the labour force.

There are two main irregularities. First of all, there is a very unfavourable sex ratio for men in Russia, despite Russian culture being patrilineal. This oddity does not contradict the map derived from the *Ethnographic Atlas*, but this is simply because Murdock was wrong about European Russia, wrongly classified as bilateral.[6] The Russian sex ratio is explained by an excessive masculine mortality linked to certain risky behaviours, including alcoholism. But the status of Russian women is abnormally high for a traditionally patrilineal system. We will encounter this Russian anomaly frequently. The opposition between a paradoxical Russian patrilineality and a Chinese patrilineality that is, as it were, normal appears nowhere more strikingly than in the analysis of suicide rates. The Russian male suicide rate is high, and its sex ratio is very skewed to the disadvantage of men, with six male suicides for one female suicide – one and a half to three times more than in Western countries (see figure 9.3). China, on the other hand, has long been characterized by a higher suicide rate for women than for men, particularly noticeable around their age at marriage.[7]

Another paradox can be found in Scandinavia. Norway, Iceland and above all Sweden, the most feminist countries in the world, have sex ratios that are not so favourable to women. We must therefore ask if the most advanced feminism doesn't also turn out to be, in the end, good for men's condition too.

Map 1.3 is taken from data from the *Global Gender Gap Report 2020*, an annual publication sponsored by the Davos World Economic Forum. This report could just as well have been called 'Report on the Situation of Women in the World'. Each country is assigned a synthetic index of the status of women, according to the criteria of health, economic power and political power. The overall distribution proposed is very compatible with that of the two previous maps. We again find the central BBO axis which leads from China to West Africa through the Middle East. This time, however, Africa appears at its true level, without the result being biased by sex ratio at birth. We also see Scandinavia at its expected level of feminism, the highest in the world. The position of Brazil (bilateral), here similar to China (strong patrilineality), is questionable; however, that of South Africa, where the status of women appears to be high, is possible since it is furthest away from the West African patrilineal hub.

Maps 1.2 and 1.3 have used the current division into states across the planet to locate continuous numerical variables. Map 1.1 had directly placed the peoples of the near past on the planisphere, characterizing

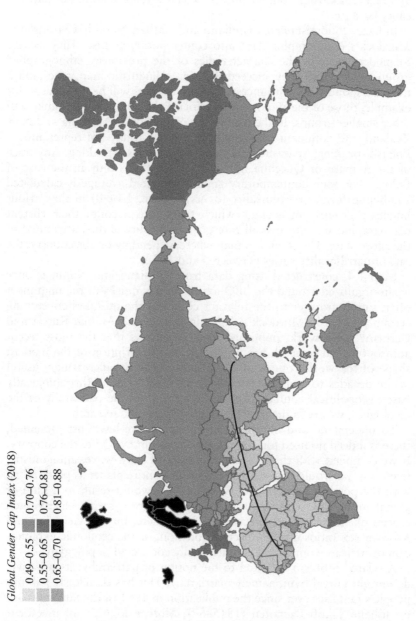

Map 1.3 The status of women today
Source: Global Gender Gap Report 2020

Global Gender Gap Index (2018)

- 0.49–0.55
- 0.55–0.65
- 0.65–0.70
- 0.70–0.76
- 0.76–0.81
- 0.81–0.88

them by a discontinuous trichotomous variable: patrilineal, matrilineal and bilateral kinship. But we now also have a representation of patrilineality by state.

In fact, economists Paola Giuliano and Nathan Nunn have translated Murdock's ethnographic data into contemporary terms.[8] They ascribe to modern peoples the characteristics of the previously ethnographed groups with which they succeeded, using a linguistic map, to establish the correspondence.[9] The ancestral characteristics will be, in Senegal, for example, those of the Wolof, Serer, Diola, Peul, Soninké, Mandinka and other smaller groups. In the case of the New World, Australia and New Zealand, the dominant ethnolinguistic groups today are represented – English-speaking, Spanish-speaking and Portuguese-speaking. Any trace of the Aymara or Quechua Indian groups remains only in the case of Bolivia. For each contemporary state a weighted average is calculated combining former patrilineality (or its absence, 1 or 0) in the various linguistic groups, an average which takes into account their current demographic size. An overall rate of patrilineality is thus attributed to the entire state. The result is a map where, depending on the country, the rate of patrilineality varies between 0 and 100%.

Map 1.4, constructed using data from Giuliano and Nunn, is once again organized around the BBO axis. The few quirks of the map most often simply transfer to the relevant countries the mistakes concerning certain peoples in Murdock's *Atlas*, in Iraq, Saudi Arabia, Russia and Germany. This work, published in 2018, shows that the most recent anthropological research has finally led to a description of the modern shape of the world, one whose applications will be increasingly useful in the decades to come, inevitably dominated by an anthropologically based geopolitical conflict. We are here far from the patriarchy of the ideologues; we are in the midst of ongoing scientific research.

To understand and interpret the four maps we have just presented, there is indeed no need for any notion of patriarchy. Quite the contrary. If we complied with the belligerent criteria of third-wave, antagonistic, feminism, we would be forced to classify the entire planet as patriarchal, with the possible exception of Sweden. This would result in a kind of global mishmash, a thick fog preventing us from seeing clearly such crucial phenomena as the recent rise in Chinese, Indian, Georgian and Kosovar sex ratios due to selective abortion, or the economic exploitation of African women that is functionally connected to polygyny.

A related problem is linked to the notion of patriarchy: its negative, downright unreal twin, namely matriarchy. This has ceaselessly fed into people's fantasies ever since the publication in 1861 of the famous work by Johann Jakob Bachofen (1815–87), *Mother Right*,[10] an investigation of the religious and juridical character of matriarchy in the ancient world, and up to the work of archaeologist Marija Gimbutas (born in

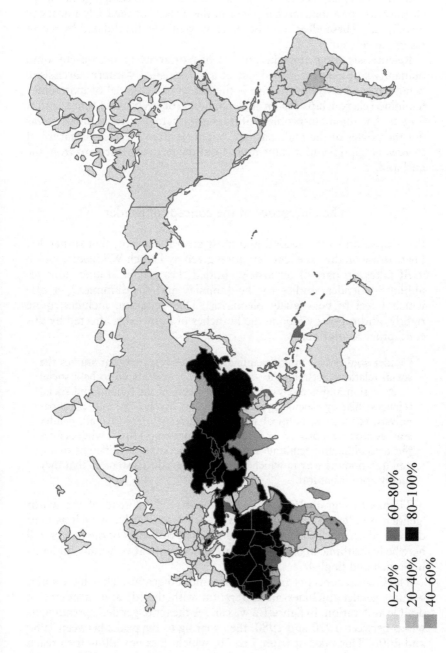

Map 1.4 The rate of patrilineality by state

0–20%

20–40%

40–60%

60–80%

80–100%

1921 in Lithuania, died in Los Angeles in 1994), who campaigned for the glorification of a matriarchal phase in the history of the early European Neolithic.[11] These ideas have been, as we shall see, invalidated by recent historical research.

Relentlessly projecting the notions of patriarchy or matriarchy onto humanity's oldest past is evidence of a self-satisfied Western narcissism. It fails to see how unpersuasive is the antagonistic model of masculine–feminine relationships for an understanding of prehistoric times, and it forgets that the main problem of hunter-gatherers or early farmers was not the power of the male partner, but survival in the face of nature. If there was oppression, it came more from the environment than from the husband.

The emergence of the concept of gender

Let's move on to the second and most central concept, that of gender. I here draw on the excellent definition given by French Wikipedia, which itself takes up part of an article entitled 'Les *gender studies* pour les nul(le)s' ('Gender studies for he-dummies and she-dummies'), a title which I feel to be vaguely pleonastic. This definition includes, quite rightly, anthropology among the branches of knowledge affected by this conceptual revolution:

> Gender studies is a multidisciplinary field of research that studies the social relations between the sexes. Gender is considered to be a social construction and is analysed in 'all the fields of the human and social sciences: history, sociology, anthropology, psychology and psychoanalysis, economics, political science, geography . . .'[12] Overall, gender studies propose a process of reflection and draw up a list of what defines the masculine and feminine in different places and at different times, and question the way in which norms are reproduced so often that they finally appear natural.[13]

Thanks to Ngram Viewer, we can observe the spread of the words 'gender' and '*genre*' in English and French respectively, as well as their derived adjectives 'gendered' and '*genré*'. The ordinates of the figures will here be logarithmic in order to capture fluctuations at very different levels in French and English.

The English concepts are innovative and indigenous. They have a nice sound: 'gender' includes an alliteration with the [d] and 'gendered' a double alliteration. In figure 1.2 we can see the term 'gender' spreading its wings between 1970 and 1980, then soaring to the peaks between 1980 and 2000. This takes it from 5 to 70, which does not allow it to reach the level of '*genre*' in French, which is never less than 100. This initially

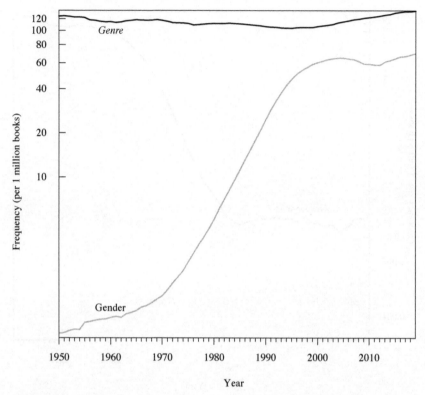

Figure 1.2 Evolution of the frequency of use of the terms 'gender' and *'genre'*
Source: Google Ngram Viewer

high level in French is, of course, explained by the fact that the term was widely used before the 'gender revolution': for the classification of species (genus), to designate good or bad social behaviour ('good or bad *genre*'), but, above all, for grammatical gender. I do not know whether its decline from 125 to 105 between 1950 and 1995 reveals a growing disinterest in grammar. The rise of 'genre' to 135, however, came 20 years after the take-off of 'gender' in English, a sure sign of the cultural domination of the Anglo-American world over France.

'*Genré*' in figure 1.3 reproduces the same cycle with respect to 'gendered'. The term is new in French, but horrible to the ear. The frequency of its use shows, like that of 'gender', the typical chronology of an imported concept. Unlike '*genre*', whose use was frequent and indigenous to France at the beginning of the period, and at the end of the period still higher than that of 'gender' in English, '*genré*' remains fifty times less

37

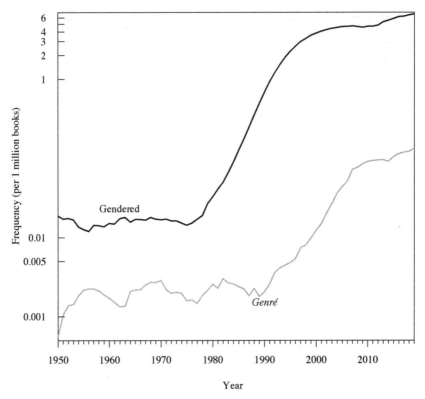

Figure 1.3   Evolution of the frequency of use of the terms 'gendered' and *'genré'*
Source: Google Ngram Viewer

frequent in the French corpus than 'gendered' in the English corpus. Its ugliness doubtless works as a protectionist barrier.

The take-off of 'gendered', starting in 1980, occurred in the period of Thatcherism (beginning in 1979) and Reaganism (in 1980). To illustrate the relevance of word frequency analysis, I have added, in figure 1.4, the rise of the English word 'vibrant', strongly associated with the neoliberal ideology that was endlessly singing the praises of 'vibrant economies' and 'vibrant societies'. Its take-off around 1980 is very pronounced. We cannot suggest, on the basis of this simultaneity alone, any cause-and-effect relationship between neoliberalism and the theory of gender. But neither can we conclude that it is a priori obvious that there is *no* relation. Such a close chronological coincidence impels one to raise the question. These coordinated time sequences confirm the interest of the hypothesis (one which I have set out in my introduction) of a possible

38

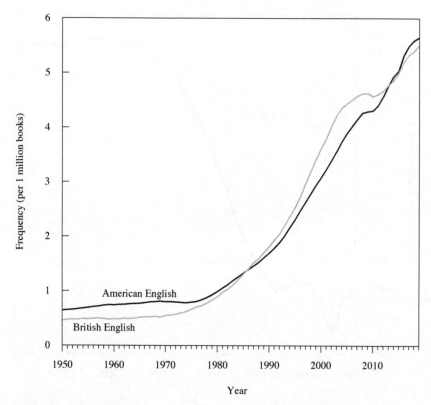

Figure 1.4   Evolution of the frequency of use of the English term 'vibrant'
Source: Google Ngram Viewer

functional relationship between the rise of equality between men and women and the decline in the capacity for collective action.

Another contextual element must be mentioned. It was in June 1981 that the Centers for Disease Control and Prevention in Atlanta identified AIDS. Throughout the following period, the sexual revolution initiated in the 1960s was to be overshadowed by tragedy, though the liberal gains in mores were not undermined. Homosexuals, a high-risk group, were not ostracized. Nor were people of African origin or intravenous drug addicts, two other high-risk groups. Such a resistance in liberal ideological evolution shows that social factors much more powerful than disease were at work. I will place women's liberation at the heart of this mechanism, and we shall see why.

For the sake of defending our national conceptual interests, I have added, with figure 1.5, the historical sequences for '*déconstruction*', the French term, and 'deconstruction', the English term. Here, we French

39

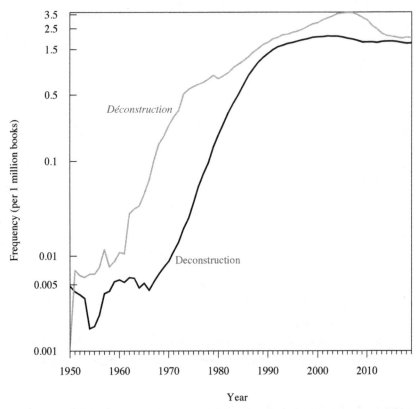

Figure 1.5 Evolution of the frequency of use of the terms '*déconstruction*' and 'deconstruction'
Source: Google Ngram Viewer

are clearly the exporters. Deconstruction was defined by Derrida as a technique for the analysis of philosophical texts.[14] This verbal innovation came from France and was imported into the Anglo-American world some fifteen years later. The term is not unrelated to our subject since deconstruction was a prolegomenon to the 'social construction of gender'. After all, Judith Butler, in her impenetrable but terribly influential *Gender Trouble*, relied on the great French authors of the previous period.[15] If France did not 'invent' the concept of gender, it provided America with the raw material of (conceptual) deconstruction.

Gender: a useless and ideologized duplication

The adjectival form 'gendered' isn't awkward in itself. Anthropology has always been interested in the relationships between men and women – this is even, as we shall see, the very heart of the profession – and it wouldn't be a bad thing to have an additional, concise term to speak of the status of women. The existence of a biological dimension and a social dimension in the difference between men and women would make it possible to imagine a distribution of roles: 'sex' for biology, 'gendered' for the social dimension. Gendered relations could thus be a concise way of saying 'relations between men and women as affected by social bias'. Nevertheless, how effective would this actually be? We would still find, in an attenuated form, the hazy, undifferentiated idea of patriarchy.

The word 'gender' is more of a problem because it places us from the outset in a situation where biological difference is denied, which doesn't seem sensible at first sight. This is an ideological diktat that leads to statistical formulations that are ineffectual because we no longer know what we're talking about.

Take the example of opinion polls. Let's sort out the samples, as American political polls often (but not always) do, according to gender. That gives us a masculine gender and a feminine gender. But how are they defined? Does the new classification mean that transgender people have reached their destination, their 'real' essence, in the results? The question has no practical consequences because the proportion of transgender people, as we will see, is lower than 1 in 1,000 and inaccessible to the opinion pollster, who usually operates with a sample of 1,000 individuals, at best with 10,000. What we actually observe is a replacement of the classification according to sex by a classification according to gender, which, it must be said, handles the basic categories 'men' and 'women' in the most traditional way. In any case, some pollsters, in 2020, came back to sorting their results 'according to sex'.

This is yet one more example of the typical American playing with words that started with 'Black'. 'African-American' attempted to replace 'Black', but lost popularity after a while. The word was meant to dominate the thing (i.e. racism), but its power ultimately appears limited. Today we say 'Black Lives Matter', and not 'African-American Lives Matter'. Perhaps it will be the same with sex and gender. I would be tempted to say that the real reason for the choice of the word 'gender' rather than sex, or (in French) *'genre'* rather than *'sexe'*, is a latent form of puritanism. With gender, it's not so much that we are introducing the social; rather, we are repressing the image of the genitalia.

There's something more serious at stake: the emotional and militant nature of the concept of gender in practice imposes a biased statistical vision because it includes a limiting condition within itself. We must only speak of men who 'oppress' women, never of women who 'oppress' men. This limitation isn't a big problem for the past, I admit. But we are living through an anthropological revolution. We can observe in certain fields that men are being overtaken by women and we need to have conceptual tools that allow us to measure these new elements.

Let's take an example of limitation by 'gender' in the *Global Gender Gap Report 2020*, which gave us the elements of map 1.3. This highly useful document integrates the educational results of men and women respectively into the calculation of the global indicator by which we can assess the gap between the sexes. It is right to do so. In a particular country, if women are catching up with men in terms of higher education, a score of 1, measuring parity, is assigned to the country concerned. Then, as 'gender' dictates, the counter on the dial gets stuck: we do not measure the growing advance of women over men in countries where women are becoming dominant in higher education, by values of the indicator which could be 1.1, 1.2 or 1.3. The concept of gender is here responsible for the mental block. But we would urgently need indicators, which, sector by sector, can measure the transition from a situation that I will henceforth systematically call 'patridominance' to situations of 'matridominance'.[16] The concept of gender, created to grasp male domination, here becomes an instrument for hiding an emergent female domination.

We will see later how the concepts of patridominance and matridominance, applied to politics, to economics, to education, to power in the decision to procreate, to the evolution of racism and homophobia, and to determining the aspirations of transgender people, actually function.

For a generalized intersectionality

We now come to the third notion linked to the concept of gender, that of intersectionality. Let's take the French Wikipedia definition, which, like the definition of gender theory given above, has the advantage of proposing a commonly accepted usage. It reads as follows:

> Intersectionality studies the forms of domination and discrimination not separately, but in their interconnections, starting from the principle that social differentiations such as gender [we can see the association with the concept of 'gender' – the term used could just as well have been 'sex'], race, class, or sexual orientation are not hermetically sealed, and the relations of domination between social categories cannot be fully explained if studied separately from each other. Intersectionality therefore undertakes to study the intersections between these different phenomena.

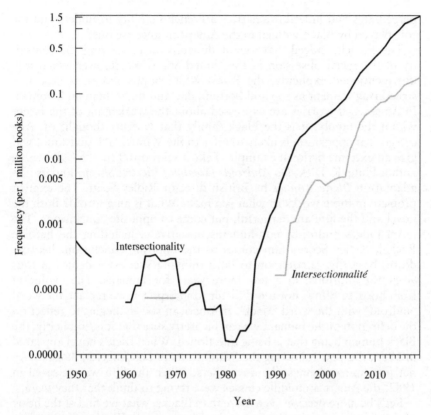

Figure 1.6 Evolution of the frequency of use of the English term 'intersectionality' and the French term '*intersectionnalité*'
Source: Google Ngram Viewer

The notion dates back to 1989 and an article by the African-American (Black) feminist scholar Kimberlé Crenshaw.[17] This legal article high-lighted a problem in the struggle against discrimination in the United States: a Black woman could bring a prosecution only as a woman or as a Black person, but not both at the same time. The obligation to choose, in the American judicial system, allowed her case as a Black person to be dismissed if Black men were not affected by the discrimination she denounced, or as a woman if White women did not encounter the same problem.

Cross-referencing categories is essential. Combining concepts, as intersectionality proposes to do, is welcome. However, the parallelism between France and the United States indicated by figure 1.6, a parallel-ism that the term seems to encourage, testifies to a misunderstanding: it

43

perpetuates and indeed dramatizes a French inability to understand the role played by Black women in the American unconscious.

The French, indeed, have great difficulty in conceiving the centrality of the racial obsession in the United States where, even when it is not mentioned explicitly, the Black–White opposition is as crucial a structuring element as top and bottom, day and night, man and woman. In America, if worries are expressed about the weakening of the father within the family, it is the Black family that is being thought of. Any categorical opposition is likely to refer to the White/Black division. I will give an extreme fictional example. Take a sci-fi novel by the Californian author Philip K. Dick, *Do Androids Dream of Electric Sheep?* and its film adaptation *Blade Runner* by British director Ridley Scott. The explicit problem in these works is: what is a man? What is an android? Both the novel and the film are masterful, but come to opposite conclusions. The novel judges androids, non-humans, negatively, including the heroine Rachel; Ridley Scott's film comes to the opposite conclusion, because death, basically, is common to both thinking species: it comes in four years for androids, in a few more years for humans. The evolution from book to film is not too difficult to interpret if we replace the word 'android' with the word 'Black'. If American society begins to reflect on the definition of the human, we can be pretty sure that it is, implicitly, the Black human being that is being questioned. When Dick's novel appeared in 1966, the year following the Watts Riots in Los Angeles, Blacks were not just human beings like any others. When the film was released in 1982, the American middle classes were trying to think that they *were*.

Let's be more precise: even more than Blacks, what we find at the heart of the American mental system is the *Black woman*. Racism, fundamentally, is measured by the refusal to have children with a woman of the dominated group, however intelligent and beautiful she may be. If, over a long period, the rate of Black men marrying White women is around 10% in the United States, the rate of Black women marrying White men is less than 2%, five times lower. These figures should be viewed with caution because what especially characterizes Black women is non-marriage – a single-parent family. When people talk about the single-parent family in the United States, whether explicitly or not, it is yet again the category of the Black woman that springs to mind – the centre of gravity, as I have said, of the national unconscious.

The original concept of intersectionality is therefore well suited to a description of the United States. However, it needs to be broadened. Why consider only the 'dominated' side of the problem? Admittedly, people talk of dominant White males in order to denounce them, but why not also study the cases (contradictory in themselves as far as domination is concerned) of White women or Black men? I propose the development of a *generalized intersectionality* which takes an interest in all intersections,

Table 1.1 Voting in the 2020 US presidential election

		Total	Men	Women
Black	Biden	87%	80%	91%
	Trump	12%	18%	8%
White	Biden	42%	40%	43%
	Trump	57%	58%	55%
Electorate overall	Biden	(51.3%)	48%	56%
	Trump	(46.8%)	49%	43%

In italics, the total effective scores, plus 1.8% of votes cast for independent candidates.
Source: Poll exits survey, Edison Research Reuters.

whether they be *harmonic* on the axis of domination (Black women are doubly discriminated against, White men doubly privileged) or *disharmonic* (White women are sexually dominated but racially dominant and Black men are sexually dominant but racially dominated).[18] To show the usefulness of this widespread intersectionality, I will briefly study the way these various categories voted in the 2020 US presidential election (see table 1.1).

If we reject the intersectional concept, we will merely see that, on the men's side, Trump and Biden are almost at the same level, with Trump at 49% and Biden at 48%, and that women show a significant difference: Trump falls to 43% and Biden rises to 56%. We will quickly deduce that American women are generally more to the left and more progressive than men – a correct conclusion, but partial and of limited interest if we really want to understand the dynamics of the American political system.

Fortunately, we've picked up the message of intersectionality and we can apply it. Blacks, both sexes combined, voted 87% for Biden, but this included 91% of Black women and only 80% of Black men. There were 8% of Trumpistas among Black women and 18% among Black men – more than double. How are we to interpret this? We again find, with different levels, a gap between Black women and Black men that we have already observed in the case of intermarriages, where it was 2% as against 10%. So here we have confirmation that Black women are at the heart of the mechanism of segregation in the United States, even more locked into the Democratic vote than Black men. The (very relative) greater liberty of Black men to vote Republican seems like an extension of their (also very relative) greater freedom of marriage into the majority community. The notion of intersectionality here allows us to connect the mixed intermarriage rate with the vote.

But let's go further and, in accordance with our project of a generalized intersectionality – one which does not just examine the dominated and the superposition of dominations (the fact of being a woman, the fact of being Black) – let's also apply the concept to White women and White men (while keeping in mind that our sketch excludes Latinos and Asians, whose vote largely accounts for Biden's majority). White women seem to change their political colour and turn red: Trump gets 55% of their votes while only 43% vote for Biden. Among White men, Trump is at 58% and Biden at 40%. So there's a small difference according to sex, but this difference is much smaller among Whites than among Blacks. The application of the (generalized) intersectional concept to recent American elections thus reveals to us that, in the dominant White group, the split between the sexes is of little importance. The concept of race is in fact more decisive in the US vote than the notion of sex, but Black women are indeed more dominated than Black men.

French intersectionality

What about intersectionality in France at present? In an excellent article published in *Libération*, Sonya Faure noted the specific impact of the concept of intersectionality in French academia, even before its dissemination in the political sphere.[19] But I feel that this academic passion has difficulty in identifying the dominated that it needs. Black French women don't fulfil the role. This is because their significance in society is not great enough, but mainly because they are not subject to an exclusion comparable to that of Black American women. If we take the decisive criterion of intermarriage, we observe for women from the Sahel an exogamy rate of 38%, i.e. nineteen times that of Black American women.[20]

We could search, but still in vain, for a French equivalent to Black American women, i.e. women of North African origin. Yet here again, the high rate of exogamy (41% for women of Algerian origin) immediately invalidates the comparison.

In the case of France, the notion of race proves to be of little use and it is difficult to superimpose the ways in which women are discriminated against. In fact, being a woman lessens ethnic, religious and racial discrimination in France. But if we do not use intersectionality simply to 'reveal the plurality of *discriminations* of class, sex and race' but also to reveal the plurality of *dominations* of class, sex and race, we can identify the brand-new ideological power of *women with a higher education* – the very women who in some cases have enthusiastically adopted the concept of intersectionality.

We mentioned in the introduction the predominance of women in higher education. In the rest of this book, we will try to reflect on the link between educational level and sex, and its ideological implications. We will then better understand the success of the notion of intersectionality in academia, now a place of matridominance and one of the centres of gravity of the new ideological power. I would never have reached this notion of ideological matridominance without intersectionality. It has become for me not just a research technique, but an indispensable source of verification. It has allowed me to escape the masculinism of my training as a historian who in human societies saw only male actors. I have learned to identify, in our rapidly changing society, the respective numbers of women and men in the various sectors of social life; I have learned to combine sex and class automatically, as it were – in the different professions, of course, but also in ideological production and in research. This has led me to write, for example: x% of authors of this collective work on witchcraft not only have a higher education but are also women, y% of the editors of this OECD study on LGBT not only have a higher education but are also women, z% of the researchers in this particular institute are women. I will not provide these figures immediately, so as to leave the reader the pleasure of discovery, when the time comes.

— 2 —

DEGENDERING ANTHROPOLOGY

Since the second half of the 1980s, anthropology has suffered from gender trouble. As both concept and experience, gender has messed things up everywhere, casting doubt on solid data and on the comparative instruments patiently developed since the end of the nineteenth century. Third-wave feminism in particular has disrupted the development of this science of the human, which had reached the stage of conceptual maturity and now had only to synthesize its findings and lay bare the general meaning of the data collected by generations of field researchers, both men and women.

A tribute to female anthropologists

To properly measure the intellectual debacle caused by the introduction of the concept of gender into anthropology, I would like to begin by paying homage, in a non-exhaustive way, to the women anthropologists who have been essential to my work since my training in social anthropology at Cambridge. This list should not hide the overwhelming male predominance in the field, even though this diminished rapidly from the end of the 1960s onwards, finally giving way to a female predominance – but, unfortunately, at a time when the notion of gender had already spread chaos in research, among both men and women in the profession.

In terms of general training, I came across the work of Ruth Benedict (1887–1948), whose *Patterns of Culture*, published in 1934, is one of the key books in American cultural anthropology.[1] In it, she shows how the cultures of the Zuni (southwestern United States), Kwakiutl (west coast of Canada) and Dobu (an island near New Guinea) model typical personalities that represent only one possibility among others of the human being, and can form individuals who are adapted, deviant or even rejected.[2]

In 1949, Margaret Mead (1901–78) published *Male and Female*, a fundamental work which contains two essential elements for our purposes here: first, the universality of the use of the opposition between men and women in the organization of societies, in very varied ways; and second, the hypothesis of a specific male anxiety linked to the less obvious and direct nature of the contribution of men to reproduction.[3] This idea was passed on to me by my mother when I was a teenager and I must admit that I still feel it, deep down, to be my mother's idea. Without Audrey Richards (1899–1984) and her article 'Some Types of Family Structure among the Central Bantu' (1950), I would not have ever understood anything about the variability of family systems of the African matrilineal belt.[4] In relation to Africa, I was also able to draw on Lucy Mair (1901–86), using not only her general introduction to anthropology, *Marriage* (1971), but above all her inventory *African Societies* (1974).[5] Without Irawati Karve (1905–70) and her *Kinship Organization in India* (1953),[6] I would never have grasped the diversity of family systems in the Indian subcontinent. Germaine Tillion (1907–2008), with *Le harem et les cousins* (*The Harem and Cousins*, 1966), gave me a good introduction to the Arabian kinship system, a structure that Claude Lévi-Strauss (1908–2009) himself admitted to not having understood.[7]

Moving on to a later generation, I must mention June Helm (1924–2004), who gave me (and many others) the key to the bilateral and horizontal organization connecting brothers and sisters, as well as their partners, in the majority of hunter-gatherer life systems, and, most likely, in *Sapiens* to begin with. Her article 'Bilaterality in the Socio-territorial Organization of the Arctic Drainage Dene' (1965) even ended up undermining the belief of many anthropologists in the patrilocality of the Australian Aborigines.[8] Chie Nakane (1926–2021) provided me with a key to understanding a particular Japanese issue with *Kinship and Economic Organization in Rural Japan* (1967).[9]

So, before 'gender', the role of women in anthropology was developing in a harmonious way; they used and refined scientific concepts that were admittedly most often produced by men, but were still 'genderless'. These male anthropologists themselves gladly admitted that having more women in their ranks would allow for a better approach to women in the societies studied. That is why Adolphus Peter Elkin (1891–1979), a specialist in Australian Aborigines, sent one of his women students, Phyllis M. Kaberry (1910–77), to carry out fieldwork. The result of this feminization, as conceptualized by a man, was the publication, in 1939, of *Aboriginal Woman: Sacred and Profane*, a work as relevant as it is well written.[10]

The list can be completed by Hildred Geertz (1929–2022), author of *The Javanese Family* (1961),[11] and Margery Wolf (1933–2017), to whom we owe *Women and the Family in Taiwan* (1972), already mentioned above in connection with Chinese women suicides.[12]

Published in 1988, Nancy Levine's book *The Dynamics of Polyandry: Kinship, Domesticity and Population on the Tibetan Border*, might seem to have come after the irruption of gender into American anthropology, but it rests, in its basic structure, on a doctoral thesis defended in 1977, and therefore falls within the tradition of a classical and efficacious anthropology.[13] I learned from it that Tibetan polyandry could not be associated with a privileged status for women because it functioned within a 'stem system' with male primogeniture. But where the Christian stem-family countries condemned younger brothers to remaining single, to the army or the priesthood, Tibetan Buddhism, less suspicious of sexuality, allowed the older brother to grant his younger brothers sexual access to his wife – so long, that is, as he himself was absent. The goal, however, remained that of any stem system: preserving the family patrimony undivided.

What about the debates on male–female relations in this anthropology which was making steady progress, and in the 1970s extended to Eurasian agrarian societies the application of methods developed for the study of the Indians of North America, the peoples of Africa and the Australian Aborigines? From the second half of the 1960s onwards, one can sense, with the second feminist wave, an ever more insistent questioning of male predominance, a questioning which was initially rather beneficial.

The collective work *Man the Hunter* was published in 1968, the year which preceded the Woodstock Music Festival, but it was the result of an international conference held in Chicago shortly before Grace Slick sang 'White Rabbit' to a rapturous audience in 1966.[14] This collective volume, despite its title, mainly highlights the importance of gathering and of women in food – and, according to this book, gathering counted more than hunting.

The implications of this were feminist, without any doubt. The question was an important one, and it opened up a fruitful debate. Ten years later, the book's male authors were rejected for their allegedly biased sample, by a woman, Carol Ember, in her article 'Myths about Hunter Gatherers'.[15] Ember is now a member of the steering committee, on the American side, of the D-PLACE project to which the present book owes so much. Ember used the general sample derived from the Human Relations Area Files to defend the idea that men contributed as much as or more than women to feeding the local group. She also thinks – wrongly it seems to me – that she has demonstrated a patrilocal predominance in the organization of groups, as well as the largely violent character of hunter-gatherers in general. On this last point, later research may have proved her right, but the case of the Indians of the inner basin of the Rocky Mountains – primordial peoples in my view, and unacquainted with war – leaves me in doubt.

Leaving aside the problem of any definitive answers to these questions, it needs to be emphasized that, at the end of the 1970s, anthropology was a normal scientific world. New questions were being posed on the balance of relations between the sexes in various types of societies, and they were being posed in adequate terms thanks to the continuity of a stabilized vocabulary. These new questions certainly reflected ongoing developments in America and elsewhere in the 1960s and 1980s, the era of the second feminist wave, centred on sexuality, the pill and abortion. It is normal, healthy even, that the evolution of the environment in which scholars live should lead them to new angles of research. Among anthropologists, the central object, the analysis of kinship systems, has always been based fundamentally on the duality of the sexes and the way in which this duality organizes society, in so many different ways. Thus, men and women could participate quite serenely in the debate. It is characteristic that, in the case of the confrontation between hunting and gathering, the 'feminists' were men, and that they were contradicted, on the basis of a dense technical argument, by a woman. True science has no sex.

I will now mention five books in order to illustrate the way the concepts of anthropology suffered a descent into hell. I will start with a book dating from 1938 to show how classical anthropology spoke of women before the era of feminism. The following four examples will show, successively, the relatively beneficial character of second-wave feminism, and the conceptual catastrophe that followed.

Julian Steward: sexual equality among hunter-gatherers described by a classical anthropologist

Killing two birds with one stone, I have chosen the work of Julian Steward (1902–72), the great anthropologist of the Indian groups of the inner basin of the Rocky Mountains and the plateau located further north, whom we will be using again later on in this study to illustrate how, on the eve of the Second World War, he raised the question of sexual equality. A quotation here is more useful than a comment.

> The matrimonial status of each sex was, with a few exceptions noted below, substantially equal. If native male dominance was to man's advantage, women's somewhat great economic importance in seed gathering offset it. There were virtually no noneconomic activities which either sex would use as a social lever. The family therefore was a well-balanced bilateral unit, neither sex having appreciable advantage.[16]

One expression of this sexual equality seems to have been the simultaneous practice of polyandry and polygyny.

I'm not arguing here for or against Steward's twofold idea that equality of the sexes resulted from the balance of economic contributions, and that polyandry was the result of this equality. I'm arguing that we need to see how, before recent feminism, classical anthropology posed with great clarity the question of sexual equality. I would add, however, that Steward also notes the predominance of a fraternal polyandry (several brothers and one wife) and of a sororal polygyny (one man and several sisters). The levirate and the sororate – the inheritance by a younger brother or sister of the wife or husband of the deceased elder partner – were also common. More generally, the human groups in this region show the importance of horizontal links between brother and sister, between brothers, and between sisters, in the association of nuclear families. This is perhaps the biggest difference between the original nuclear family and the nuclear family of the modern West which has weakened these horizontal links between siblings. Note that the brother–sister relationship is a variety of bond between men and women that seems to be of little interest to third-wave feminism, much less in any case than the husband–wife bond, which can lead to femicide, or the father–daughter bond, which can lead to incest of domination.

I now come to the study of the relation between men and women in recent anthropology.

Martin King Whyte: anthropology just before gender

The Status of Women in Preindustrial Societies, by Martin King Whyte, is a classic.[17] It was published in 1978, on the eve of the massive dissemination of the concept of gender. It was, of course, a response to the question of the balance between the sexes which was then arising in the Anglo-American world, but it's clear that the feminist movement was influencing research in a positive way at this stage.

Martin King Whyte analyses the status of women (and, therefore, let's not forget, the status of men) in pre-industrial societies by using a sample of just over ninety societies, itself drawn from Murdock's *Ethnographic Atlas*. It mixes hunter-gatherer societies with peasant societies, some of them advanced, but excludes industrial and urban societies. This nuanced book distinguishes between many dimensions in the status of women and the relationship between the sexes. It notes, with regard to the acquisition of resources, 16% of societies where the role of men is greater than that of women, 23% where the role of women is greater than that of men and 61% where the roles of men and women are equivalent. When he goes on to the question whether men might not feel obliged to dominate their women, he finds 67% of societies where this is indeed the case, but 30% where there is no question of this. (The total here is less than 100%,

because some societies do not give a clear answer.) When he examines
the right to beat one's wife, he observes 62% of societies where this right
exists, 25% where no physical violence between spouses, in either direction, is tolerated, and 13% where the spouses can fight symmetrically. As
for the sex of the gods, he records 13% of societies where all the gods
are male, 55% that possess gods of both sexes but with a male predominance, and 31% of complete divine egalitarianism.

Such an observation may perhaps slightly contradict current French
opinion polls (see chapter 15): the pre-industrial world, for the most
part, did not adhere to the stereotype of the zombie Christian world that
men have sexual needs superior to those of women, a belief to which
only 18% of societies subscribe. In 77% of the societies in the sample,
men and women have equivalent sexual needs, and in 4% women have
superior sexual needs, a belief shared by the Protestant and Catholic
witch-hunters of the sixteenth and seventeenth centuries.

Many of the figures in Whyte's book – and not just in the examples
I have given – suggest a one-third–two-thirds distribution: two-thirds of
societies show a male predominance, but in a third of societies, Martin
King Whyte observes no such thing.

There are two areas that fall outside this two-thirds rule, in different
senses: procreation and politics.

Let's start with the respective roles of the two parents in procreation:
in 87% of societies, they are thought to be equal, in 8% the father has
a more important biological role than the mother, and in 5% women
predominate. This 5% includes some societies which, like the Australian
Aborigines, deny the biological father's role in procreation. I will return
to this important point. My personal feeling is that an understanding of
the biological equivalence of both parents is in fact universal and that
the deviations from this awareness are cultural constructs, denials of the
obvious rather than manifestations of natural ignorance. Identifying the
equality of these biological contributions of men and women does not
exclude men's doubts as to the value of their contribution, given that
nature has dispensed with them from gestation.

The second exception to the two-thirds 'rule' is the set of variables
that involve political power, leadership in the group and the practice of
war: masculine predominance is in this case very clear, with proportions
higher than 80% or 90%.

Martin King Whyte comes to the conclusion that the status of women
in the pre-industrial world is very varied and that, for many societies,
according to his indicators, we cannot speak of a masculine predominance:

Many writings by both partisans and skeptics of the women's liberation
movement depict existing and previous societies as universally emphasizing male dominance over women. For the feminists this universal

53

male dominance is seen as the result of factors that can and will change (such as the past importance of male strength in subsistence activities), while the skeptics are more apt to search for biological and genetic arguments for why this dominance will remain inevitable in future societies. Our findings lead us to qualify the statements and assumptions coming from both sides. We do not find a pattern of universal male dominance but much variation from culture to culture in virtually all aspects of the position of women relative to men. Our findings do lead us to doubt that there are any cultures in which women are totally dominant over men [. . .] Yet from this it does not follow that in all societies men are absolutely dominant over women. Rather, there is substantial variation from societies with very general male dominance to other societies in which broad equality and even some specific types of female dominance over men exist. Women seem never to dominate men in all of social life, but the degree of male dominance ranges from total to minimal.[18]

In short, this is a (very good) book which proves that the notions of women's status and the relations between men and women (with their various social variabilities) were fully included in anthropology, before gender seized power, and without any need for conceptual innovation.

Henrietta Moore: The first disruptions

Let's jump forward ten years to find ourselves in 1988, the date by when, as shown in the previous chapter (figure 1.3), the word 'gendered' had begun its ascent. This was two years before the publication of Judith Butler's *Gender Trouble*. That same year saw the publication of the book by the English scholar Henrietta Moore, *Feminism and Anthropology*.[19] Its objective was to show what feminism had contributed to anthropology, including the notion of gender. When we read this book, it isn't always clear whether its author agrees with what she is describing or not. Right from the first lines of the first chapter, it is suggested that the feminist critique of anthropology is hardly justified. This criticism assumes that women have suffered 'neglect in the discipline'. But Moore is obliged to recognize that 'unravelling the history of that neglect is difficult', since 'women were not ignored by traditional anthropology' and that 'kinship and marriage' lie at the heart of its concerns.[20]

While Moore cites the work of Martin King Whyte on China, she does not mention his seminal book on women, which is, to put it mildly, a curious omission – or, more significantly, the start of the obliteration of the real history of women by third-wave feminism.

She evokes the idea of the mother as a cultural construction; in other words, she attempts to denaturalize the mother's biological functions. The examples she gives are hardly convincing. Placing the nannies of

Victorian English families – who effectively raised the children of other women – at the centre of human history is touching at best. As for her speculations about absent fathers, they refer, without it being said, to the Black American family, where, at this time, the role of the father was disintegrating.

This shows one of the great pitfalls of these third-wave feminist texts: while being accompanied by a denunciation of Occidentalism, they display a stunning Anglo-American narcissism. Moore seems to ignore the very specific character of the Black American family which, after stabilizing in the first half of the twentieth century, was shaken, from the 1960s onwards, first by the libertarian cultural revolution, then by neoliberalism. Likewise, she hardly recognizes the special character of the middle-class English family, where parents are traditionally distant from their children.

Feminism and Anthropology nonetheless remains an informative and interesting book. It contains an idea that may at first seem obvious but that we still need to constantly remember: relations between men and women are not only relations between husband (or companion) and wife or between father and daughter, but also the relation between mother and son, and between brother and sister (if we stick to the nuclear family). Though this was doubtless far from being Moore's intention, this thoroughly banal idea reveals that gender theory is half-blind. It pays hardly any attention to the relations between brother and sister, which are admittedly somewhat tenuous in the West, but above all it ignores the bond between mother and son – a bond which, as much as the bonds between father and daughter or father and son, albeit in a different way, raises the question of dominance and power.

Marilyn G. Gelber: the monstrous man

As early as 1986, the worst kind of ideas could be found in the work of American anthropologist Marilyn G. Gelber. Her book *Gender and Society in the New Guinea Highlands: An Anthropological Perspective on Antagonism toward Women* predates Moore's by two years.[21] It nevertheless marks a new low in the way anthropology was plunged into chaos through the notion of gender. Maybe we should ascribe Moore's 'belatedness' to the legendary restraint of English women.

Gelber indicts the object of her study, those New Guinean males who, having had the misfortune to survive the irruption of the Europeans into their world, are reproached for their way of life, one that was admittedly hardly favourable to women. But this is a step backwards to the nineteenth-century colonialism which passed judgement on the life of savages. New Guinea is one of the seven places on earth where agriculture was independently invented – which was not the case for Europe. Over the millennia, the heart of the highlands of this very large island has, like the Middle East, China, northern India and West Africa, witnessed the development of a patrilineal hub leading over the long term to a low status for women (see chapter 5). Gelber's book reaches the zenith of Western narcissism when she identifies American males with New Guinean males:

> Strangely enough, the respect [sic] in which the societies of the New Guinea Highlands most resemble our own seems to be in the personality of adult men. Once again, Highland society seems to echo or even caricature elements of American society: the forceful, invincible, maneuvering, and self-assured personality of Highland men is an exaggerated form of a certain ideal of manly behavior in our own society.[22]

Third-wave feminism denounces men in their masculine generality. Fine. The problem is that, when applied to historical anthropology, the denunciation of male predominance comes down to denouncing the whole of human history. And even to abolishing it. We enter the dream of a history that didn't happen but that *should have* happened. What does such an approach represent, intellectually? Coming 'from the left', it nevertheless seems, in its relationship to science, very close to the creationism that rejects Darwinism because it doesn't conform to the Bible – that other history which *should have* happened but didn't.

Janet Carsten: Decomposition

That brings us to the final step, decomposition, with *After Kinship* by Janet Carsten, published in 2003.[23] In it, we see how the notion of gender has had its fullest impact on anthropology, in a process that is quite logical despite some confusion in its general expression. After describing her childhood memories from the perspective of the household, Carsten expresses a rejection of the overly technical anthropology of kinship, which she doubtless sees as typically masculine: 'The study of gender played a crucial role in the gradual shift in attention in anthropology from the functioning of social institutions to the symbolic construction of people and relations.'[24]

From Murdock's ambition to create a global classification of concepts and cultures, we dive into the supposedly crucial importance of new but statistically very insignificant practices, such as assisted procreation, in the context of the definition of new forms of kinship. Carsten's discussion of the judgement of the Orthodox rabbis of Israel on artificial insemination has certainly rekindled my fondness for the Judaism of my maternal ancestors. The rabbis came to the (irrefutable) conclusion that artificial insemination complies with the Law if the sperm donor is not Jewish, because a good Jew doesn't masturbate and the matrilineal definition of Jewishness makes the father's biological contribution secondary from the religious point of view. However, this gem cannot compensate for the weakness of the rest: Carsten, for example, does not seem aware of the fact that the self-assurance of women increases with age in the Chinese family and she suggests the opposite. Such a blunder reveals an ignorance of the classics.[25] So there's no more comparative analysis of family and kinship systems in the world; we have to bid farewell to the quest for a global vision of the cultures invented by human beings, while the potential applications of an anthropological reading to other economic or political fields of human history are ruled out of court. Carsten demands that we focus more on emotions, the intimacy of the home and the personality, and on the body.

The ultimate result of this contribution of gender to thought is stupefying: Carsten ends up legitimizing the most hackneyed stereotypes about what differentiates women from men, intellectually and emotionally.

Let's rely on the *Sex Role Inventory*, which examines the traditional roles attributed to men and women, developed by the American psychologist Sandra Bem and published in 1974. Let's complete it with the stereotypes listed in the 1975 article by John E. Williams, Susan M. Bennett and Deborah L. Best, 'Awareness and Expression of Sex Stereotypes in Young Children'.[26] Here are the ideal types of traditional masculinity and femininity that we get:

- man is strong, active, dominating, independent, more rational, but at the same time more prone to take risks than woman, more outward-looking but at the same time more selfish than she is;
- woman is weak, passive, emotional, dependent, more intuitive, but at the same time more cautious than man, more turned towards interiority (whether it be the home or feelings), but at the same time more altruistic, more capable of compassion, more delicate.

And there you have it. With gender, anthropology – a discipline for which the study of the relationship between men and women had always been central, an instrument for comparing and understanding human societies – has dissolved into a narcissistic reverie, into the caricature of some psychology magazine for housewives under fifty. The extraordinary women who had contributed to the blossoming of the discipline are no more.

57

An insufficiently feminist history

When I say that I think the most recent feminism has damaged anthropology, it would be a mistake to believe that I am passing a general judgement on all of the human sciences. I was a historian before I became an anthropologist and I wouldn't in the least come to the same conclusions about the contribution of feminism to history, a contribution that is absolutely positive.

Male predominance is more entrenched and more resistant in the discipline of history. The evolution of the distribution of doctorates by sex, in both disciplines, in the United States for example, shows as much. Towards 1970, 25% of doctorates were already going to women in anthropology, but only 12% in history. From 1985 onwards, the proportion of women PhDs in anthropology caught up with men PhDs and, in 2007, 60% of doctorates in anthropology went to women.[27] Clearly, between 1985 and 2007, anthropology moved to a situation of matridominance. In history, the male sex has continued to resist: the number of female doctorates reached 49.3% in 2012 but fell to 48.9% in 2014.[28] In chapter 11, I give the equivalent figures for France.

I am convinced that a little more feminism in history, a little earlier, would have averted a monumental mistake, a blind spot in the well-known Laslett typology of households.

In his seminal *Household and Family in Past Time* (1972), Peter Laslett distinguished households according to whether they included just a conjugal family (a 'simple family household'), a conjugal family plus one or more unmarried individuals (an 'extended family household'), or several conjugal families (a 'multiple family household').[29] In addition to these three basic concepts he describes the categories of 'no family' (no couple) and 'solitary' (an individual alone). All over Europe, thousands of analyses of nominative listings of inhabitants were produced thanks to the methodical application of this typology, which is essentially effective – largely because, being standardized, it allows comparisons between one community and another. But Laslett had forgotten to make his typology say whether the aggregations, in the 'extended' and 'multiple' categories, were created by bonds on the side of the husband or the wife in the main couple. In other words, the Laslett typology does not capture the usual anthropological categories of patrilocality and matrilocality, although these had been formalized in the early 1930s in an article by anthropologist Paul Kirchhoff (1900–72), who was also the inventor of the concept of Mesoamerica.[30] Laslett's oversight resulted in a huge loss of information about the place of women in domestic organization. It considerably slowed down the encounter between history and anthropology. Such a blunder would not have been possible if the question of women in history had been asked earlier.

Recent research on witchcraft reveals a persistent inability on the part of male historians to incorporate into their models the fact that around 80% of witches executed at the dawn of modern times were *female* witches, women who were usually past the age of forty. While the superb essay by Hugh Trevor-Roper, *The European Witch-Craze of the 16th and 17th Centuries*, which dates from 1967, does highlight how Alpine and Pyrenean areas acted as initial incubators, and points out the balanced contributions of Protestant and Catholic elites in the massacre, it completely overlooks the question of the sex of the victims. Forty-six years later, *The Oxford Handbook of Witchcraft in Early Modern Europe and Colonial America* counts witches according to sex and age, country by country.[31] It establishes the centrality of the Germanic areas in this phenomenon. It shifts the focus from the madness of elites and sees it as the responsibility of rural communities, thus seeming to confirm that today the common people are less appreciated by historians than they were during the more democratic 1960s. But the *Oxford Handbook* fails to reach the radical feminist conclusion, which is also mine, that a murderous war on women was involved. Alison Rowlands, in a chapter titled 'Witchcraft and Gender in Early Modern Europe', admittedly reminds us that feminists of the first, second and third generations had identified a war of the sexes operating under the veil of magical and religious obsessions.[32] Patriarchal oppression, misogyny, gynocide ... I am less disturbed by these expressions, applied to the Germanic world of the sixteenth and seventeenth centuries, Switzerland included, than by the application of the terms 'patriarchy' or 'femicide' to France at the beginning of the third millennium. That period and that place witnessed the coming of age of the stem family, carrying a level 1 patrilineality. There was a certain overestimation of the extent of the massacre, but the feminist interpretation is the most likely. Characteristically, historians of witchcraft remain mostly male, and Alison Rowlands, a woman, treats her male colleagues with elegant tact, nuancing the idea of the centrality of sex in the way witch hunts were prosecuted. A count reveals that 19 out of 26 (73%) of contributors to the *Oxford Handbook* are men, and the book can be defined as heavily patridominated.[33]

The origin of the opposition between anthropology and history when it comes to the feminism–masculinism axis is not very mysterious. Anthropology's centre of gravity is the analysis of relations between men and women, at the heart of the life of pre-industrial societies and their kinship systems, and so it attracted women early on. In earlier generations, men's liking for history often stemmed from the time they were boys playing at war in the playground or with their tin soldiers. That's my case. Before reaching the sophistication of *Annales*-style history and delving into ordinary life, history is the tale of battles and conquests. Alexander, Caesar and Napoleon lie behind many vocations. I'm a little ashamed today to have preferred Sparta to Athens. We will soon know whether the integration of women into Western armies will eventually break down male dominance in the study of history.

— 3 —

THE TOOLS OF HISTORICAL ANTHROPOLOGY

After showing the harmfulness of the notions of patriarchy and gender for anthropology, let's see how its classic instruments can help us understand women's history. This chapter is certainly the most difficult of the book but, given that the history of women is the history of one half of humanity, it would be disrespectful to dispense with technical rigour in the approach to the subject.

Analysing family systems amounts to defining the status of women which, within each such system, is higher or lower. I will give a quick description, for each major family type, of a 'developmental cycle in domestic groups', a notion that was clearly formalized in anthropology from 1958 onwards, and an account of what each of the cycles implies for the status of women, without claiming to be exhaustive.[1] The types I will describe were those of the peasantry or the residual hunter-gatherers on the eve of industrialization and urbanization, obviously not the current types. The persistence of values – of authority, for example – after the disappearance of complex households in cities means that we could (in the same way that we speak of zombie Catholicism or Protestantism) describe a zombie stem family or a zombie communitarian family. This would make the going rather heavy, so I will just talk of a 'stem' culture, temperament or country for Japan or Germany, and of a 'communitarian' culture, temperament or country for Russia or China.

The nuclear family

Let's start with the simplest type, the *pure nuclear family* and its developmental cycle. The reader is likely to recognize this as what is usually considered to be the modern family. A wedding takes place and a couple comes into being; they have children and, when these reach adulthood, they go on to found other independent conjugal units. In this type of

61

family organization, the marriage system will be called *neolocal* since the young couple leaves.

Compared with that of the pure nuclear family, the developmental cycle of the *tempered nuclear family* is different in one significant way. The departure of the children does not take place abruptly, since there is generally a phase of *temporary co-residence*. When a child gets married, he stays with his parents or those of his spouse, often, but not always, until the birth of the first child. The very nature of the system is to be flexible and a bit fuzzy. After this, the young couple will leave, while tending to stay close to the parents. If temporary co-residence is on the husband's side, we call this a *virilocal* marriage. If it is on the wife's side, it's a *uxorilocal* marriage. If, finally, it follows the preferences of the individuals concerned, what we have can be described as a tempered nuclear family with *bilocal* temporary co-residence.

At the heart of the nuclear family, whether pure or tempered, we find the couple. Such a system, in which the fundamental bond is that between the spouses, implies a solidarity between them and therefore a degree of sexual equality, in a context of moderate patridominance. In the case of the nuclear family with virilocal temporary co-residence, there is a bias towards men; in the case of the family with uxorilocal temporary co-residence, a bias towards women. But in no case can the status of women be really low, precisely because of the principle of solidarity and mutual aid between spouses – a basic condition for economic survival.

If we want to get an idea of the neolocal pure nuclear family, we need just think of the English or American family, or the French family from the Parisian Basin. In the case of England and France, it can be observed from the seventeenth century onwards, described in detail, individual by individual, in lists of inhabitants drawn up by the vicar or the priest.

The nuclear family with temporary co-residence, whether virilocal, uxorilocal or, more often, bilocal, is typical of hunter-gatherers. In its virilocal variant, it is also characteristic of peoples of the Eurasian steppe (Kazakhs and Mongols), the nomads of Iran, and much of peasant southern India. In north Italy, we observe a proximity to the parent couple rather than a residency with them. In all these cases of virilocality, women's status is ambiguous since it combines the importance of the couple with its insertion into the patrilineal network defined by father–son ties. The uxorilocal variant of the tempered nuclear family dominates Southeast Asia and corresponds to a high status of women there, both in Buddhist countries such as Burma and Thailand and in Muslim countries such as Malaysia and Indonesia.

Bilocal temporary co-residence is characteristic, for example, of Indian hunter-gatherers of the inner basin of the Rocky Mountains, and of Belgians.

I have not so far mentioned the criterion of monogamy, or its negative, polygamy in its polygynous and polyandrous modalities. But we need to add to this summary description of the family the concept of a religious norm concerning marriage, a norm that is present or absent depending on the case.

Christian marriage prohibits polygamy and marriage between cousins far beyond the first degree. It does not interfere, on the other hand, with temporary co-residence. The marriage standard will be used here only in the case of Christianity, as the Muslim and Buddhist worlds behave differently. Islam allows polygyny up to four wives and often coincides, even if it does not demand this, with a preferential marriage between cousins; Tibetan Buddhism, as we have seen, admits polyandry and of course polygyny.

The work done for this book on berdaches and family systems among Indians of California, the inner basin of the Rocky Mountains and the plateau have influenced my typological vision. I ended up admitting that placing the tempered nuclear family of the Belgians or Icelanders and the tempered nuclear family of the Shoshone or Paiute Indians studied by Julian Steward into the same category, because they all practised bilocal temporary co-residence, was an oversimplification. The Belgian or Icelandic family can be more accurately described as a tempered nuclear family standardized, for marriage, by the Christian religion, and the Shoshone or Paiute family as the tempered nuclear family not standardized for marriage.

The stem family

The next step leads us to the complex family systems born from the emergence of the patrilineal principle. This principle, let us remember, preferentially associates a father and a son or, better, a father, a son and a grandson. It could take various forms. Let's focus first on the oldest, the *stem family*.

Let's go back to our developmental cycle and start from the same theoretical couple. They again have children, but this time, rather than all leaving upon marriage or soon after, one of them is selected to ensure the succession of the parent couple. The simple existence of a succession mechanism suggests that there is something to transmit. The stem family presupposes, in fact, some kind of possession, land, right of use over a place, or a craftsman's shop – and therefore sedentary societies, most often already endowed with agriculture. But there were also rules of primogeniture among the Kwakiutls mentioned above, those salmon fishermen from the west coast of Canada: in their case, fishing grounds, houses and 'noble' titles were the possessions likely to be transmitted.

63

The patrilocal stem family mainly appeared, however, quite logically, in the first centres of civilization born of agriculture, in Sumer during the third millennium BCE and in China around 1100 BCE.

Insofar as it's a matter of designating an heir, the question is the following: do we choose a boy, a girl, or one or the other indifferently? In fact, the *patrilocal* stem type (and no longer simply the *virilocal* type, since there is here a stable and definitive association of two generations), where it is the eldest of the sons, or more rarely one of the other sons, who is chosen, represents at least 75% of cases. It is one of the modes of emergence of the patrilineal principle, which is indeed accompanied by a new lowering of the status of women. But here we are dealing with a level 1 patrilineality which cannot go very far: demographic vagaries mean that not all families have a son to transmit anything to. The demographic situation of the seventeenth and eighteenth centuries in Europe and Japan, for example, meant that 20 to 30% of couples had no male descendants. The stem system thus usually allowed transmission to a daughter, whose husband was taken into the family.

Moreover, if this patrilocal stem system is favourable to men without being absolutely so, it is also because it treats younger boys like girls. It basically admits that some boys and some girls are worth the same – that is, in terms of inheritance, nothing at all. Girls have to go and find a husband elsewhere, of course, but sons who do not inherit must also leave, ideally to find an heiress in a family without sons. Such a system thus retains considerable ambiguity in the distribution of roles between the sexes and it cannot radically lower the status of women. The corresponding kinship systems generally remain bilateral in the sense of the term generally accepted by anthropologists, with paternal and maternal ascendants being equally important in the definition of the child's general social status. This is the case with German and Japanese stem families. Patrilocal stem family and bilateral kinship system: this means that Germany and Japan can be perceived as Western countries along with those bordering the Atlantic, nuclear by family and bilateral for kinship: these countries include England, the United States and northern France. The bilaterality of kinship, which corresponds both to nuclear and to stem families, also makes it possible to bring together, in a certain harmony and within a single country, the stem families of the southwest of France and the nuclear families of the Paris Basin.

My level 1 patrilineality, derived from the stem family's patrilocality, therefore does not fall within the patrilineality of classical anthropology, designed to describe a kinship system beyond the household; this latter generally includes only my level 2 and level 3 patrilinealities.

Male ultimogeniture, where the last-born boy is chosen as successor, generally corresponds to a weak stem type, less authoritarian and less favourable to boys than those who practise primogeniture. It represents the imperfectly transformed form of a nuclear family with temporary co-residence in which the elderly parents were looked after by the last-born. Ultimogeniture could be observed in Switzerland, in the canton of Bern in particular, and in the northwest of Germany, in Lower Saxony or in Friesland. Often the 'ultimogeniture stem' type and 'temporary co-residence nuclear' type are muddled together in the censuses: thus, the 1980 Thai census describe as 'stem' households those which include three generations but embody a nuclear family type with temporary co-residence in which the youngest of the daughters, along with her husband, looks after her elderly parents, a typical procedure in the uxorilocal tempered nuclear systems of Southeast Asia.

Korea, with its stem family system but with patrilineal kinship, is an exception. If a couple has no sons, they will choose a successor from the husband's lineage rather than transmitting their property to a daughter. This patrilineality explains the surge of selective foeticide which took place in South Korea from 1981 onwards and took the sex ratio to 113 boys for every 100 girls among births in 1988, falling to 106 in 2007 (but it was still 114 for the third child at this date).[2] Control of fertility in Korea has therefore led to sex-selective abortions by the parents in order to maximize their chances of having a boy, especially after the first birth if their first child was a girl. This surge of selective foeticide had no equivalent in Japan, which verifies the hypothesis that there is a persistent bilaterality in that country, and a status of women that is admittedly lower than in the United States or France, but nevertheless higher than in Korea. The fact that the surge was brought under control in Korea, thanks to government intervention, shows that patrilineality in Korea is still lower than in China, where the sex ratio still hasn't returned to normal. This very sensitive statistical indicator allows us to observe, in the present, the action of family systems beyond the rural world in which they were born, at the very heart of the modernity of birth control.

I have long considered Sweden as a country of stem families, after reading an article by Orvar Löfgren in the first half of the 1970s.[3] Swedish historians struggle to break away fully from this category. I considerably nuanced this description of Sweden in 2011 in my *L'Origine des systèmes familiaux*, as I felt that its stem type was very weak except on the coast.[4] In the context of a study of the status of women, and because Sweden presents itself as the world champion of applied feminism, I will eventually have to proceed, in chapters 12 and 13, to a complete re-examination of family history in that country. This re-reading will allow us to understand the deep logic of a matricentral social authoritarianism that has very little to do with the stem family, and is in any case distinct from those in Germany and Japan. In order to find significant points of comparison, this specific authoritarianism will have us looking towards the Atlantic, in Brittany, Ireland and Portugal.

There are stem systems where the child chosen to inherit is a girl. The classic case is that of the Garos and the Khasi of northeast India, as analysed in detail by Chie Nakane, already mentioned for her description of Japanese families and kinship patterns.[5] The Garos have a system of *primogeniture*, the Khasi one of *ultimogeniture*.

In another possible configuration, the choice falls on the eldest child regardless of sex. The Basque valleys are the classic example; this system can also be observed in some villages in Tohoku, in northeast Japan.

Among these types, we find slight differences in the status of women. This will be higher within the *matrilocal* stem family (as opposed to *uxorilocal*, as the aggregation of generations is stable) and within the *bilocal* stem family.

Any static vision of these systems would involve succumbing to a fixist illusion, a common mistake in anthropology, particularly among functionalists. For example, in the patrilocal version, things tend to become more rigid over time. In Japan, for example, where it emerged in the thirteenth century, the stem family did not reach a maximum level of perfection – along with its corresponding patrilineality – until the nineteenth century, in the Meiji period, when Japan entered Western modernity. The rule of primogeniture was then applied to the imperial family itself.

The stem family was identified by Frédéric Le Play, the first major analyst of family systems; his study of stem families was revitalized by the Cambridge scholar Peter Laslett's critique. The dispute ended with the essentials of what Le Play had described being validated by Richard Wall, Laslett's pupil and assistant – a triumph for nineteenth-century French science.

In addition to the nuclear family and the stem family, Le Play had described a third, more complex family type, which he had called the *patriarchal family* and which I designate by the expression *communitarian family*. Anthropologists from India and the Anglo-American world would call this the *joint family*. These transformations of terminology turn out to be successful in usage since they protected post-World War II anthropological work from the distortion of the term 'patriarchal' by the feminism of the years 1980–2020.

The communitarian family

The stem family, in its majority patrilocal variant, constitutes a first stage in the emergence of the patrilineal principle, which does not lead to a general reorganization of kinship. The high level of Korean patrilineality is the result of a Chinese influence, not the effect of a dynamic specific to its stem family. The emergence of the patrilocal communitarian family implies, on the other hand, that of a patrilineal architecture of kinship.

Let's go back to the developmental cycle in domestic groups: the original couple produces children again, but this time, it's not only the eldest son who, after his marriage, remains with his parents, but all the sons. Unlike the stem system, the communitarian system cannot function without sons. The continuity of the domestic group is not a problem for it. When the father dies, the sons divide the inheritance more or less quickly. With the patrilocal communitarian family, we move to a potentially lower status of women since they are no longer at the heart of the family organization: on one side there are all the men, who have the same value, and, on the other, all the women, who also have the same value, but this is a low value since they are exchanged between families like so many parcels.

We must bear in mind that this system, like the stem system, has a history and evolves: it has a time to appear, a time to improve, and then, often, as we will see in chapter 5, a time to become fossilized. Initially, the status of women is not very low. This explains the coexistence in Russia, where the communitarian family dates only from the seventeenth century, or even the eighteenth, of a perfect patrilineal architecture with a status of women that remains quite high. Russian communitarian family structures are striking when one examines the village censuses of the nineteenth century, with their vast family aggregates where all bonds go through men.[6] But the average age gap between spouses is nil, and many women are older than their husbands. This paradox makes it possible to understand why we feel close to Russian literature. If the status of women in Russia had been as low as in Chinese or Arab cultures, Western women wouldn't be able to identify with the Natasha of *War and Peace* or the eponymous heroine of the novel *Anna Karenina*. The fact remains that Anna Karenina's divorce causes her to lose her son, as befits any self-respecting patrilineal system. Russian onomastics put the father's first name before the family name, for both girls and boys, for Bolshevik leaders – Vladimir Ilyich Ulyanov (Lenin), Lev Davidovich Bronstein (Trotsky), Joseph Vissarionovich Dzhugashvili (Stalin) – as for Tolstoy's heroines Anna Arkadyevna Karenina and Natalya Ilyinichna Rostova (Natasha). It would be a lapse of taste not to mention the revolutionary Alexandra Mikhailovna Kollontai.

I dare not attribute to Russia more than a level 1 patrilineality, as in Germany, and even this is rather lenient for Germany. My personal feeling is that the German patrilineal stem family has, over time, led to the woman's status being a little lower than in the Russian communitarian family. We could, admittedly rather superficially, take the incapacity of German literature to produce a Natasha or an Anna Karenina as evidence of this. But if we are comparing Russia and Germany, a more solid parameter such as the sex ratio in higher education (125 women for every 100 men in Russia, 106 women for every 100 men in Germany) supports the hypothesis that Germany is less feminist than Russia.

The drama of the communitarian family is played out in the later phases of its development: the patrilineal architecture has its own dynamics which leads to an ever greater decline in the status of women.

In China, the communitarian family is older and patrilineality has reached level 2. The old infanticide of girl babies followed, at the heart of modernity, by selective foeticide, is sufficient proof. These days, selective foeticide also occurs in Georgia, Azerbaijan and Armenia, but certainly not in Russia.

Confinement seems the right criterion for defining a level 3 of women's oppression. The Arab family system unproblematically falls into this category. The case of northern India is a bit more complicated. Here, the confinement of women (purdah) is found together with infanticide. If I were to award a prize for the lowest status given to women, it would therefore probably be in this region. I even sometimes wonder if it wouldn't be appropriate to speak in this case of a level 4 patrilineality, but the absence of marriage between cousins, and thus of absolute confinement in close kinship, forbids me to make this conceptual leap.

According to 'Arabic marriage', which values marriage between the children of two brothers, the ideal daughter-in-law is a niece, which partly explains the rejection of infanticide by the Arabic world. Endogamy, which confines women a little more within their families, infantilizes them but also protects them. These remarks apply to Iran and Pakistan, which practise marriage between cousins. Islam certainly led to the spread of 'Arabic marriage', but there is no Qur'anic prescription about it.

My description of the communitarian family of the Arab–Persian world is schematic here. A closer look would reveal innumerable nuances, the most important of which would certainly be the feminist inflection of Shiite-influenced cultures. As N.J. Coulson has shown in his classic *Succession in the Muslim Family*,[7] in the absence of a son, a daughter inherits the bulk of the father's estate in the Shia variant of Islam, while the bulk of the estate goes to the more distant male relatives in the Sunni tradition.

The communitarian family can exist in matrilocal forms, with an aggregation of couples around women. We find this form among the Hopi Indians of the southwestern United States, and in Amazonia. In this configuration, there is no lowering of the status of women, of course. But we need to realize that these cases are rare. The same applies to the bilocal communitarian family, which links brothers and sisters and their respective spouses. This kind of system may seem exotic but it used to be found on the northwest edge of the Massif Central, between the Dordogne and the Nièvre, where, without being necessarily a majority practice, it was quite frequent. Here, the assumption of a lowering of the status of women is also implausible.

In Western Europe, the only example of a fully developed patrilineal communitarian family system is found in central Italy. It doubtless dates back to the Lombard invasion of the sixth century. As regards the lowness of the status of women, I would place it halfway between China and Russia, close to that of Germany. Without practising female infanticide, this part of the world produced, in eighteenth-century Florence, an influx of abandoned female newborns entrusted to the Hospital of the Innocents. Once, while I was working on my thesis, I found many of them placed in peasant families and recorded in the parish records of Pratolino, designated by the expression *degli Innocenti*.

The local group and marriage

The definition of family types by the principles of co-residence, viri- and uxorilocality, and patri- and matrilocality should not make us forget that, around the family, there is the local group, itself organized according to the principles of bilocality, virilocality and uxorilocality. The family never lives alone; it is part of a community just as necessary to its survival as is solidarity within the couple and/or between generations.

Marriage outside the family group, known as exogamous, presupposes the existence, not only of a local community, but also of a population of at least a thousand people if we want to avoid all marriages between first cousins.

The local group can be isolated by family endogamy which, in the Arabic–Persian world, as we have just seen, favours marriage between cousins born to two brothers, or, if the right partner is not available, between all types of cousins. In the central Arabic world, there is an average of 35% of marriages between first cousins; in Morocco and Iran, the figure reaches only 25%. In Pakistan it reaches 50% – a rate maintained among second-generation emigrants in Bradford, England – and Pakistan probably has the most stifling type of endogamous communitarian family. Muslim Malaysia practises cousin marriage, but not, it seems, the bulk of Indonesia. The case of Malaysia, which is matrilocal, shows us that neither Islam nor endogamy lead systematically to a low status for women.

There is another major model of family and therefore local endogamy, namely marriage between 'cross-cousins', children of a brother and a sister. It is combined, in southern India, with a tempered nuclear family with virilocal temporary co-residence. It highlights the importance of a bond between brother and sister, and thus expresses or nourishes a status of women that's much higher than in northern India. The better status of women clearly explains the notably higher educational performance of southern India, and the presence in the Deccan of the most dynamic cities, including those IT capitals, Bangalore, Hyderabad, Mumbai and Chennai.[8]

So we see that, from a few simple elements, we can describe dozens of family forms and get a sense of their persistent affects in the most recent modernity. Maybe it's this kind of Meccano which really annoys Janet Carsten, whom I criticized in chapter 2. She prefers to tell us all about 'intimacy', and what *really* happens inside the home. Yes, we should hear about it, it would be wonderful ... to know everything about everything. Astrophysicists would also probably like to visit black holes or, more modestly, the heart of the sun. But how are we to compare the intimacy, the secret feelings, of an English family with those of a French, German, Russian, Chinese, Arab, northern Indian, southern Indian, or West African family? The problems of intimate life are everywhere, but how can we situate the peoples of the world with regard to each other in terms of intimacy by means of objective criteria? How can we make sense of women's history if every anthropologist loses him- or herself in their subjectivity? The discipline ends up, once gendered and patri-archized, being less effective than comparative literature. You might as well read Tolstoy and Turgenev, Jane Austen and Agatha Christie, Guy de Maupassant and Maurice Leblanc, Stefan Zweig and Thomas Mann, Tanizaki and Kawabata, Ed McBain and Philip K. Dick, if you want to understand cultures. Classic anthropology, with its combinations and permutations, as precise as they are rich, is even more effective when it comes to understanding the diversity of the world, and even, if one has a little imagination, to approaching the infinite variety of subjectivi-ties involved, and understanding the individuals behind the populations. I can guarantee that knowing the specific importance of the brother–sister bond in southern India will help you crack some excellent jokes to a Brahman from the middle classes of Bangalore.

— 4 —

IN SEARCH OF THE ORIGINAL FAMILY

We Westerners have a wrong idea of the 'modernity' of our family and what we are. We perceive the Arabs and the Africans as being 'behind'. We are less inclined to describe the Chinese in this way nowadays, at the time of the Covid epidemic, when we depend on them for our masks and our toys, or the Indians of South Asia, producers of software and medicines. Nevertheless, in the Arabic–Muslim world, in West Africa, in northern India and in China, we find complex family systems in which the status of women is lower than in the West, and the common view is that these peoples represent our past. We have evolved, we have become individualists, and finally granted women the status of fully fledged individuals. Such a representation justifies our insistence on demanding that these other countries adapt. Their destiny, we feel, is simply to catch up with us. To improve the fate of women was one of the justifications for the twenty-year-long occupation of Afghanistan. We know how that turned out.

Nothing is more false than this vision of the history of family systems. Those systems from the patrilineal block, which we consider to be retrograde, are from the point of view of history, as we shall see, the most evolved and the most complex. Westerners in the narrow sense, that is to say the Anglo-Americans, the French of the Paris Basin, and the Scandinavians, in short, the peoples of the western fringe of Eurasia, have the most archaic types of family organization.

Classical anthropology and the original family

Classical anthropology understood that the original family was nuclear. It came to this understanding by comparing the residual hunter-gatherers with the agricultural peoples of societies with or without a state. One conclusion was obvious: the family was much simpler among hunter-gatherers than among most of the agricultural peoples who had developed state systems.

As early as 1875, Frédéric Le Play, in a short – and actually quite ideological – book, *L'Organisation de la famille* (*The Organization of the Family*), ascribed the nuclear family, which in his view was also the 'unstable family', to the Gauls and the 'Indian hunters who still populate, at the same latitudes, vast forests in North America'.[1] The nuclear family, which separates married children from their parents early on, and in which relations between generations are distended, may seem logically deducible from the fact that the parents have very few assets to pass on to their children. It would be erroneous to argue this way: we must never deduce an external 'reality' from an a priori drawn from our brains. That would be the anti-empirical attitude par excellence, the attitude of the Descartes who was wrong. Le Play avoids this pitfall: he draws his description from the original 'unstable' family of the observations of eighteenth-century French missionaries and explorers on the Indians of North America. His argument is based first and foremost on observation. His rigour fails him when he comes to the Gauls: he probably deduces their 'unstable family' from their legendary indiscipline, without possessing the least data.

After him, in 1891, Edward Westermarck, in his *History of Human Marriage*, came to the same conclusion.[2] As we saw in the introduction, Westermarck explained, in a way that, for his time, was very modern and Darwinian, the success of the human species through the effectiveness of the monogamous nuclear family in rearing its young. *The Origin of Species* dated from 1859. One element in Westermarck's conclusion, however, left him perplexed: the resemblance between the Western family system and that of the primitives. To explain this, he described a cycle leading from the simplicity of primordial times to a complexification, followed by a return to simplicity. This idea of a cycle was taken up. In a 1956 article, Lévi-Strauss also noticed this oddity: the family appeared to him to be simple in structure both among primitives and among the most modern peoples.[3]

The idea of an original nuclear family forms a consensus among American anthropologists: the Americans Robert H. Lowie (1883–1957) and George P. Murdock endorse it.[4] There was nothing remarkable about this: their subjects of study were the Indians of their own continent, whose family nuclearity was glaringly obvious. British anthropologists, whose field was mainly Africa, a continent where the family systems are on the whole very complex, either patrilineal or matrilineal, had a much harder time of it. The best-known examples of nuclear families in Africa are scattered and visibly residual: the Bushmen[5] from the south of the continent or the Pygmies of the equatorial forest, hunter-gatherers, and the Amharas from the Ethiopian highlands, a Christian people integrated into a state system.

Martin King Whyte comes to a similar conclusion about the evolution of the family, from the nuclear to the complex (and therefore to the patrilineal), when moving from hunter-gatherers to dense peasant societies controlled by states. The status of women, overall, declines. He attributes the increase in the power of men to the new opportunities offered by the increasing economic and social complexity:

[T]hrough a series of variables, we can compare cultures that have features that emerged early in the scale of human evolution (pottery making, nomadic bands) with cultures having features that emerged relatively late (the plow, settled towns and cities). It is this sort of comparison that shows the strongest and most consistent results. In the more complex cultures, women tend to have less domestic authority, less independent solidarity with other women, more unequal sexual restrictions, and perhaps receive more ritualized fear from men and have fewer property rights, than is the case in the simpler cultures.[6]

There is, however, a seemingly relevant criticism of the idea of an original nuclear family of *Homo sapiens* derived from the sole examination of residual hunter-gatherers. Those who survived the Neolithic (i.e. agricultural) and industrial revolutions cannot be considered representative of their prehistoric counterparts. In ancient times, all sorts of groups may have lived in different ecological contexts, better or worse, depending on location and climate. Think of the Ice Age reindeer hunters in the Dordogne, to whom we owe Lascaux, or their successors who set out to conquer northern Europe after the thaw. And of so many others in Asia and Africa. The fact remains that if, everywhere on the periphery of the inhabited world, we find nuclear family systems, borne by populations separated by the oldest migrations (*Sapiens* reached Australia 60,000 years ago, according to the most recent estimates, Europe 40,000 years ago, North America 15,000 years ago – these dates are obviously approximate), this is because this nuclear system was a common trunk. And if, moreover, the so-called modern peoples of the periphery of the inhabited world are also the bearers of a nuclear family structure, we are very close to a general solution for the perplexity of Edward Westermarck, Claude Lévi-Strauss and Martin King Whyte. Here I will propose my general hypothesis on the evolution of family systems, firstly as it was proposed in *L'Origine des systèmes familiaux* for Eurasia, then by extending it to the entire planet, by the new cartographic use of the Murdock Atlas that I announced in the introduction. In chapter 6, I will examine in detail the problem of the Australian Aborigines, a problem that has unnecessarily complicated anthropology, sociology and psychoanalysis for over a century. I will show that, freed from the prejudice of an intrinsic Western modernity, we can quite easily situate the Australian Aborigines, not at

73

the source of history, but as influenced by the evolution of New Guinea, which lies so close to them.

The block in anthropology

While classical anthropology had seen that the original family was nuclear, and of the tempered variety according to my categories, it did not manage to draw the most important conclusions from this discovery. The block resulted from its reluctance to include 'developed' Westerners in its field of study. It had, at best, like Westermarck, imagined a historical cycle going from simplicity to complexity and then, again, towards simplicity. It ignored the essential: the kinship of hunter-gatherers and Western Europeans. The latter have not 'returned' to simplicity, they quite simply never left it.

The 'developed' man, who feels developed, seems unable to get rid of the presupposition that anthropological analysis 'is not for him' and should only be applied to primitive people.

The conservatism of peripheral zones: English, Americans, French, Shoshones, Bushmen, Eskimos, Chukchi and Agtas in one humanity

As far as I am concerned, I managed, with the help of my linguist friend Laurent Sagart, to come to the conclusion of a tempered nuclear original family, not by comparing hunter-gatherers with agricultural societies, but by applying, in a way unprejudiced by Occidentalism, in my reading of the map, the principle of the conservatism of peripheral zones (PCPZ).[7]

We have placed all peoples on the same logical plane, without taking account of their level of development on the eve of urbanization. We need to treat in the same way the English, the French, the Shoshones, the subarctic Denes, the Eskimos, the Siberian Chukchi, the Tagalogs and the Agtas of Luzon, as they are all nuclear; the Germans, the Japanese, Rwandans, Bamilekes of Cameroon, the Kwakiutls of western Canada, all of whom observed rules of primogeniture; and the Russians, the Chinese, the Indians of Uttar Pradesh, the Persians and the Arabs from the Mashreq to the Maghreb, the Tallensis of northern Ghana, and the Mossis of Burkina Faso, who all have communitarian and patrilineal family structures. We avoid the definition of anthropology as a science of primitives.[8] Let us also apply, when interpreting the maps, the explanatory principle of the conservatism of peripheral zones, well known to American anthropologists before the Second World War, but stupidly

74

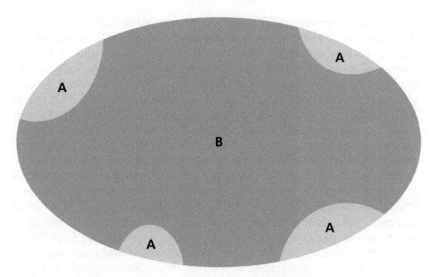

Figure 4.1 The conservatism of peripheral zones: typical diagram
Source: Emmanuel Todd, *L'Origine des systèmes familiaux*, vol. 1, *L'Eurasie* (Paris: Gallimard, 2011), p. 24

rejected by Murdockian or Levi-Straussian structuralism afterwards. What does it tell us?

The PCPZ makes it possible to read a history in the geographical distribution of phenomena captured at a given moment. Take the spatial distribution of two features, A and B (see figure 4.1). If feature B completely occupies a central zone and if feature A is distributed across several separate peripheral zones, it is likely that feature B was an innovation that has spread towards the periphery: the zones characterized by feature A represent the residual implantation of a previously predominant feature over the entire mapped space. The likelihood of this explanation increases with the number of peripheral A zones.

However, if we look at the distribution of current family types, focusing solely on Eurasia for now, what do we see? We find, inter alia, the pure nuclear family in England, in France, in the Paris Basin, in central and southern Spain, in central Portugal, and the tempered nuclear family in Iceland, among the Lapps of northern Scandinavia and the Kola Peninsula in Russia.[9] But we also find a tempered nuclear family among the Palaeo-Siberians of northeast Siberia, throughout Southeast Asia, from Burma to the Philippines, via Cambodia and Indonesia, as well as in the Andaman Islands, between India and Burma. Sri Lanka provides the case of a nuclear family of yet another kind. I won't go into the details, but the peripheral distribution of the nuclear family is not in doubt.

Patrilocal communitarian systems are observed in China, in Vietnam (or rather, in north Vietnam), in northern India, in the whole of the Middle East as far as the Maghreb and West Africa, and in Russia, occupying a vast connected mass, along an axis that I named (above) the Beijing–Baghdad–Ouagadougou (BBO) axis. The developmental cycle leading from father to sons is the same everywhere even in this vast space, but the marriage system varies. It is endogamous in the Arab–Persian world, radical exogamous in northern India and in Russia, tempered exogamous in China, massively polygynous in West Africa, with more than 35% of women there sharing a husband with a co-wife.[10]

The interpretation of such a map is a simple matter: the original system of humanity was the nuclear family, in its various tempered variants. Then came the innovations that led to the predominance of the patrilocal communitarian family in the central block. The presence of the stem family in Germany, Japan and Korea further supports this hypothesis. It is intermediate in complexity between the nuclear and communitarian types, and also by geographical position. It is commonplace, in Japan anyway, to feel that Germany and Japan have something similar in terms of mentalities; this is an effect of the stem family, of the discipline of behaviours it fosters, and the economic and social efficiency it makes possible. Of course, Japan is far from Germany, which is so close to us, but these two countries have in common the fact that they are located on opposite sides of the great mass of Eurasian patrilocal communitarian structures. They are distant but similar.

If we convert these geographical observations into a chronological sequence that focuses on women, we are forced to admit that, in Eurasia, the status of women did not rise with modernity in a vast movement towards family nuclearity and individualism. We are confronted, on the contrary, with a history in which the original, nuclear family, where women's status was quite high, was replaced, first by the stem family which marks a first lowering of the status of women, then by the communitarian family which conceals within itself several possible and successive stages in the lowering of this status. The pioneer regions in this evolution were Mesopotamia, followed by China and then by northern India. The extent of the lowering of women's status is roughly proportional to the time that has elapsed since the stem innovation. I reproduce in figure 4.2, with some modifications, the diagram which concluded *L'Origine des systèmes familiaux*; it shows the chronological thickness of this transformation in the geographical spaces which make up Eurasia.

In *Lineages of Modernity*, I extended to Africa the sequence leading from the nuclear family to the communitarian family.[11] The zone of innovation is in West Africa, inland, where we find the densest communitarian forms, while more nuclear forms have survived in eastern and southern Africa, with a higher status of women. In two intermediate

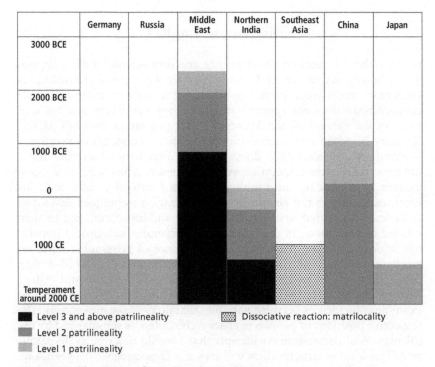

Figure 4.2 The stages of patrilineality in history
Source: after Emmanuel Todd, *L'Origine des systèmes familiaux*, p. 593

zones, between southern Benin and southern Cameroon on the one hand, and in the highlands of the east and in particular in Rwanda on the other hand, we observe stem forms.

The model is complicated in Africa by the addition of a mass polygyny, at a maximum in West Africa but decreasing towards the east and the south. Hunter-gatherer groups, pygmies of the equatorial forest and southern Bushmen, the most peripheral because they are protected by the forest or by distance, are nuclear and monogamous, closest to the original simple form. The Amharas of Ethiopia likewise, despite their complex state society, because they were protected from polygyny and patrilineality by their position of refuge on the highlands and by the preference of early Christianity for family nuclearity. I will return to this point in chapter 8, devoted to the co-evolution of family and religion. The Amhara nuclear family, however, like that of the Pygmies, has a virilocal bias, the effect of patrilineal diffusion.[12]

Saving Private Murdock

I confess that I do not find Lévi-Strauss's structuralism useful when applied to the family. As shown by Laurent Barry in *La Parenté* (*Kinship*), his elementary matrimonial exchange – marriage with the matrilateral female cross-cousin – does not appear statistically very significant: just 4.2% of cases in the version of the Murdock *Atlas* put online by D-PLACE.[13] A theory based on such a small number of cases cannot get us very far.

Murdock's structuralism doesn't get us anywhere either, but for a different reason than quantitative insufficiency. Murdock, as a good student of American anthropology, collected extensive data with his team, extending to the planet the standardization techniques developed at Berkeley by Alfred Kroeber (1876–1960) and his school. But he then refused to map them, in the name of a structuralist categorical imperative which denies, on principle, the importance of geographic diffusion mechanisms, although these were studied by Franz Boas (1858–1942), Clark Wissler (1870–1947), Robert Lowie (1883–1957) and Alfred Kroeber, his masters. Murdockian structuralism is therefore content to examine coincidences between variables that do not take into account the respective positions of peoples in space – coincidences summarized by the calculation of correlation coefficients that I would describe as despatialized. This kind of structuralism will seek a correspondence between, say, dense agriculture and patrilineality (a correspondence that does indeed exist, but is not absolute), but will refuse to examine the spreading of patrilineality to hunter-gatherers or nomadic herders who live next to patrilineal farmers, and admire them as soon as these possess writing, bronze and a state – and then imitate them. The subsequent diffusion of patrilineality acquired by the nomads, now organized into formidable warrior clans thanks to the association of father, sons and cousins – from the Huns to the Mongols – will not be examined by structuralists. In other words, patrilineal diffusion in Eurasia, intuited by Lowie in *Primitive Society*, will not be identified. Let's not even think about the nomadism of the African Sahel as another factor of diffusion.

Still, unlike Lévi-Strauss, Murdock left us a monument of knowledge, the *Ethnographic Atlas*, and his structuralist errors are, in the grand scheme of science, a venial sin. We are going to show, in a few maps, that once we have freed ourselves from the anti-diffusionist prejudice, we can draw from the *Atlas* the sketch of a history of the relations between men and women for the whole world and no longer just for Eurasia.

Murdock's sample is very deficient as regards Europe, but it nonetheless attributes to enough Western peoples a system of kinship, a type of residence after marriage, a family organization and a level of the ban on marriage between cousins. So let's put the 1,291 peoples of the *Atlas*

78

in its latest version on a map. The reader will have had a first glimpse of the results that can be drawn from Murdock in chapter 1, with map 1.1, on patrilineality, matrilineality and bilaterality, which, as we have shown, anticipates the distribution of sex ratios (map 1.2), and the map of the composite indicator of feminism from the *Global Gender Gap Report* (map 1.3). Map 1.4 converted the Murdock data so as to define a rate of patrilineality for most states on the planet, a version of map 1.1 for our own era. We will now read time in space, and history in geography.

We started by mapping kinship systems because data on the family, in the sense of a domestic group, are less reliable in the *Atlas*. The developmental cycle of the domestic group is a late concept in anthropology – it was created in 1958 by Meyer Fortes (1906–83) and Jack Goody (1919–2015) – and so the description of family forms in the *Atlas* is rather imperfect. One might as well start with what's clearest.

Map 1.1 of patrilineality, derived from the *Atlas* (p. 39), is very simple. It shows the principle of diffusion at work. It clearly shows a vast unified patrilineal zone along the BBO axis, central and therefore innovative. This spreads from West Africa to China. We find the bilateral and matrilineal systems on the periphery of Eurasia. In Africa, matrilineal systems are in contact with the central patrilineal zone while, further south, among the Bushmen, we find bilateral kinship systems, as in Sri Lanka, in the Andaman Islands, near India and throughout Southeast Asia. The patrilineal patch located in South Africa corresponds to a very recent breakthrough of peoples through the matrilineal belt. The patrilineality observable in New Guinea, whose shadow across Australia can be perceived, should be seen as an independent innovation, just like the patrilineal patch to the east of the US Great Lakes. If we consider the New World as a whole, we can see how dominated it is by bilateral kinship systems in spite of some irregularities. As regards the patrilineal pockets of southern California and the Amazon rainforest, I cannot say anything at the current stage of my research, as I don't know whether the data need to be interpreted or refuted. The mass of bilateral kinship systems in the New World confirms the image of a primordial continent, unaffected by the anti-feminist family transformations of the Old World. New Guinean patrilineality, with its Australian annex, alerts us to the fact that Oceania is part of the Old World.

Not all of Murdock's data can be taken as indisputable. His main errors relate to Eastern Europe. Map 1.1 suggests that all kinship systems there are bilateral. However, with the exception of Poland, they are in fact more or less patrilineal and should therefore appear as such.[14]

What is stunning, however, is how merely projecting three categories – bilateral, patrilineal, matrilineal – onto a planisphere makes possible a global approach to the history of human beings.

We now come to the family, grasped as much as possible through the development of the domestic group. Let's start with the residence of spouses defined by marriage, in two cartographic stages. Map 4.1 distinguishes between patrilocality and matrilocality, which point to a complex family system stably combining two adult generations, virilocality and uxorilocality that involve temporary co-residence or proximity to one of the families of origin, on the side either of the husband or of the wife: the tempered nuclear family, in other words. We say 'point to' because the correspondence between viri- or uxorilocality and the tempered nuclear family is far from automatic in the *Atlas*: German and Japanese stem families also appear as virilocal, despite the stability of the bond between the father and the son who is his successor. It is true that the other children leave, which creates a very partial patrilocality. Avunculocality, as defined by the typology of Paul Kirchhoff, designates the cases where the young groom will settle with the family of his maternal uncle, a movement most often associated with a matrilineal organization of kinship.[15] The young man does indeed succeed to the property of his maternal uncle. Often, this procedure is accompanied by a marriage with the daughter of this uncle, the matrilateral cross-cousin dear to Lévi-Strauss. The corresponding family structure is most often nuclear as will be shown by map 4.3; it does not lead to stable co-residence with the uncle.

The category 'other' of map 4.1 is broken down in map 4.2 into its subcategories: neolocality, which suggests the pure nuclear family, and ambilocality according to Murdock, a marriage procedure that can evoke either a bilocal tempered nuclear family, or a larger but more nebulous structure, associating such families in a structure that is ill-defined – complex in Murdock's view, but not if we follow my categories. The ambilocality also includes the Basque stem family which chooses the eldest child, whether girl or boy, as successor.

Map 4.1 describes a world very close to that of maps 1.1 (kinship), 1.2 (sex ratio) and 1.3 (current feminism). We can measure how close the concepts of patrilineality and patrilocality are in practice. The peripheral position of the virilocal, uxorilocal, avunculocal and 'other', all of which refer to the nuclear family and a status of women that is not too low, or even not low at all, is evident. The central position of patrilocality, which in turn suggests the communitarian family, is obvious and, here again, the BBO axis works.

On map 4.2, which distinguishes neolocality from ambilocality, we observe even better than on the previous one, albeit in reverse, the central patrilineal effect: the distribution remains perfectly peripheral when compared to our BBO patrilineal axis, which crosses northern India and the Arab–Persian world with a void. The small number of cases of separate residence clearly designate New Guinea as the epicentre of the antagonism between men and women, in a patrilineal context.

80

Map 4.1 Residence of spouses: after their marriage
* See next map
Source: Ethnographic Atlas

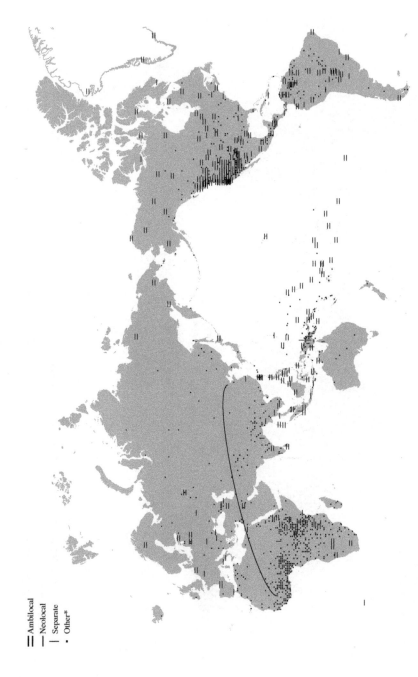

Map 4.2 Residence of spouses: neolocality and ambilocality
* See previous map
Source: Ethnographic Atlas

Legend:
- ‖ Ambilocal
- — Neolocal
- | Separate
- · Other*

The *Atlas* also offers a usable description of nuclear family types.[16] Map 4.3 depicts the monogamous nuclear family, the nuclear family with limited polygyny, and the 'independent family' if polygyny is statistically frequent, further distinguishing cases of 'atypical' polygyny.[17] It has the merit of clearly showing the importance of the independent family in Africa and among the Australian Aborigines, but it calls for caution regarding the way the *Atlas* uses the patrilocal category of map 4.1 for these regions: for, if the family is independent, several married men cannot be associated within it by stable co-residence. Virilocality might have been a better term. But we here have to face the fact that there is a certain blurring of the concepts of patrilocality and virilocality in the *Atlas*; this, rather than false data, is the problem.

These few maps reveal the power of an interpretation in terms of diffusion. They allow us to grasp the origin of the human family. We can see the emergence of a sort of ideal-type of the original, peripheral, nuclear or independent family, most often tempered, monogamous or moderately polygynous, and where the status of women remains high. We can see the correspondence between bilateral kinship systems and neolocal or bilocal, virilocal and uxorilocal residence after marriage.

We can complete this description of the simple origin of the family, of an individualistic and free birth of mankind, by projecting onto our planisphere the type of choice of spouse.

The Western bias of seeing a stifling complexity in the past, and an individualist simplicity in the present, often extends to the taboo on incest. However, Westermarck had demonstrated its natural character concerning the relationship between brother and sister or parents and children. Saint Augustine had noted the Romans' avoidance of cousin marriage in the absence of an official ban, a proof, according to him, of its natural character. It should be understood that the prohibition on marriage within kinship defines an obligation of choice in an open world, that the *ban* on marriage between cousins implies a certain *freedom*.

Map 4.4 of preferred or forbidden marriages, derived from Murdock's data, allows us to verify a dominant prohibition on marriages between first cousins – i.e. freedom – not only among hunter-gatherers but in all peripheral regions of the world. Again, Western Europeans and American Indians are close, but also close to the Bushmen of South Africa and the Australian Aborigines.

A geographical analysis of the information contained in Murdock's *Ethnographic Atlas* thus allows us to make a simple test of the idea that human marriage has evolved from exogamy to endogamy.

Arab endogamy – between the children of two brothers, of two sisters, or of a brother and a sister – is central on the map. It marks a step forward from patrilineality, with a preference for marriage between the children of two brothers that expresses their affection beyond the

○ Nuclear, monogamous
◐ Nuclear, limited polygyny
▲ Polygyny, typical co-wives pattern
△ Polygyny, atypical co-wives pattern
▶ Polyandrous
• Other

Map 4.3 The nuclear or independent family
Source: Ethnographic Atlas

○ Maximal exogamy
◑ Intermediate exogamy
● Minimal exogamy

Map 4.4 Exogamy and endogamy
Source: Ethnographic Atlas

present. Women, as we have said, are confined even more effectively by the Arab or Persian endogamous communitarian family than by the Russian pure exogamous communitarian family or the Chinese tempered exogamous communitarian family. The endogamous marriages indicated by the *Atlas* for Christian Europe are errors of categorization that we have left in place in order to be faithful to our source.

Marriage between cross-cousins, that is to say between the children of a brother and a sister, is mainly concentrated in intermediate regions close to the BBO patrilineal axis, such as southern India or the African matrilineal belt. The similar case of the Amazon concerns populations with a complex history, close to the destroyed Inca Empire, that have since regressed technically, going back partly or completely from agriculture to fishing, hunting and gathering. Cross-cousin marriage is, as to the status of women, ambiguous since it values the brother–sister axis, and therefore a solidarity between the two sexes. It seems to be, as it were, a moderator of patrilineality. It highlights, like marriage carried out by the exchange of sisters between two men, the archaic importance of horizontal relations among siblings. Marriage between cross-cousins seems overall to be intermediate between exogamy and endogamy in its effects on the status of women and in its geographical position.

A new geography of the world

We will now attempt a simplified planetary geography. Let's divide the planet into six spaces: Asia, Europe, Africa, the Americas, Inner Oceania, centred on New Guinea and Australia, and finally Outer Oceania, following the Micronesia–Polynesia axis.

Asia and Africa comprise the main patrilineal central space on the BBO axis. Central Oceania represents another hub of patrilineal emergence, in New Guinea, a region whose influence is felt in Australia and throughout Melanesia.

The other three spaces are peripheral and the patrilineal hubs are either fragile or non-existent in America, Outer Oceania and Europe.

Consider three variables in their individualistic form: bilateral kinship, nuclear family (defined by ambilocality, neolocality, virilocality, uxorilocality or avunculocality) and complete exogamy (defined by a quadrilateral prohibition on marriage with all first cousins). We measure in table 4.1 the frequency of these individualistic traits in the six major regions that we have just defined.

The distribution of the three variables – kinship, family, exogamy – reveals the systemic proximity of America, Europe and Outer Oceania, with respectively 71%, 80% and 56% of the peoples there possessing a bilateral kinship system; 78%, 90% and 67% preferring a residence after

Table 4.1 Survival of original traits

	Bilateral kinship	Nuclearity	Quadrilateral exogamy
America	71%	78%	72%
Europe	80%	90%	81%
Outer Oceania	56%	67%	72%
Africa	20%	23%	57%
Central Oceania	33%	29%	65%
Asia	32%	36%	38%

marriage that evokes family nuclearity; and 72%, 81% and 72% practising quadrilateral exogamy there. *Bilaterality, nuclearity and exogamy appear very dominant in the three major peripheral regions of the world.* The principle of conservatism of peripheral zones defines these three elements as archaic.

A second set includes Africa and Central Oceania, where quadrilateral exogamy has resisted statistically, with 57% and 65% of cases, but where nuclear family forms no longer represent more than 23% and 29% of cases and bilateral forms of kinship just 20% and 33%. A correction of patrilocality into virilocality by the 'independent' family organization of map 4.3 would raise the proportion of nuclear family forms and would bring eastern and southern Africa, just like Australia, closer to the original and peripheral human type.

That leaves Asia, at the heart of history, where statistically the whole of the old substrate has given way: here we find only 38% of quadrilateral exogamy, 36% of nuclear family forms and 32% of bilateral kinship forms.

We still have to explain the patrilineal transformation which, across most of the planet, starting in several places, triggered the decline in the status of women.

— 5 —

THE CONFINEMENT OF WOMEN: HISTORY COMES TO A HALT

The differentiation of family types from the original type – nuclear, bilateral and relatively feminist – followed, after a certain delay, the Neolithic revolution, i.e. the invention of agriculture as defined by the Australian and British archaeologist Gordon Childe (1892–1957).[1] The Neolithic revolution launched humanity on all sorts of experiments – the city, writing, the state, the successive metals of copper, bronze and iron – and these experiments had a big impact on the family. There have been seven independent inventions of agriculture throughout history, shown in map 5.1, including two that are controversial. This plurality of similar processes provides us with a splendid field for comparison. The zones where the independent emergence of agriculture is not in doubt include the Middle East, China, the central Mexican plateau, the zone currently occupied by Peru and, as we have seen above, New Guinea. The controversies relate to West Africa and the upper Mississippi.[2]

Several of these places of agricultural innovation coincide with hubs of patrilineal innovation. The Middle East pioneered agriculture and also patrilineality, even if the stem family appeared in Mesopotamia, a little to the east of the initial Neolithic zone located between the current territories of Israel and Syria. The same geographical coincidence between agricultural innovation and patrilineal innovation is observable in China, as well as in New Guinea.

The correspondence is not general. I have started to work on the cases of the central Mexican plateau and Peru for the future second volume of *L'Origine des systèmes familiaux* (*The Origin of Family Systems*) and it seems that at the time the Spaniards arrived, a full and complete patrilinealization had not been established, even if today the Nahua family systems on the one hand, and those of the Quechuas and Aymaras on the other, found among the Indian[3] peasants who survived the Conquest, are indeed patrilocal – in my terminology – and almost patrilineal. As I don't need to establish any correspondence with the categories of Murdock's

88

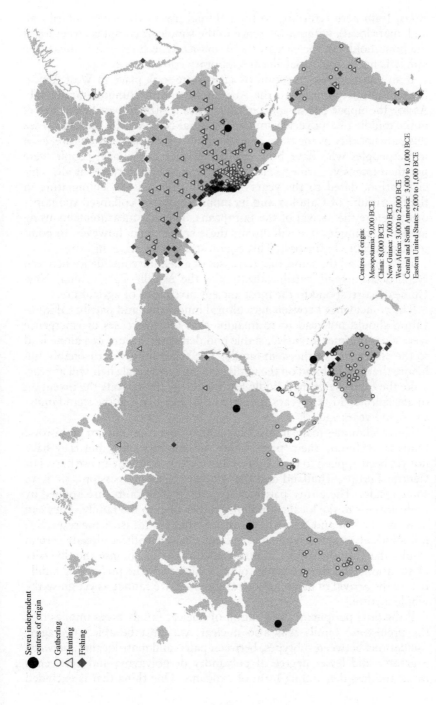

Seven independent
centres of origin

○ Gathering
△ Hunting
◆ Fishing

Centres of origin:
Mesopotamia: 9,000 BCE
China: 8,000 BCE
New Guinea: 7,000 BCE
West Africa: 3,000 to 2,000 BCE
Central and South America: 3,000 to 1,000 BCE
Eastern United States: 2,000 to 1,000 BCE

Map 5.1 The original hubs of agriculture
Source: Binford database

Atlas, I am here returning to my habitual use of the terms 'patrilocal' and 'matrilocal', without reference to the simple or complex structure of the household.[4] In the case of the Aymaras, Quechuas and Nahuas, the family is nuclear with patrilocal temporary co-residence.

If an autonomous invention of agriculture took place in West Africa, it corresponds perfectly to the African patrilineal communitarian hub. As for the upper Mississippi, it constitutes a bizarre patrilineal pocket in the middle of an overwhelmingly bilateral New World. Should we see this patrilineality as the trace of a missing Mississippian agriculture, even if the peoples who have been ethnographed as patrilineal people were not then intensive farmers, and sometimes not even farmers at all? This civilization, dated to the years 1000–1400 of our era, culminating in the flourishing of Cahokia and its mound-builders, collapsed spontaneously before the arrival of the Europeans. The first measurements using modern techniques (we will discuss these below) tend, however, to point to matrilocality in the past. This region still has surprises in store.

Let's note, all the same, that the cases of a definite coincidence between Neolithization and patrilinealization – the Middle East, China, New Guinea – correspond to the most ancient inventions of agriculture.

The coincidence between agricultural innovation and patrilineal innovation should not lead us to imagine that the two cases of emergence were close in time. Intensive, stable and dense agriculture can alone lead to the emergence of the stem family. The space must be reasonably full before the need to hand on the undivided land to a single heir will appear. Take the example of the Middle East: 6,500 years separate the invention of agriculture, 11,000 years ago, from the emergence of the stem family, say 4,500 years ago.

New techniques make it possible to measure the mobility of prehistoric humans, including their 'patrilocality' or 'matrilocality', but they have not yet been applied to the Middle East in a way that we can use here. For Central Europe, Thailand and the America of the Mississippi, we have some results. The terms 'patrilocality' and 'matrilocality' are applied by prehistorians to the local community rather than to the family. They can now use the ^{86}Sr and ^{87}Sr isotopes of strontium to measure the respective mobilities of men and women in ancient times. The three already certain results that I am going to summarize allow us to glimpse the diversity of situations and therefore the complex history of the prehistoric family before the arrival of dense agriculture, though we cannot as yet grasp the whole picture.

If the final peripheral distribution of nuclear family types implies that the prehistoric family was also nuclear, we must be able to imagine oscillations between subtypes, between patri- and matrilocality, between a greater and lesser degree of polyandry or polygyny, and between a more and less demanding form of exogamy. One thing that is excluded is the crystallization of a dense patrilineal and communitarian family before intensive agriculture. New Guinea is the exception that proves the rule, because while it appears on maps derived from Murdock's *Atlas* as patrilineal and patrilocal, and with extensive agriculture, this is because its horticulture falls by convention into the same category of extensive farming as that of the Indians of the eastern United States as they were observed in the seventeenth and eighteenth centuries. But the highlands of New Guinea often revealed, when they were penetrated in the 1920s, much higher densities. Indeed, this is why the Papuans, unlike the Iroquois, the Cherokees, the Choctaws and the Timucua, still exist.

The quantitative ratio between the two strontium isotopes found in tooth enamel shows whether the human beings from which this element comes were brought up and nurtured as children in the same place as they were found buried. The $^{87}Sr/^{86}Sr$ ratio varies according to the nature of the terrain; sedimentary soils reveal a lower ratio than primary terrains, which are more radiogenic and generally higher in altitude. The $^{87}Sr/^{86}Sr$ ratios of individuals taken from a cemetery or from land surrounding houses can therefore be compared with the local $^{87}Sr/^{86}Sr$ ratio. In fact, if the human remains permit, two different ratios can be calculated for an individual, because the more or less early growth of molars can distinguish two of the initial stages of life. Once the ratios of the individuals have been established, they are placed in order on a diagram, with the abscissa, for example, representing the strontium concentration, with males being distinguished from females, and we can see what proportions of each fall into the band of values of the ratio typical of the site. In other words, we can see the proportions of males and females born and raised outside the community who nonetheless died in it. If more women are born outside, the variability of their $^{87}Sr/^{86}Sr$ ratios, summarized by their standard deviation, will be higher than that of men, and the social model will be said to be patrilocal. If more men are born outside, the opposite will be the case and the social model will be said to be matrilocal. A European example, a Thai example and a North American example, the last measuring the morphological variability of skulls rather than the radiogenic variability of strontium, show how varied prehistoric situations could be.

The best-studied culture at this stage is the so-called *Linearbandkeramik* culture or LBK (usually known as the 'linear pottery culture') which colonized Central and West Europe along the Danube valley between Hungary and the middle valley of the Rhine between 5500 and 4700 BCE. The many analyses carried out in the longhouses and vast cemeteries have led to a diagnosis of patrilocality, a term which, I repeat, cannot be taken here in its classical anthropological meaning. The cemeteries reveal a greater stability of buried men, therefore more local origins than those of women; but we also find, before any measurement of the strontium in

91

the teeth, an overall deficit in the number of young men, which suggests that the movement of agricultural colonization continually drew some of these young men towards the west, in a phenomenon of male mobility that can hardly be considered 'patrilocal'.[5] The general model raises the question of potential marriages between men farmers and women taken from the groups of hunter-gatherers already present, usually located in the highlands – a question that will one day be completely resolved by palaeogenetics. I do not know of any study suggesting a matrilocal model for the early Neolithic period in Europe or for the phases that succeeded it through the Bronze Age and then the Iron Age, whatever the technique used (strontium, genetic analysis or osteoarchaeology).

Prehistoric Thailand provides us with a very different case: the Ban Chiang community where men and women were symmetrically mobile in hunter-gatherer times. The arrival of rice cultivation led to a local fixation of women, whose $^{87}Sr/^{86}Sr$ ratios are quite sharply restricted to local values shortly before and after 900 BCE, while those of men remain fairly variable. Here we can diagnose the appearance of a matrilocal pattern.[6] But, as noted by the authors of the article from which these results are taken, a mixed hunting–gathering–farming system persisted. We can surmise that the hunter-gatherers borrowed from agriculture, in a process quite different from monolithic and demographically invasive agricultural colonization by LBK groups.

The arrival of maize in an American Indian community in midwestern Illinois reveals a matrilocal emergence similar to that of Thailand,[7] one which this time is measured by a greater morphological variability of male skulls than of female skulls. The study's authors realized that the statistical method applied to strontium in teeth could also be applied to any physical characteristic allowing the calculation of standard deviations for both sexes. Lyle Konigsberg and Susan Frankenberg prefer the terms viri- and uxorilocality to those of patri- and matrilocality. With the increase in the variance of male skulls, they measure the change from virilocal to uxorilocal with the introduction of maize into the Mississippi area when agriculture there was becoming intensive. This intensity, as we have seen, disappeared later with the collapse of the mound-builder civilization.

Let us note in passing that, thanks to its researchers, prehistoric archaeology seems on the point of escaping the curse of its androcentric history. Among the authors of the four articles I have just been using, there are twelve men and ten women (55% and 45%). In the remarkable survey *The First Farmers of Central Europe*, published in 2013, there are sixteen men participants and twenty-one women (43% and 57%).[8] The ages of the authors would show even more clearly the feminization of this branch of science, something which struck me while I was compiling the whole of my prehistoric bibliography. I didn't notice any change in scientific style corresponding to the modification of the sex ratio of researchers, as happened in anthropology, for example. A few extremist incursions of the idea of 'gender' into archaeology can admittedly be noted in other places. But one has to admit that, in a fairly technical discipline where the determination of the biological sex of a skeleton is already a problem, any speculation on 'gender' can only be a conceptual burden, particularly in the current general context where the word 'gender' is increasingly replacing the word 'sex', erasing all nuance in meaning between the two terms.

These specific analyses of patrilocality and matrilocality confirm that the introduction of agriculture started to shift the respective statuses of men and women in the acquisition of resources and social organization. Did women, who specialized in gathering among hunter-gatherers – we will see later to what extent – and who had a better understanding of plants, actually invent agriculture? This is an old but reasonable assumption. Three maps derived from the *Ethnographic Atlas* suggest that it should be considered. These maps comprise an anthropological overview of the world with regard to the respective contributions of men and women to agricultural activity among the peoples for whom such activity is the main resource (map 5.2), and also with regard to the patri- or matrilocal orientation of the family organization of the peoples in question, distinguishing between them according to whether their agriculture is intensive (map 5.3) or extensive (map 5.4).

Map 5.2 shows that the regions in which agriculture is performed by men alone are distributed, in the Old World, around the BBO (Beijing–Baghdad–Ouagadougou) axis. The central Mexican plateau and the southwestern United States also fall into this category. There are many points of male predominance in agriculture in Polynesia, a region of the world where settlement by populations of Austronesian language happened late. However, there is a female predominance in Micronesia and Melanesia, areas that were populated much earlier.

We observe a pre-eminence of women in agriculture in the eastern two-thirds of the United States, in the Indian American era of course, and more generally throughout America before the Europeans. Africa above all, around and south of the equator, shows a predominance of women in agricultural work.

The zones of female predominance are peripheral on the global scale and may represent an ancient state of affairs. The hypothesis of a Neolithic start led by women is therefore compatible with map 5.2. But, faced with these very partial data, the existence of several hubs of independent agricultural innovation means we cannot conclude that agriculture in general was invented by women. Invention by the opposite sex in the Middle East, the original place of LBK colonization, cannot be ruled out. I have mentioned the ubiquity of the patrilocal hypothesis for Neolithic and post-Neolithic Europe, which seems difficult to reconcile with that

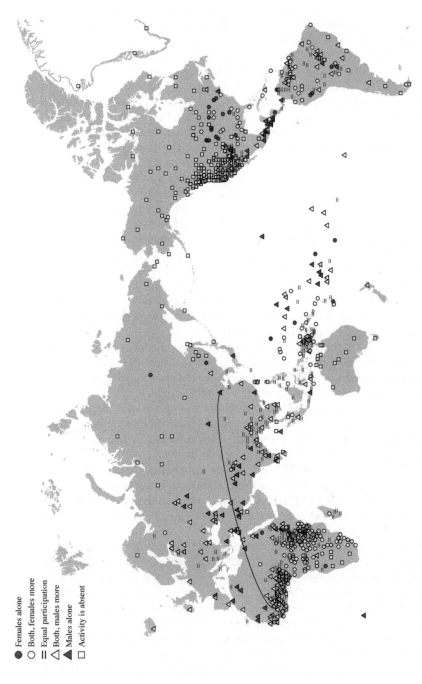

● Females alone
○ Both, females more
≡ Equal participation
△ Both, males more
▲ Males alone
□ Activity is absent

Map 5.2 The role of women in agriculture
Source: Ethnographic Atlas

of a female predominance in agricultural work. And why exclude from the outset the hypothesis that agriculture was invented by *both* sexes? It would be superficial to think in principle that the history of agriculture follows a single unilinear pattern. It was invented in seven regions of the world; it evolved in those regions but also subsequently spread to others, either by demographic expansion of Neolithic populations at the expense of hunter-gatherers, or by transmission to hunter-gatherers of the new mode of subsistence, or by a combination of the two. It is in this third case that mixtures of populations must be considered, either by quite egalitarian intermarriages, or by the enslavement of hunter-gatherers, or by other factors.

The regions of agricultural matridominance are characterized by extensive farming. The most likely historical hypothesis is that a male takeover of agriculture accompanied, in a second phase, the transition to intensive agriculture. In other terms, there is no increase in agricultural efficiency without a reorientation of male activity. It is at this stage of agricultural intensification, which has led to higher densities and full spaces, that there may have appeared rules of undivided succession, the stem family and an initial patrilineality (of level 1, according to my terminology).

Maps 5.3 and 5.4 allow us to observe the strength of the patrilocal principle among peoples who derive their existence from agriculture, which we need to contrast with the dominant bilocality of hunter-gatherers. But we can also see that, on the eve of urbanization, and on a global scale, there was only a slight difference between the peoples who practised intensive farming (62% patrilocality and 12% virilocality, in Murdock's categories) and those who practised extensive agriculture (56% patrilocality and 11% virilocality).

Despite the huge contribution in terms of work made by African women around and south of the equator, most of the extensive agriculture of this continent coincides with patrilocality, and only the avunculocality of the matrilineal belt is an exception. The Africa of extensive agriculture is classified by Murdock as 74% patrilocal. Even if, in view of our doubts about the term 'patrilocal' as used by the *Atlas* for this region, we convert this 74% into virilocality, adding it to the 7% virilocality already identified, this would make 81% virilocality. It is impossible to get rid of this male predominance in the orientation of family life, even where agricultural life is dominated by women. In central and southern Africa, patrilocality has supplanted bilocality or matrilocality for reasons that are not purely economic.

Note that, symmetrically, intensive agriculture has not pushed Europe or Southeast Asia into patrilocality. People who practise intensive agriculture are only 9% patrilocal in Europe; 50% of them are still virilocal. Extensive agriculture is too poorly represented in Europe for the figures relating to it to have much meaning.

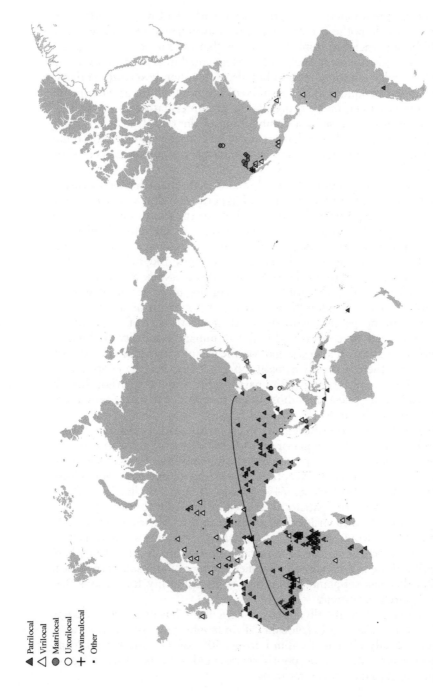

▲ Patrilocal
△ Virilocal
● Matrilocal
○ Uxorilocal
+ Avunculocal
• Other

Map 5.3 Residence of spouses in intensive agriculture
Source: Ethnographic Atlas

Map 5.4 Residence of spouses in extensive agriculture
Source: Ethnographic Atlas

Patrilocal ▲
Virilocal △
Matrilocal ●
Uxorilocal ○
Avunculocal +
Other ·

I'm not going to examine in detail all the data of these maps: the aim of the present essay is to understand the new antagonism between men and women and the crisis of sexual identities in the modern Western world. The important thing here is to realize that a diffusion of patrilineality and patrilocality, and an associated decline in the position of women in the social system, may have occurred regardless of the type of agriculture, by diffusion around the hubs of intensive agriculture. We noted above that structural analysis is content to detect coincidences and correlations, and that only mapping can suggest and measure diffusion mechanisms in space, distorting the initial structural coincidences.

It would be unreasonable to expect more from this cartographic sketch than what we have just surmised: the hypothesis of a matridominated phase in the history of the initial extensive agriculture in certain places, followed by an intensification of agriculture which coincided with a rise of male power in production. We have added the secondary hypothesis of the diffusion mechanisms of family forms that are not bound by agricultural logic.

Nomads and the history of the family

In *L'Origine des systèmes familiaux* I noted the contribution made by nomads, as specialized pastoralists emerging from and detached from agriculture, to these mechanisms of dissemination. They acquired the patrilineal principle from the cities of Mesopotamia or China at the stage of the stem family and drew from it the possibility of forming patrilineal clans, vast symmetrized structures of kinship. In doing so, they acquired a formidable organization and a competitive advantage in the field of war: indeed, if we examine the typical outline of a patrilineal clan system, we cannot fail to be struck by its resemblance to a bureaucratic or military organizational chart. A group of nomadic herders organized by the patrilineal principle is an 'army in civilian clothes'. It can invade the sedentary society which had transmitted the initial patrilineal principle to it. In return, the nomads impose their own innovation, the symmetry of brothers.

Clans – Amorites in Mesopotamia, Huns, Turks and Mongols in the heart of Eurasia, Arabs between the Middle East and the Maghreb – in their turn conquered towns and countryside. Imposing their principle of symmetry on the stem family, they transformed it into a communitarian family in which all the sons, and not only the eldest, stay with the father. Details of this story for Eurasia can be found in *L'Origine des systèmes familiaux*. Map 5.5 also suggests something of a similar role for pastoralists in the Sahel and East Africa.

Map 5.5 allows us to observe the patrilocal (and patrilineal) homogeneity of herding peoples along and around the BBO axis: 84% patrilocality

Map 5.5 Residence of spouses among pastoralists
Source: Ethnographic Atlas

△ Patrilocal
△ Virilocal
● Matrilocal
○ Uxorilocal
✛ Avunculocal
· Other

in the world as a whole and 9% virilocality; 85% patrilocality in Africa and 11% virilocality. America, lacking the goats, cows, sheep and horses needed for nomadic breeding until the arrival of the Spaniards, is not involved here.

This map confirms that during the second stage of patrilinealization and the lowering of the status of women, nomadic peoples played a decisive role, in interaction with the sedentary farmers, in the Middle East, China, northern India and Africa.

Among the nomads themselves, the symmetrization of brothers did not involve too great a lowering of the status of women. Their conditions of existence forbade it. Patrilineal ideology allowed the emergence of clans without preventing the mobility of nuclear families within the encompassing structure. Father and son, brother and brother, collaborated in breeding activities, but in the event of tension or conflict they could separate, temporarily or permanently. In the steppe or the desert, you can distance yourself from a father or a brother that you can't stand any more. By the grace of this patrilocality, which cannot be absolute, women retain a relatively high status. The ability of Mongolian women to make decisions and take action is a historical commonplace, the most classic example being Genghis Khan's mother, a widow able to protect her offspring in difficult circumstances.[9]

It was different in the sedentary societies conquered by the nomads. There, the principle of symmetry of brothers would, over time, dramatically lower the status of women. We witness, first in the Middle East, later in China and elsewhere, the great undivided patriarchal family of Le Play, tied to the ground by agriculture: rooted, so to speak.

Patrilineality and social stratification

Patrilinealization and the status of women are inseparable from the complexification of societies. We have just seen that dense agriculture led to the stem family, then, interacting with the nomads, to the communitarian family. However, we mustn't forget that these complex family forms develop in societies that are also becoming more complex overall, as a consequence of an increasingly sophisticated division of labour, bringing together peasants, craftsmen, priests, administrators and soldiers.[10] Writing and its scribes were important figures in this process.

I noted in the previous chapter that Martin King Whyte had associated the lowering of the status of women with this general phenomenon of a diversification of social tasks. There is no doubt that the new division of labour worked to the advantage of men. Less hampered by reproduction and its constraints, they were able to take advantage of new opportunities created by complex societies nourished by intensive agriculture.

100

The link between population density and patrilocality or patrilineality is striking. The agricultures that corresponded to the matrilocal peoples of ancient North America and Southeast Asia were generally extensive and supported low-density populations. I noted in *L'Origine des systèmes familiaux* that, around 1800, China, with a patrilineal level 2, had about 330 million inhabitants; Japan, with a patrilineal level 1, had 30 million; and the whole of Southeast Asia, bilateral through the kinship system but matrilocal, had only 28 million.[11] The rulers of Southeast Asia sought extra men rather than land, a relative rarity – hence the importance of slavery in this region of the world.

Alfred Kroeber highlighted the disturbing fact that the American Indian farming populations of eastern North America had lower population densities than Californian gatherers.[12] His explanation for this takes us far from an idealized vision of matrilocal peoples: this agriculture, considered as an accessory, in particular allowed the Indian groups in the east to wage more war, an activity whose contribution to population growth is hardly positive.[13] Matrilocal societies whose agricultural activities are led by women have therefore not escaped the principle of male predominance, here seen in its absurd warlike effects – contrary to what Marija Gimbutas and her faithful feminists might have dreamed.[14]

Even if, in the Balkans between Romania and Serbia, a matrilocal phase may have preceded the colonization of Central and Western Europe by the 'patrilocal' LBK groups, nothing allows us to fantasize about a matriarchal golden age. The matrilineal Iroquois were a warlike and ferocious people. The matrilineal Nayars of Kerala in southern India were a military caste. Matrilineality may not lower the status of women as does patrilineality, but it mainly replaces the husband by the brother as male authority. However, we must avoid falling into the opposite excess which suggests that matrilocal or matrilineal societies are more warlike than patrilocal and patrilineal societies. The Hopi and Zuni Indians of the southwest United States were rather peaceful, unlike the Navajos who surrounded them. They can all be defined as matrilocal or matrilineal.

It is appropriate, when analysing a patrilinealized society – and above all one that has not been completely patrilinealized – to keep in mind that the status of women varies according to social class. I abruptly realized the importance of this element in Japan (incomplete patrilinealization, level 1), a country which I regularly visit. For a long time, I met only people from my own background, mainly academics and journalists. I observed, despite the huge progress made by women in higher education, the persistent domination of men in the public space, and the difficulty the sexes have in communicating with one another – something which the Japanese gladly talk about, and which they deplore, but which remains a problem. In 2011, however, during a survey in the devastated

101

region of Tohoku, in the northeast, a few months after the tsunami and the Fukushima disaster, I met ordinary Japanese people – men and women belonging to the administrations of towns that had been flattened, farming couples, workers, fishermen and hairdressers. Relations between the sexes turned out to be more egalitarian and relaxed here than in the upper middle classes of Tokyo, and therefore much closer to the situation familiar in France.

The patrilineal concept most often appears within the aristocracy of a society before spreading downwards to the wealthy peasantry and then the small farmers and, in all cases, affecting these two categories more profoundly than agricultural workers who most often escape its impact. As long as it has not reached all of the categories of the people, the patrilineal principle remains, quite logically, stronger at the top than at the bottom of society.[15] Diffusion expresses a phenomenon of domination, and this is the reason why, after the Second World War, it was rejected by anthropology, which saw structuralism as a way of considering all cultures as 'equal'. Thinking that some peoples or groups were superior to others had appeared unbearable to scholars confronted with the Nazi delusion of racial superiority and then, in the years that followed, with the colonial problem. We can understand the reaction of that generation. Unfortunately, in history, phenomena of domination do exist, and while fine feelings can sometimes improve the future, they have no retroactive effect. Diffusion by cultural or military domination existed and produced centre–periphery geographic distributions as well as top–bottom social stratifications in family forms.

When we tackle the description of families and their history, account must therefore be taken of socio-economic stratification, which interacts with the patrilineal principle and the practice of patrilocality. Landowning peasants, as I was able to observe from the lists of inhabitants of Cornouaille in Brittany in the eighteenth century and of Swedish Scania at the beginning of the nineteenth century, just like the big farmers of Artois in the eighteenth century, reveal, despite a bilateral kinship system, a patrilocal deviation: the transmission of property mainly took place via men, and the latter therefore had a greater geographic stability than women. In contrast, agricultural workers showed an opposite matrilocal tendency, here in relation to the village since their family was nuclear. Men, rather than women, moved from village to village, initially as servants.[16]

However, we cannot generalize about the class distribution of nuances in family organization. Among the Tuscan sharecroppers of the eighteenth century, there was no economic necessity for the patrilineal organization and patrilocality of the communitarian family, even if the size of the domestic group could be explained by the demands of production. Communitarian families of similar sharecroppers on the northwestern edge of the Massif Central had only a weak patrilocal deviation that enables them to be classified as bilocal.[17] In both cases, however, the Communist vote proved very strong in the twentieth century.

The fate of primogeniture was socially and nationally differentiated in Europe. In France, from the end of the tenth century, male primogeniture seduced the Capetian dynasty and then the aristocracy but not the lower classes, apart from in Occitania where the stem family became a kind of peasant ideal-type. In Germany, on the other hand, the stem family imposed itself in the middle peasantry, which led the aristocracy to see primogeniture as a sign of servitude, and to decide that being noble, and free, meant being able to divide your inheritance between your sons. This attitude explains the proliferation of microstates – Hesse-Darmstadt, Hesse-Cassel, Saxony-Anhalt, Saxony-Coburg, etc. At the lowest level, however, in Germany, among the proletariat, we find both a lesser influence of male primogeniture and a higher status of women. August Bebel (1840–1913), the historic leader of German social democracy, is remembered as the author of a classic work on women's liberation, *Die Frau und der Sozialismus* (*Woman and Socialism*, 1879). The strength of primogeniture, which embodies masculinity and inequality, in the middle classes of German society explains why the democratization of Germany – beginning with the political activation of the petty bourgeoisie and the well-to-do peasantry – provoked an upsurge of inegalitarian and authoritarian sentiments rather than an adoption of the ideals of the French Revolution.

Note that we are here referring to systems of kinship which, apart from the Tuscan communitarian family, remain bilateral. What happens to the social distribution of family types where patrilinealization has come to an end?

Patrilineality is absolute in the Arab world, where it has been made complete by the confinement of women through endogamy, that is to say marriage between cousins. In the Arab world, we currently observe these specific features of family organization more deeply rooted in the lower-class categories, including marriage between cousins. Recent *Demographic and Health Surveys* (*DHS*) show us that endogamy is more frequent among the least educated women than among those who have college degrees.

The patrilineal impasse

With the endogamous communitarian family we reach the culmination of the patrilineal transformation which, starting out in the most dynamic zone in the world in the third millennium before the common era, namely Mesopotamia, found its consummation in the same region, present-day

103

Iraq, which became a training ground for the American army, after centuries of historical slumber. So what happened in this part of the world that had invented primogeniture? Is there a relationship between patrilineality and the end of history?

Societies that have finished moulding themselves according to the patrilineal principle have indeed experienced a long and slow tragic cycle. After having invented everything – writing, the state, the first written reflections on death with the *Epic of Gilgamesh*, and the first economic globalization, in the Bronze Age – they got bogged down.[18] This great inertia, which we then see in China and India, and in Africa (in societies that could not write but did know how to work iron), is one of the great mysteries of history. Perhaps *the* great mystery of history. My own explanation is that it resulted from the lowering of the status of women.

The more advanced regions of the world fell into a trap. The first stage of family development, the stem family, which lowers woman's status a little, makes for a high level of educational and economic efficiency. The stem family was invented to transmit things – writing, craftsmanship, the art of war and the cultivation of the soil. When you can remember the skills you have acquired, you can benefit from a competitive advantage and, as a first step, acquire an additional dynamism. As we have seen above, within the stem family, the status of women, over time, declines and the family system becomes rigid. This trend has been observed in Germany and in Japan. We can imagine the unfolding of the same sequence in Mesopotamia or China. But, in these places where the stem family was invented, the transformation has gone further: communitarization by nomadic clans meant that the trap snapped shut.

Societies that deprive themselves of a full contribution from half of their population – women, in the front line for the upbringing of children – cannot remain dynamic. In *The Causes of Progress*, I scrutinized the relationship between family structures and level of development, focusing in particular on the speed at which societies became literate.[19] I analysed family systems in the light of two criteria: the level of authoritarianism in the parent–child relationship, and the status of women. I came to the empirical observation that family systems in which parent–child relationships were authoritarian (as a good child of May 1968, I was very sorry to learn this) and the status of women was still relatively high (no conflict there with my preferences) were the most educationally effective. (This is another way to describe the German stem family or the matrilineal communitarian family of the Nayars of Kerala.) Nuclear systems had an excellent capacity for absorbing innovation. And the patrilineal communitarian systems, with their very low status for women, lagged behind, with the exception of the Russian system, protected by the fact it still granted a high status to women. I do not have any reason to revise these conclusions, except to add this nuance: the autonomous capacity of the

104

stem family to become rigid explains the social and economic blockage, at a high educational level, of Germany and probably of Japan, before the Industrial Revolution – initiated by a more nuclear and more sociably flexible England – launched these two countries on a process of rapid development, under concurrent pressures.

I have nevertheless made advances in my understanding of the mechanism by which societies are blocked by increasingly patrilineal communitarian family structures. The oppression of women remains at the heart of the extinction of social dynamism, but I have finally realized that the individual woman was not the only one to be confined by the patrilineal principle. In the patrilineal communitarian family, *everyone* is confined: women, of course, but men too. The clan infantilizes all its members, men perhaps even more than women.

This idea resolves a modern paradox: women coming from patrilineal and complex systems can perceive the men formed by American or French family systems, feminist in nature, as completely masculine. The reason for this? While the men from nuclear and bilateral family systems may be terrorized by the women of their country, they are accustomed to deciding and acting as individuals. This is not true of the collectively dominant males of a patrilineal system; on the contrary, they present a weaker individual decision-making capacity. A Frenchman can therefore appear reasonably manly, in comparison to men formed by a patrilineal system. We are here close to a solution to one of the paradoxes offered by American culture, which juxtaposes simultaneously strong images of women and men. Pure individualism partly explains the origin of this phenomenon.

The same reasoning, reversed, can be applied to the status of women in a matrilineal system. We then observe women de-individuated by a system that nevertheless treats them as vectors of the transfer of property. In *The Status of Women in Preindustrial Societies*, Martin King Whyte showed that the existence of matrilocality or matrilineality coincided, for several variables, with a rather high status for women. But if we look carefully at his table measuring this effect with regard to control over property, to the value given to women's lives, to their work, and to their ability to live through collective rituals, we see that matrilocal systems do better than matrilineal systems.[20] Why? Matrilocality (which here includes matrilocality and uxorilocality) can correspond to tempered nuclear family systems, which do not really integrate the individual into the extended family. In the case of the matrilineal system, on the other hand, if status and property actually pass (from the genealogical point of view) through women, this vector role does not prevent them from being diminished as individuals, representing only cogs in a system which transcends them – just like men in a patrilineal system. In matrilineal systems, male authority theoretically goes to the brother, and the increased freedom of women most often results from a tension between the predominance of the husband and the predominance of the brother. Patrilineality and matrilineality debase the individual, whether male or female.

Societies that have innovated on the family level have obviously not been aware of the risk they were taking. The stem family, with its initial patrilineality, was at first an effective innovation. Up to and including the Greeks and Romans, advanced peoples thought that male domination was equivalent to modernity. A Latin historian such as Tacitus (*Germania*) or a Greek ethnographer such as Strabo (*Geography*) considered a high status of women as a sure sign of underdevelopment.

Sitting at the end of the world, Western Europe mostly escaped patrilineality. This delay was a piece of good luck for it. The Middle East transmitted to it what defines civilization: agriculture, writing, the city, the state. What was missing was patrilineality, the absence of which finally allowed northwest Europe to make its later ascent.

— 6 —

A DETOUR BY WAY OF AUSTRALIA

The general project of this book, once we have tidied up the analytical instruments of anthropology, is first to define the original nature of the relationship between men and women, and then to compare it with the most recent development of this relationship. We are looking for the right point of comparison for the recent model of the feminism of resentment, as well as for the current crisis in feminine and masculine identities, including the development of bisexuality and the ideological centrality of the transgender question.

The previous chapter has shown us that the right point of comparison is not the patrilineal world of the heartlands of Eurasia and West Africa – whether Arab, Chinese, northern Indian, Burkinabé or Russian. The history of family systems has shown us that these regions fell prey to a long historical impasse, leading, by patrilineal stages, from the stem family to the exogamous communitarian family. Mass polygyny and endogamy brought to an end the millennia-old lowering of the status of women. The result was that history came to a halt. Germans and Japanese, on the fringes of this vast central region, were affected, at stage 1, by the patrilineal transformation and the beginning of a lowering of the status of women.

The West in a narrow sense – the Anglo-American world, the France of the Paris Basin and Scandinavia – has for the most part escaped patrilineality, and has retained nuclear family systems and a high status for women, though this has never excluded, even in Sweden – as we shall see – a moderate male predominance.

It is therefore already obvious at this stage that the right point of comparison for our recent evolutions is the original hunter-gatherer family – nuclear, bilateral, exogamous, so close to us. A more detailed examination of the division of roles between men and women in hunter-gatherer societies will allow us to spell out the meaning of the partial leap into matridominance that we are currently performing.

But, even before describing the sexual division of labour among hunter-gatherers, in chapter 7, we will need to get rid of a traditional analytical deadweight, the Australian question, which could lead to a critique of the idea that women enjoyed a relatively favourable status to begin with. Australian Aboriginal women, whose status is unenviable, are not our anthropological Eves. To demonstrate this, I am going to propose a new interpretation of the case of Australia. What might appear as a digression is actually essential. However, as we have provided evidence in the previous chapter of how agriculture and patrilineality functioned in New Guinea, our task will be quite easy.

The debate on the Aborigines

The hunter-gatherers of Australia are the only peoples for whom the existence of an original nuclear family and a high status of women has been debated. They numbered about five hundred groups when they were discovered by Europeans at the end of the eighteenth century. For the anthropology of the second half of the nineteenth century, these Aborigines did not even have a 'family': their high rate of polygyny, certain 'swinger' moments in their social life, their refusal to see the father's role in procreation, had encouraged a belief in their primitive sexual communism. Their metaphysics describes spirits of children hovering over the land, able to enter into women to be incarnated.

Residence after marriage was generally defined as patrilocal, as was belonging to the territory, even if this element has been somewhat challenged by recent studies that have underlined the similarities between the bilocality of American hunter-gatherers and the statistical rather than theoretical bilocality of Australian Aborigines.[1] The transmission of totemic affiliations, on the other hand, is invariably matrilineal. Adolphus Peter Elkin has underlined the link between the rejection of the role of the father in procreation and matrilineal totemic organization.[2]

These Aborigines, whose physical appearance seemed to place them further away from Europeans than were the American Indians, were once considered the most primitive form of human beings, a source type, which inspired the reflections of Durkheim, Freud and many others on totemism. The last significant representative of this school is Alain Testart, who made the Australian Aborigines his type A hunter-gatherers, older than the type B hunter-gatherers, which includes all others.[3] Testart has little interest in the family, however, insisting as he does on matrimonial exchange, in a very Lévi-Straussian tradition. The sophisticated Aboriginal rules of attributing spouses according to membership in classes and subclasses have been, and remain, an object of fascination for kinship technicians. From this point of view, Australians can hardly be considered as living in simple societies. Placing them at the source would therefore bring us back to the old interpretive scheme of an ascent towards individualism, relentlessly leading humanity from the complex to the simple. This would also lead us to perceive a march of women from oppression to freedom.

Australian Aboriginal systems give women a very low status, almost the opposite of that of the Shoshone women described by Julian Steward and summarized in chapter 2. At birth they are assigned to men much older than they are, to the extent that Australian systems can be described as gerontocratic. Every elderly man is entitled to several wives and polygyny is very widespread. A large age difference between spouses is necessary for the functioning of polygyny so that the number of 'married years' of men and women will be balanced in the community.

Maps 6.1 and 6.2, derived from Binford's database on hunter-gatherers (much more complete on the subject than the *Ethnographic Atlas*, and also made accessible by the D-PLACE project), show the special place occupied by the Australian Aborigines, whose high polygyny rates and average age differences between spouses contrast with those of other hunter-gatherers. Before agriculture, we find such a huge rate of polygyny only among certain Indians of the Great Plains, peoples whose productivity as hunters was greatly increased by the acquisition of the horse, introduced by the Spaniards in the sixteenth century. These Plains Indians are thus not an archaic social type; for them, basically, hunting on horseback comes after agriculture.[4] Binford's sample further confirms that, when we talk statistics about hunter-gatherers, we are depending mainly on North America and Australia, which provide the largest battalions of them.

Nothing in the lives of Australian Aborigines separates them from other hunter-gatherers. If we focus our analysis on the domestic group and the acquisition of resources rather than totemic organization and the marriage system, following Durkheim, Freud and Testart, we come back, in Australia, to the notion of a nuclear Aboriginal family or, if the idea of nuclearity seems exaggerated because of the presence of several wives, to the notion of a *polygynous independent family*. A husband and his wives – that's what we observe in the life of the encampments.

As early as 1913, Bronisław Malinowski (1884–1942) demonstrated, in his *The Family among the Australian Aborigines* – a book far less well known than his model monograph on the inhabitants of the Trobriand Islands – that the father–child bond was, contrary to nineteenth-century fantasies, stable in Australia.[5] Indeed, the father's affection for his children was remarkable. A.P. Elkin places the married family at the centre of social life, inserted into a local group that is rather fluid although attached to its territory.[6] In 1939, Phyllis Kaberry demonstrated that the status of the Aboriginal woman was not as abominable as people

109

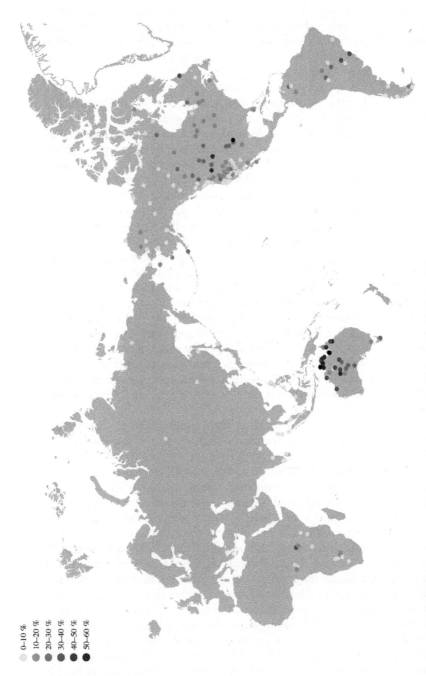

Map 6.1 Polygyny among hunter-gatherers according to Binford (in %)

Source: Binford database

126

Legend:
0–10 %
10–20 %
20–30 %
30–40 %
40–50 %
50–60 %

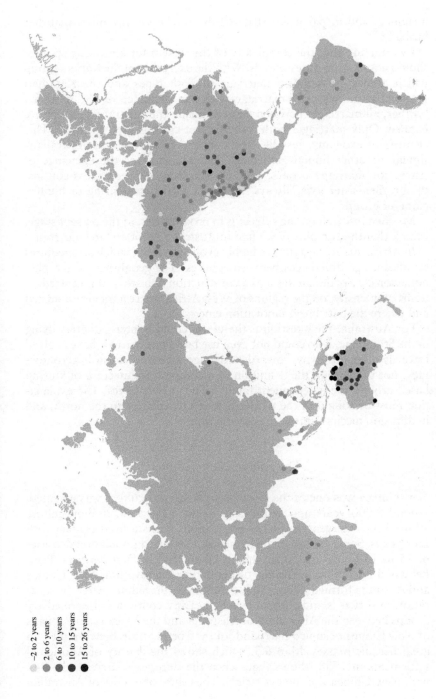

Map 6.2 Differences in age at marriage among hunter-gatherers according to Binford
Source: Binford database

−2 to 2 years
2 to 6 years
6 to 10 years
10 to 15 years
15 to 26 years

imagined, and in particular that she did not work any more than her husband.[7]

I would add that the complexity of the system for allocating spouses should not obscure the essentials. With the exception of the Kariera group which allows cross-cousin marriage of both types and the Karadjeri group that allows only marriage with the daughter of the mother's brother, all marriages between first cousins in the Australian groups are banned. Only marriages with more distant cousins are organized. This element of exogamy, just like the conjugal family, makes Australians similar to other hunter-gatherers. The frequency of the exchange of sisters for marriage evokes, as does marriage between cross-cousins, the brother–sister axis, always important in the structuring of hunter-gatherer groups.

My own research on the subject is in progress but, at the present stage, I think that the complexity we find in Australia is not an 'archaic' trait.

In Africa, mass polygyny is a highly evolved system, which also requires significant age differences between spouses. The geography of the phenomenon clearly designates it as a construction of history: it is centred, in terms of intensity, on the regions of West Africa where agriculture started and where the patrilineal innovation emerged.

For Australia, the question is therefore: could hunter-gatherers living in the Stone Age, who could not even use bows and arrows, have evolved towards mass polygyny, towards large age gaps and towards gerontocracy, not to mention the definition of a complex architecture of kinship based around the independent family? The answer is yes. The explanation must be sought in the world located immediately to the north, and in diffusion mechanisms in prehistoric times.

The role of New Guinea

New Guinea was one of the seven areas where agriculture was invented, around 9,000 years ago in its case. As we have seen, its horticulture allowed the emergence of dense populations that survived contact with Europeans. Some valleys in the highlands supported population densities of 75 to 150 inhabitants per square kilometre.[8] In *First Farmers*, Peter Bellwood notes that in the age of agricultural innovation, New Guinea and Australia formed a single island-continent, the Sahul.[9] After the separation into two islands, exchanges by seaway continued. Intermediary groups between the Aborigines of Australia and the Melanesian Papuans of New Guinea occupied the islands of the Torres Strait, between the two great oceanic masses. Map 6.3, which shows the density of Aboriginal settlements in 1788, shows that, when the Europeans arrived, the link with New Guinea was always visible. The centre of gravity of Australian

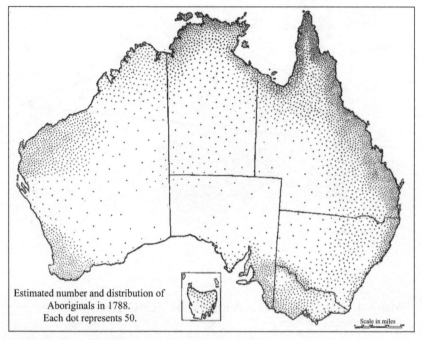

Estimated number and distribution of
Aboriginals in 1788.
Each dot represents 50.

Scale in miles

Map 6.3 Australian Aborigines in 1788
Source: Australian Bureau of Statistics, Year Book of Australia 1929, archival issue,
chapter 24, 'Population', pp. 671–2

Aboriginal settlements was clearly along the north coast, facing New
Guinea.

The non-expansive nature of New Guinea agriculture is a historical
problem on which many researchers have reflected. Testart notes that the
Australians rejected other innovations, but we cannot assume that none
of the New Guinean innovations influenced Australia.

However, New Guinea also appears to be a hub of patrilineal innovation. There are traces of primogeniture in some peoples there. The majority system is a strong patrilineal type, whose originality is, as we have
seen above, a frankly antagonistic relationship between men and women,
to the point that there are peoples where the dominant model is separate
residence. I add that this is neither an old and amiable case of 'living
apart together', nor an anticipation of the tensions in the relationship
between men and women in the United States during the years 1950–80,
or even within the French middle classes at the beginning of the third
millennium.[10]

Patrilineal and matrilineal concepts were able to travel. Maps 6.4 and
6.5 of kinship systems and type of residence of spouses reveal a New

113

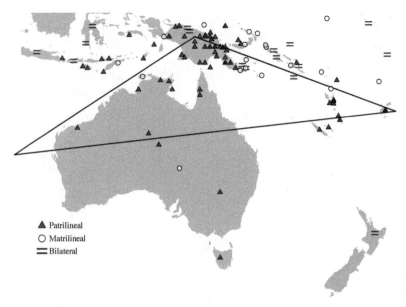

Map 6.4   Kinship systems in Australia and New Guinea
Source: *Ethnographic Atlas*

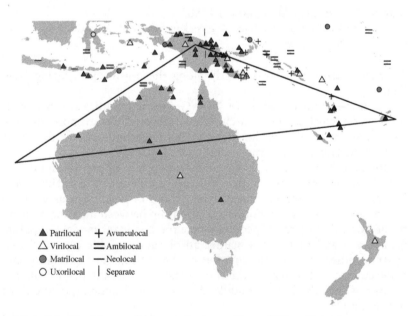

Map 6.5   Residence of spouses in Australia and New Guinea
Source: *Ethnographic Atlas*

114

Guinea–north Australia set, symbolized by a fairly flat isosceles triangle on the maps. Murdock's sample is not very abundant for Australia, presumably because few field studies contained sufficient data. But it accurately presents a bias to the 'north', which reproduces that of the settlement map in 1788.

The patrilocality of the territorial group and the matrilineality of Australian totemic groups – the latter illustrated by the negation of the role of the father in procreation – seem to me constructions, systems that have evolved, rather than being primordial.[11] I noted in *L'Origine des systèmes familiaux* that matrilineality – in Kerala in southwestern India, among the Na of China, among the Garos and Khasi of Assam, and across the entire African matrilineal belt – was positioned geographically on the contact front of patrilineal diffusion. The groups subject to patrilineal pressure, initially the carriers of a bilateral kinship system that attributed to both parents symmetrical roles in the definition of the child's social status, react as follows: 'You think that only the father counts. We, on the contrary, have *always* considered it to be the mother.' Resistance leads to the definition of an equally innovative system. This is what George Devereux (1908–85) calls *dissociative negative acculturation*.

Could Australia be an exception? The denial (much more than the ignorance) of the father's role in procreation is, as a logical form, very similar to the rejection of the patrilineal principle. Patrilineal and matrilineal elements are mixed together in Australia but, in either case, we can see the influence of New Guinea, by direct diffusion as far as patrilocality goes, by dissociative negative acculturation for the elements of matrilineality.

Let's keep it simple: men who can make a fire, design tools such as the boomerang and complicated marriage systems, and draw on rock, cannot be incapable of a hypothesis connecting the penetration of a woman's sex by the erect male sex to the fact that, a few months later, as if in return, a child arrives by the same route. Here is an empirical observation: men, everywhere, understand this. In fact, by its absurdity, the denial of the paternal role in procreation seems to me the best proof of the constructed and innovative character of the Australian systems.

The blockage at the technical level of gathering and hunting raises a theoretical problem but one which may not be insoluble either. Why not apply to these hunter-gatherers our hypothesis of a lowering of the status of women which blocks development? In Australia, we would have the opposite theoretical case to that of Western Europe which had taken everything from the Old World – agriculture, metals, state, city, writing – except patrilineality and the lowering of the status of women. Australia would have taken an embryo of patrilineality and a substantial lowering of the status of women, and nothing else. In this case, the hypothesis of a complex history of Australia, leading to the elaboration of the sophisticated forms observed among its Aborigines, cannot be rejected.

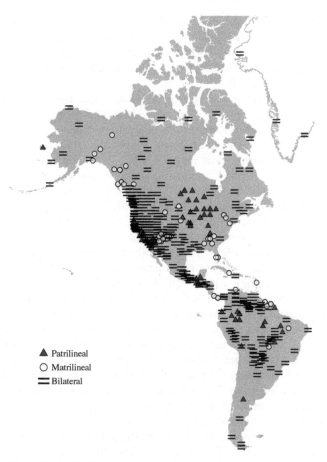

Map 6.6 Kinship systems in the Americas
Source: *Ethnographic Atlas*

The existence of the nuclear family with limited polygyny – and the corresponding quite egalitarian status for women – among the !Kung Bushmen of South Africa, is bound to remove any last doubts we may have.[12] Australian Aborigines are indeed a separate branch, one which evolved in an original way, but they do not represent the origin of mankind. If, following Testart, I were to define a tree of separation-evolution, I would make Australian Aborigines a type B, separated from the common trunk of a type A, represented by American, African and Asian hunter-gatherers.

Let's end this chapter with a final return to America, our real origin, and with two maps, enlargements of the world maps 1.1 and 4.1 adapted for the American continent. Maps 6.6 and 6.7 describe kinship systems

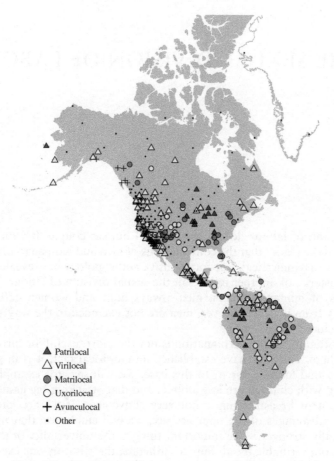

▲ Patrilocal
△ Virilocal
● Matrilocal
○ Uxorilocal
+ Avunculocal
· Other

Map 6.7 Residence of spouses on the American continent
Source: *Ethnographic Atlas*

and the residence of spouses between the Bering and Magellan Straits: we find a massive predominance of bilateral kinship, the nuclear family with temporary co-residence, most often bilocal but sometimes virilocal. Such are the origins of mankind, in this second humanity, separated from the rest for 15,000–20,000 years – with this paradox, that the terms bilaterality, bilocality and virilocality could just as well apply to the peasantry of the Atlantic fringe of Europe. It was themselves that Westerners, in this case aptly named, found on the other side of the ocean – themselves, but at the stage where, in Mexico, the age of writing and metals was just beginning.

117

— 7 —

THE SEXUAL DIVISION OF LABOUR

A division of labour defines the original human couple. It won't have escaped the reader that the contributions of men and women to making a baby are asymmetrical. But comparative anthropology has revealed to us the existence of another universal: the sexual division of labour. Within groups of hunter-gatherers, men always hunt and women gather, an activity from which, however, men are not excluded in the way women are excluded from hunting.

As often in history, explanation is not the most 'useful' or 'profound' thing here. Once we have established an empirical fact, it is in general easy to find 'causes' for it. In this case, we will say, for example, that women with children are less mobile, and that attacking big game when pregnant or breastfeeding is not very convenient. If we are interested in the advantages of the opposite sex, we will emphasize that men are physically stronger.[1] The important thing is the universality of the phenomenon, verifiable for all hunter-gatherers; there is only one exception, mentioned above: the Agtas from the Philippines – a weak exception, since the few Agta women who hunt do so only rarely.[2]

In fact, the correct objection to the universality of the way women are excluded from hunting would be the berdache women of the Indian tribes of North America, a case to which we will return in chapter 16, devoted to the social construction of transgender: having adopted male roles, they could and did hunt, and did it well. However, their adoption of a general male role means that they obey the rule: once they have become men, they have the right to hunt.

Going beyond hunter-gatherers and considering all the populations of Murdock's *Ethnographic Atlas*, we have drawn map 7.1 on the role of men and women in hunting, with three theoretically possible categories: men alone, mixed activity (with men more involved), and societies without hunting. This is the most extraordinary map of the distribution of a social trait that I have ever contemplated in my life: there is no variation. It is the men who hunt. I beg the reader to immerse him- or herself in this map, then go back to look at the maps in the previous chapters with all their variations. The level of homogeneity for hunting is staggering.

The universality of men's hunting monopoly resists all the other variations. It is observed for farmers and pastoralists as much as for hunter-gatherers. Among hunter-gatherers themselves, there is no variation despite the fluctuating level of the importance of hunting, a level that rises ever higher as one moves from the equator towards the pole, towards the cold and the absence of plant resources.

Though we can observe variations, bilocal and virilocal, in the structure of the tempered nuclear family, there is none in the sexual division of labour when it comes to hunting.

This division of labour between the sexes is found in other areas of economic life (see maps 7.2–7.7), without, however, having the same absolute character as it does in the case of hunting, with one exception: boat building (see map 7.4). In gathering, the domination of women is certainly overwhelming, but it is not total: men do take part, and in some cases, close to the equator, they even predominate in this activity (see map 7.2).

In fishing, we come close to an absolute male predominance, without actually reaching it (see map 7.3). Let me remind the reader that the peoples represented here are those of the Murdock sample, not just hunter-gatherers but pre-industrial humanity in general.

Female predominance reappears in pottery work (see map 7.5). It is only threatened along the BBO axis.

A very strong male predominance reappears in house building with, in the latter case, a few exceptions in the heart of North America and in steppes and deserts (the Sahara in particular) (see map 7.6). The houses there are tents and their making is associated with the work on fabric and skins. The map of work on skins shows the involvement of women in nomadic zones: in North America, in Siberia and in the Sahara (see map 7.7).

What is striking about these maps is how much less variability there is for economic specializations than for family forms.

Can we situate these various activities in relation to our modern division of labour? In current terms – which are not as anachronistic as all that – one could say that the hunting, fishing and gathering of hunter-gatherers belong to the primary sector of the economy (today agriculture and extraction of raw materials), and so are shared between men and women. The manufacture of tools, houses and boats as well as pottery, the manufacture of baskets and fabrics and leather work define a secondary sector (today industry) that is predominantly male, but without any monopoly since pottery is predominantly female. Child rearing and food

▲ Males alone
△ Both, males more
□ Activity is absent

Sources: *Ethnographic Atlas.*

Map 7.1   Role of men and women in hunting
Source: Ethnographic Atlas

Map 7.2 Role of men and women in gathering
Source: Ethnographic Atlas

Legend:
● Females alone
○ Both, females more
= Equal participation
△ Both, males more
▲ Males alone
□ Activity is absent

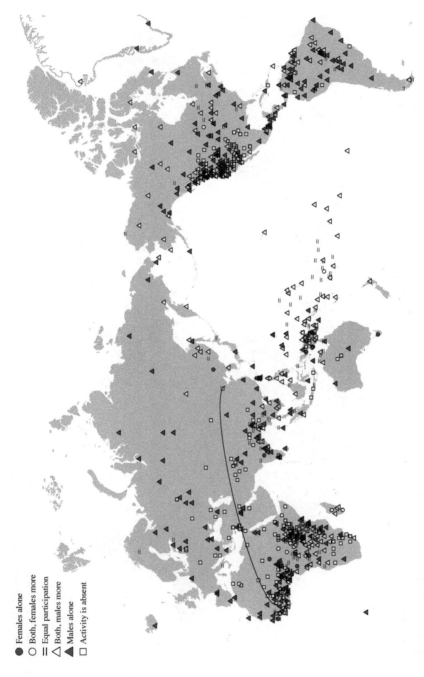

● Females alone
○ Both, females more
= Equal participation
△ Both, males more
▲ Males alone
□ Activity is absent

Map 7.3 Role of men and women in fishing
Source: Ethnographic Atlas

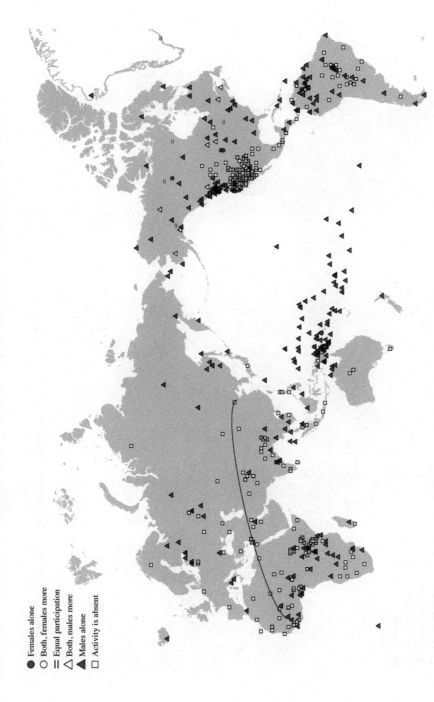

● Females alone
○ Both, females more
= Equal participation
△ Both, males more
▲ Males alone
□ Activity is absent

Map 7.4 Role of men and women in boat building
Source: Ethnographic Atlas

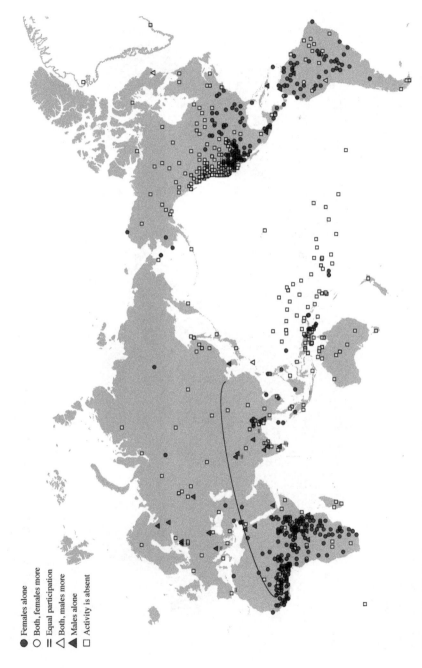

● Females alone
○ Both, females more
≡ Equal participation
△ Both, males more
▲ Males alone
□ Activity is absent

Map 7.5 Role of men and women in pottery
Source: Ethnographic Atlas

● Females alone
○ Both, females more
= Equal participation
△ Both, males more
▲ Males alone
□ Activity is absent

Map 7.6 Role of men and women in house building
Source: Ethnographic Atlas

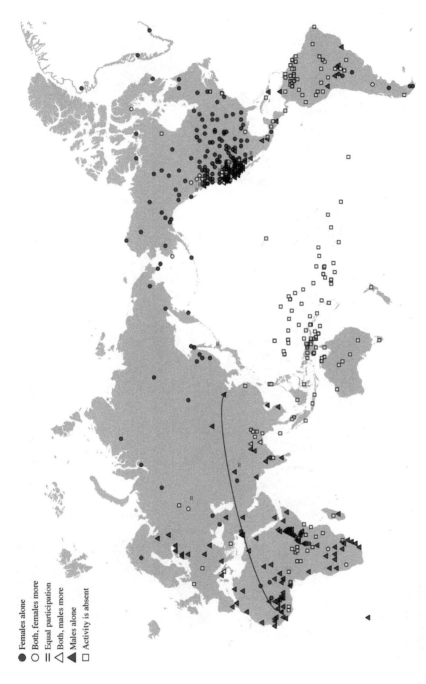

Legend:
- ● Females alone
- ○ Both, females more
- ═ Equal participation
- △ Both, males more
- ▲ Males alone
- □ Activity is absent

Map 7.7 Role of men and women in leather work
Source: Ethnographic Atlas

preparation can be considered as a proto-service sector and are highly female-dominated. We will see the relevance of this classification when we analyse the most recent evolution of economic activities according to sex. Let's return to the invariant of hunting and the ideological tensions it has aroused.

Ideology versus reality

Some try to deny the universal phenomenon comprised by the male monopoly of hunting. Recent feminist ideology, which wants everything to be a social construction, struggles against a statistical wall that clearly indicates that it is a fact of nature.

Alain Testart played a part in this denial of reality. In one of his first books, *Essai sur les fondements de la division sexuelle du travail chez les chasseurs-cueilleurs* (*Essay on the foundations of the sexual division of labour among hunter-gatherers*), he gave, in the wake of Murdock, a good factual analysis of the division of labour, in all its dimensions, with several nuances.[3] However, he could not help mentioning, in his chapter 2, the 'failure of naturalistic explanations'. This engineer, a graduate of the École des Mines, then presented the sexual division of labour as an ideological phenomenon. But this male ideological monopoly on hunting is found in all the peoples of the earth, who diverged spatially at various dates, from 100,000 BCE (if we take departure from Africa as a starting point), or 200,000 BCE or 300,000 BCE (if we take into account previous intra-African separations). This ideological monopoly can be verified among the Aborigines who arrived in Australia around 60,000 BCE, then among the Europeans who settled around 40,000 BCE, and the American Indians, who crossed the Bering Strait around 15,000 BCE at the latest. This 'ideological' transformation therefore intervened at the source, at the very origin of humanity; it was permanent, since it is found everywhere another 3,000 generations later. Describing the sexual division of labour as 'ideological' rather than 'natural' in such a context is merely playing with words. The universality of the male hunting monopoly seems to me very close to other universals such as: men can learn to speak, have opposable thumbs, and can't see very well in the dark.

But the debate, or rather the denial, continues to rage, and may demonstrate the ability of an era and an ideology – a real ideology – to destroy scientific knowledge. In November 2020, a new assault against the statistical wall was launched. An article published in the journal *Science Advances* was picked up by the major media; it was titled 'Female Hunters of the Early Americas',[4] and was based on *one* skeleton found in the Andes with a small amount of hunting equipment, dated to

7000 BCE, as well as a few other skeletons whose link with the previous one is poorly understood. The article came to the conclusion that there was a time before ideology when women hunted as much as men. Apart from the fact that, statistically speaking, all this is worthless: 7000 BCE is very recent. If the fact were significant, we would be facing a late or intermediate innovation. This exception is even less important than the Agtas or the berdaches.

Ideology against itself

The ideological revolt against the original sexual division of labour can lead to even more surprising results. Feminist prehistoric anthropology, in particular, may inadvertently come to some very distressing conclusions for feminism itself.

In an article from 1979, i.e. very early but already consonant with the denunciation of male domination, Paola Tabet carried out, unbeknownst to herself, a conceptual breakthrough that was dangerous for the very interests she believed she was defending.[5] From a perspective that I would call prehistoric hyper-Marxism, she first explains to us that the oppression of women is a universal. So here we are again, back in the condemnation of a human history that should not have taken place. But Tabet makes a fascinating point: it would not be enough to consider activities such as hunting or gathering. Consideration should also be given to more fundamental activities such as the manufacture of tools – stone axes, spear-throwers or bows which make hunting possible, and the building of houses and boats: the means of production, as it were. It was by manufacturing these instruments, she says, that men ensured their domination. Does she even realize the implications of such an assumption? If men controlled history and women by their control of the production of tools, we come to the insane conclusion that humanity itself is masculine – that what made mankind a species that had emerged from nature was the appearance of a male individual who could make tools. All the credit for human success would thus go to the males![6] Female predominance in pottery and the role of women in agricultural innovation, luckily, are there to reassure us that this was not so.

This strict division of labour should not overshadow an essential underlying phenomenon: man and woman collaborate in the acquisition and preparation of the necessary resources for the family. The pair is a production–consumption unit, even if some resources, such as meat, are (as we shall see) distributed through the entire local group. Various uncertain debates, often conducted in bad faith, have questioned the male contribution; the reality is that both members of the pair are necessary for survival and for bringing up children. It should also be noted that among hunter-gatherers, the father sees his children more than in most other socio-economic formations, right from birth.[7] As early as 1939, Phyllis Kaberry showed, as I noted above, that even Australian Aboriginal women, supposedly the slaves of their old husbands, did not work any harder than the latter.[8]

Collectivist men versus individualist women

This debate on hunting may seem redundant. But the challenge it poses today is more important than ever because it involves the definition and functioning of the collective. Hunting is not just killing animals. While hunting is practised by men individually or collectively, depending on the type of game, its product, among hunter-gatherers, is always shared. Here is a new invariant. We often observe that the man who succeeded in bringing down a beast has a slight advantage, but, overall, unlike the products of gathering, which remain within the household, what reigns in the case of hunting is a principle of distribution at the community level – something which is rather a nuisance for individualist ideologues of the American school.

As for the male monopoly of the act of hunting, we can immediately find reasonable reasons for this sharing: in the absence of cooling equipment, meat must be consumed quickly and therefore shared out. But, again, this isn't the main point. What is interesting is that men are associated with a principle of communitarian division of the proceeds of their specific activity while women, in their activity as gatherers, represent the individualist half of the group. The sexual division of labour reveals an unexpected binary opposition: the individual assumes a female sex and the collectivity a male sex.

This orientation of men towards the collective, it should be noted, has little to do with altruism – and probably nothing at all. Among hunter-gatherers, while hunting sometimes requires a group action, and always leads to a sharing of the meat, it is above all an opportunity for a man to show his efficiency, his bravery, and in no way to show empathy towards those who are in need or suffering. War, that other male activity, brings out the non-altruistic orientation of this specialization in the collective. A better ability to care for the weak, for those who suffer, is, on the other hand, one of the stereotypes precisely associated with the female role.

There is no contradiction between the fact that women are at once more altruistic and more individualistic. This duality is inherent in the maternal function. Altruistic in her relationship to the child, the mother may be intractable against competitors in the acquisition of the resources needed for it. This duality is a problem only for the 'modern' individualist rationalist.

129

Still, we have to face, deep down in human history, the reality of men specialized in the collective of the local group and women specialized in the individuality of the family. We can push the analysis further by accepting that the collective, among hunter-gatherers, is a modality of equality.

The issue of equality: we are not chimpanzees

Hunter-gatherers are still the object of some passionate research. Since Rousseau, at the latest, asking the question of primordial humanity amounts to questioning human nature itself. The origin of inequality, for example, always gives rise to debates that are basically quite funny. Hunter-gatherers, we can well imagine, form relatively undifferentiated communities. Not that men are equal in them: there are good and bad hunters. But, in the absence of transmissible wealth, there can be no inequalities of inheritance.

However, in the Anglo-American world, a number of researchers, ideologues of neoliberalism, want to see inequality as the expression of a profound human nature. Hunter-gatherers and their rather egalitarian societies are a thorn in their delicate flesh. The perfectly simple facts of the impossibility of accumulation and the effectiveness of cooperation among hunter-gatherers trouble them. They worry about the weakness, in these original men, of the mechanisms of dominance between individuals that can be observed in our chimpanzee cousins.[9] While it may be nicely amusing to identify Anglo-American academics with the inegalitarian male chimpanzee, it loses sight of the essential thing: the radical break between the two species. On one side, we have a male chimpanzee crushing the male competition to spread his sperm in all the females, engendering the maximum number of children whom he will neither know nor raise, in a group that will continue to live in trees, and is essentially frugivorous. On the other hand, there is a mainly monogamist man who brings up his children over a long time and whose quite egalitarian and solidary groups will set out to conquer the planet and doubtless, one day, the stars. This academic identification with the chimpanzee occurs in an Anglo-American society where a powerful feminism flourishes, and where the men of the educated classes, unlike male chimpanzees, strive through contraception to avoid too numerous a progeny and often even practise vasectomy to avoid their sexual partners becoming pregnant against their will and running away with their offspring and part of their property.[10]

But this ultimate inegalitarian ideological contortion commands respect because it goes, albeit in an opposite direction, as far as communist egalitarianism: it asserts that primordial sharing was an imposition and necessitated the establishment of an egalitarian mechanism of repression.[11] On this view, sharing behaviour would be, in primitive societies, not natural. *Homo sapiens* forced himself to overcome his nature and foster equality, until the emergence of agriculture, that is, for 200,000, even 300,000 years, if we rely on the most recent estimates by Jean-Jacques Hublin for the appearance of our species. I propose – just for fun – introducing a difference between men and women which would widen the field of possible contortions. If we associate collective redistribution with egalitarianism, we fix the egalitarian principle on the male sex, and the resistance to equality on the female sex. Logic would then lead to considering women as more human than men because they don't impose the constraint of equal sharing on themselves. I'm joking. The question of equality or inequality didn't interest hunter-gatherers, whose problem was the survival of the group and the individual in the group.

However, one troubling question still remains for us, as we experience the liberation of women and a rise in inequalities. Should we reflect on the possibility of a functional relationship, from 1950 to 2020, between the collapse of male power in the anthropological order and the decline of equality in the economic order?

— 8 —

CHRISTIANITY, PROTESTANTISM AND WOMEN

Nuclearity of the family, bilaterality of the kinship system, exogamy and a relatively high status of women: hunter-gatherers appear close to what Westerners were, around 1950, but only if we restrict ourselves to these basic anthropological elements. It would be absurd to deny the existence of significant differences created by more recent history. Europe has absorbed from the Mediterranean several elements: agriculture, a sedentary habitat, the state, writing, and a monotheistic religion that is quite strict on sexual issues.

The tempered nuclear family of hunter-gatherers usually fits into a local non-hierarchical group of twenty-five people on average, itself part of a 'people' of a thousand or so individuals. Our pure nuclear family can't work in a vacuum, either. What allows the tempered nuclear family to become pure is the emergence of a complex social organization: the central state and its army, of course, but also, at the local level, an embryonic administrative apparatus. In England, for example, the registers indicate with certainty that the pure nuclear family existed from the second half of the seventeenth century onwards. It resulted from a transformation that lasted several centuries, completed by the establishment of a socially interventionist state under the Tudors and Stuarts. Rural communities were able to enforce 'poor laws' to tax for the maintenance of orphans and old people.[1] The French egalitarian nuclear family ended up emerging with the absolutist state, inserted into a rural world dominated, like southern England, by large farms and in the context of villages tightly grouped around their churches. It's hard to imagine a pure nuclear family without the large farms that allowed children to leave to find jobs as servants.

But I will focus here mainly on the control of Western family life by religion, the most important element when it comes to the status of women. Early Christianity, born in the Roman Empire, was originally strongly committed to a nuclear ideal of the family and an egalitarian status of the relations between the sexes. Its most peripheral, archaic residues, in Kerala in southern India, among the Amharas of the Ethiopian plateau, or among the Maronites of the Lebanese mountains, still show this Christianity to be associated with the nuclear family, admittedly with a virilocal bias, but in an environment of much denser and more complex family types, either matrilineal (Kerala) or patrilineal (Lebanon and Ethiopia). Christianity has, moreover, whenever it has been able, transformed statistical monogamy into absolute monogamy – its greatest failure here was polygynous Christian Africa along the Gulf of Guinea – and it has expanded the natural avoidance of marriages between first cousins to a much wider taboo on marriage between close relations. The transformation affected all these domains in Western Europe. Classical Greece and Republican Rome were, however, already absolute monogamists. These religious norms have been applied to the nuclear family with temporary co-residence in Belgium, Iceland and Brittany, to name just some examples of regions for which it is not possible to speak of a pure nuclear family.

Religion is at the heart of major historical interactions: it has evolved with the state and we can consider the Church of the High Middle Ages, after the fall of the Roman Empire, as a bureaucratic remnant and a model for future state reorganization.

A thousand years later, the Protestant Reformation gave control of the Church to the state, but it simultaneously made the individual delve deep into him- or herself: by demanding access for all to the Holy Scriptures, and therefore the acquisition of the ability to read, it favoured the development of a new interiority. The human being alone, faced with a text that expresses God, and living not only in the cities but also in the countryside, was a historical and anthropological novelty. The Reformation thus completed the Christian project of transformation of the individual, which included bringing one's sexuality under control, an exercise that in the Middle Ages was essentially the preserve of a few clerical virtuosos specialized in asceticism. (By virtuosos, I mean in Max Weber's sense, i.e. a category which does not include all religious but an elite that lived its faith intensely, and the chastity that went with it – in general, monks rather than priests.)

In many ways, the Catholic Counter-Reformation followed the Protestant Reformation. In *Lineages of Modernity*, I showed that the years 1550–1650 were those of a mental transformation. This change destroyed the bilateral kinship network that oversaw the family. It marked the moment of the fundamental break with the family of hunter-gatherers, and in particular the end of an essential component in the original naturalness: the importance of sibling relationships. The universal but abstract brother in Christ replaced, even among the peasants, and no longer simply in the monasteries, the concrete brother of primordial times.[2]

Conversion to Christianity and the Protestant Reformation are the two most important steps in the co-evolution of family and religion. In this short chapter, I will note how these two stages changed the status of women, in a positive direction as far as the general conversion to Christianity goes, but in a negative sense as far as Protestantism is concerned. Without integrating these religious elements into our study, we would not be able to understand the evolutions of the years 1950–2020, which saw the final extinction of all forms of Christianity, including American Protestantism – the most resilient, since only between 2000 and 2020 did it lose all its social force.

Early Christianity and women

The role of aristocratic women – Roman, Germanic or Slavic – in the establishment of Christianity as the state religion is familiar to historians. Clotilde encouraging her husband Clovis to get baptized is just one example among many others. The Church, with its values of peace and non-violence, its cult of the Virgin Mary and its convents, was, throughout the Middle Ages, a hub of resistance to male brutality. Even today, opinion polls reveal that women tend to be more religious, a fact which sociologists have explained in various ways. An overall interpretation of this feminine religiosity, like so many others, would force us to resolve one question – a difficult technical problem: the respective importance of social and biological factors in the determination of this sexual difference. My own view is that that the extreme variability in the levels of religiosity between countries, the diversity of differences in religiosity (high or low) between men and women in these same countries around 1995–6 for example (table 8.1), suggests an overwhelming preponderance of social factors. The lesser degree of direct integration of women into social life, a difference that is admittedly residual in the developed world, is enough to explain their slight 'lagging behind in secularization'.

Several centuries after the conversion of the Latin, Greek and barbarian chiefs, the alliance of women and the Church was renewed, in the Central Middle Ages, through the sanctification of marriage as implemented from the eleventh century onwards. By imposing the principles of mutual consent and indissolubility, the Church offered women a metaphysical and administrative protection against male instability, as well as a counterweight to parental authority, including a curb on marriage arranged against the bride's own feelings. A woman could then, in theory, freely choose her spouse and not risk being abandoned by him. Even more, in the twelfth century, the theory of presumed marriage developed: if a man promised a woman he would marry her and a sexual act followed

Table 8.1   The religiosity of men and women in the mid-1990s

1995–1996 World Values Surveys	Percentage defining themselves as a religious person		
	Men	Women	Gap (Women–Men)
France	47.4	53.7	6.3
United States	77.2	87.0	9.8
New Zealand	42.6	52.5	9.9
Ireland	66.9	77.5	10.6
Italy	78.8	89.4	10.6
Canada	65.0	76.5	11.5
Sweden	25.0	38.1	13.1
Switzerland	49.1	62.2	13.1
Australia	52.3	65.6	13.3
Netherlands	53.1	66.8	13.7
Great Britain	49.6	64.1	14.5
Germany	50.1	67.2	17.1
Portugal	65.1	83.5	18.4
Denmark	63.2	81.8	18.6
Norway	37.0	55.7	18.7
Spain	57.4	76.8	19.4
Russia	45.8	67.9	22.1

Source: Rodney Stark, 'Physiology and Faith: Addressing the "Universal Gender Difference in Religious Commitment"', *Journal for the Scientific Study of Religion*, 4 (3), 2002, pp. 495–507.

that promise, consent was presumed and the marriage was considered as contracted.[3]

The Church and sexual security

Rodney Stark, a great sociologist of religion, has hypothesized, in an amusing but unconvincing way,[4] that the precocity of men in the process of secularization rests on their greater predisposition to take physical risks than is found in women.

Hormonal development does indeed cause the appearance, at puberty, of an accidental excess mortality of boys that only the increase in male risk behaviours can explain. Demographer Joshua Goldstein has even used the evolution of the 'hump' in the quotient of male mortality in adolescence to follow the lowering of the average age of puberty that characterizes our times.[5] Stark, a follower of rational-choice theory, shifted from physical risk to metaphysical risk. He quotes Pascal, and suggests that betting that God doesn't exist involves taking a risk, something that is more difficult for women.

The notion of risk, absurdly applied by Stark (who is himself not afraid of intellectual risk), does, however, albeit accidentally, lead us to a sensible idea. The attachment of women to the Church was indeed an insurance against a certain risk, but this was a risk much more real than Hell.

One sometimes wonders whether certain male theorists of the difference between men and women have ever sincerely wondered what a woman's life was like. The absence of periods, that monthly reminder of the autonomous life of the body, undoubtedly predisposes men to a certain detachment from the reality of the world. But there a certain risk did exist for women of the pre-industrial age, and even up to the decades that followed the Second World War – a risk more immediate than divine punishment, and one which men don't have to face: gestation and childbirth, which have certainly killed many more women in human history than war or car accidents have killed men. Maternity included a high risk of death. Some figures: Hector Gutierrez and Jacques Houdaille have measured a maternal mortality of 11.5 per 1,000 births in eighteenth-century France.[6] By 2010–12, the figure had fallen to 9.6 deaths per 100,000 births, i.e. a division of the risk by 120. Women have moved, in just a few generations, from a situation of maternal risk largely equivalent to the male risk entailed by heavy work, fishing and war, to a situation of relative security.

Once we have established this ancient context, we can understand why many women adhere to the Christian rejection of sexuality. The Church placed chastity above marriage and legitimized the refusal to procreate by the potential choice of celibacy. The ban on contraception in marriage immediately comes to mind, and warns us against any idealization of the Church's feminism. However, the negative attitude of Christianity to sexuality also extended to marriage and could be an ideological weapon against marital rape. Christianity often allowed women to refuse the sexual act to their husbands.

If we want to explain the alliance between women and the Church, this context of the danger associated with childbirth and the brutality of sexual mores seems to me more reasonable than Stark's metaphysical elucubrations. Women may have a heavenly soul; but, before that, they have an earthly reason.

Protestant patricentrism

Because the historical hubs of modern feminism are found in Protestant countries – in England with the suffragettes, in the United States with the contraceptive pill, in Sweden with the first feminism of national identity – it is a little difficult to perceive the religion of Luther, Zwingli and Calvin as unfavourable to women. Yet it was, and it is quite possible that an ever-active zombie Protestantism in these countries represents a discreet but powerful counterweight to the liberation of women, after having been one of the reasons for their rise.

Protestantism was born in Germany in 1517 with the Ninety-Five Theses of Martin Luther (1483–1546), affixed to the door of a church in Wittenberg in Saxony. Ulrich Zwingli (1484–1531) in German-speaking Switzerland, and Jean Calvin (1509–64) in the French-speaking world, produced their versions of the new belief. In these three cases, the geographical seat of Protestantism was a zone of emergence of the first patrilineal principle, at the very time when the stem family was reaching maturity. This was true of central Germany, of German-speaking Switzerland and of 'France', since Calvinism found its areas of strength in Occitania, along a La Rochelle–Geneva arc passing through the valleys of the Garonne and the Rhône. The stem family meant the emergence of fathers, and the inequality of sons with regard to succession – a mechanism reflected in the Protestant doctrine of predestination: men are called, by a decree of God preceding their birth, to death or eternal life. There is a perfect functional correspondence between the concrete inequality of sons and the metaphysical inequality of men. However, with the metaphysical inegalitarianism of Protestantism there comes an earthly egalitarianism.[7] All men must speak directly to God without the intermediary of a priest, and for this purpose they must be able to read the Holy Scriptures. The transition to the Reformation therefore brought about, as if mechanically, the extension of literacy to everyone and, *by accident*, a century or two later, the economic take-off of the peoples concerned.

Protestantism requires a man-priest. He closes the convents and monasteries. He demands that everyone be married. This man-priest will not be a human being in general, but the father of a family, a male individual. In his *When Fathers Ruled: Family Life in Reformation Europe*, on Germany and Switzerland, Steven Ozment has tried to show that the power of the fathers did not stop women enjoying favourable conditions, and that there could be affection in the families of the Reformed Churches.[8] In her *L'homme protestant*, Janine Garrisson-Estèbe has a chapter with a puzzling title: 'La femme protestante: de la modération au dépassement' ('The Protestant Woman: From Moderation to Overcoming').[9] Neither of these writers could hide the fundamental masculinism of Protestantism (we would have called it the Protestant attempt at patriarchy, were it not for the recent distortion of the term 'patriarchy'). The upper-class wife lost the possibility of escaping marriage through the convent, which Eileen Power (1889–1940) had shown

137

could, in the Middle Ages, be a refuge from the power of men.[10] For Protestantism, a woman must be a good wife, and cannot avoid this fate. The texts of Luther, and in particular his *Small Catechism*, give a central place to the father of the family.

One of the first concerns of Protestant leaders was to abolish the secret marriages legitimized by the medieval Church. In certain cases, as we have seen, these allowed the young woman to choose her husband freely.[11] Leaving the mediaeval Church led to a loss of female autonomy. The Protestant movement also contributed a return to the reading of the Bible, that magnificent text of the patrilineal mentality, with its original Eve who leads to an equally original sin. The decline of the Virgin in favour of Eve in religious thinking was not good news for women. Erich Fromm (1900–80) and, with him, the Frankfurt School clearly judged Protestantism to be patricentric: 'Protestantism [. . .] has done a thorough job of expurgating the matricentric traits of Christianity.'[12]

The spread of literacy in Germany, the heart of the Protestant conquest of souls, is the finest illustration of this patricentrism. In *Lineages of Modernity*, I noted that the literacy gap that opened up between men and women in Germany between the sixteenth and the seventeenth centuries was one of the largest ever observed in the world during a process of learning how to read and write: towards the end of the eighteenth century in Germany, 80–85% of men could read at the time of their marriage, but only 25–35% of women could.

This religion of men conquered Scandinavia, Great Britain and the Netherlands where the only stem family zones were Scotland, the interior of the Netherlands and western Norway. Elsewhere, in Denmark, in Norway around Oslo, in Holland, and in England, the family terrain was nuclear and favourable to women. The anthropological terrain of the nuclear regions that converted to the doctrine from Eastern Europe ensured the progressive deformation of Protestant metaphysics, which gradually lost its dogma of predestination. Without becoming equal, sons in these countries recovered the free will of the original Christian doctrine. In chapter 13, I will discuss the case of Swedish egalitarianism, after a re-examination of its family type.

Let's call this group of countries that surround the North Sea the 'western Protestant world', while the 'central Protestant world' refers to the set of countries that includes Germany, Switzerland and Occitania. In the western Protestant world, the importation of Protestantism had the usual effects in terms of literacy and even economic take-off, even more intensely than in the centre of Europe since the flexibility of the nuclear family did not subsequently block development. But the new doctrine led to a decline in the status of women, eloquently described by Lawrence Stone (1919–99) in *The Family, Sex and Marriage in England 1500–1800*. His chapter 5, 'The Reinforcement of Patriarchy', is devoted to the Protestant will to consolidate the power of the father. The ideal subordination of the wife to the husband is illustrated by a striking phrase from John Milton (1608–74): 'He for God only, she for God in him.'[13]

In the Germanic world that was then being transformed by a powerful patrilineal impetus, fear of the devil followed in the wake of Eve's rise to power. Here, it unleashed the great witch hunt, a war waged on women by men. These women were all the more threatened if, having passed forty or fifty years of age, they had become self-assured. The Catholic regions of Germany, where the stem family also prevailed, were the Protestants' equals when it came to fear of the devil and the executions that followed. The witch hunt was a European phenomenon, with a certain particular intensity in western areas such as Scotland and the Basque Country, stem family regions – non-patrilineal in the latter case, admittedly, since the eldest child, whether a boy or a girl, inherited the property.

But half of the witches executed were on the territory of present-day Germany; the whole of the Germanic Holy Roman Empire and Switzerland combined yielded three-quarters of the victims, 80% of them women. Elsewhere the intensity of the phenomenon was divided by a factor of around 10. In Sweden, there were just over 300 witches executed, again the vast majority being women. In England, in the county of Essex, between 1560 and 1675, 313 witches were put on trial, 93% of them women. In New England, 342 were accused of witchcraft, 78% of them women. The survival of evidence from the trials is patchy, but it is clear that European diversity has an anthropological significance.

In France, little documentation has survived, but in the jurisdiction of the Paris parliament, a little more than half of the appeal trials involved men. In Normandy, between 1564 and 1660, 278 of the 381 accused were men. France did not experience the great patrilineal impetus and relatively few of its witches were women, even if in Franche-Comté and in the Nord department, on the margins of the Empire, the figures for women were 76% and 81% respectively.[14] The witch hunt affected Catholic and Protestant countries, but the exceptions to the anti-feminine character of the trials or executions were squarely in Catholic countries. In all Protestant countries, the proportion of women among those condemned reached at least 80%.

Western feminism was born in a Protestant country, but certainly not because Protestantism was inherently favourable to women. On the contrary. Feminism was to a large extent a reaction to Protestant masculinism. Here we hold a very important interpretative key.

Not everything in Protestantism, however, was an inversion of early Christianity. In its hostility to sexuality, it was faithful to the Fathers of the Church. In *The Body and Society*, Peter Brown has clearly demonstrated the anti-sexual extremism of the early Church, so many of whose glorious representatives were true masochists of the body.[15] Here Protestantism, of which the English branch has given us the word 'Puritanism', from the name of the hardline Protestant party during the first English Revolution, brought about, for all people, the rejection of the body and of sexuality on this earth. Christian Europe was, in this rejection, a world of sexual obsessions – something we cannot in the least say about hunter-gatherers – and we need to take into account this dimension of the religious experience of the West if we are to understand the sexual revolution of the 1960s, gay identity in the 1980s and the transgender fixation of the 2010s.

Part II

Our revolution

— 9 —

LIBERATION: 1950–2020

Now that we have established the place of Western women in history, as the direct descendants of their ancestors the gatherers, the time has come to make the big leap: we need to try and grasp what is happening today. I will distinguish three short phases. First, the post-war period (1950–65), an era of apparent conformity. I will then move on to the anthropological transformation of the years 1965–2000. We will then see how far back it was that women started to overtake men educationally, and what this means for our present. Finally, I will examine the years 2000–20, our immediate world. Drawing on the concept of generalized intersectionality, I will study how the division between the sexes interacts with class relations. Our aim will be to understand the plurality of dominations rather than the plurality of discriminations.

This chapter, like the next two, will focus on France. But we will also draw on the case of the United States, which was up to a generation and a half ahead of us in the feminist revolution, and constitutes an indispensable point of comparison. Sweden will also be a necessary point of comparison. It became the self-proclaimed standard bearer of global feminism and its case allows us to identify some of the limits of the anthropological revolution that we are experiencing.

1950–1965: the height of petty-bourgeois conformism

For the period 1950–65, in the West, it is impossible to claim that women's status was low. The situation in Western Europe and the United States was very far from the situation in the Maghreb, in China or even in Japan and Germany. In Western mentalities – around the Atlantic, the North Sea and the Baltic – there reigned, from the point of view of historical anthropology, a basic, natural equality between men and women which did not prevent a political predominance, in the broad

143

sense, of the male sex. But – and this is what induces our often mistaken perception – Western societies are very specialized in their masculine and feminine functions.

In this economically and socially diverse post-war world, with regard to the status of women, it is necessary to distinguish the middle classes from the working-class world. Contrary to what current elitist and anti-working-class stereotypes suggest, the working-class world, though of course very differentiated in terms of male and female roles, was, in many dimensions, quite matricentric, as shown by the above-mentioned studies of Michael Young and Peter Willmott on England[1] and Olivier Schwarz on northern France.[2] The role of women was important in these areas – an always normal situation when the existential objective is survival rather than self-fulfilment. Of course, in the *Trente Glorieuses*, the thirty-year boom in postwar France (1945–75), the workers began to dream they were petty bourgeois and thereby adopted certain types of behaviour less favourable to women. But even if the man earned the household income and his wife stayed at home, he gave her his pay and she controlled the way it was used.

The epicentre of what is now called the oppression of women (the soft 'patriarchy' of the West) was found within the upper and petty bourgeoisie. Questions of survival arose less in these classes, and the predominance of men in obtaining income was more intense than in the working-class world. This is where we can observe, as was already the case in the nineteenth and eighteenth centuries, patrilineal inclinations and the strongest 'puritanism' – a moralizing term that can be translated (to keep the language technical) as 'control of women's sexuality'. The working-class world was more relaxed in its mores. An article by Guy Desplanques and Michel de Saboulin tells us that in 1952–4, premarital conceptions (a sign that couples have made love before getting married) accounted for 11.6% of births in the upper middle class and for 22%, almost double, among manual workers.[3] In her *History of Homosexuality in Europe*, Florence Tamagne points out that the working-class world was also more tolerant of homosexuality.[4]

The sexual liberalism of the working class should not be idealized. Let's not in our turn be the bourgeoisie of the nineteenth century fantasizing, albeit in a positive way, on the freedom of the lower classes. Clellan S. Ford and Frank A. Beach point out that in the American society of the 1950s, the only one for which we have indications at that time, the erotic sophistication of college graduates was a little higher: they neglected the oral stimulation of the breasts and female genitalia less than did men with only a high-school education.[5] America was a pioneer in the study of sexual behaviour, so it has unparalleled retrospective data, and we will never know if the same could be said of French graduates from the same period. American sociology comes to us from a world where young people, even before the invention of the pill, had the right to get laid in the backseats of cars. However, the sex was a hasty affair and relied to an immoderate degree on fellatio. Without being completely inexperienced, they were essentially virgins when they married.

Even in America, therefore, sex before the pill was as much a risk as a pleasure. To make love was to take a risk – for a woman, the risk of becoming pregnant; for a man of 'getting a girl pregnant'. Birth control was obviously practised, but with unreliable means: a mixture of condoms, the temperature method, coitus interruptus and, above all, abstinence, the surest technique for avoiding accidents. The girls were not, contrary to the current commonplace, kept under a watchful eye out of sexism, but for their own protection, since becoming 'baby mamas' entailed a difficult existence. It's a little facile today to denounce the sexual double standards of yesteryear, which deprived girls of the sexual freedom left to boys.

The prohibition on abortion, which resulted from the French populationism of the law of 1920, or more often from a Christian religious prescriptivism, aggravated sexual insecurity and the risk of fatal accidents resulting from clandestine interventions. The religious monitoring of sexual life had here reduced the freedom of Christians to less than that of hunter-gatherers.

This context often led, outside or in marriage, to brief and unfulfilling relationships. We could probably apply to the ideal-typical sexual relationship of the pre-pill years Thomas Hobbes's formula for human life in a state of nature: 'solitary, poor, nasty, brutish, and short'.

The educational and sexual revolution: 1965–2000

To understand the social and cultural movement of the past seventy years, let's go directly to society's educational subconscious, that easy-to-trace axis of human history, and see how, at this level, the balance, or imbalance, between men and women evolved.

In France, from 1900 onwards, literacy was a universal achievement for both sexes in the younger generations. It was how many people passed the baccalaureate that mattered throughout the twentieth century.[6] In 1896, according to national statistics, there were 7,241 male *bacheliers* but no female *bachelières*. In 1897 (the year of the publication of *Le Suicide*, by Durkheim), for the first time, two female *bachelières* were recorded, for 7,549 male *bacheliers*. The number of *bachelières* then rose slowly to 400 in 1914, for 7,139 boys. Just after the Second World War began, in 1940, there were 9,292 *bachelières* for 18,485 *bacheliers*: two-thirds boys and one-third girls. In 1950, there were 14,106 girls for 19,039 boys: two-fifths girls to three-fifths boys. The regularity of the catch-up is striking.

In 1960, parity was almost achieved: 29,864 girls for 31,635 boys – even though this was at the very heart of the conformist and petty bourgeois apogee described above. The definitive turning point took place in 1968 (the year of my baccalaureate!). It was a special baccalaureate for many reasons. It has often been forgotten that this was when the girls (87,930 *bachelières*) crushed the boys (just 81,492 *bacheliers*).

I would like the reader to share my astonishment at these figures. When I started researching this book, I thought I was studying a change in the power relationship between the sexes that was destined to flourish in the future. On the educational level, the shift took place more than half a century ago!

The evolution of mores accompanied women's liberation in education – even before the authorization and availability of modern contraceptive methods. Fertility began to drop sharply in France between 1965 and 1970. From 1965 to 1969, an increase in premarital conceptions was observed. From 11.6% in the upper middle class in 1952–4, as we have seen, these conceptions rose to 18% in 1965–9, before falling, in 1970–4, to 16.6%. Among workers, premarital conceptions rose from 22% in 1952–4 to 27.3% in 1965–9, and, without falling, reached 30% in 1970–4. One of the great illusions of the present age is to believe that it was the upper classes of society that drove the sexual liberation movement. The relaxation of mores was stronger and more rapid among the workers than among the bourgeois. Because this evolution occurred in a working-class world that was not then concerned with the baccalaureate, we can deduce that the evolution of mentalities must be perceived as a global, multidimensional phenomenon. We must assume a women's liberation that crosses all social categories.

The pill was authorized by the Neuwirth law in 1967 and voluntary termination of pregnancy by the Veil law in 1975. In 1971, when the decline in fertility was already well underway, only 6% of women were on the pill or intrauterine device.[7] The great leap forward in modern contraception took place between 1970 and 1975, when 25% of women used it.

If modern contraception makes the sex lives of both men and women more pleasant, it makes procreation a female decision. The loss of male power is total here, but this phenomenon has been masked by the complexity of romantic relationships: everyone thinks of men who don't want to commit, of women who don't love their partners enough to 'give them a baby', and so on. This confusion of feelings hides a simple reality: in the last instance, it is now the woman who decides whether or not to have a child. The position of weakness has changed sex: the man whose sperm is disdained has replaced the baby mama.

Women, services and industry

I said in the introduction that I will not separate the educational, anthropological and economic variables, and I reject any hierarchy between them. Let's now move on to the economy, without considering jobs as a priori less important than education, marriage or one's sex life, even if the massive arrival of women onto the labour market came somewhat after 1975 and then advanced at the same rate as secondary and higher education. This access to employment destroyed a certain dependency, abolishing the economic necessity of men, at least at the microeconomic level of individuals. We could simply say that it allowed women to divorce. But, far beyond that, it seemed to suppress the need for the human couple. This is a major difference with hunter-gatherers. But the notion of the uselessness of the couple applies here, I repeat, only at the level of individuals. It still leaves us with the question of the macroeconomic and macro-demographic viability of a society that moves beyond the human couple.

The employment rate for men was 73.8% in 1975 and 75.3% in 2019 (+1.4%). During the same period, the rate for women rose from 43.4% to 68.2% (+24.8%). The stability of the male rate hides a fairly broad shift, in the group and not among individuals, from agriculture and industry to services. In the case of women, while they may have withdrawn somewhat from employment in agriculture and industry, their direct entry into services needs to be emphasized. It should be noted that the arrival of women on the labour market did not constitute an 'addition' to a stable industrial world. This period was also that of a drop in the industrial workforce which began between 1975 and 1982.

From 1958 to 1964, the proportion of the active population employed in industry had continued to increase, reaching a peak of 40%, which was maintained for a little over a decade.[8] By 2014, this proportion had fallen to 13.9%. In 1968, the year when girls definitively overtook boys in obtaining the baccalaureate, men held 53% of jobs in services, 67% of agricultural jobs, 71% of jobs in the processing industry, 91% in fishing, 95% in construction, and 97% in extractive industries. The sexual division of labour had not changed much since the days of hunter-gatherers or intensive agriculture. I refer the reader to the maps in chapter 7 and to the male monopolies on hunting, fishing, boat building and the construction of permanent (e.g. brick) houses, as well as the sharing of agricultural tasks, which is more variable; see also my categorization of child rearing and care of the elderly as more feminine tertiary activities. There is no doubt that by removing textile activities, which are more feminine than the others, from the processing industry, we would bring the sexual division of around 1968 even closer to what it had been during the previous 100,000 years.

In 1946, 42% of women were already employed in the tertiary sector and this proportion had reached 59% by 1968. If we try to think simultaneously about the economy and the relations between the sexes, we must conclude that industry was masculine and that the development of the tertiary sector has enabled accelerated growth in female employment. To measure the fall in industrial employment is to chronicle the decline of male occupations.

Let's not rest content here with a mechanical vision of the development of the economy, a realization of the model developed by Colin Clark (1905–89) and then Jean Fourastié (1907–90), which describes a shift in human activity from primary to secondary then from secondary to tertiary, at the rate of the differential development of the physical productivity of the agricultural, industrial and service sectors. We will see in the last chapter of this book that the movement towards the tertiary sector did not occur at the same rate in all advanced countries, and that nations with a patrilineal tradition were much less quickly and fully tertiarized than the West narrowly speaking. In Germany, for example, the higher education of women progressed more slowly, and industry was more resistant; women there have not been 'liberated' to the same degree as in France, Sweden, England or the United States. We must acknowledge the possibility that women's liberation, so visible in education, has been one of the driving forces behind the development of the tertiary sector.

Just as the second phase of the Neolithic, intensive agriculture, coincided with the development of the patrilineal principle and a lowering in the status of women, the post-industrial revolution coincided with women's liberation and an elevation of their status.

Educational matridominance: 2000–2020

Thus, in the space of a generation, between 1965 and 2000, society changed. But on the educational level, the ratio of men to women shifted beyond what is generally imagined. The baccalaureate was only one step. Because this qualification gives one access to higher education, a female preponderance has finally established itself in the most educated part of the French population.

The INSEE 'Jobs' surveys indicate the highest qualifications obtained according to age and sex in the working population.[9] Around 2018, to find an age group in which more men than women had completed long-term higher education, we have to go to the 55–64-year-olds, with 14.5% of men and 12.1% of women. As soon as we go to the 45–54-year-olds, the balance is reversed, with 18.3% of women and only 17.9% of men. Thus, when we speak of an overtaking of men by women, we are not nowadays talking of kids or young people, but of people who are already mature. The trend is accentuated in more recent generations. Among those aged 35–44, 28.6% of women but only 24.7% of men have had higher education. Among the 25–34-year-olds, it's 36.1% of women and 29.6% of men, i.e. a sex ratio of 122. The younger generations have passed into educational matridominance. The student population is predominantly female.

The evolution was rapid, as is well known. The problem of retrospective perception, as for the baccalaureate, lies in the date: all this is already ancient history. People who are 50 today, and whose generation has experienced the inversion of the sex ratio in higher education, were 20 years old in 1990.

From hypergamy to hypogamy

For an anthropologist, the most important aspect of this inversion of the sex ratio has been the transition from hypergamy to hypogamy. The tradition, statistically speaking, was for women to marry older, wealthier and/or more educated men. We described this as hypergamy of age, wealth or education. Men at the bottom or periphery of the social structure – farmers, farm labourers and manual workers – thus had more difficulty finding a wife, and their rate of remaining single was higher than average. At the top and in the centre of the social structure, highly educated women, sometimes senior executives, did not find the men they wanted in the strata above them, and were often single.

I am here using the term 'marriage' as we do in anthropology to designate a de facto union with a minimum of stability, which can be consensual without being legitimized by civil or religious registration. Hypergamy expressed, at a variable level, male predominance in all human societies up to ours, but it was of very uneven intensity, depending on the culture. The obligation to marry a man of higher status, with a dowry, was so strong in the Rajput castes of northern India that it led, in families with too many daughters, to the massive infanticide of female babies. France was far from this explicit rather than statistical hypergamy – another difference that the notion of patriarchy would disguise.

Our moderately hypergamous world is no more. We suspect that, in a society where women are more educated than men, the perpetuation of a model according to which women mostly marry men with more qualifications than they themselves have is becoming impossible. In a 2015 article on 'the reversal of female hypergamy over cohorts [i.e. generations] in France', Milan Bouchet-Valat measured a decrease, then a disappearance, of hypergamy, and finally an inversion into hypogamy.[10] It is now men who, statistically, marry above their educational condition. Bouchet-Valat's study does not concern just college graduates but all levels, primary, secondary and higher, with – as groups between which the movements are noted – those with 'no diploma', those with a 'certificate of primary studies', the 'CAP, BEP and BEPC'[11] grouped together, the 'general, technological and professional baccalaureates', the 'higher education diplomas below first degree level', and finally the 'higher education diplomas with a first degree or higher'. What is striking, once again, is that the shift occurred much earlier than one would imagine: at the latest, for the generation born in 1955, those who therefore reached the age of marriage around 1980. When we include the intermediate educational levels, and not only those between higher education and the rest, the shift therefore appears even earlier.

Milan Bouchet-Valat, who helped me a great deal in accessing and understanding these data (without being in any way responsible for my possible errors), told me of his own surprise when he discovered the precocity of the transition to hypogamy. If we no longer take into account this or that generation, but the entire population, hypogamy becomes more frequent than hypergamy around the year 2000.

Bouchet-Valat asks himself whether the shift to hypogamy was held back by norms. To do this, he compares the random distribution of unions that would have been created by the respective proportions of men and women having reached such and such a level of education with what actually happened. His conclusion is fascinating: no cultural norm seems to have opposed the formation of hypogamous couples. There may even have been, on the contrary, an intensification of hypogamy compared to what should have existed. In any case, the hypothesis of a resistance of society favouring a principle of male domination does not hold, at least as long as we consider society as a whole.

Differences according to social class

Let's here introduce the notion of a generalized intersectionality, which, applied not only to the dominated but also to the dominant, allows a realistic and reasonable representation of society. To consider women as a whole would confine us a priori to a pure sex-based logic, to an opposition between men and women. But raising the level of education has not affected all women and all men in the same way. It has even led to a new stratification of society into primary, secondary and higher education and to an absolutely new phenomenon in history: a direct differentiation of women among themselves rather than through their spouses. Before the mass spread of education, and simplifying somewhat, women were differentiated by the social being of their husband: one was the wife of a bourgeois, a minor civil servant, a peasant or a worker. The hierarchization of the entire population by the educational machine has resulted in women being themselves socially sorted even before they enter working life and/or marriage.

Milan Bouchet-Valat's work as a whole, to which we can add the conclusions of Christine Schwartz and Robert Mare on the United States, leads to the observation of two fundamental phenomena which combine sex relations and class relations:[12] in the majority centre (60–80%) of the social structure, there are many marriages outside one's own group (social exogamy) and a predominance within this exogamy of hypogamy.

At both ends of the social structure, however, one can find 'dysfunctions': persistent homogamy at the top, that is to say a tendency to marry a spouse with a level of education equal to one's own, and a good number of single-parent families at the bottom, that is, non-marriages.

Seeing specific phenomena at the top and bottom of the social structure is, in a sense, inevitable, since women and men in the upper strata have no one above them with whom to practise hypergamy or hypogamy, and women and men in the lower strata have nobody below them with whom to practise hypergamy or hypogamy. I will show later that the situation at the top of the social structure is only this simple when the top corresponds to higher education defined in a fairly broad way, without distinguishing a higher stratum within the higher level itself.

The survey known as the 'Étude des parcours individuels et conjugaux' (Épic: 'Study of individual and marital careers'), conducted by the Institut national d'études démographiques (INED: National Institute for Demographic Studies) in 2013–14, shows, at the top and bottom of the hierarchy of qualifications, a specific resistance to hypogamy *on the part of certain women*, with 25.6% of women with bac +5[13] who won't easily accept the idea of marrying a man with fewer qualifications than them, compared to only 10.1% of men who won't easily accept the idea of living with a woman with more qualifications than them.[14] The attitude of some women without a diploma is paradoxical: 21.5% of them would not accept a partner with fewer qualifications than them – more than a rare pearl, this would be a social being who simply cannot exist. But this response no doubt represents, metaphorically, the rejection of a man who doesn't earn much, and it is crucial to understanding the accumulation of single-parent families at the bottom of the social structure.

For all women, the rejection of hypogamy is 17.8% and for all men, 9.5%. Any survey triggers an exaggeration of the conscious and socially accepted response, and it is likely that the vast majority who accept hypogamy mask an even deeper resistance, especially on the part of women.

Dysfunctions at the extremes can be explained by a hidden remnant of preference for hypergamy, not in society as a whole, and especially not in men, but among some women. After all, the marital life of men, at the top and bottom of society, has hardly changed. They easily manage to get married at the top of the hierarchy of diplomas, professions and income

151

(they can even practise successive polygamy in these strata), but they have some difficulty in finding a wife at the bottom of society (whether this bottom be defined by education or income).

Bouchet-Valat's very detailed studies concern first unions, strongly marked by the educational levels reached at the beginning of life. However, the author also shows that occupational hypogamy will follow educational hypogamy, after some delay, since the hypergamy of socio-professional category has ended up declining in its turn, again in the case of first unions. After the first unions, which are its statistical target, there is the rest of life, the professional successes and failures of all those involved, divorces, finding a new partner or leading one's life without a spouse. A new field of possibilities then opens up for hypergamy, with some men who succeed and can find a woman easily and others who do not.

In her book *Amours clandestines: Sociologie de l'extraconjugalité durable* (*Clandestine Loves. A Sociology of Enduring Extra-conjugality*), the sociologist Marie-Carmen Garcia has described, with finesse and cruelty, the socially inegalitarian structure of some adulterous couples.[15] The study is qualitative but describes the underground re-emergence of a certain form of male domination which, however, cannot be said to stem from the desires of the men themselves: the women concerned participate actively in the perpetuation of this inegalitarian mechanism. Reading this book leads one to suppose – in a hypothesis that needs to be confirmed or invalidated by wider statistical work – that this represents a certain return of the repressed. It seems to me that, beyond the data which now show a majority hypogamy, many things remain to be said, that the case is not proven, and that the decades to come could bring us some surprises, including the persistence among some women of the search for a dominant male, of the kind called 'Prince Charming' in fairy tales.

Leaving to one side extra-marital love affairs, what we need to take from Bouchet-Valat's studies is that one cannot seriously study hypergamy and hypogamy without integrating single-parent families into the set of all matrimonial mechanisms, that is to say situations of non-marriage that have produced children, or of broken marriage. The rejection, by certain women, of hypogamy or even of homogamy, and the persistence of a dream of hypergamy, dysfunctional at a time when women are better educated than men, contribute to explaining the accumulation of single-parent families at the bottom of the social structure.

Poverty and single-parent families

Let us dwell for a moment on this problem of single-parent families, which, in the overwhelming majority of cases, are single mothers with children.

In a first phase, the sexual revolution led to the appearance of 'modern' single-parent families in the educated categories. This phase turned out to be very brief. Subsequently, the weakening of the marital bond was mostly concentrated, in a much more traditional way, at the bottom of society, while in the middle and at the top, discreetly – beyond all the discourse on sexual tolerance, the acceptance of homosexuality and of the transgender phenomenon – people behaved well: marriage and life as a couple are solidified again in the middle classes. Single-parent families are now mostly located at the bottom of the social structure, but in different ways depending on the country. In 2004, Sara McLanahan was the first to highlight, in the United States, the phenomenon of the concentration of single-parent families in underprivileged areas.[16] She observes that educated people live much more often together as a couple. This stabilization of the family in the middle and upper strata and its growing weakening in the lower categories are fundamental.

A 2018 article, 'Middle-Class Single Parents',[17] gives for a certain number of countries the proportion of single-parent families who do not belong to the disadvantaged working classes: 30% in the UK, 35% in the US, 40% in France. In Sweden, the proportion of middle-class single-parent families is higher: 48%. The relatively socially undifferentiated character of Swedish society is evident here, as for many other variables. But the trend in Sweden is towards Western normalization: while, in the mid-1980s, the proportion of single-parent families from working-class backgrounds there was only 35%, it has now reached 52%. The middle classes in the West are once again becoming cautious, in a world that is once again economically dangerous.

The current cultural atmosphere in fact points to an inverted bourgeois hypocrisy, which one could express, with a slight exaggeration, in the following way. In the nineteenth century, the officially puritanical middle classes allowed their men to take mistresses and their sons to frequent prostitutes or to have flings with the servants. Today, the middle classes, officially open to all sexual experiences, are secretly returning to the security of married life.

Poverty, family disorganization and pro-life attitudes in the US

The questioning of the right to abortion by the US Supreme Court in June 2022 was, without question, a regression of the right of women to freely dispose of their bodies. I will not discuss here the legal and political elements of the problem, the fact that in the United States a central authority can take a decision contrary to the wishes of the majority opinion. The Pew Research Center tells us that in 2022, 61% of Americans nationwide believe that abortion should be legal in most cases, and only 37% believe it should not be legal in most cases. Some of the causes of the counter-revolutionary move are to be found in the crisis of American liberal democracy. But what will interest me here is the social location of the minority pro-life movement and how it is best explained by poverty and education.

It is in the underprivileged part of the American population, in terms of both education and occupation, that we find the greatest support for the anti-abortion movement. Why is this so? Let's make the hypothesis that the ideology and praxis of the educated classes – sexual liberalism and matrimonial neo-conformism – have left American working-class families, threatened by disintegration and the single-parent family, in a state of abandonment. The model of behaviour and opinion coming from the top of society no longer makes sense to them. In this vacuum, regression has become possible.

Single parenthood is not restricted to Blacks in the US. While its overall rate of 19% (more than twice the average Western European rate of 9%) includes the 48% of Black single-parent families, it also includes the 13% of white single-parent families. Lower-class American families are struggling, and those that don't go under are living on the edge of disorder. This threatened world is probably in search of 'norms' – in search of any order, however absurd. The demonization of abortion, which dates back to the time when the white evangelical movement was flourishing among the less-educated, in the early 1970s, has survived the weakening of religion since the early 2000s.[18] We will see later in this book the importance of this retreat from religion in the emergence of a tolerant attitude towards homosexuality. But hostility to abortion, despite a slight decline, has persisted, and its ban has become the banner of a pro-life movement that relies less and less on religion and more and more on a diffuse fear of emptiness in a world that is increasingly physically threatening. While religion, the promise of eternal life for some, has declined in the US, mortality on earth has increased. In their *Deaths of Despair and the Future of Capitalism*,[19] Anne Case and Angus Deaton point to the rise in mortality among white Americans aged 45–54, since the early 1990s, from alcoholism, suicide and opioid-based drug abuse, affecting, of course, those with no more than a high-school diploma. Since 2015, Blacks with the same level of education have joined them.[20]

It is in relation to this pro-death objective environment that we must situate support for the pro-life movement, as it appears in the major 2014 Pew Research Center survey, which allows us to drill down into the analysis by education and sex across the US. At that time, the national proportion of people who thought abortion should be legal in most cases was slightly lower than today, at 51%, and the proportion of people who were against it, i.e. pro-life, was slightly higher at 43%. The difference in attitude between men and women in their opposition to abortion was small: 45% of men as against 41% of women. This 4% difference is small when compared to the chasm that separates Americans with a complete higher education (college and above), only 33% of whom express opposition to abortion, from Americans who remained at the high-school level, 51% of whom express opposition to abortion – a gap of 18%. The hypothesis of a working-class world in dire disarray, ready to cling to any norm, is beginning to be verified. The hypothesis of a 'pro-life' slogan flourishing in a world concretely threatened by the increase in mortality is also starting to be confirmed.

We can go further and understand the ability of some American states to effectively ban abortion thanks to the Pew Center's detailed survey. It gives us, for the majority of states (not all of them, due to low sample sizes), the proportions of pro-lifers by education and sex. In eighteen states we find higher percentages of women opposed to abortion than men. We should not take these distributions too literally: the samples are small. However, the sex gap falls to 1.5% (relative to the national 4%) if we average the states for which sex attitude estimates are available. In the case of education, the gap between college and high school obtained by averaging the rates by state remains at 14% (18% nationally).

In clearly pro-choice states like New York, where only 32% of respondents are pro-life, the rate rises to 42% of respondents with only a high-school diploma. In California, where only 38% are pro-life, the rate rises to 48% among high-school graduates. In Pennsylvania, an economic, cultural and political frontier state, the pro-life rate, already 44% overall, rises to 51% among the less educated, which means that among them, in this state, the pro-life movement is the majority. When the higher educated are few in number in a state, the culturally dominant popular world can use local institutions that allow it to ban abortion. In a sense, American educational, economic and social evolution has created *lower-class states* and *upper-class states*, where, although not necessarily in the majority, the higher educated control the cultural system. Social control operates at two levels, since the post-graduates themselves control the mass of the college educated. The upper-class states constitute a world of order and hierarchy, but one that is liberal and pro-choice. The lower-class states represent the opposite model of societies not controlled by the social elite, anarchic and intolerant at the same time.

A very simple calculation allows us to measure the power of educational and, by inference, economic determination, since education increasingly determines professional destiny. The negative correlation coefficient between pro-life attitudes and college degree is –0.77 (60% of explained variance), which means that a low educational level explains 60% of the opposition to abortion. Such a level of determination is all the more astonishing given that Blacks, who are often poorly educated, deviate from the

155

attitude of the white population by a much higher pro-choice alignment, whatever their level of education. How are we to interpret these figures, calculated using the US states as units of statistical aggregation? We must forget about regional histories, about cultural variations within the US, and about history. We must perceive the US states as detached from their anthropological roots, as almost chemically pure class states. The low-education states are pieces of the working classes, capable of expressing, in a poll or in a partisan vote, their class nature and the moral attitudes attached to them. One can always underline evangelical or Catholic traces, or their absence. But what predominates is a class refusal of abortion. In *Les Luttes de classes en France au XXIème siècle* (*Class Struggles in Twenty-First-Century France*),[21] I noted a new capacity of French *départements* to express directly the attitudes associated with their educational levels, independently of all their previous history – a sign of the disappearance of all traditional anthropological, religious or ideological anchoring.

The middle classes in survival mode

In the educated middle strata, economic difficulties are rising and, in reaction to this, a stabilization of the family, which now requires two salaries. The economic backdrop to the evolution of mores is no longer the expansion of the post-war boom of 1945–75, but an incessant contraction of opportunities and incomes. And even the salaries that are rising, in the financial professions or in consulting, are in reality simply following real-estate prices: the winners are treading water. The difficulty of the times is taking those most aware of the problems back to the rationality of hunter-gatherers, those men whose objective was survival rather than fulfilment. The heart of the economic survival mechanism (through hunting, gathering or fishing) was the solidarity of the couple. Here we are forced back to the unspoken assumptions of the contemporary middle classes, masked by a certain form of ideological inertia: we are supposed, above all, to love one other, in mind and body, but two salaries make it possible to love one other with more serenity.

In the past, it was taken for granted that a woman sought to marry a man who earned a decent living. Now, with women also working, we have moved into a world where, especially in the educated middle classes, men prefer to live with a woman with a good income. This explains the easy acceptance by men of hypogamy, even if this interpretation upsets the stereotype of the dominant male.

This mechanism operates at full capacity in the middle strata of society, whereas at the bottom, where solidarity is most needed, the couple is more unstable: the attitude of rational survival is weaker here, probably due to its rejection by women.

Forgive me for speaking like a cynical American researcher. For a long time, I found Gary Becker's theories on economic rationality in families very irritating.[22] But, faced with these data on the fall of hypergamy and the proliferation of single-parent families among the less educated, I must admit that American sociology excels in its description of the relationship between men and women as resulting in part from an economic transaction in a market. The rational-choice school will not hesitate to say – taking American racism as a given – that a white woman who marries a rich Black man compensates for the handicap of colour by an advantage of resources. The same school will stop seeing the hunter-gatherer as an irrational moron and will define the good hunter-gatherer as a good thing for a woman. If it de-poeticizes the conjugal bond somewhat, this attitude has the merit of reminding us that a couple is an economic unit – among hunter-gatherers a unit of production and consumption, in the post-industrial world, outside of agriculture and small trade, a consumer unit. Living as a couple isn't just about loving each other, making love and building up a store of good memories. It *is* all of this, fortunately, but it's also finding somewhere to live, eating and paying for the children's studies. Divorce has now become the moment of anthropological truth, the time when we convert sentimental problems into money problems.

Paradoxically, we can find a more optimistic vision of the couple if we consider a massive return to conditions of survival rather than maintaining a goal of self-fulfilment in a society of abundance. If it's a question of not dying, the opposition between economy and sentiment becomes specious: mutual aid within the human couple once again becomes the very expression of love.

The American attitude finds its axiomatic limit when it comes to explaining the birth of children. Raising children does not bring in anything economically. Having children remains the altruistic act par excellence and, faced with the power of natural selection (we are all the descendants of people who have reproduced), the rational-choice axiom flounders. All that economic rationality can explain today is the choice not to have children: the establishment of secure pensions has released us from the old days when children, when they became adults, took care of their parents. If one takes early retirement, one can envisage a very old age without children. Obviously, if all individuals make this calculation and refuse to procreate, there will be no retirement pension for anyone.

Women at the risk of anomie

Women's liberation from the 1960s onwards made free subjects of them. But freedom has its dark side: it is accompanied by a rise in anxiety, a turmoil, which we must examine. An INSEE article can help us to pose the problem: it concludes that 'in 40 years, the social mobility of women has progressed; that of men has remained almost stable'.[23] Specifically, this study measures the upward mobility of women over the past decades, as well as the beginnings of a downward mobility for the most recent generations. What we basically discover from it, all of a sudden, is women facing the once purely male problem of an autonomous social destiny. The authors tell us that 'the social mobility of women in relation to their mothers has increased by 12 points in 40 years'. This is a 'structural change', as many mothers had no job or very low jobs in the social ladder. We therefore see (and this is to be expected) four times more upward than downward mobility for women compared with their mothers. But we also observe a more curious phenomenon: more downward mobility for the daughters of executive mothers than for the sons of executive fathers. Executive status seems more resistant in the male lineage than in the female lineage, with a weaker female capacity for social reproduction. Compared to their fathers, the trajectory of women is even more often downward: '61% of the daughters of an executive father occupy a lower social position (compared to 53% of the daughters of an executive mother).' This points to an emancipated, socially higher, but unstable feminine world.

What this article suggests is that liberation has brought women, now come of age, in difficult economic times, into the once male-only mental world of social anxiety. The hour of Durkheimian anomie has struck for them, something which the author of *Suicide* defined thus, in a more optimistic economic period:

> Appetites, not being controlled by a public opinion become disoriented, no longer recognize the limits proper to them. [. . .] With increased prosperity desires increase. At the very moment when traditional rules have lost their authority, the richer prize offered these appetites stimulates them and makes them more exigent and impatient of control. [. . .] But then their very demands make fulfillment impossible. Overweening ambition always exceeds the results obtained [. . .]. Nothing gives satisfaction and all this agitation is uninterruptedly maintained without appeasement.[24]

The concept of anomie should not lead us to a mechanical reproduction of the interpretation given in *Suicide*. Durkheim made anomie a central explanatory element of the increase in the suicide rate at a time of increasing prosperity. We are experiencing a drop in suicide, male as well as female, and a drop in prosperity (see figures 9.1 and 9.2).

While we can diagnose a growing anomie among women, we must also observe, among them as among men, outside the United States, a drop in the suicide rate since 1985. In any case, the central phenomenon is the decrease in the rate of suicide, something which I had interpreted in

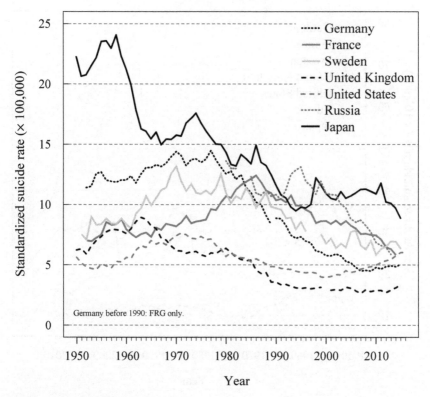

Figure 9.1 Female suicide rate
Sources: CDC WONDER (USA) and WHO Mortality Database. Author's calculations

Les Luttes de classes en France au XXIe siècle as pointing to an overall fall in the degree of anomie, the result of a collapse of expectations in an ever more impoverished society – one that is, moreover, debilitated by the evolution of mores. A general reduction in expectations calms everyone down, while weakened 'superegos' entail fewer suicides in the event of social or moral failure.[25]

The concept of soft anomie

So I come to one of the major paradoxes examined in this book. I have just successively suggested a rise in anomie among women, and a decline in anomie in society as a whole, even though this society is becoming more feminized.

We can take this paradox further: the psychological revolution

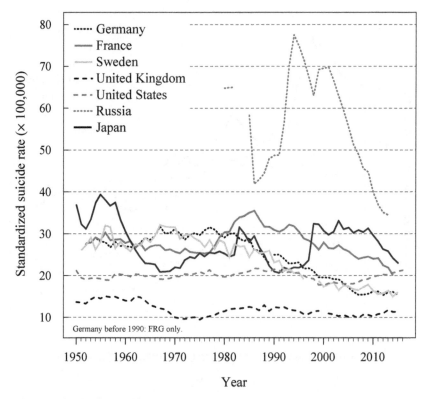

Figure 9.2 Male suicide rate
Sources: CDC WONDER (USA) and WHO Mortality Database. Author's calculations

that has favoured the fall in the suicide rate owes a lot to women. It is commonplace to emphasize their predominant role in questioning the typically male self-repression of personality. Women are the big consumers of psychological interviews and the literature of self-development. They have also allowed the emergence of a male ego less subject to the dictatorship of the superego. According to Thierry Jobard, author of a cruel and funny book on 'personal development', it seems that we are witnessing a 'masculinization' of personal development. 'While it was intended for a middle-class, largely female audience, personal development is diversifying its offer horizontally and vertically. Horizontally by addressing, via certain publications, a male audience; vertically, by also targeting less well-off social strata.'[26] We here have a phenomenon of diffusion from women to men, an index of matridominance.

160

But how can we reconcile our two main observations: women's access to anomie, plus a decrease in overall anomie resulting from the arrival of these same women at the heart of the psychological life of society? A dynamic, i.e. historical and evolutionary, conception of the processes provides us with a solution.

Women's liberation and the demographic convergence of the two sexes

If we look at the sex ratio of suicide rates, no general convergence seems to emerge. Perhaps in the United States, where women's liberation began earlier, we see a slight decline in male excess suicide rates, a correlate of the rise in female suicide. In France, Germany, the United Kingdom and Italy, things seem to be quite the reverse (see figure 9.3).

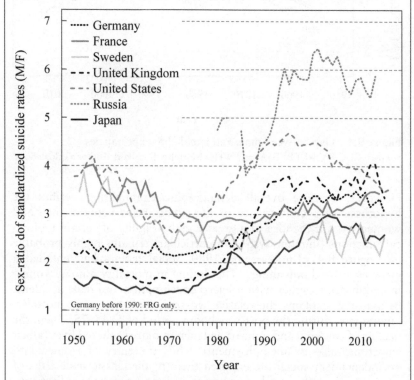

Figure 9.3   Sex ratio of suicide rates
Sources: CDC WONDER (USA) and WHO Mortality Database. Author's calculations

161

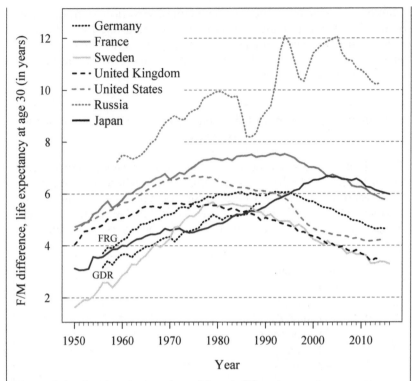

Figure 9.4 Gap between male and female life expectancies
Sources: CDC WONDER (USA) and WHO Mortality Database. Author's calculations

However, a more overall demographic examination verifies the hypothesis of a convergence of life expectancies between men and women, even if the idea of a greater male fragility of certain biological functions (immune system in particular) remains highly probable (see figure 9.4). Until around 1980, social factors had entailed a growing male disadvantage. The decline in mortality among women in childbirth, together with tobacco consumption and male accidents in industry, explains the relative worsening of the excess mortality among men during the post-war boom period of 1945–75. Then, the decline of smoking and industry led men to more sheltered lives (albeit sometimes also to unemployment), while the entry of women into an independent social life exposed them to the classic male risks of smoking, alcoholism, other narcotics and road accidents. All of this, of course, has taken place, until recently, in the context of rising life expectancies for both sexes.

Women are entering mainstream social life with traditional characteristics, i.e. without carrying the *Homo sapiens* mental burden of male
self-repression, the view of a man who must be a 'real' man in a group of
men, a hunter who must shine among his peers and manage the collective
while being submissive to it – committing suicide, perhaps, but, above all,
not crying. These new women are modifying the psychological tonality of
their society through a better attention to the well-being of the self – I am
here drawing, albeit quite unironically, on the posture of the anthropologist Janet Carsten described in chapter 2. As I said, Carsten demands
that we pay more attention to the emotions, to the intimacy of the home
and to the personality, to the body. These women dilute the superego,
individual as well as collective. The suicide rate of men is falling; their
right to cry is recognized. But, having become free individuals, women
themselves are insidiously being led into the old male concerns of dissatisfaction with their social expectations – to a distortion between their
level of education and their economic or personal success, for example.
If we take on board this double movement, which occurs against a
background of economic stagnation, we can conceive of a society that
is less demanding for the individual in general but that is simultaneously
becoming anxiety-provoking in a new way for women. It feeds into
low-level dissatisfaction without raising the suicide rate. I propose to
describe this new and probably transitional situation of women in our
society as a form of 'soft anomie'. Perhaps, in order to measure this soft
anomie, the suicide rate used by Durkheim to measure anomie should
be replaced by the frequency of suicide attempts, which have long been
known to be more characteristic of women. In 2017, in France, 61% of
hospitalizations after attempted suicide were those of women. But such
an indicator poses serious methodological problems of measurement and
it is therefore not certain that it allows the kind of retrospective analysis,
since 1950 for example, that the suicide rate makes possible. The fact that
suicide attempts mainly involve younger subjects than those who commit
suicide tells us a priori that the existential dissatisfaction captured is a
matter of impatience rather than a feeling of terminal failure.

In this book, we are seeking to explain the rise of an antagonistic
vision of relations between the sexes, even though so many objective
indices reveal a massive improvement in the situation of women. These,
it should be remembered, have taken precedence over men in educational
terms, and they have arrived en masse on the labour market, including
in positions of responsibility. In France, their proportion in the National
Assembly, which before 1997 had never exceeded 10%, rose to 26.9%
in 2012, and reached 38.8% in 2017, approaching the Swedish level of
45%. Things are getting better, at an accelerating pace. And society is
not resisting. Men marry women who are more qualified than they are
without complaining. So why this new antagonism? Could it be that

the rise of a negative vision of the male sex is partly a result of this new freedom for women, generating a soft anomie, a new kind of dissatisfaction, as much as it produces freedom? We certainly hold part of the explanation here, but only part of it. A certain type of male domination persists, at the very top of society; this is what we must now examine.

— 10 —

MEN RESIST BUT THE COLLECTIVE COLLAPSES

Women's liberation in Western countries since the 1960s has been a massive, rapid phenomenon, which has not met with much opposition within the societies it has so profoundly shaken. This doesn't mean, as we have seen, that one cannot at present observe nuances depending on whether the women (and men) belong to the middle classes or to the working classes. Nor does it mean that women's liberation is not currently coming up against certain limits. In this chapter, we will first note the persistence of a sexual division of labour which is very close to that of the hunter-gatherers. I will then abandon the too simple opposition between working classes and middle classes to focus, not on the top 1% as is now done for the critique of globalized capitalism, but on the top 4% defined by educational stratification, the upper group of the upper group, which remains patridominated. This is the best-known limit to women's liberation: the resistance of a very thin male layer at the top of society.

I will not explain this by the evil machinations of a sex that I will no longer dare to describe as 'strong', since its domination is now so fragile. The contradictions of the feminine condition and the uncertainty of the masculine condition explain, much better than oppression, the omnipresence of male figureheads at the top of the social structure. The weakness of this residual male dominance actually helps to explain the West's main fragility, the collapse of the collective sentiment. But I admit in advance that, when I suggest that the excesses of neoliberalism result, in part, from women's liberation, I will be positioning myself on the very frontiers of scholarly study, opening up a path rather than presenting a conclusion.

The persistent sexual division of labour, yet again

To take the full measure of the persistence of the sexual division of labour, let's start with the most advanced feminist country, Sweden, whose position as world number one on map 1.3, taken from the *Global Gender Gap Report 2020*, we have already seen. Its limit will be our limit. Its official, militant but honest statistics, published in *Women and Men in Sweden 2018: Facts and Figures*, reveal astonishing occupational disparities by sex.

Let's start with the government: 52% of ministers are women and, at the lower level of secretaries of state, women comprise 54%. There continues to be some resistance, on the other hand, at the level of top administrators, 57% of whom are still male. We will find these male bureaucrats, proliferating without control, in France too. But, in Sweden, in the state as a whole, there is no problem: a more or less satisfactory parity can be measured. In the field of party politics, in the Riksdag for example, the results remain good but have levelled off: from 1998 onwards, 42% of MPs are women; in 2002, 45%; in 2010, still 45%; in 2014, 43%. It's not bad, even if the big battalions of politics remain predominantly male.

The most interesting feature, however, lies elsewhere, in the private sector. Its managers are 69% men while those in the public sector are 65% women. In 2017, the distribution by sex within listed companies shows that 94% of chairpersons are men, who also comprise 92% of CEOs and 68% of members of boards of directors. In the upper echelons of the private sector, therefore, male resistance in Sweden is extraordinary. This is confirmed by the examination of limited companies, where presidents are 85% men, who comprise 76% of the members of boards of directors.

When it comes to differentiation into professions, sexual division is further accentuated. On the maps in chapter 7, which concerned pre-industrial societies, we saw a clear division between men who hunted, or built boats and houses, and women who devoted themselves to gathering or pottery. In Sweden, the differentiation of occupations according to sex persists: 93% of nurses, 87% of those who take care of the elderly, 84% of social workers, 83% of assistants or secretaries and 82% of those working with children are women. Finally, 80% of kindergarten teachers are female. Conversely, masons, carpenters and electricians are 98% male. Among metalworkers and mechanics, the proportion of men is always above 95%.

The massive entry of women into employment therefore most often conceals a strong and almost complete resistance on the part of the sexual division of labour. Women specialize in trades which seem to be the salaried counterparts of their tertiary functions in the family of hunter-gatherers: caring for young and old and teaching, with housekeeping now becoming the administrative management of the house-nation.

As Sweden has set our maximum expectation, I will not repeat the overall demonstration for France, contenting myself with emphasizing the current sexual division of labour in a few highly skilled trades, within the educated middle classes. I will examine executives, doctors and mathematicians in turn.

The sex of the state

In the 2017 edition of *INSEE Références*, we find an article entitled 'Access of Women and Men to Executive Positions at the Start of Working Life: A Convergence in Motion?', written by an apparently mixed team – Vanessa Di Paola, Arnaud Dupray, Dominique Epiphane and Stéphanie Moullet.[1] 'In 2013, for the first time, the proportion of young women who, three years after entering the labour market, occupied executive positions became almost equivalent to the proportion of young men.' So there was a catch-up. This, the authors continue, 'is also happening with salaries [. . .]. The fact remains that the increase in the number of women in executive positions at the start of their professional lives is still not commensurate with the importance of their educational investment. With characteristics and diplomas identical to men, they still have 30% less chance of becoming executives, whether or not the position is associated with hierarchical responsibilities.' This is quite correct: while the number of men and women executives is equivalent, while there are more women graduates, these are at a disadvantage in the transition from their studies to their profession. If we based economic structure on qualifications, we would achieve a resolutely matridominated society.

The crucial information, however, is still to come. It concerns the persistence of sex-based specialization within the category of executives. Women are overwhelmingly executives in the public sector and men in the private sector. 'Young female executives work twice as often in this [public] sector as men (31% compared to 16% in 2013).' There are major differences according to categories: 'Young women thus represent 62% of hierarchical executives in public service, 69% of teachers and scientific professions, 62% in the arts and entertainment information professions, but 46% of supervisors among administrative and commercial business executives and only 22% of engineers and technical business executives.' Here we are again in a – gentler – world of hunter-gatherers: men continue to make tools and to transform matter.

The medical profession

The division of labour observed at the level of the major sectors, secondary and tertiary, private and public, as well as at the level of professions, persists if we go down a further notch in the analysis and examine the most feminized professions from the inside. It is then possible to identify new, more finely sex-based divisions that did not exist before women entered the sector.

Let's take the example of medicine. In France, 7,978 students chose their internship specialty in 2017. Women were in a large majority: 57% of the workforce. *Le Quotidien du médecin (The Doctor's Daily)* analysed the assignments.[2] Women are over-represented in paediatrics, endocrinology and dermatology. In these specialties, their proportion exceeds 75%. It now reaches 98.4% in gynaecology. Men are over-represented in surgical specialties. The numbers are small but the difference is significant: neurosurgery comes first (76.2% men), followed by oral surgery, then orthopaedic and vascular surgery.

Male involvement in surgery strangely reflects their predominance in industry and technology. It again points to an attraction for the manipulation of matter, here living rather than inert. Ophthalmology was also dominated by men (59.6%) but less so than surgery. To qualify, you had to be ranked among the top 2,134. This may explain the over-representation of men in this highly sought-after discipline. Men are on average better ranked: 52.2% among the first 1,000. We see a higher male layer emerging, which no ideological intervention seems capable of ridding us of. I'll come back to this later.

Mathematics

Technology and the transformation of matter seem to constitute the heart of masculine resistance. We have further proof of this when we examine the respective relationship of men and women to scientific studies.

If we stick to individuals, it is obviously not difficult to think of some women who are equally adept at high-level mathematics as some men. But, statistically, scientific studies remain a male bastion and UNESCO reports express concern about this.[3] This is the negative side of the shift in higher education towards matridominance: it is massive in the humanities, in the human sciences (with, as we have said, some resistance in history), and in the medical and judicial sector. But the percentage of women with doctorates in science, mathematics and computer science was only around 35% in 2007 (compared to 65% for men according to

UNESCO), France being close to this average and Sweden just exceeding the 40% threshold.

Pure science is the heart of abstract thought, with mathematics at its ultimate centre. The evolution of higher education does not, however, point to abstract thought as the ultimate and central hub of resistance of the male sex. It is an education leading to an engineering career that constitutes this anchor point. Here, the European female average falls to 25% against 75% for men, France being at 23% and Sweden at 27%. This discrepancy observed between abstract science and technology is important because it establishes a continuity (yet again!) between the current male resistance and the old sexual division of labour in *Homo sapiens*, where the manufacture of tools and, as we have seen, boats was the preserve of the male sex (see again the maps in chapter 7) – denounced by Paola Tabet as a strategy of male domination.

Undoubtedly, the importance of the French scientific *grandes écoles* and their ability to provide executives and leaders beyond industry make them one of the instruments for perpetuating the thin upper layer of patridominance, still observable in all advanced nations. In 2011, in France, the proportion of women at university was 57.2%; in business schools, 49.9%; in the preparatory classes for the *grandes écoles*, 41.9%; in engineering schools, 27.8%.[4]

However, today, in our tertiarized world, the transformation of matter only ensures a very limited domination. If engineers want to make a really good living, they often have to escape into finance. Workers who feel abandoned vote for the National Rally in France, for Trump in the United States or for the Sverigedemokraterna in Sweden. And we observe that the industrial collapse of certain societies is contributing to the erasure of patridominance.

The top 4%: a residual patridominance

Let's go back to the highest educational category. The massification of higher education poses a problem of description analogous to that of income. Thomas Piketty's great contribution to the study of income inequality undoubtedly lies in targeting the 1% within the top 20% (the two upper deciles dear to the OECD) and in showing the whole world that it was in this 1% that the beneficiaries of the globalized economic system in its current state were to be sought.[5] The next 19% lost their elite status as a result and were transformed, thanks to the statistical analysis of tax revenues, into a weakly oppositional global petty bourgeoisie.

Let's apply a similar type of targeting to academia. If 40% of young people (the modelling figure) are now completing higher education, it's obvious that they will not constitute a 'mass aristocracy', the absolute oxymoron. An upper level of the upper level emerges on the practical and symbolic planes: in the United States or in England, the best universities (a category wider than just the Ivy League or Oxbridge); in France, the best of the *grandes écoles* and the high-school classes that prepare pupils for them. The place held by this upper level of the upper level is difficult to measure with precision because of the combinations and permutations in student courses, but we can assess it, in France, as 10% of total students, based on the number of students in engineering schools and preparatory classes. Ten per cent of 40% would be 4% of a generation. This percentage is interesting because it allows us to foresee the emergence of a new stratification in France: with this 4% in the upper levels, we are not taking all the higher intellectual professions which represent (again by modelling) 20% of the working population.

I am aware of the difficulties presented by this scheme. It is obvious that a certain number of former students of the *grandes écoles* subsequently find themselves, in terms of income, in the sociological 'standard' middle-class categories. Think of the *normaliens* who become high-school teachers.[6] And, conversely, a certain number of persons who can only be placed in the most dominant category did not attend the *grandes écoles*. Françoise Bettencourt Meyers, the heiress of L'Oréal, has only the baccalaureate.[7] Her eldest son, Jean-Victor, does not seem to have particularly distinguished himself during his studies either.[8] In fact, while income is indeed partly based on educational qualifications, there are of course limits to this.

However, men make up more than two-thirds of the workforce in the *grandes écoles*. The division of the highly educated into two categories makes it possible to situate, at the source, the maintenance of the patri-dominated upper layer. This top 4% can then spill over to the top of the structure of professions, since the economy follows education. Following the work of Milan Bouchet-Valat, I have described a homogamy at the top of society, but this is true only if the description of higher education is not too detailed. We can push the analysis a step further here and imagine that if we cut finer, we will even find a hypergamic bias within the upper level of the upper level. A woman from the École centrale who marries a man from the École polytechnique could be counted, like a Rajput woman, as entering into a hypergamic marriage.[9] I do not have such precise statistics but I know two couples of this type, one of which, moreover, has managed to produce a son who went to the École normale and a daughter who went to Polytechnique.[10]

Even higher: capital has no sex

Let's just say at this stage that the top level of society is still patridominated. This top level will not remain on top for long. Social reality is not stable in an economic world which is indeed moving towards a decline in the overall standard of living, but also towards the accumulation of fortunes for those with the top 1% income and perhaps even more so the 0.1%. The work of Louis Chauvel[11] and Thomas Piketty[12] has shown that, for the generations born after 1970, there was an increase in income from capital compared to income from labour. However, French inheritance law ensures equal shares for girls and boys. If capital continues to increase in the definition of income for future generations, at the top of the social structure, inevitably the ratio of men to women will tend to balance out, by the simple process of inheritance.

Combining the results already presented in this chapter and the previous one, we can define a sex-based social structure:

1. At the bottom, a working-class world in which the couple is weakened. Women are less and less inclined to marry poor and/or uneducated men, or else they separate from them. Single-parent families result. The fragility of the couple reveals a latent remnant of the value of hypergamy in women.
2. In the young petty bourgeoisie, with matridominance, we have a homogamous or hypogamic modern family. Believing his wife is a fantastic companion is a psychological imperative for a man. She will contribute (roughly) half to the income, and decides whether to procreate.
3. Above that, a situation of patridominance for 4% of the population, where very high incomes, and strong social prestige, sustain male power and hypergamy.
4. Even higher, in the future, an upper bourgeoisie, or (who knows?) a new hereditary nobility (between 1% and 0.1% of the population), within which the egalitarian inheritance of property will ensure a balance between the sexes. Just for fun, we can postulate, in these ethereal spheres, a world which will be homogamous and endogamous.

I will not venture into the obscure terrain of apparent intellectual inequalities between men and women to explain patridominance in the 4%; this is far from being a male monopoly, and, as we have just seen, it is ultimately threatened by the rise of capital, which nowadays is sexually undifferentiated. I postulate that a difference in will power, and in the mobilization of intelligence, is sufficient to explain the essential inequalities between men and women within the same field of competition, whether in medicine, mathematics or nuclear physics. I do not exclude a priori the possibility of natural differences in aggressiveness or even simply in physical resistance, but this is not my area of expertise. I will therefore go no further than Margaret Mead in terms of explanation: men cannot produce children and are forced by nature to concentrate all their anxiety and activity on studies and work. This is quite simply why, after the educational slack period of puberty, associated as we have seen with risky behaviour and accidents that are not all physical, men succeed marginally better in higher-level studies.

But we can add something to Mead, who speculated about male anxiety at a time when women were not in the majority in higher education. Male anxiety is now echoed by a female contradiction: the existence of a twofold career opportunity – they can follow a profession or procreate. This twofold feminine potential entails Durkheimian anomie: I said in the previous chapter that women, now free of their destiny, had access to the doubts and dissatisfactions that had previously, in modern times, been a male preserve. Their situation is, in reality, even more complex, because men, at least, do not really get to ask themselves whether to procreate, a decision which they have ultimately lost even if it remains theoretically open for longer in the absence of a strict male equivalent to menopause. Modern contraceptives have effectively transferred the power of choice to women, and exercising it places additional anxiety on them. The constraint is really strong. Pregnancy only takes nine months but it involves the whole body and can transform it permanently. And for more highly educated women, if they finished their studies at 25, the time for deciding to procreate isn't long: fertility drops significantly from the age of 35. Liberation has not given women a simple life, but a difficult freedom. No wonder men focus more easily on their studies, at least if they did not suffer an educational crash as teenagers, which happens frequently; the age of fifteen or so is the most dangerous crossroads as regards their schoolwork.

Let's see how their loss of marital power has increased the need for these men to work.

Divorce at the heart of the system

Male over-investment in work proves resistant because it is at the heart of a 'system'. To perceive the logic of this, we must refuse the atomized vision of a social life made up simply of independent elements, and return to a minimal sociological functionalism. I would, for example, happily draw a link between the greater identification of men with their profession and divorce settlements, which always grant the mother custody of the children, when they are young, if she so wishes and is neither alcoholic nor insane.

Around 2009, children of all ages combined, 76% of children were entrusted to their mother after a divorce, 9% to their father, the remaining 15% being placed in joint custody.[13] Less than a tenth of fathers responsible for the care of their children look after boys or girls who have passed beyond early childhood; only 15.3% of them then get any money from the mother for their child, compared to 61.2% of mothers.

Joint custody is developing but cannot be isolated from the overall social structure since it is a class phenomenon: the proportion of children in joint custody doubled between 2010 and 2016, but it is characteristic of couples with relatively decent incomes.[14] From 5% in the lower income decile, the proportion of children placed in joint custody at the time of divorce rises to around 20% in the ninth decile, to fall slightly in the upper decile.

Joint custody is therefore typical of the petty bourgeoisie of executives and higher intellectual professions, a world that has passed into educational matridominance in its youngest generations. Joint custody is, however, far from being the majority practice in this social group. It cannot be said that it implies an equality of men and women, since the decision to go for it is made in a context where, basically, only the mother has the right to grant it, in fact if not in law. Joint custody therefore does not exclude latent matridominance.

Once this element of specialization between men and women in the face of divorce has been established, the system unfolds its implacable logic. Men's concentration on their jobs is assured. They have little choice in a society where a woman can freely decide to divorce (75% of divorces are requested by women). The man, who, as we have seen, finds it difficult to find a wife if his income is insufficient, has every interest in continuing to consider his job as essential to his social survival. It is symmetrically obvious that assigning the children by lot at the time of divorce would destroy this aspect of the sexual division of labour in one fell swoop. Apparently, the most radical reformers do not ask for this.

The masculine collective and its disintegration

Social and ideological attention is rightly being focused today on the persistence of male dominance in the highest managerial and supervisory positions in society. The existence of this thin upper layer of male dominance partly explains the persistence of sexual harassment problems. The continued existence of male 'heads' (in offices, departments, editorial divisions, etc.) everywhere in a highly feminized tertiary society has multiplied the opportunities for a sexual overflow of the hierarchical relationship. The appalling situation of young people on the labour market, an automatic effect of free trade, has also increased the power of small bosses over their subordinates and optimized their opportunities for harassment.[15]

We have just found the start of an explanation for the origin of this higher layer in a specific concentration of the men on their professions and by a division within feminine existential objectives. There is another possible explanation, complementary rather than contradictory, which involves the sexual division of functions in hunter-gatherer societies. The men were in charge of the collective. The product of their hunting was divided up within the community; defence against other communities was also their domain. Let me warn the reader in advance that I will not legitimize the current residual male predominance but, on the contrary, emphasize its parodic and even degenerative character.

We can now find female executives everywhere, much more in the public sector than in the private sector. But even in the public sector, the highest managerial staff are male. In the French state education system, directors in central administration are male. In the health sector, recent reforms to liberalize and apply private standards in hospitals have caused, as in national education, an influx of male bureaucrats. Could the persistence of a superior layer dominated by men have a relationship with the ancestral male specialization in the management of the collective? After all, the management of central systems is the management of the collective at the level of the whole society. It is as if men knew better, and more spontaneously, how to organize themselves into networks than women. In a 1969 book, *Men in Groups*, the American sociologist Lionel Tiger looked into this phenomenon.[16] He had noted the specific ability of men to organize themselves into groups, their propensity to be attracted to each other without this constituting homosexuality. And he had concluded that because of this, it would be impossible to dislodge them from their position of dominance.[17] The absence of a link between a sense of the collective and male homosexuality is not obvious to me. We could even give a very nice illustration of their association. I will devote a whole chapter of this book to the evolution of homosexuality, but we can already note here an association between male homosexuality and the collective and, symmetrically, an association between female homosexuality and individualism. In an excellent book, *L'Atlas mondial des sexualités: Liberté, plaisirs et interdits* (*The Global Atlas of Sexualities: Freedom, Pleasures and Taboos*), Nadine Cattan and Stéphane Leroy focus on the spatialization of homosexuality.[18] But what do they find? Collective communitarian mechanisms leading to the appearance of gay neighbourhoods for male homosexuals on the one hand, and 'lesbians without territory' on the other. There was no female Marais.[19]

174

I cannot resist the pleasure of recalling the persistent masculinity of the ENA,[20] the official heart of the management of the collective in France, and also a symbol of its collapse. The principle of parity struggled to impose itself in this factory of dominant male bureaucrats; from 2010, the proportion of women granted admission to it oscillated violently, between 30% and 45% of the successful candidates. The high levels of 2013 and 2020 appear to have been the result of wilful manipulation rather than a natural evolution. The ENA thus illustrated rather well the idea of an indestructible superior male social layer. True, patridominance manifested itself here in the central institution of management of the French collective – but this was an institution which adhered to a neoliberal ideology which denied the economic importance of the state, and thus of collective action. The ENA in fact largely contributed to the economic collapse of France, thanks to this negative sense of the collective, which made it deify an individualist dynamic of the markets – a dynamic which it did not in the least understand.[21] Similarly, the bureaucrats of the French national education system and hospitals have enjoyed high salaries, but, faithfully reflecting the dominant ideology in the ENA, have made it their mission to bring market forces and scarcity into their sectors. This mission was accomplished, as we saw during the Covid crisis, with hospitals being overwhelmed and universities emptied of their students. This management of the collective was undoubtedly overwhelmingly male. If the ability to hold together the sphere of the collective is indeed reminiscent of the original situation among hunter-gatherers, it is clear that our state bureaucracy is no longer able to hunt for and distribute meat.

We have seen that the fundamental organizational model of *Sapiens*, that of hunter-gatherers, was based on a division of labour: women took care of gathering for the family, the men hunted for the community. The consequence of this dualistic model was that women were the custodians of the strongest individualistic and family rationality, and men were more anchored in the collective. We have just briefly described a degenerated sense of the male collective in the state apparatus. But the essential lies elsewhere.

Between 1980 and 2020, the Western world was submerged by a neoliberal ideology and a set of policies that stubbornly persist despite their obvious failure. The standard of living is falling, free trade has destroyed our factories, those that remain have proven unable to provide us with protective masks and medicines during the Covid epidemic. But there has been no massive, industrialist and protectionist collective reaction. We could obviously attribute our inability to act, and more precisely here to react to danger, to the autonomous and abstract power of ideology. We could, as I did in *Les Luttes de classes en France au XXIe siècle*, go a little deeper in our analysis by locating the cause of our mental and practical immobility in an individualist problematic of the weary ego, following

175

Alain Ehrenberg.[22] I propose here to dig even deeper and ask ourselves if the feminist revolution is not also contributing to our inability to act collectively.

Let's have another look at our model of the hunter-gatherer society. And let's stop focusing on men for once. I have pointed out the predominance among women of an individualistic family orientation of economic activity. The products they gather remain in the household and are not intended for distribution throughout the group. They are for children and for parents. But are we here so far from our post-industrial and consumer state of mind? How can we avoid the hypothesis that a new female predominance is accentuating the individualistic orientation of society and weakening its sense of the collective? In order to support this kind of explanatory sequence, we don't need to postulate an individualistic biology of women and a collectivist biology of men: a persistent trait going back 300,000 or 200,000 years would hardly be shocking in the context of a transformation that in its current stage stretches out over a mere seven decades, if we fix its starting point in 1950.

I therefore posit that the collapse of collective beliefs and the flourishing of neoliberalism are linked to women's liberation (dynamic functionalism). Admittedly, economics remains a rather masculine discipline, probably as a result of its mathematizing degeneration. But let's stop taking the thought of Milton Friedman or Friedrich Hayek as *causes* of social evolution: rather, let's see their popularity as a *symptom* of this evolution. If we seek to capture the spirit of the times, our *Zeitgeist*, by getting past those dogmatic, boring books that carry an unrealistic vision of man (here including woman), we can imagine a feminization of concerns that contributes to the dissolution of collective feeling and of the action that can result from it, especially if we accept that collective action is not only health and education (the 'left hand' of the state, to use Bourdieu's expression) but also the creation of material resources. Collective action can be an economic management that integrates fiscal stimulus, industrial investment by the state and national protectionism. This collective action in the broad sense depends, as much as social security and *national* education, on a belief in the nation – which itself is an enlarged form of the group of hunter-gatherers.

Such a hypothesis will not consider the 'theory of care' as a feminine negation of the individualism of men but as a revival of individualism, admittedly in a benevolent and gentle form. Care – more precisely mutual care, as Agata Zielinski puts it, as it envisages only relationships between individuals – takes us a little further away from collective identification, a phenomenon in which individuals accept that they are part of a more important group.[23] As I said above, the collective is not always about kindness: it is as much about warring against other human groups as it is about hunting game or building a dam intended for fishing.

I readily admit that I am not giving a 'proof' here, in the restricted sense in which today's virtuosos of statistical modelling understand the word 'proof'. But, just as an experiment, let's formulate the opposite hypothesis: 'There is no relationship between women's liberation (one of the most important phenomena of our time) and the flourishing of neoliberalism (one of the most important phenomena of our time).' Isn't it implausible? As for the relationship between feminism and the theory of care, which succeeded neoliberalism in time, it is transparent.

It is true that postulating the existence of a relationship between women's liberation and the neoliberal revolution does not guarantee that the causal mechanism proposed – the superior family and economic individualism of women gatherers – is the correct one. I am open to any other explanation for this striking temporal and social coincidence. But any competing explanation must still, according to the principle of parsimony (also known as Ockham's razor), have the same simplicity.

— 11 —

GENDER: A PETTY-BOURGEOIS IDEOLOGY

In the development of relations between the sexes since the war, it is usual to distinguish, in France, between a dimension which is so to speak spontaneous, resulting from the dynamics of interactions between individuals in the society (a dynamics which goes back some time), and an ideological dimension which is more recent. In this country, which has always had a rather egalitarian family structure, one that is not particularly oppressive for women, liberation – raising the educational level of women, the fact they have overtaken men in education, and now have access to the labour market and to positions of responsibility – initially followed a spontaneous evolution, on which, over the last twenty years, with ever-increasing force, there has been superimposed an ideological stratum calling for the full realization of this spontaneous movement. There was, so to speak, first the natural course of history, then the awareness of this course, an awareness that then became a demand, manifesting itself in political action and norms.

Such a representation only really fits France, a country which Anglo-American commentators still described, in the late 1980s, as a country where women's liberation had taken place in the absence of a feminist movement worthy of the name. There was nothing comparable in France to the English suffragettes or the American feminists of the 1970s. France was the country where men and women liked each other, and considered a relationship based on mutual seduction as a positive thing. Such at least was the psychological state of the middle classes when I was 20 or 30 years old, between 1970 and 1980. French people viewed the antagonism of the sexes in the United States and their separation in England (if they were aware of it) as Anglo-Saxon quirks. I personally attribute the Anglo-American sexual tension to the Protestant background, studied in chapter 8, which, following Luther and Calvin, had taken an anthropological background that was egalitarian as far as daily relations between men and women were concerned, and superimposed on it a dream of male metaphysical domination and, of course, a renewed Christian horror of sexuality.

Republican France remained on a Catholic trajectory, in which the Virgin Mary, at the kindly suggestion of the Italian Renaissance, was to be stripped bare but respected, turned into Venus – and certainly not the ominous Eve of the Bible. The worldwide success of a publication like *Elle* expressed this peaceful and, for non-French people, rather seductive dimension of women's liberation, French-style. Nothing foreshadowed the emergence of an antagonism between the sexes in our country. In the Anglo-American world, however, there was a persistent long-standing antagonism, and it is not even certain that we can diagnose any real aggravation of this in recent decades.

These cultural tendencies are obviously characteristic of the middle classes. In the West, the working-class world, more determined by questions of economic survival than by the expansion of consumption, was more egalitarian in the relations between the sexes, even if these relations were harsher.

Research, however, must avoid nostalgia. What we need to analyse and understand is the antagonistic ideological shift in relations between the sexes in the French middle classes. I say and repeat 'ideological' because it is not certain that the ideological antagonism represents the basic tendency. We need to bear in mind the stabilization of marriage – in the anthropological sense of a stable union – in the educated and hypogamous middle classes. Single-parent families, as we have seen, are increasingly characteristic of working-class backgrounds. Ideology still exists, however, even if it is an inversion of the deep social reality. It has consequences and deserves to be explained.

France in the face of the Anglo-American world

Any difference between a certain French evolution, on the one hand, and an Anglo-American evolution, on the other, must draw our attention to certain recurring oppositions between two cultures that are otherwise very close. They share, as far as our present concerns go, a dominant individualism and a rather high status of women to begin with. The fundamental difference concerns the value of equality, with here an opposition that we can identify at the levels of family structures (unconscious), religious metaphysics (unconscious or conscious depending on the period) and modern political ideologies (conscious).

In the egalitarian nuclear family of the Paris Basin, brothers and sisters are strictly equal, to the point that, long before the French Revolution, the division of inheritances was here carried out, in the peasantry, however poor, with obsessive precision. In the Anglo-American absolute nuclear

179

family, brothers, and a fortiori brothers and sisters, were not radically unequal but they were not equal.

English Calvinism, followed by the American variant, brought its doctrine of grace into conformity with this non-egalitarian but liberal family structure in the relationship between parents and children by getting rid of the predestination to death or to life formalized by Luther and Calvin. Without becoming equal, men regained their free will. There is no better proof of the influence of family structure on metaphysical form.

France was distinguished by an early religious collapse, by two-thirds, centred on the Paris Basin and the Mediterranean facade, from the second half of the eighteenth century onwards. The equality of men, hitherto ensured by Catholic baptism which, as we know, washes men and women of original sin, was suddenly replaced by the equality of citizens of the French Revolution. They beheaded nobles, and the king, and the queen, to show that this was not just a vague promise. The fall of English Protestantism did not take place until between 1870 and 1930, but it allowed the confirmation across the Channel of a non-egalitarian secular liberalism. The process was completed in the United States very recently, in the first twenty years of the third millennium, with the collapse of the last bastions of Protestant religiosity.

Three elements therefore characterize majority France if we compare it to the Anglo-American world:

1. an older and stronger unbelief;
2. a self-assured egalitarianism, undoubtedly boosted by the resistance of a periphery of France that had to be convinced or subjugated;
3. an egalitarianism extending to women since girls and boys inherited in the same way in the Paris Basin, if we exclude Normandy from this vast region, which practised the exclusion from inheritance of daughters, once they had been given a dowry.

In France, unbelief and egalitarianism ensured the predominance of class oppositions over racial oppositions. Equality between the sexes may explain the atmosphere of camaraderie between men and women in the early stages of sexual liberation. In this country where girls had long inherited as much as boys – this is in fact a rule that can be traced back to the Later Roman Empire, formalized by the Code of Justinian – the potential for conflict was lower than in the Anglo-American world, where the distribution of inheritances, without being absolutely unequal, nevertheless favoured the eldest son in the aristocracy and the well-to-do peasantry. In the United States as in England, especially, the principle of difference between children, applied to the two sexes, led to the idea of essential differences between the two sexes. In France, the equivalence

180

of children of both sexes led to the idea of a universal man who could also be a woman. In *Le Sacre du citoyen* (*The Consecration of the Citizen*), Pierre Rosanvallon has noted the difference between the specific woman of the Anglo-Saxon world, who acquires the right to vote earlier, as a woman, and the woman who must become a citizen in general to benefit from the right to vote. Rosanvallon is seeking to explain French resistance to the political liberation of women, and I am here seeking to understand the way the French could relax when they were liberated by the pill, but the underlying idea of an Anglo-American sexual differentialism and a French sexual universalism seems to me common to both interpretations.[1]

However, we mustn't forget Protestant Puritanism, which for centuries had forced the bodies of men away from those of women even more surely than late Catholicism. The secularization of the eighteenth century had also done much to ensure that France, on the eve of the 1914–18 war, enjoyed a deserved reputation as a country of sexual freedom. It was then a century ahead in the spread of birth control, initiated in the small towns of the Paris Basin before the 1789 Revolution. In 1900, the fertility rate there was 2.8, compared to 3.6 in the United Kingdom and the United States, and 5 in Germany. The Republican version of birth control combined condoms, coitus interruptus, abstinence and the brothel; its peripheral Catholic version put its faith in abstinence.

We still remember, I hope, a once sexually repressive America and England, hunting down homosexuals at a time when French justice took no interest in them. But above all, we must free ourselves from a vision of the Anglo-American world as being more favourable to women in all dimensions. As I pointed out in chapter 8, Anglo-American feminism was certainly born in reaction to Protestant patricentrism. The existence of women vicars today should not make us forget history. The weakness of conscious French feminism results, in part, from the absence of the Protestant patriarchal dream (here the word 'patriarchal' assumes its full meaning), and from the need to fight it in Britain and the United States.

This enables us to locate our current problem more precisely: in France, in a culture which did not predispose men and women to an antagonistic relationship, an ideology emerged at the beginning of the third millennium which undoubtedly *does* advocate such an antagonism. The phenomenon is recent and its durability is not certain. Let's try an application of Ockham's razor, explaining as many facts as possible with the simplest hypothesis. When we contrast France with the United States, we almost always end up, ever since the eighteenth century, with the conclusion that what really differentiates these two nations is a predominance of race in the United States and of class in France. Tocqueville would not contradict me on this point. We saw, in chapter 1, the predominance of the racial question in American-style intersectionality. So let's cut to the chase: doesn't a generalized French-style intersectionality suggest to us that French antagonistic feminism is a class problem? I will answer in the affirmative, but without claiming that the explanatory weight of the class distinction is greater than that of the sex distinction. Both concepts are necessary for an adequate description of the French crisis, and I will stick to the methodological postulate announced in the introduction: we must not establish any a priori hierarchy between anthropology (the relations between men and women) and the economy (the relations between classes).

The sex of social classes

To begin with, let's get rid of the archaic vision of social classes defined by the male sex alone. Our aim here is to take women's liberation seriously. Women now make up almost half of the employed workforce. I will try to look at the class structure from the point of view of women who are at last free and define social groups independently of their spouses. This is the lesson of the previous chapters which described how girls overtook boys in terms of numbers passing the baccalaureate half a century ago, and noted a transition to matridominance in higher education for the generation which turned twenty around 1990, and a general shift to hypogamy around 2000. There was a time when the head of the household, who was still a man, determined the placing of the family in such and such a socio-professional category. This mechanism is no longer automatic, but the habit persists of perceiving the class structure through a masculine prism. In a certain way, official statistics maintain this rather stagnant vision; with the best of intentions they tirelessly compare women to men in their professional performance. This persistence of a male-centric view is ridiculous. Unfortunately, statistics only rarely select the figures that would allow us to effectively compare *women with each other*, in terms of income or belonging to socio-professional categories – the only presentation that would allow us to arrive at the definition of a feminized class structure.

I will give an example of an exploratory overview of the 'feminine' class structure through the socio-professional categories of the INSEE. The 2019 mass-release data fail to sort out executives, middle management and others by age and sex, which alone would make it possible to observe the pattern emerging in younger generations. I call here for the help of young researchers, who will not fail, I am sure, to search the job surveys and censuses for the figures that we are lacking. At the current stage, in readily available data, the ultimate reality is more obscured than captured by the very heterogeneous category 'executives

Table 11.1   Class structure according to sex: a first approach

	Men	Women
Executives and higher intellectual professions	27%	17%
Intermediate professions and skilled employees	30%	50%
Unskilled workers and employees	37%	28%
Total	94%	95%

Artisans, small traders and farmers are not indicated. Source: INSEE.

Table 11.2   Class structure according to sex: ideal-types

	Masculine classes	Feminine classes	
Capitalist hyperclass	ε	ε	Egalitarian
Salaried or liberal upper middle class	20%	10%	Patridominated
Middle middle class, petty bourgeoisie	35%	60%	Matridominated
Working class	45%	30%	Sexually disorganized

and higher intellectual professions'. This category now appears to be slightly patridominated, but finer data would divide it in two, according to income, into a patridominated upper half (the thin layer studied in the previous chapter) and a matridominated lower half that we could add to the matridominated intermediate professions. The importance of female teachers in the lower half by income and of male executives in the private sector in the upper half by income guarantees these opposing orientations of sex-based dominance in the lower and upper parts of the category 'executives and higher intellectual professions'.

A distribution, however crude, into three social groups nevertheless allows us to identify two contradictory class structures, one polarized for men, the other averaged out for women (see table 11.1).

Projected into the future by targeting the younger generations and after dividing the 'Executives and higher intellectual professions' category into upper and lower halves, this distribution would reveal a ternary structure that I model in table 11.2, pending refinement by future studies. At the top of the table I have, for the record, indicated by two epsilons a capitalist hyperclass defined as sexually egalitarian by the customs of inheritance.

Combining sex and class, we define an egalitarian hyperclass, a patridominated salaried or liberal upper middle class, a matridominated middle middle class, or petty bourgeoisie, and a sexually disorganized working class, where there are more men in the labour force but where the instability of the marital bond, born of the resistance of certain women to hypogamy, increases the number of single-parent families.

This simple model allows us to define confrontations between classes in which, so to speak, classes have a sex. At the very top, a hypothetical bisexual capitalist class; below, a male upper class, below that an immense female petty bourgeoisie, and at the bottom an asexual working-class mass.

The female petty bourgeoisie includes the biggest battalions who have followed long or short courses at college. This is where we should look for the ideological foundation of the ongoing feminist revolution, the site of a new kind of Gramscian hegemony. The concept of ideological matridominance demands that men in these classes adhere to the new feminist doctrine. Statistical hypogamy makes this condition reasonable since it assumes a minimum of harmony in the lives of couples.

The male upper middle class still wields technological and economic power, even if the relentless rise of capital points to an ultimate horizon of sexual equality.

The capitalist hyperclass will no doubt be indifferent to the issue of a balance between the sexes. But we don't need this distant and uncertain future to understand the class tension that is currently shaping France: *a female petty bourgeoisie is challenging a male upper middle class*. This structure exists throughout the West, but class antagonism does not contribute to antagonism between the sexes anywhere as much as it does in France.

Anger as a general social phenomenon

In *Les Luttes de classes en France au XXIe siècle*, I described a new type of class confrontation, regressive in nature and characteristic of a period of economic decline, in which a blockage of upward social mobility probably even comes with the start of downward social mobility.[2] Let's place recent feminist anger within this general model.

It is to be expected that women's liberation should have led to a feminist ideological revival; it is absolutely to be expected that women's freedom should have generated in them a wave of Durkheimian anomie, a specific anxiety about a freedom that for hundreds of thousands of years had been a male preserve. On the other hand, the general pessimism of the current feminist wave, and the antagonism which characterizes it, do not, in my view, involve women specifically: they are only the incarnations, in the universe of relations between the sexes, and in a particular social class, of a regressive tendency which characterizes all categories and all groups of a French society that is now launched on a downward trajectory.

184

I also analysed a 'cascade of descending contempt', from the state-financial aristocracy towards the CPIS petty bourgeoisie[3] (executives and higher intellectual professions), from the CPIS petty bourgeoisie towards the proletariat, and from the proletariat towards immigrants and their children, where everyone sought, beneath themselves, an object of contempt, a scapegoat.[4] I see no reason to exclude antagonistic feminism from this infernal mechanism. It is true that the model that has just been traced – a female petty bourgeoisie looking upwards at a male upper middle class – would bring us closer to a healthier class struggle, in which the group at the bottom challenges the group at the top. But, according to this new ideology, the male being is indeed designated as a moral inferior and I doubt that the hypogamous men of the petty bourgeoisie, inferior to their wives in education, are completely immune to antagonistic feminism. Anger pervades social and sexual categories. It is everywhere. It is the *Zeitgeist*.

Taking women seriously thus allows us to define the social basis of the new ideology: a female-dominated middle or petty-bourgeois class, disadvantaged in terms of income but dominant ideologically through its grip on teaching and research sectors in the humanities. I will now develop somewhat the study of the Gramscian mechanisms of the new ideological hegemony. Gramsci gave us a superb Marxist vision of the phenomena of ideological hegemony linked to education, journalism and the production of books. Gender theory and, more generally, third-wave feminism have reached a situation of Gramscian hegemony that we must examine.

We have already met, in chapter 1, when presenting the concept of intersectionality – a concept that emerged from the problem of Black Americans – the social group that is producing and driving this concept in France, namely a feminized French university system, inflamed by the problem of Black American women (excluded from the white matrimonial market), even though Black women are not subject to such discrimination in France (their rate of intermarriages is very high). And we see more and more educated Black women on television, intelligent, beautiful women, terribly French in their demeanour, demanding a representation of Black people in cinema that would be the equivalent of that of the United States. Do they also want the taboo on intermarriage that is functionally associated with this American visibility? The representation of Black women will come to France naturally, without any ideological effort, because the French cultural system does not place any taboo on them and considers them as 'universal women' just like the others. In the United States, there is unfortunately a functional relationship between racial segregation and representation. It is therefore easy to point out the absurdity of the ideological import of American racism. Let's try to get past this facile irony and try to detail the mechanisms of French-style female ideological domination.

Ideological hegemony in the feminine: doctorates

The sex of social actors is important. It is customary to count women in political assemblies, in ministries and at the head of administrations or companies. But it is essential, in our perspective of generalized intersectionality, not to restrict ourselves to sectors where they remain in the minority, or sectors where they are in the majority but which are themselves dominated. If an ideology is dominant, its female producers and consumers are dominant. So, in order to validate our initial questioning about the matridominated character of recent ideological developments, we need to stop speaking about the human sciences or the social sciences as if they had no sex and to examine the sex of the authors of texts and job holders. Our first approach to the phenomenon must be a numerical count. Let's study the case of France more systematically, by analysing the number of doctorates.

The theses.fr portal lists all the theses defended in France since 1985 and allows a quantitative study of the changes in higher education in terms of sex.[5] For each thesis, it indicates the name of the doctoral student, the title, the discipline, and the date of defence or, for a thesis still being written, of first registration (see table 11.3).

Table 11.3 Theses: proportion of women by university discipline and year of thesis defence

Discipline	2001–2006	2016–2020
Psychology	65.8	68.0
Anthropology	61.7	65.5
Literary studies	60.3	66.9
Biology	53.6	58.5
Sociology	50.3	54.6
Management studies	48.2	51.8
Law	48.1	48.7
History	46.4	51.0
Chemistry	43.6	44.8
Economics	40.8	38.4
Political science	40.5	49.4
Geography	38.6	48.5
Philosophy	30.8	39.8
Mathematics	24.0	27.6
Physics	22.5	27.6
Engineering	19.7	24.8
Information technology	19.0	26.0

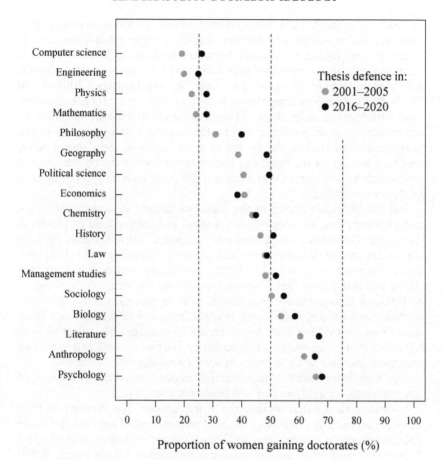

Figure 11.1   The sex ratio of French theses

I have downloaded the set of data from theses.fr, i.e. entries relating to over 480,000 theses.[6] They do not directly mention the sex of the individual, but the first name is a good indicator (see figure 11.1). To infer the sex from the first name, we used the INSEE's first-name file,[7] which provides the number of female and male carriers of each first name born every year since 1900. It tells us, for example, that, since 1960, 86,048 Alices of the female sex and 17 Alices of the male sex have been born, i.e. approximately 99.98% of Alices born since 1960 are women, or that 99.99% of Bernards born in the same period are men, or that 65.3% of Dominiques are also men.

To each doctoral student mentioned in theses.fr, we can assign a probability of being a woman.[8] It is then possible to calculate a sex ratio by discipline and year of defence.[9] In France we see the same specializations

187

at work as in the United States, with a strong matridominance in psychology, anthropology and literary studies; a clear matridominance in sociology and biology; a balance between the sexes in history, law and management; and a resistant patridominance in mathematics, physics, information technology and engineering. The trend between 2001–5 and 2016–20 made engineering the main hub of male resistance, even more than information technology. Matridominance in biology is linked to matridominance in medicine and to the ancient role of women in the management of bodies: the bodies of their children, their own bodies, and to some extent the bodies of their partners, since the counterpart of this female specialization was a certain difficulty men had in taking care of their own bodies.

But the matridominance in the theses of literary studies, psychology, anthropology and sociology covers a good part of the field of ideology. These are 'Gramscian' disciplines par excellence. There remains the very interesting case of disciplines in which women, a minority in 2001–5, have made the most progress: philosophy, geography and political science. These are disciplines that I would describe as 'holistic': their object is to think of human beings as a whole, in their society, on this earth, or in their deep nature, and I think that the irruption of women into these disciplines means that their lesser ability to manage the collective is in the process of being eroded or, even better, that we can instead expect an imminent increase in the female capacity to manage the collective.

Our technique allows us to go further in our intersectional analysis of sex and class, an analysis that combines sex and class.

Sociology theses that include the word 'gender' [i.e. '*genre*'] in their titles are an excellent indicator of the dissemination of the concept in the French university system – a central place for the evolution of ideological hegemonies and a Gramscian space par excellence. Of the nearly 9,000 sociology theses in the corpus, this is the case for 181. However, if 49% of sociology theses whose subject *is not* gender are written by women[10] – parity achieved – the 181 'gendered' theses are in 85% of cases the work of female doctoral students (figure 11.2). In other words, the concept of gender has a sex. For each male doctoral student interested in the concept, we find six female doctoral students. Admittedly, the concept of gender is most often presented as an instrument in the fight against male domination, and how can we be surprised that women, rather than men, use it as a weapon? The rate of 85% indicates this. This justification, however, appears to be completely spurious once we become aware of the overwhelming predominance of women in the specialties concerned: far from fighting against domination, the concept of gender expresses a domination.

Note that the same type of analysis, but this time carried out on the word 'sex' and its compounds (sexuality, homosexuality, etc.), shows

188

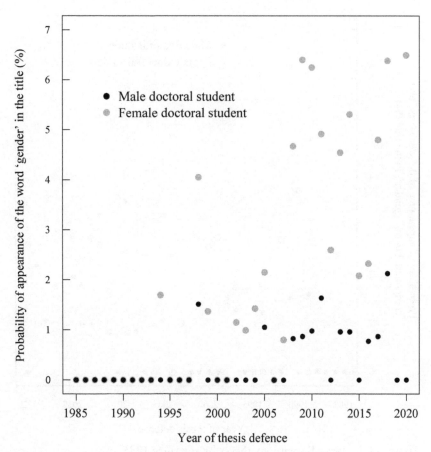

Figure 11.2 'Gendered' sociology theses by sex since 1985

a very different development: the male–female gap is smaller (overall, women are no longer 85% but 68% of authors) and is in the process of narrowing, thanks to growing male interest in the word (figure 11.3).

Theses can also be located in time, in this case thanks to their defence date. The defence in fact registers the changes with some delay: a thesis defended in 2009 will have been started in 2006 at the latest. But we can observe the explosion, from the end of the 2000s onwards, of the use of the word 'gender' among sociologists who were born women. For the first time in 2009, more than 6% of sociology theses defended by women dealt with gender. Male enthusiasm for the concept remained low throughout the period under study. But the gender crisis is so recent in France that we cannot be certain that it will last.

189

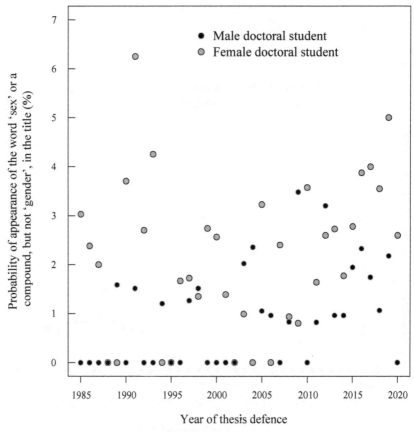

Figure 11.3 'Sexed' sociology theses by sex since 1985

Matridominance at the OECD as well as at the INED

There are therefore hubs of female domination in France with regard to the determination of social attitudes: this has long been true in education and justice (I will talk about justice in the next chapter, which is devoted to the exercise of authority by women). The rise of women in journalism is rapid but incomplete: statistics on the allocation of press cards for the year 2018 tell us that 'women are even in the majority among newcomers (53%), also in the majority among those with insecure jobs, since they represent 53% of freelancers. On the other hand, only 19% of women hold a '"director's" card'.[11]

The conflict between male upper middle class and female petty bourgeoisie is acute in journalism. It overflows into the relationship with poli-

190

tics. The high frequency of known couples comprising a *female* journalist with a *male* politician suggests, if we stick to the traditional view that politicians are superior to journalists, the persistence of a hypergamic mentality; but if we perceive politicians as powerless figureheads and journalists as real opinion makers, these couples express, on the contrary, a shift into hypogamy. I must confess to having no opinion here.

In the ideological state sector, on the other hand, the male principle has already lost.

I will continue the exercise at the global level but without leaving Paris. A study by the OECD, *Society at a Glance 2019*,[12] which I will also use for the analysis of the LGBT phenomenon, allows us to pose the problem. The Organization for Economic Co-operation and Development was founded after the Second World War to help monitor the Marshall Plan for reconstruction aid in Europe. It has been extended to all advanced countries with liberal economies and produces, year after year, an abundant comparative literature, initially economic, but since extended – with the PISA surveys – to education. We are not leaving Paris, since the institution is housed near Porte de La Muette in the 16th arrondissement. The OECD represents, better than the Davos Forum and on a par with the World Bank, a place of ideological power.

Produced on the eve of the Covid epidemic, which would highlight the industrial deficiencies of many member countries, *Society at a Glance 2019* made the protection of LGBT minorities a global social priority. This volume was supervised by a woman, the head of the department, and edited by a woman, assisted by three other women and a man. Six men and six women are acknowledged as additional contributors. This is a case of massive matridominance. I cannot guarantee that my definition of sex is operational for the calculation of the sex ratio since the report waxes indignant that some countries do not accept that one can change 'gender' just by saying so. We must consider the possibility that some authors are transgender women (biological males at birth) or transgender males (biological females at birth).

In truth, it was this question of the calculation of the editorial and ideological sex ratio that made me understand that the names of cisgender individuals (those living in accordance with their sex) no longer publicly indicated their sex with any certainty (I specify for the reader that I am male by biological sex at birth). I will come back to these questions. The important thing here is to note an apparent matridominance in a research and publication group; this perhaps led to an interest in a specific social issue. I will show later that women's liberation led to the liberation of homosexuality and the emergence of the transgender question. The world of research in the human sciences is shifting into matridominance. I should point out that this volume, like most OECD publications, is of excellent quality.

Table 11.4   INED researchers by sex and age around 2019

Age (years)	Men	Women
20–29	1	11
30–39	13	15
40–49	8	14
50–59	3	6
60 and above	9	8
Total	34	54

I will give another example, drawn from my own professional experience. When I joined INED in 1984,[13] it was a world of men, dominated by *polytechniciens*[14] implementing an elegant mathematical approach to population issues, a bridge between the human sciences and biology. Table 11.4 presents the breakdown by sex and age of the researchers in the 2019 report of the institution from which I am now retired.

The Institute is now 61.4% female as far as researchers are concerned, with a peak of 91.7% among 20–29-year-olds. I will here mention one last time my reservations as to the significance of these sex ratios because we can no longer know if the statistics tell us about sex at birth or on the day of the survey.

The reversal of the sex ratio was accompanied by a change in research orientations at INED. The mathematical heart has atrophied. Its psycho-sociological periphery has swelled in proportion, obviously including an interest in 'gender'. Here too we see gender operating as a feminine concept. Here is how a very recent publication by the Institute, edited by four women, entitled 'Violence et rapports de genre' ('Violence and Gender Relations') is presented:[15] 'Carried out in 2015 among 27,000 women and men, the "Violence et rapports de genre" survey (Virage) constitutes a major tool for measurement and analysis. By questioning both women and men, it makes it possible to compare statements with the analysis of the effect of gender norms on the violence to which women and men are subjected.'

The displacement of the sexual centre of gravity in the human sciences, and soon, or perhaps already, of ideological commentary in the media, is real, even though I admit that my examples are not in themselves a demonstration. Nonetheless, drawing attention to the fields of power – even ideological power – in which women dominate seems to me to open up a promising area of research. This is what I call generalized intersectionality.

Farewell to reality

Ideology is a travesty of reality, according to Marx's initial concept: an inability to see the world without class prejudices, here those of a matridominated petty bourgeoisie. Ideology was nationalism when it allowed the European petty bourgeois to think that they belonged to exceptional peoples; ideology was Marxism–Leninism when it assured the proletarian that it was a dictator; and ideology was Nazism when it made the German petty-bourgeois members of a superior race. All these crazy movements were patridominated, without any argument.

Ideology is sometimes a pure and simple farewell to reality. I will use two examples to show that current feminism fulfils this condition perfectly. It is a hegemonic farewell to reality, i.e. one validated by society: an ideological hegemony creates a situation in which one can affirm without risk any absurd proposition if it conforms to orthodoxy, with the approval of official institutions and – why not? – being financed by them.

In *Le Journal du CNRS* (CNRS, may I remind you, is the acronym of the Centre national de la recherche scientifique (National Centre for Scientific Research), we find, on 14 January 2020, under the title 'La Ménopause est-elle une construction sociale?' ('Is Menopause a Social Construction?'), an interview with Cécile Charlap, the author of a book on the question,[16] an interview that was among the top ten for readers of this publication. We learn that the term 'menopause' is quite recent, first found in 1821 in France and in 1990 in Japan – less as a social constructor of gender, it is suggested, since it referred just to ageing. But why make this positive reference to a tolerant, doubtless non-gendered Japan, when this country is a level 1 patrilineal country, and much less feminist than France? Its terminological hesitations about 'menopause' did not prevent it from rejecting the birth control pill until June 1999, when the urgent acceptance of Viagra and international pressure led it to a dramatic rebalancing of the freedom of both sexes?[17] Even in 2018, only 2.9% of Japanese women were as yet on the pill.

We would be wrong just to smile. This impossible thesis, 'menopause as a social construction', is not an aberration but the product of a certain logic. If any difference between the sexes results from social phenomena, we will end up having to 'demonstrate' – inevitably – that the biological difference between men and women is itself of social origin. So we will need to demonstrate that the 20-month delay in puberty of boys compared to girls (in France 14.8 years as against 13.1 – the ages at which half of the boys' voices have broken and half of the girls have had their first period) is a social construct;[18] and of course we will need to show that the pregnancy of women is itself of social origin. I look forward, in the interests of sexual egalitarianism, to a thesis on the 'social construction of prostate problems'. The other strange contribution I will mention, again to illustrate the concept of hegemony, is *Hommes grands, femmes petites: Une évolution coûteuse* (*Tall Men, Small Women: A Costly Evolution*), by Priscille Touraille, published in 2008 by the Maison des sciences de l'homme, another state publisher.[19] Its subtitle is 'Les régimes de genre comme force sélective de l'adaptation biologique' ('Gender regimes as a selective force of biological adaptation'). This book questions sexual dimorphism – the biological difference, in particular of stature, in the same species, between males and females. It is not uninteresting, it really isn't: it contains information. But natural selection is there only to be lamented over. The goal of research is no longer to understand human history but to wax indignant about it.

The notion of ideology includes being separated from reality. This separation does not necessarily involve the entire population. It is hard to imagine that the majority of women will one day experience their menopause as an act of aggression on the part of society.

A provisional summary

At the current stage (2021), the relative importance of men and women in the various areas of social life is not the same.

First, a situation of matridominance can be observed at the educational and therefore ideological levels. With regard to the concept of 'gender', we can speak of a Gramscian hegemony. It is now omnipresent in official world and European literature (OECD, Eurostat, World Economic Forum, etc.), most often replacing the word 'sex', without altering its practical meaning.

Second, a persistent patridominance can be observed in the field of technology and the private economy. Its future elimination is not a certainty. Capitalism remains a male domain.

Third, politics and the state – the public sector – seem to be an area of tension between patri- and matridominance. The most senior personnel remain male, in government and in the administrations, but the role of women is increasing rapidly at these higher levels, while they represent an overwhelming majority at the lower and middle levels. The tension between the sexes is here expressed by a confrontation between a feminine 'middle class' and a masculine 'upper class'. The notion of generalized intersectionality is fully operational here. It saves us from choosing, at this stage, between an interpretation in terms of class struggle and an interpretation in terms of the struggle between the sexes. We simply observe that there is a matridominated petty bourgeoisie confronting a patridominated upper bourgeoisie.

I will not reproduce here my previous logical errors, when, for example, after examining the political divergence between France, England, the United States and Germany in the 1929 crisis, I drew the conclusion that family values absolutely determined national trajectories. I had forgotten, as I said in the introduction to the present book, the economic crisis, a factor common to the four nations, without which neither Hitler, nor Blum, nor Baldwin, nor Roosevelt would have expressed these different anthropological tendencies. The error here would be, on the contrary, to assign to the economy, through the class structure, an exclusive capacity for determining antagonistic feminism. The difference between men and women exists and evolves historically, and it takes a feminine dimension as much as a threatened petty bourgeoisie to produce the antagonistic feminism of today.

We can, however, measure the extent to which this new feminism differs from the previous ones in its class insertion.

The first feminist wave, fostered by women from the middle classes, demanded female suffrage for all women and clearly followed the model of the French Revolution, launched by the bourgeoisie but egalitarian and universal in spirit.

The same can be said of the second feminist wave, that of sexual liberation, which also came from the middle classes but which demanded freedom of the body for all women. Neither the first nor the second wave were anti-masculine. I would even tend to perceive the second as liberating for men too, since contraception has allowed both sexes to have much more pleasant physical relationships, and fathers as well as mothers to stop worrying so much over their daughters.

The third wave – symbolized by #MeToo – on the other hand, is anti-masculine, without the least shadow of a doubt. Its conflictual dimension reveals its class nature. It was initially fostered by a larger group than the first two waves, a matridominated petty bourgeoisie, increased in numbers by the spread of higher education. But it cannot have positive effects for all women. In the working classes, where couples' relations are already destabilized by unemployment and a remnant of hypergamic aspiration, the antagonistic model is disastrous in its psychological effects. The world of single-parent families does not need more confrontation between the two sexes, but more trust. The anti-masculine atmosphere may be an instrument in the struggle of the petty bourgeoisie against the patridominated ruling stratum, but it leads to a worsening of living conditions where the solidarity of the couple is most necessary for the realization of a minimum of economic security.

— 12 —

WOMEN AND AUTHORITY

Taking women seriously means considering them no longer just as victims of history, but as its full-fledged actors. The question here is not whether their specific attitudes are transitional with respect to a heritage from the past or anchored in the genes of the species. To understand the present, it is enough for us to admit that 100,000–300,000 years of human habits cannot be erased in seventy years, if we place the beginning of the great transformation in 1950.

Let us study further what the rise to ideological power of women, and more precisely the emergence of a matridominated petty bourgeoisie, has brought, in terms of values and typical behaviours, to our society in transition.

Women as less racist

Women, as we have seen, did not carry the collective consciousness of the original *Homo sapiens* group and we considered them, for this reason, as more economically individualistic. We should therefore not be surprised to find that they are also less hostile to outside human groups. In the United States, their greatest tolerance concerns Blacks; in France, it concerns immigration. We have excellent data on this.

Let's start with the United States. True, we noted in chapter 1 that, at the 2020 presidential election, white women supported Trump; it was the massive vote of Black or Latina women that explains why women, overall, were more supportive of Biden than were men. In political choices, the variables of 'race' therefore remain more relevant in the United States than do those of sex. But significant sex differences can be found if we focus on more general and diffuse attitudes, and then we find white American women more sensitive to Black suffering than white men. A 17 June 2020 poll, conducted by Quinnipiac University, tells us that 56% of white American women were then in favour of the Black Lives Matter movement compared to only 46% of white men.[1] Intermarriage especially demonstrates that women in the United States are less racist than men, a fact that must weigh even more heavily than politics in our overall assessment: five times as many white women live with or marry Black men as white men live with or marry Black women.

The Black question isn't of much concern to the French – outside academia, the world of cinema and the media – as the French are more bothered by Islam, which gets bundled together with immigration. The general perception of immigration is negative in France and there is hardly any difference between the sexes here. According to an IFOP poll of November 2018, 54% of men find that there are too many immigrants, and 52% of women.[2] If we ask about the positive or negative consequences of immigration, there is no significant difference either: 59% of men think that they are negative, and 57% of women. When it comes to the concrete problems posed by immigration and the causes of the slowdown in integration, the two sexes begin to diverge. While 49% of men believe that integration is difficult because immigrants refuse to integrate, only 39% of women share this judgement, which places responsibility for any difficulties on the 'other'. Similarly, while 26% of men believe that immigrants' religion prevents them from integrating, only 16% of women do so.

Let's turn to France's responsibilities. Attitudes continue to diverge: only 18% of men attribute the problems of integration to economic difficulties, but 28% of women do so. On the question of secularism as a negative element in the integration of immigrants, 66% of men agree, 57% of women do.

The maximum gap is reached with regard to family reunification, which 59% of men reject and only 46% of women, who are more individualistic and more humane. The most surprising thing concerns sexual equality: admittedly, 45% of women think that immigrants pose a problem for sexual equality, but . . . 54% of men think this is the case.

All of these results on the attitude of women to foreigners therefore bring us back to the question of their attitude to the group, to the defence of the collective. In the United States as in France, men still tend to be more the bearers of collective identification and are therefore, in principle, more hostile to foreign groups. Women turn out to be more humane, but maybe this is quite simply because they do not bear the burden of national identity to the same degree.

If we consider that the principle of vaccination includes an element of collective responsibility, we find that women are relatively reluctant: in November 2020, before opinions had evolved on the subject, an IFOP poll recorded that 53% of men did not intend to be vaccinated against

Covid-19 against 65% of women.[3] The greater opposition of women involves both college graduates and non-graduates and cannot be interpreted in terms of cultural level. It's all about sex.

The weakening of the collective, but not of authority

Analysis in terms of the differences between men and women therefore allows us to considerably broaden our understanding of the individualist crisis and to understand why no purely economic argument can bring us back to strong collective decisions (such as those which I defend – protectionism and state investment in industry). On the other hand, it is evident that the dilution of collective feeling by feminization has not been accompanied by a weakening of authority. The prisons are full and politicians are engaged in fierce competition for ever more repressive measures. The neo-republican order is becoming, day after day, the fantasized 'imaginary' solution to all our problems.

The ageing of the population largely explains this new authoritarian hard line. The average age of registered voters is now fifty and it is therefore not surprising that politics in France is expressing a need for order, a priority for security. The health crisis has shown the power of the gerontocratic mechanism, which, without perhaps reaching the levels of the Australian aboriginal gerontocracy, has nevertheless managed to lock down France's youth for more than a year, and put on hold the higher education of 18–25-year-olds to protect those over 70. All this political authoritarianism, however, involves fairly classic notions of a public order managed by the police. I will now try to grasp the emergence, alongside this classic political authoritarianism, of a new type of authoritarianism, more diffuse and fundamentally ideological – one which affects the young as much as the old, and which we cannot understand unless we include women's liberation in our reflections.

There is a specific female authority, quite different in its causes and effects from male authority. This chapter does not claim to deliver a firm and intangible truth, and must be considered, on the contrary, as speculative, as the pure expression of a certain liberty of thinking. It will also allow me to identify and interpret certain shortcomings of my previous work on the relationship between family structures and ideology.

The origin of Prohibition?

During my intellectual life, the question of women's authority has presented itself to me via two different paths: the study of the United States in the years 1920–60 on the one hand, and certain anomalies I have observed in the relationship between political ideologies and family structures on the other.

While working on immigration, I had come across a series of articles in which American psychiatrists in the 1940s and 1950s attributed their patients' schizophrenia to domineering mothers.[4] In *The American People*, published in 1948, Geoffrey Gorer (1905–85) put forward the general interpretation of a certain American matriarchy.[5] In a chapter entitled 'Motherland', this Englishman, whose promise was spotted by Margaret Mead, who then trained him in anthropology, studied a recent moralizing and authoritarian deviation within American culture, the Prohibition of the years 1920–33. He attributed it to the cultural domination of overly virtuous women, not only mothers but also the large majority of women involved in secondary education. Since then, I have looked into the question of the evolution of secondary education in the United States and I have verified that, as Gorer pointed out, women occupied a preponderant place among teachers. But above all, I noted that during the development of American secondary education, more than a generation before it happened in continental Europe, the educational level of women had for the first time exceeded that of men.[6] This shift occurred precisely when Prohibition was being imposed.

Having noted the contribution of this English anthropologist, we can allow a German psychoanalyst who emigrated to the United States, Erich Fromm, to take us even further. We have already encountered him, diagnosing Protestantism as patricentric. He was one of the first to identify the mistake that Freud had made by overestimating the role of the father in the formation of the child and his/her neuroses and, at the same time, underestimating the role of the mother. 'Freud's idea – that the child especially fears his father – reflects another of Freud's "blind spots", based on his extreme patriarchal attitude. Freud could not conceive that the woman could be the main cause of fear. But clinical observation amply proves that the most intense and pathogenic fears are indeed related to the mother; by comparison, the dread of the father is relatively insignificant.'[7] It was logical for Fromm to come up with this idea. He had been brought up in the Germanic sphere, like Freud, that is to say in a society which presented a patrilineal inflection of level 1, where fathers were 'visible' everywhere, especially in Luther's *Small Catechism*. Moving to the United States, he was confronted with very visible mothers. It is now a psychoanalytical commonplace: a patient, male or female, who has read a bit of Freud comes to a consultation fully prepared to talk about his or her father, but leaves the session having spent a considerable amount of time talking about his or her mother.

If we want to study female power, we must therefore focus on the relationship of the mother to her children and, more specifically, to her sons. This asymmetrical relationship goes beyond any interpretation in terms of male domination. It is then that, as a child, the man is in a position of inferiority, including physical inferiority, compared to the woman.

Ideological anomalies

The second way in which the question of female authority imposed itself on me was my work on the relationship between family structures and ideological systems. In *The Explanation of Ideology*, first published in French in 1983, I highlighted an excellent geographical correspondence between authoritarian peasant family structures and the emergence, in the phase of modernization, of authoritarian ideologies.[8]

Two types of family structures were involved: the exogamous communitarian family, with its strong patrilineal principle, had produced communism. This was true of Russia, of course, as well as of China, Serbia, central Italy and Vietnam. The stem family, of a generally lower patrilineal level, had produced social democracy, Christian democracy and, in a period of religious collapse and economic crisis, Nazism. The causal link was simple. An authoritarian father is replaced, when the peasant family disintegrates, by an authoritarian party or state. If the sons are equal, we will obtain communist egalitarianism; if they are unequal, we will have at best the coexistence of unequal social classes, at worst the idea of a race superior to all others. Note the patricentric character of the interpretation, which focuses on the relationships between the men in the family.

The spatial coincidence is striking. But, as in all correlations, there are irregularities. In some regions of Europe and the world, we observe emerging authoritarian ideological systems without being able to identify a corresponding authoritarian family type. And in some regions of the world, we observe authoritarian family types that refuse to produce the corresponding authoritarian ideology. I came to understand that all of these exceptions had a common factor, and that common factor was a specific female authority, either very high or very low.

In the south of Portugal, in the Alentejo, there are large farms and, if you look at the censuses, the only type of family you find is the nuclear family. However, this region was characterized, after the democratization of Portugal at the end of the 1970s, by a very strong communist vote. In inland Brittany, between Côtes-d'Armor and Finistère, there was also a significant implantation of the Communist Party without exogamous communitarian families. In Iceland, in 1945, the communist vote had reached 19.5% of the vote, though the only type of family in this country was a nuclear family with temporary co-residence – an interesting anomaly in a Scandinavian world that has been rather refractory to communism, if we except Finland, where one could observe, on the part of the territory adjoining Russia, a very fine communitarian family type. If we cross the Atlantic, we come across the only communist regime on the American continent, Cuba, where there are certainly communitarian structures, but where the family is more of a matrilocal type and certainly not patrilineal. We could add Kerala, in southern India, where several associated communist parties have risen to power, causing a few constitutional crises in the country. There is no classic exogamous communitarian family here, either. That said, in this case, the riddle has quite a simple solution: quite specific matrilineal communitarian systems explain how authority values could operate in the absence of a patrilineal communitarian family.

Let's move on to the cases where we would expect a stem family. In Ireland, this type of family is very uncertain and above all belated. However, this country is characterized by a very intense Catholic authoritarianism, the effects of which can be gauged today through the scandals of paedophilia and child abuse in orphanages.

Swedish family types

Another example, which will play a central role in the following chapter, is Sweden, which, following an article by Orvar Löfgren, I wrongly classified as a stem family country. It took me thirty years to free myself from this inaccurate vision, which nevertheless presented itself, in Löfgren's article, as cautiously exploratory. This is a fine example of interpretative bias, the explanation of which is as follows: I was confronted with an obvious long-lasting difference between Danish individualism, very close to that of England, and the Swedish order, close to that of Germany – an opposition very well perceived by the Scandinavians themselves, and one that even affects their respective senses of humour. Indeed, Sweden is fully the equal of Germany, the largest of the European stem countries, when it comes to the discipline of its social behaviour. In both countries an extraordinarily powerful social democracy has flourished and we observe great political stability there (from after the post-war period in the German case, well before the war in Sweden). It would have been logical to find the stem family underlying both cases. I was still in possession of a theory, verified in at least 90% of cases, which highlighted a coincidence between family structures of the stem type and authoritarian stratified societies.

Löfgren's approach suited the theory so well that for thirty years I ignored the accumulating data that made the categorization of Sweden as occupied by a stem type questionable. These data showed that (1) it was impossible to find, in post-Second World War censuses, many households including three generations; (2) the national inheritance rules did not include primogeniture; and, above all, (3) women enjoyed an exceptionally high status, something that is by its nature incompatible with the patrilineal stem family. Around 1977, David Gaunt noted the omnipresence of the stem family in Swedish ethnological literature;[9] but in 1995, Christer Lundh and others signed its death certificate, stating that the stem family did not exist in Sweden, but the practice of inheritance allowed one of the children to compensate the others and take possession of the property.[10] In reality, divisibility seems to have been very active until the end of the eighteenth century, and it was only later that the fragmentation was slowed down by the redemption of the shares of the brothers and sisters. Compensation was then scrupulously paid, which clearly shows that the principle of equality was real and absolutely opposed to the inegalitarian ideal of the stem family.[11] The fact remains that in the heart of central historical Sweden (Svealand, the lands around Stockholm and the great lakes), in the seventeenth century, where noble mansions did not dominate, a large majority of people over sixty lived with their children, who were usually married, as Gaunt found.[12] Jonas Lindström, the author of a magnificent monograph on the nearby Björskog community, was kind enough to provide me with a tabulation of households according to Laslett's categories. We see a rapid decrease in 'multiple' households, comprising several married couples, between 1643 and 1814, i.e. even before the industrial age: the figures dropped from 36% to 18%.[13] My feeling is that the recuperation of Gaunt's parents and the multiple households of Lindström corresponded to a rather archaic system of nuclear family with temporary co-residence. The mobility of individuals suggests it. This means, in the functioning of rural communities, that there is less sense of the rigidity of the stem family.

To conclude this discussion, we must introduce the notion of Swedish geographical diversity, as studied for the 1890s and 1900s by Mark Magnuson.[14] In this modernized rural world, the proportion of over-60s living alone or with their spouse, and in a nuclear form of the family, is particularly high in central Sweden and in the south, in Skåne (see maps 12.1 and 12.2). The correlate of a larger agricultural proletariat can be observed in these two regions. My impression is that the stem family could have existed in western Götaland and on the island of Gotland in the heart of the Baltic. But Svealand was dominated by an archaic family system with temporary co-residence. Jonas Lindström, in his monograph on the parish of Björskog, noted the frequency of marriage by exchange of sisters, an archaic trait if ever there was one.[15] Note that the power of the social-democratic or communist left was at its maximum, according to map 12.5, outside the stem family regions, where the agricultural proletariat was most numerous – the sign of an underlying nuclear family (map 12.3). The presence of a huge industry does not seem to have been a determining factor in the vote for the left at the geographical level (map 12.4).

Map 12.1 The three major Swedish regions

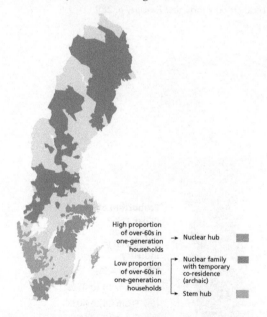

Map 12.2 Nuclear and stem hubs in Sweden around 1900

Source: Interpretation of the map by Mark Magnuson in 'Regional Variations in Farming Household Structure for the Swedish Elderly, 1890–1908', *Journal of Family History*, 41 (4), no. 4, 2016, pp. 378–401, map p. 394

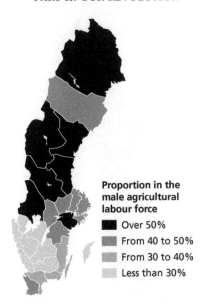

Map 12.3   Agricultural employees in Sweden in 1960
Source: Todd, *L'Invention de l'Europe*, p. 289

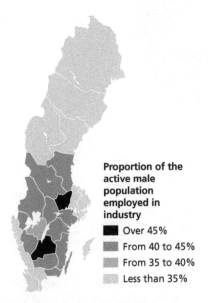

Map 12.4   Workers in Sweden in 1970
Source: Todd, *L'Invention de l'Europe*, p. 288

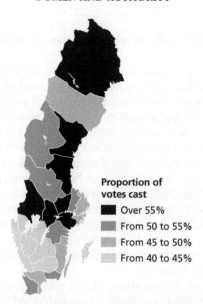

Map 12.5   Social democracy in Sweden in 1968
Source: Todd, *L'Invention de l'Europe*, p. 289

It's never too late to correct your mistakes. I did so in *L'origine des systèmes familiaux* (*The Origin of Family Systems*), published in 2011, where I defined the Swedish stem family as weak or even dubious.[16] As is often the case, admitting an irregularity in the data opens up an important interpretative perspective.

But, to escape any Eurocentrism, let's also take a look at the case of Thailand. In 1950, John F. Embree described it as a 'loosely structured social system', contrasting the fluidity of its family organization with the order of the Japanese patrilocal stem family.[17] The Thai family can be described as nuclear with matrilocal temporary co-residence. The last-born child traditionally provided care for elderly parents. We can indeed describe Thai political and ideological life, with its respected monarch, its interventionist army and its student or popular revolts, as being not just fluid, but conceptually elusive. The flexibility of the family seems to be echoed by that of ideology. In chapter 14, on the liberation of LGBT groups, we will observe the exceptional plasticity of Thai conceptions of sexuality. However, the fact remains that, if necessary, Thai society is capable of strong discipline. Its ability to control epidemics – AIDS and then Covid-19 – reveals a hidden order, more likeable than that in Ireland but related, as in that country, to a specific feminine power.

205

The riddle of authoritarian feminism

Let's focus on Europe. How are we to explain the authoritarian anomalies of southern Portugal, Brittany, Ireland, Iceland and Sweden?

In all these cases we are dealing not only with political discipline, but with a diffuse social authoritarianism. In the absence of authoritarian family structures, where can this come from? The key seems to me to be the specific importance of women observable in these five regions. Here, the anthropological literature has detected what is called a matriarchal deviation. This applies to the whole of Portugal, which is often wrongly associated with Mediterranean countries, but whose features are, as can be seen here, clearly 'Atlantic': women's sexual autonomy has always been strong and the proportion of illegitimate children high. In the north of the country (as in Spanish Galicia, for that matter), there are even systems, stem systems in this case, but matrilocal, with a clear preference for transmission by women.

As far as Brittany is concerned, the phenomenon is a commonplace since in 1983 and 1984 two books were published which bore in their titles the expression '*matriarcat breton*' ('Breton matriarchy').[18] We find in one of them the now classic example of Breton children who were asked to depict their families: they drew a tiny father and a huge mother. In Ireland, the matriarchal inflection manifested itself in extremely late marriages or no marriage. The men who were interviewed sometimes replied that if they had married so late, or not at all, it was so as not to upset their mothers. I haven't come across anything like this in Sweden. Is it really necessary anyway? After all, this country has put women at the heart of its identity, a position that we also find, in a miniature form, in Iceland. We will come back to this in the next chapter. These higher statuses of women have a geographic point in common: their location is on the extreme fringe of Eurasia, along the Atlantic or on the western shore of the Baltic. And Cuba, Thailand and Kerala are also far from the heart of patrilineal Eurasia. The peripheral presence of a high status of women should not surprise us. These are regions where the patrilineal principle has been rejected (see map 12.6).

No paternal authority without maternal authority

We have just examined societies whose family structure was not patrilineal communitarian but which nevertheless produced communism (Alentejo, Cuba, Kerala, inland Brittany, Iceland). The reverse configuration – patrilineal communitarian family structures that did not produce communism – also exists. The Arab family, despite being a communitarian family,

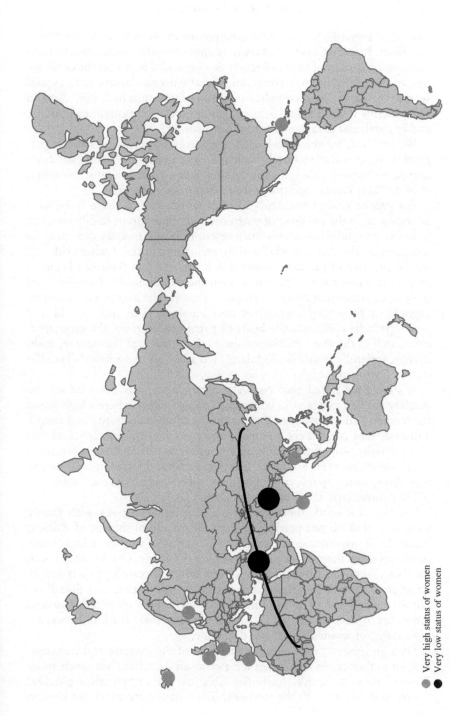

● Very high status of women
● Very low status of women

Map 12.6   Exceptional women

has never engendered a dominant communism, at most a dysfunctional socialism. It is true that this family is endogamous, favouring marriage between cousins, and that endogamy is a powerful brake on the constitution of the state. No impersonal bureaucratic organization – army, social security or party – can completely escape penetration by family clans in the societies it dominates. But endogamy does not explain everything, and in particular it fails to account for disorder.

We can also and above all find the (massive) case of an *exogamous* patrilineal communitarian family which did not produce a significant communist movement either: northern India, from which we must, however, exclude West Bengal and the part of Bihar adjacent to it.

But precisely what the Arab–Muslim world and northern India have in common, in the universe of patrilineal communitarian family systems, is an exceptionally low status for women. In both cases, we can speak of a certain confinement, symbolized by endogamy in the Arab world, and by the practice of purdah in northern India. We can therefore begin to suspect that too low a status for women ends up disabling the capacity of these communitarian family systems to provide the authoritarian norms capable of projecting themselves into ideology. The Arab world and northern India constitute the heart of patrilineal Eurasia, the geographical as well as the theoretical opposite of the peripheral Portuguese, Irish, Breton, Icelandic, Swedish, Keralan, Thai and Cuban societies where the status of women is high.

It should be noted that concrete communism was invented by the country with an exogamous communitarian structure where a high status for women had survived, as if the coupling of male authority and female authority had created the optimal conditions for the emergence of this exceptionally powerful ideological authoritarianism. Perhaps it is time to break down parental authority into a masculine dimension and a feminine dimension, capable of adding to or subtracting from each other?

Let's summarize these discordant data.

On the one hand, then, we have countries or regions with family structures that do not predispose them to the establishment of efficient hierarchical organizations, but where the status of women is high; these countries show themselves to be capable of discipline. On the other hand, the exact opposite: countries or regions which, because of their family structures, should be able to demonstrate organization and discipline, but do not manage to do so, and which, moreover, have greatly lowered the status of women. The conclusion is obvious: there is a link between a high status of women and social discipline.

Such an observation raises the question of the exercise and transmission of authority, in terms that are not at all Freudian, but much more Frommian, so to speak. Authority isn't just the father; it's a parental couple and therefore it's the mother too. It is important to restore women to their rightful place in this area as well. The case of the family systems of northern India and the Arab world which, despite their communitarian family structures and their patrilineality, can't produce enough discipline to bring about a serious communism, even suggests that, if the status of women falls too far, there is no longer enough paternal authority either. In a sense, the authority of the father must be validated by some level of maternal authority.

The mother at the centre of the family

In a world that is getting rid of the principle of male social predominance, we must be able to perceive the reality and the centrality of mothers, who, let me remind you, are women. A comparative study by the World Health Organization on the European younger generation allows us to measure the levels of interaction between mother and daughter, between mother and son, between father and son, and between father and daughter around 2013 (see table 12.1). The WHO study used a survey of children aged 11, 13 and 15 to gauge whether their communication with one or the other of their parents was easy. I have chosen to look at what proportion of 15-year-old children felt that they could speak easily with their mother or with their father, because at this age we are very close to adulthood and power relations in society in general.

For Europe as a whole, we find 80% of boys talking easily or very easily with their mother, and 78% of girls too; 75% of sons speaking easily with their father, but only 59% of daughters speaking easily with their father. The strategic pre-eminence of the mother *for both sexes* is obvious – with this little surprising detail that communication seems

Table 12.1   Parent–child communication around the age of 15

	Speak easily			
	With their father		With their mother	
	Girls	Boys	Girls	Boys
Sweden	64	75	81	83
Denmark	59	73	80	80
United Kingdom	53	71	72	81
Germany	46	69	74	76
France	33	56	60	66
Europe	59	75	78	80

Source: World Health Organization, Europe, *Growing Up Unequal: Gender and Socioeconomic Differences in Young People's Health and Well-Being*, 2016.

marginally easier between son and mother than between daughter and mother. Communication between son and father remains at a high level, even if it includes, as we often know, around the age of 15 and later, an element of conflict. Communication between daughter and father seems the most difficult. Here is a source of ideological fragility for men if society becomes matridominated.

The central position of the mother is confirmed: her communication with her son is probably the very essence of feminine power. I have extracted from the table the data for the Western European countries that are most discussed in this book, although it is doubtful that the survey can really compare such intimate relationships from country to country. The fact remains that Sweden has the highest levels of communication between all the elements of the elementary family group. France stands out as a champion of non-communication.

Constructed authority and natural authority

The authority of each of the two parents does not act at the same psychological level. In traditional peasant societies, the role of fathers as authority models begins quite late in children's lives. It's a little earlier, as we saw, among hunter-gatherers. But everywhere, maternal authority is exercised immediately, let's say, for the sake of simplicity, at the stage of breast-feeding, according to an unconscious mechanism which precedes the acquisition of language. It is deeper, more diffuse, less conscious than the authority of the father. I would tend to say that male authority is socially constructed and female authority natural. Let's move from the way children see their mothers and fathers to the way mothers see their children.

I feel somewhat embarrassed at this point because we live in a world saturated with ideology, where the most obvious and reasonable axioms of thought are no longer accepted, while the most delusional postulates no longer need to be justified. Such is the world of ideological hegemony, which can make the cautious researcher a pariah and the crackpot ideologue a representative of the state. With every step, even stating the blindingly obvious seems to entail the odd feeling that one is taking a risk. This is why I had to remind the reader, in my introduction – trembling at my own audacity – that what differentiated a woman from a man was that she could bear a child. I must here, terror-stricken, proceed to a second assertion, one that is hardly less banal: having created children in their own bodies, mothers have a 'natural' capacity for expression of authority over them that fathers do not have. We will see the importance of this distinction when we examine parental decisions about the hormonal treatment of dysphoric children, i.e. those

210

who think they belong to a sex other than the one biologically defined at conception.

In a nuclear, bilateral family system, the father's authority is delayed, uncertain and negotiable – even in the father's own mind. It is the man's very uncertainty that will create a need for explicit assertion, and sometimes express itself in a violent way. Maternal authority, much earlier in the child's mind, and much surer of itself in the woman who made this child, goes without saying. Deciding for the child is an easier action for the mother, and arouses less doubt than for the father. Until women's liberation, all of this concerned only the internal functioning of the family. Liberation has brought women to power in a number of areas, ideological areas in particular (though not exclusively), and we must consider the possibility that their exercise of authority differs somewhat from the exercise of authority by men. We can imagine it as being less violent but more assured.

A first area of verification would be the judicial system, which seems to attract women to the point that, in this social field, the male presence is being liquidated. Justice is not a field where modern salaried work covers and reorganizes old female economic specializations such as health, education or retirement homes.

In France, in 2017, 66% of judges were women, a proportion that rose to 84% among judges aged 30–34.[19] The profession's transition to matridominance is, like the general educational shift, long-standing, since it is necessary to go back to judges aged over 65, obviously few in number, to find a majority of men. The filling of prisons, and the repression of the *Gilets jaunes* (yellow vests), have not given us, in recent times, the vision of a justice that is getting any softer.[20]

The case of the judiciary allows us to measure a certain French advance in this field. The proportion of women judges is only 53% in Sweden, 50% in the United States and 39% in England (see table 12.2). Moreover, France is the only one of the four countries where women are in the majority, at 53%, at the highest level of the hierarchy. We French can therefore reassure the supporters of authority in the three Protestant

Table 12.2   Proportion of women in the judiciary, 2016

Proportion of women 2016	Professional judges	High Court judges
France	66%	52%
Sweden	53%	39%
United States (2019)	50%	
England and Wales	39%	25%

Source: European Judicial Systems. Efficiency and Quality of Justice. CEPEJ Studies no. 26, 2018 Edition, 2016 data. For the US: Judge Demographics (2022)

countries that the likely arrival of a larger majority of women judges will not weaken the application of the law.

Let's move on. Let's agree for a moment that the public sphere has been penetrated by a new feminine authority, less violent, more diffuse but more self-assured; this is particularly important in the sector of ideology where women are now in a majority. We can then resolve one of the paradoxes of the present time. Previous generations (especially mine) experienced a collapse of collective ideologies. This fall raised the promise of unlimited freedom of expression. However, gradually and simultaneously, we have on the contrary observed the rise of an ideological intolerance of another, more diffuse nature, in the form of political correctness, currently reaching a new peak with cancel culture, which provides a theoretical underpinning for the prohibition of certain opinions.

Once again, I would point out that I am putting forward a hypothesis and not coming to a conclusion. But I cannot abstain, in the face of recent ideological developments, from reformulating Gorer's interpretative proposal on American Prohibition. This followed an overtaking of men by women in the educational field and the establishment of an ideological matridominance in secondary education. We are now experiencing comparable phenomena at a higher educational level. Women are now better qualified than men; they dominate the key sectors of education and justice. Soon they will dominate journalism. While capitalism and, more generally, economic power remain unquestionably patridominated, we have passed, in the West, into a matridominated ideological system. However, we are immersed in an ever-expanding world of mental and verbal prohibitions. Again, not to examine the possibility of a connection between the two phenomena would be sociologically negligent. Again, the opposite view – that there is no relationship between the new conformism of thought and the majority situation of women in the field of the production, control and dissemination of social thought – would be even more difficult to demonstrate.

So, we will have to do our sums, and give cancel culture a sex, for example. As an admirer of the American school of anthropology, I was devastated by the erasure of Alfred Kroeber's name from a building at UC Berkeley. He was absurdly accused of having defiled Indianness, even though he had served it all his life. Exit the Kroeber Hall. But the main actors in this nihilistic act, among student agitators as well as among the administration, were women. I repeat, I am speculating without drawing any conclusions. I require extensive and complex statistical work. Is there an over-representation of women in cancel culture on both sides of the Atlantic? We now accept without difficulty the historical fact of a masculinity of Fascism in Italy and of Nazism in Germany. Should we consider the historical possibility, yet to come, of a female despotism, nonviolent, diffuse, but equally capable of destroying our cultural heritage?

— 13 —

THE MYSTERY OF SWEDEN

Sweden, the number one country for feminism according to the *Global Gender Gap Report*, deserves a chapter to itself. The social sciences can work on average values, or correlations that connect the variables for all countries and regions. But sometimes, according to an inverse methodology, they need to examine extreme cases.

I have already used Sweden to define a theoretical limit in terms of the disappearance of the sexual division of labour. We have observed that no efforts in favour of women have succeeded in abolishing this sex-based distribution of tasks which, in Sweden as elsewhere, remains strong.[1] In the previous chapter, I diagnosed a 'non-patrilineal-stem' origin (of the German or Japanese type) for Sweden's exceptional social discipline, and in a sense demonstrated the feminine (even more than feminist) identity of this country, by seeing the authority of women as lying at the source of its powerful social democratic, trade union and cooperative tradition. (I am referring here only to the style of social reform and not to the totality of struggles in the whole of Swedish history.)

From the fourteenth and fifteenth centuries, the sources of democracy in the north were in fact found in peasant revolts, supported by the autochthonous nobility and targeting rulers and nobility of Germanic origin. The dynasty established by Gustav Vasa, king from 1523 to 1560, was closely linked with the peasantry that was mobilized and even institutionalized in the states of the kingdom which included a peasant 'order', an exceptional case in Europe. The Swedish tradition is not just feminism; it is also the way that a peasantry, politically active from the end of the Middle Ages, was wedded to a strong state, an original coupling that explains the military expansionist phase of the seventeenth century. This coupling would make Sweden a major participant in the Thirty Years War, with a peasant and noble army capable of living as predators on the soil of the Germanic Holy Roman Empire for several decades. The nobility made heaps of money there; the peasants ended up as heaps of dead. The Crown later recovered a share of the land acquired by this enriched nobility. The state revolution from above in the 1680s and 1690s, known as the Great Reduction (*Reduktionen*), returned the share of landed property held by the nobility to its sixteenth-century level.[2] The monarchy then resumed its lasting connection with the peasantry. Sweden's Baltic hegemony was finally overthrown by Russia in the Great Northern War between 1700 and 1721.

While it has been socially 'democratic' for a long time, Sweden has not always been the country of tranquil wisdom. The recent rise of active Russophobia in the country suggests that it has never truly forgiven Russia for shattering its greatness. It restored military service in 2017. With its 10 million inhabitants, Sweden has thus been a busy wasp, representing the anti-Russian West. Despite being unconvincing as a strategic leader against Putin, Sweden has won a position as an accepted feminist leader, so we need to push our research into the causes of its feminism further. Does it result from an originally elevated position of women, or even – why not? – from an ancient matriarchal order?

Against the myth of an original matriarchy

American feminism has revitalized the myth of an original matriarchy in parts of Europe.[3] Bachofen, as we saw in chapter 1, invented the myth of an original matriarchy in his *Das Mutterrecht*. The American drive towards a historical matriarchism stems from the works of Marija Gimbutas.[4] This excellent archaeologist had correctly located the origin of the Proto-Indo-European populations somewhere in the steppe of Ukraine and southern Russia. But she also built a myth around 'old Europe', the first European land to have received agriculture, in the current territories of Greece, Bulgaria, Serbia and Romania. An impressive civilization flourished there, with huge uniform agglomerations numbering up to tens of thousands of inhabitants, and lasting until the Copper Age. On the basis of admittedly fascinating statuettes and figurines, Gimbutas represented this society as a matriarchal world, an idea taken up by New Age feminists in California. Gimbutas imagined this world then being destroyed by the 'patriarchal' Indo-European thrust from the steppe, and her matriarchal fantasy then joined forces with the patriarchal fantasy of the Indo-Europeanists, which we find, for example, in Émile Benveniste, who published the original French version of his *Dictionary of Indo-European Concepts and Society* in 1969.[5]

These theories have been demolished by subsequent research.[6] For example, in a cemetery near Varna, in Bulgaria, on the shores of the Black Sea, the graves of men have been unearthed that are filled with far more goods than the graves of women. I mentioned above the patrilocality of the LBK (linear pottery culture) that emerged directly from this old Europe long before the Indo-Europeans spread.[7] It came into being around the shores of Lake Balaton, in Hungary, and ended up colonizing the heart of the European continent as far as the Rhineland. Its long-houses, slightly modified, are found in the early Scandinavian Neolithic.[8] Sweden was not converted to agriculture by any matriarchal momentum.

I am here going to suggest, contrary to 'mythological feminism', that the particular status of Swedish women is rather recent and dates back only to the eighteenth century; and I will show that this feminist inflection appeared in a system of bilateral kinship with patridominance.

The Sweden of the origins

By examining the past of pre-Christian Scandinavia, between the fifth and thirteenth centuries, we encounter societies which show all the signs of a classic bilateralism with patridominance.[9] In other words, the status of women is, on the whole, high, but in a world dominated by men.

To get a more precise grasp of this, we need to give priority to quantitative methods and not content ourselves with an example taken out of its context, such as the Viking leader from Birka, in the heart of Svealand between Stockholm and Västerås, whose palaeogenetic analysis tells us that she is a woman, despite being 1.70 metres tall (much taller than the average as Scandinavian women in the Iron Age were 1.62 metres tall and those of the Viking Age 1.58 metres tall).[10] As Charlotte Hedenstierna-Jonson, who highlighted the female genetic characteristics of the Birka skeleton, rightly notes, we here have a situation in which social rank is more important than sex.[11] In the aristocracy, belonging to a lineage meant that a woman was more than just a man of low estate.[12] However, this case is not devoid of meaning since, between 550 and 1050, many women of princely rank were buried in this region, as was common, under boats, during the so-called Vendel and then Viking periods.[13]

But once we take a systematic interest in the quantitative distribution of traits, patridominance is visible in Scandinavia during the Vendel and Viking periods.

Take the case of the *gullgubber*, a kind of anthropomorphic amulet that dates from this period, or at least its central phase, the end of the Vendel period and the beginning of the Viking Age. So far, about 3,000 of them have been found. The deposits are mainly in Denmark, but there are some in central Sweden as well. We will have to content ourselves at this stage with an overall Scandinavian approach. For a Danish sample of 845 units, 25% have no determinable sex, but among those whose sex can be defined, there are 409 men, 173 couples and 57 women, a distribution absolutely characteristic of a bilateral society (the significant frequency of couples) with patridominance (the male majority).[14]

Interpreting the runic steles

Let's move on to the end of the Viking era, which was that of Christianization. A magnificent statistical study by Birgit Sawyer of steles bearing inscriptions in runes, the Old Norse alphabet,[15] allows us to grasp the relations between men and women in the upper stratum of Scandinavian society. These memorial stones bear the names of the individuals to whom they were dedicated and of the people who erected them. They are in fact declarations of succession, by which the living claim the property and titles of the dead. Birgit Sawyer has analysed the ties between dedicators and dedicatees, distinguishing between regions.[16] These stones are much more common in the heart of historic Sweden, Svealand, around the lakes just inland to the immediate west of Stockholm, where the female boat graves are located. Again, patridominance is clear. Ties between male dedicators and male dedicatees (son–father, brother–brother, father–son, undetermined man–man and between male relatives, or between male associates) account for 68.8%, the ties between female dedicators and male dedicatees (wife–husband, mother–son, daughter–father, sister–brother) account for 20.2%. That leaves 11% of other ties.

We can see that widows occupy an important place and Birgit Sawyer clearly shows that, by inheriting from a son who died young – a fairly frequent case – a widow could recover part of her husband's property and pass it on to her lineage (reverse inheritance). Ah, the joys of bilaterality! But all the dedicatees are men. It is indeed a bilateral or undifferentiated kinship system in action that we can observe here, as Birgit Sawyer herself says, using these same terms.

Women occupy a more important place in the heart of historic Sweden: 26% in Uppland and 21.9% in Södermanland (the two coastal provinces of Svealand), as against 10.3% in Denmark. But the most significant difference concerns the respective proportions of son–father ties, absolutely dominant in Svealand, and brother–brother ties, important in Denmark. This difference is explained by the fact that the stones, less numerous in Denmark, were there erected by an aristocracy; they are more frequent in Sweden, where they were erected by what Birgit Sawyer calls, apologizing for the anachronism, a 'gentry', a broader and more diffuse upper class. Kinship on one side, a more nuclear family on the other.

But, again, we can simultaneously observe a predominance of men and a substantial presence of women who can exercise property rights and act. This is typically the environment of the Icelandic sagas; though

216

shaped in the thirteenth century, they tell of the interactions between Norway and Iceland in previous centuries. Some are real family romances and depict kinship ties: it is still a world of dominant men but in which also impressively autonomous women can act. Ties between men do not involve brothers alone, but also brothers-in-law, the absolute marker of bilaterality, since the tie passes through a woman.[17]

Peasant patrilocality from the seventeenth to the twentieth century

The written documentation that resulted from the literacy of the sixteenth and seventeenth centuries allows us to achieve true precision for the modern period. Swedish inheritance law, in the countryside if not in the towns and cities, then became clear and original. It established the equality of the sons, but gave daughters a share that was half that of their brothers. It would be easy to joke that, at this point in the analysis, the Swedish countryside seems to have adopted the rule of inheritance in the Qur'an, which says exactly the same thing about the respective shares of brothers and sisters. However, fieldwork monographs show that, in the Arab world, the rule is not applied and daughters are de facto excluded from inheritance.[18]

In Sweden, by contrast, as Maria Ågren has shown through a careful study of legal actions, daughters' right to inheritance was scrupulously protected.[19] The Swedish rule tells us that it is indeed the boys who must inherit, but that the share of the girls plays a very important role, especially as the brothers must buy back plots from each other or compensate each other completely when there is not enough land for more than one holding in their generation. These compensations between brothers also reveal – as I said in the previous chapter – a rigorous application of equality, even in the case of a single successor to the farm: this is quite different from the renunciation of the younger brothers of southwestern France. In this French region of stem families, threatened by the egalitarianism of the *Code civil*, younger brothers uncomplainingly accepted an undervaluation of the property which allowed for a very symbolic compensation. In his monograph on Björskog, Jonas Lindström has studied the burden of the debt, which for the successor was more than a mere formality.[20] His in-depth analysis of the mechanisms of family reproduction enables us to estimate a resulting patrilocality of 60% to 65%.[21] This is not much, considering that the standard value for the patrilineal stem family is typically 75%. Murdock's *Ethnographic Atlas* classifies a society as patrilocal when two-thirds (66%) of married couples move in with the husband's family. By this criterion, rural Sweden would not even be patrilocal.

217

The depiction of a male-dominated bilateral society is yet again confirmed. But we must also conclude from this investigation that nothing in seventeenth-century peasant Sweden points to a particular position for women. The same patrilocal inflection, despite a rule of inheritance more favourable to girls (whose theoretical rights were equal to those of boys) would have appeared among the winegrowers of the Seine valley in the eighteenth century. And there was nothing comparable in Sweden to the dominant matrilocality of inland Brittany in the middle of the nineteenth century.

The birth of the 'Swedish woman': literacy in the seventeenth and eighteenth centuries

The first definite appearance of matridominance in Swedish history occurred in the midst of the spread of literacy fostered by the church and thus also by the state – for Lutherans, these were the same. Egil Johansson, the pioneer of studies on literacy, shows that the ability of women to read had exceeded that of men in Sweden as early as the eighteenth century, both male and female rates being high much earlier than elsewhere.[22] Writing would come only in the nineteenth century.

The identity-based element of Swedish literacy was highlighted by Ian Winchester in a fascinating four-page article: he noted that, at the start of literacy campaigns, the state provided Swedish families with correspondence tables between runic and Latin letters – the sign that the habit of writing in runes, probably for short messages written on birch bark, had survived from the Viking Age until the Reformation.[23]

But it was in the eighteenth century that the specificity of a particularly feminist Sweden emerged, in a bilateral or undifferentiated Scandinavian region. Literacy studies for Denmark are less advanced, and reveal nothing of the sort. I have found statistics for just two Danish prisons, but it is clear that among the prisoners, who represent working-class backgrounds in jail fairly well, eighteenth-century women showed a marked lag in literacy compared to the men.[24] I doubt, however, that the extent of female backwardness could have reached a German-type level in Denmark, since, as we saw in chapter 8, devoted to Protestantism and its patricentric character, it was in Germany, in the seventeenth and eighteenth centuries, that the gap created between men and women by literacy was greater than anywhere else in the world. In that chapter, I stated that the German patrilineal character had been intensified through literacy. I would be tempted here to evoke the symmetrical emergence of a Swedish matricentrism (as Erich Fromm would put it) fostered by literacy. The two phenomena are not unrelated to each other, since it is the interaction created by German Lutheranism

218

that seems to have led Sweden to a reaction of partial dissociative negative acculturation.

Let's remind ourselves of what Georges Devereux called dissociative negative acculturation. This is the rejection by a people of a cultural import, with the definition of an opposite trait which is no longer the original state of its own culture. Regarding the status of women, this will produce: 'Ah you think that men count for more . . . but for us, women are particularly important.' The spread of a patrilineal doctrine produced the emergence of a matrilineal doctrine in Kerala and in the Ashanti regions of southern Ghana and the Ivory Coast, and among the Na of China.

Let's go back to Sweden, where state and clergy adopted Lutheranism and put it into action. Sweden is even more peripheral in Europe than Denmark – it is basically, even more than Denmark, an island – and even more peripheral than Norway, controlled by Denmark. More than its Scandinavian brother in the south, at that time its enemy, Sweden was able to resist and modify Protestantism, while also adopting it, and in particular its patricentrism. Luther's texts, in particular his *Small Catechism*, give a central place to the father of the family and Maria Ågren confirms the latter's importance in Swedish Lutheranism.[25] The interaction between Germany and Sweden at the time of the Reformation was not only ideological, moreover, but also human, since the Church of Sweden imported pastors from Germany, mainly from Rostock and Wittenberg. We can imagine a Swedish awareness of the importance of women in their culture that arose as a reaction to the Protestant influence, which in this case was a German influence. Let's put it in the most mechanical way: the German patrilineal thrust seems to have triggered a counter-thrust of matricentrism in Sweden.[26]

There is an alternative explanation for the feminine inflection of Swedish culture which does not contradict the religious interpretation and appeals, paradoxically, to the temporary transformation of Sweden into a warlike state in the seventeenth century. The army that gave Sweden its century of greatness in European military history was made possible by massive conscription in the countryside (*utskrivning*), which eventually bled the peasantry of a good part of its male population. The disappearance of many men, in fact, gave women a special role in this phase of Swedish history. One example studied in detail by the historian Jan Lindegren shows the extent of the losses: between 1621 and 1639, 230 men from the parish of Bygdeå were called up to serve; only ten returned intact, five were crippled and 215 were killed.[27] The parish lost 40% of its male population. There were then three women for every two men in the community. This was an extreme case, but this type of demographic drain affected the whole kingdom. The imbalance in the sex ratio put women at the centre of Swedish local life in the eighteenth century.[28] I cannot see any contradiction between the two explanations – one by male mortality, the other by dissociative negative acculturation – especially since the Thirty Years War brought the men of the Swedish army, en masse, into concrete contact with a Germany where the status of women had been notably lowered, at a time when witch hunts were raging in the Empire. The Swedes certainly burned a few witches, but in proportion to their population ten times fewer than the Germans. The survivors of seventeenth-century Swedish military hubris were in a position to recognize the high status of their women, and they felt the need to affirm it.

Sweden and Denmark

Let's pursue the comparison between Sweden and Denmark up to our time. The #MeToo movement offers us a fine example of historical continuity within a Scandinavian world that is globally recognized as the leading light of planetary feminism. Everyone in the Scandinavian sphere obviously took #MeToo seriously, at first. But Sweden really went overboard about it, while Denmark, though initially adhering to the concept, was quick to express resistance. This gap allows us to distinguish between a Danish feminism, 'classic' or 'standard' one would be tempted to say, that is very close to that of the Anglo-Saxon world, and a Swedish identity-based 'hyperfeminism'.

A very fine article by two academics (both women) provides a comparative analysis of press reactions to #MeToo in the two countries.[29] It has some statistical value. With the media, we are at the heart of ideology. Here are the most significant passages:

> In Sweden, the hashtag rapidly snowballed into a large public outcry, with street demonstrations, torchlight rallies and other protest events organised across the country, prompting journalists, politicians and other observers to call #metoo [sic] 'a revolution', 'a catharsis in all institutions', 'a historic moment in Sweden' and the 'largest social movement in the country since women fought to secure the right to vote'. Leading politicians, including the Prime Minister, Stefan Löfven (S [Social Democrat]), the Minister for Foreign Affairs, Margot Wallström (S [Social Democrat]), and the Minister of Culture, Alice Bah Kuhnke (MP [Greens]), showed public support by participating in political meetings, panels and demonstrations. Several public figures, including leading politicians and ministers, also came forward with personal stories of assault and experiences of sexism. [. . .]
> Several books have been published, some focusing on personal testimonies, others debating rape culture, power and the underlying societal structures of sexual harassment. In May 2018, the affirmative consent

law, recognising sex without consent as rape, was passed in parliament becoming effective from 1 July that same year.[30]

After this account, no one will doubt Sweden's feminist identity. Let's see how things stand in Denmark:

In Denmark, the media coverage was much less extensive (the number of Danish articles was less than a fifth of the number of Swedish articles) and public debate around #metoo took a rather different turn. In its initial phases, during October 2017, the movement was covered extensively by most news media, but political responses and voices were absent in the coverage and a backlash occurred as voices that criticised or opposed the movement started to gain a foothold and dominate the debate. In Denmark, there were fewer organised calls for action or pushes to change legislation and only a few street demonstrations, which were poorly attended. In October 2018, a year after the hashtag fuelled a global movement, an opinion poll commissioned by the public broadcaster TV2 showed that one in four Danes believed that the #metoo movement had had a negative impact on how Danes treat each other and that the majority of Danes considered the movement a joke.[31]

The article ends with some more general considerations on the differences between Sweden and Denmark on feminist issues in recent years. Drawing in particular on the work of political scientist Drude Dahlerup (who has dual nationality, Danish and Swedish), the authors attribute these divergences to the difference in political cultures:

Since the 1990s, progress towards full gender equality has stagnated in Denmark and concurrently feminism as a concept and a label to describe the struggle towards gender equality has largely disappeared from official political lingo in Denmark. In comparison, the majority of party leaders in Sweden declare themselves feminists. Overall, the general conservative and neoliberal turn in Denmark in the past decades has given prominence to the widespread idea that feminism has 'gone too far'. Such ideological currents of recent years should be understood in relation to Denmark's historical role as 'the libertarian of the north', where resistance to quotas and state interventionism in general is pervasive.[32]

In *L'Invention de l'Europe* (*The Invention of Europe*), I brought out the contrast between Danish liberalism, close to that of England, and Swedish authoritarianism, similar to the German model.[33] Once we have got rid of the stem family model for Sweden, and identified a specific Swedish feminism emerging in the seventeenth and eighteenth centuries, we can see that the authors of the paper reverse the likely explanatory sequence. It is the feminist bias that is the origin of the authoritarianism and highly unusual statist tendency of the Swedes. It is not political structures that underlie the persistence of Swedish feminist radicalism.

The case of Denmark is of theoretical importance because it is close to the Anglo-Saxon world in its individualistic temperament, associated in both cases with the absolute nuclear family, liberal in the relationship between parents and children, non-egalitarian in the relationship between children. In the case of Denmark, there is a mechanism of resistance to militant feminism which has no equivalent in Sweden but does have its equivalent in the United States and in England. Donald Trump, after all, was seen as a big old macho man, and I wonder if Boris Johnson is not also expressing the reassertion of a certain masculinity.

— 14 —

HOMOPHOBIA: A MALE BUSINESS

The main theme of this book is the way women have, as it were, 'come of age' in anthropological and social terms, and emerged from the principle of patridominance, so that we can consider them no longer as manipulated objects, but as free subjects and actors in history. The emergence of a specific female anomie, the division into classes independent of the socio-professional category of the spouse, the social localization of a new female ideological hegemony, and the identification of a particular style of female authority, have been, in chapters 9, 11 and 12, the first applications of this principle. The way in which women's liberation led to that of male homo-sexuality is a fourth, dealt with in this chapter. I will stop numbering these themes from now on, because the points of application of the principle of women's autonomy are flourishing in countless ways. Women now make history, along with men. Their independence thus allows the growth of female bisexuality and the affirmation of its dominant place within the LGBT bloc, a phenomenon also studied in the next chapter, as well as the emergence of 'transgender ideology', examined in chapter 16; this will lead us to the centre of our collective doubts. A final chapter will raise the question of the historical viability of the Western model as it stands today, engaged as it is in a set of unprecedented economic and sexual transforma-tions. To ask a question is not the same as to answer it and I will admit to remaining, quite sincerely, in a state of real doubt.

Orders of magnitude and causal sequences

In the next three chapters, which deal with quantitatively measurable but minority phenomena, I will apply a common-sense axiomatics.

1. First, I will see how the majority phenomena (heavy) lead to the minority phenomena (light) rather than the reverse.

2. I will then confirm axiom 1 by temporally sequencing phenomena to define possibilities and causal impossibilities. If A precedes B, it can be its cause. On the other hand, it is not possible for B to cause A.

I will therefore note a few statistical orders of magnitude before I begin. Women's liberation concerns half of society and appears as a continuous phenomenon since the beginning of the twentieth century, if we consider the movement of education. This movement, which in fact affects the whole of society through the predominance of heterosexual relations (around 85% at a minimum), will lead to the liberation of male homosexuals (under 10% of men – I will come back to these figures later), then the affirmation of female bisexuality in consciousness and social practice (it is changing: it is no doubt currently more than 5% of women, and much more in the younger generations), then the affirmation of the transgender phenomenon. A critical analysis of the figures leads to an assessment of the proportion of transgender people in the United States, the epicentre of the ideological phenomenon, not at 0.3% but more likely at 0.5‰. The constitution of an LGBT bloc does not affect this axiomatic since adding these minorities all together only leads to the constitution of a slightly larger minority.

LGBT: a tactical alliance

The acronym LGBT, without even going as far as LGBTQ or LGBTQI (lesbian, gay, bisexual, transgender, queer, intersexual), is a portmanteau concept that masks the current shift from male predominance to female predominance even within minority sexual behaviours. It was to be expected that the sexual oppression that was quite general around 1950–60 should engender, in a phase of struggle, an alliance of the oppressed. But a minimal critical analysis of the terms compacted by the expression 'LGBT' reveals a fairly fragile ideological construction over the long term.

Lesbians are women who do not feel the desire to love men, gays are men who do not feel the desire to love women. Lesbians and gays are women and men who separate out. Bisexuality somehow represents the opposite, an attraction to both sexes, and it should be seen as something of a unifying force. Being transgender is something else again – the feeling of belonging to a sex other than that defined by biology: a biological man who thinks of himself as a woman, a biological woman who feels she is a man. Common to the lesbian, gay and transgender categories is the fact of taking the distinction between man and woman very seriously, to the point of making it the central element of social identity. Bisexual seems a sociologically opposed concept since it weakens the difference between

224

men and women. But, as bisexuality is – in the Christian West – much more frequent among women, we will see that it does not unify anything at all.

Words before things

The examination of terminological frequencies by means of Google Ngram allows a first approach, semantic and historical, to the temporal shifts masked by the term 'LGBT' (see figures 14.1–14.4). These frequencies measure ideological evolution. They do not say what is actually happening, in physical interactions for example, but what people are talking about, and above all, they reveal what is important from the point of

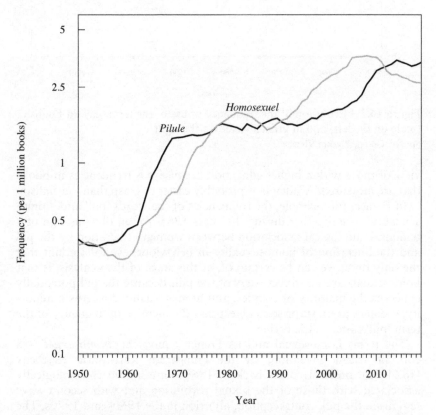

Figure 14.1 Evolution of the frequency of use of the terms '*homosexuel*' ('homosexual') and '*pilule*' ('pill')
Source: Google Ngram Viewer

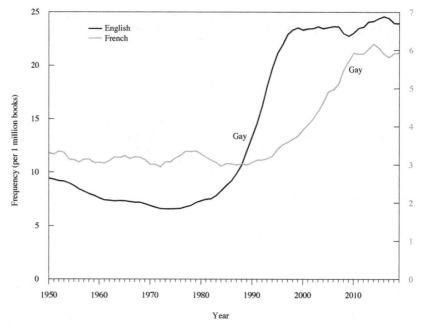

Figure 14.2 Evolution of the frequency of use of the term 'gay' in English (scale on the left) and in French (scale on the right)
Source: Google Ngram Viewer

view of those with a higher education because it is frequencies in books that are measured. Academia is probably easier to grasp than journalism.

In France, for example, the frequencies of the words 'pill' and 'homosexuality' rose together during the years 1965–75, an obvious sign of a temporal and logical association between women's liberation by the pill and the liberation of homosexuality in behaviour, even if I admit that the only thing we can be certain of, at this stage of the analysis, is that homosexuals are not direct users of the pill. Because the pill potentially concerns the majority of couples, and homosexuality concerns a minority, it comes as no surprise to detect that the increase in frequency of the term 'pill' came a little earlier.

The terms homosexual and its French equivalent *'homosexuel'* – a concept whose invention, by the Hungarian Karl-Maria Kertbeny (1824–82), probably dates back to 1869 – are indeed chronologically associated with those of the sexual revolution and with second-wave feminism: the pill, contraception, abortion in the 1960s and 1970s. The second feminist wave must therefore be considered, given the mass of the group concerned (women) and the chronology (the pill, invented by Gregory Pincus, was authorized for contraceptive use in the United

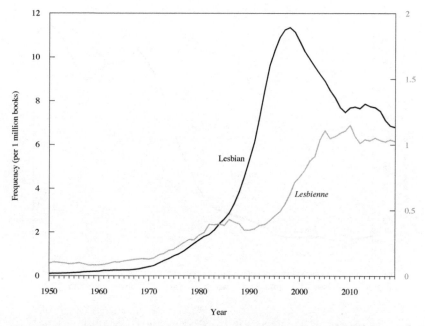

Figure 14.3 Evolution of the frequency of use of the terms '*lesbienne*' (scale on the right) and 'lesbian' (scale on the left)
Source: Google Ngram Viewer

States in 1961), as the general driving force behind the evolution of mores. Indeed, the liberation of homosexuals appeared, at the beginning of the 1970s – I remember it very well – to be a complement to women's liberation. My father, Olivier Todd, was head of the 'Notre époque' department when, on 5 April 1971, *Le Nouvel Observateur* published the Manifesto of the 343 women who publicly said they had had an abortion during their lifetime. My grandmother Henriette Nizan had signed it. I can still hear my father expressing enthusiasm shortly afterwards for Guy Hocquenghem's *Le désir homosexuel*, published in 1972.[1] On 10 January of that year, Hocquenghem had published a column in *Le Nouvel Observateur* under the title 'La révolution des homosexuels' ('The Revolution of Homosexuals'). As far as I'm concerned, I was then wading through a difficult sexual apprenticeship, and I tended to agree with my grandfather Paul Nizan in thinking: 'I was twenty years old, and I won't let anyone say it's the happiest time of your life.'

Returning to our semantic analysis, we see the terms 'gay', 'lesbian' and 'bisexual' all become more common later, between 1980 and 1995 in the Anglo-American world, although at very different levels of frequency. The term 'gay' leads the dance quantitatively, while 'lesbian'

227

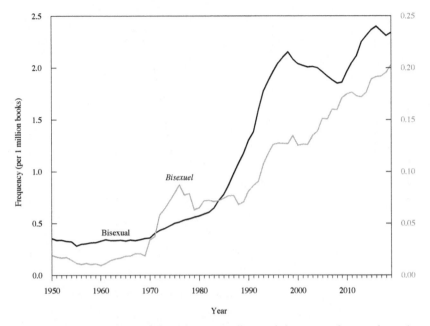

Figure 14.4 Evolution of the frequency of use of the terms '*bisexuel*' (scale on the right) and 'bisexual' (scale on the left)
Source: Google Ngram Viewer

and especially 'bisexual' seem to be only minor partners. From 1997 to 1998, the ascent stops and, above all, the terms diverge. 'Gay' plateaus out, 'lesbian' declines and 'bisexual', after drooping a little, resumes its ascent, but, I repeat, at a much lower level. Bisexuality becomes a dynamic junior partner (see figure 14.4).

The evolution is quite similar in France, but with a time lag and at a much lower level for the three series of frequencies (divided by four at the end of the period for '*gay*', by six for '*lesbienne*', and by ten for '*bisexuel*'). In the case of France, however, the three concepts diverge according to the same modalities as in the Anglo-American world. '*Gay*' plateaus out, '*lesbienne*' falls and '*bisexuel*' rises, in this case uninterruptedly.

'Transgender' and French '*transgenre*' did not appear until the 1990s. In this case, we are dealing with a brutal innovation.

Homosexuality, a natural human behaviour

The aim here is to study homosexuality in its relationship to women's liberation, and not in itself. Above all, there is no question of produc-

228

ing an interpretation of what homosexuality is in general. Let's content ourselves with a few simple introductory data. First, homosexuality is a universal human practice. It is found everywhere, in all cultures, at all times. Exclusive homosexuality, that which for the individual is not one sexual practice among others, is specifically human. Homosexual behaviour is a commonplace of animal nature, but the individuals of the sexed species who practise it almost never refrain from heterosexual behaviour.[2] What is commonplace in nature is thus bisexuality, far more than homosexuality. In the case of human beings, it would be better to speak not of a homosexuality, but of homosexualities in the plural, as the meaning of the practice differs with society and context. There is, for example, a male homosexuality associated with rather feminine behaviour, a virile homosexuality among Greek warriors and samurai, and even a functional homosexuality in certain environments deprived of women such as prisons or long-distance ships.

The first to have raised the question of homosexuality in primitive communities was, yet again, Westermarck. In *The Origin and Development of the Moral Ideas*, he drew up an inventory of the data then available, leading, still rather cautiously, to the observation that homosexuality existed in all human groups.[3] Westermarck was himself a liberal, probably homosexual, at a time when there was still considerable repression in the English-speaking world.

Research has become more systematic and it is now time to return to Murdock's *Ethnographic Atlas*. Here we can find data on the frequency of homosexuality in primitive communities which confirm Westermarck's thesis. In *Patterns of Sexual Behavior*, published in 1951 in the wake of the Kinsey Report, Clellan S. Ford and Frank A. Beach systematically compared the sexuality of the Americans of their time with that of people in simpler societies, and with the sexuality of higher primates.[4] For their study of simple human societies, they relied on a sample of seventy-six societies, all taken from Murdock's *Atlas*, which – hunter-gatherers as well as farmers – had the advantage of being located far from the Beijing–Baghdad–Ouagadougou axis, and were thus preserved from any contamination by the patrilineal principle. These societies were all characterized by relatively high status of women. Even the African societies they selected, in the east and in the south, belonged to regions where the status of women was not really low. Their conclusion was that in 64% of the seventy-six societies for which information was available, homosexual activities were considered normal and socially acceptable. We would certainly find a correlation between a relatively high status of women and a high level of tolerance of homosexuality, a correlation which, as we will see, remains fundamental. *Patterns of Sexual Behavior* also teaches us that female homosexuality is never a problem for societies and, unlike its male counterpart, never gives rise to repression.

229

The fundamental question that arises from the point of view of general anthropology is why sexual behaviour that does not lead to reproduction has not been eliminated by natural selection. It is possible that the high or low proportion of actively heterosexual males is not a factor limiting the production of offspring. The presence of homosexuals in a group may also have essential social functions. It is not impossible that homosexuality, by contributing to the behavioural heterogeneity of the group, helps to make it more creative and effective. The conquest of the planet by *Sapiens* required constant adaptations. The invention of agriculture and its consequences repeated this demand for adaptability. To cope with novelty, it is preferable to have several psychological types living together and cooperating in a group.

Let me be clear: I'm not talking about the interest of homosexuality in itself. I could just as well have given the same function to some religious minority or other. I'm just saying that different behaviours lead to different attitudes, different visions of the world, which can prove beneficial for a group that must constantly adapt.

To show how neutral the question of sexuality is in this interpretation, I will take an example which may strike the reader as somewhat malicious. John Maynard Keynes (1883–1946) started as a homosexual at a time when homosexuality was normative in Cambridge. My English great-grandmother Dorothy Todd (1883–1966), of exactly the same generation, was also homosexual. However, in his conformist sexual phase, from the point of view of the social context, Keynes showed little originality in his writings as an economist; these demonstrated a banal classicism. His original contribution to science followed his conversion to heterosexuality – a scandal in his milieu – and his marriage to the Russian woman Lydia Lopokova.[5] The real unconventionality in Cambridge between the wars, if you were a man, consisted in loving women. I don't know if the reasoning would apply to my great-grandmother, who, despite her sexual conformism, was editor-in-chief of the English edition of *Vogue*.

In their decidedly fundamental *Patterns of Sexual Behavior*, Ford and Beach tell us that the most common homosexual practice is anal penetration.[6] Fellatio and mutual masturbation are rarer. Sexologists have long recognized the erogenous nature of the anal area. In this sense, homosexuality has a physiological basis and can be considered natural. The human body provides us with this possibility of pleasure, a heritage of the phylogenesis of the species.

It will not have escaped the reader that so far, by mentioning the Ancient Greeks and the samurai, prison life and anal penetration, I have spoken solely – if we put aside a quick allusion to my great-grandmother – of male homosexuality. This is no coincidence: in all the anthropological and sociological literature, female homosexuality is conspicuous by its absence. As a problematic, it does not, so to speak, exist – neither in anthropological data concerning primitive or past cultures, nor in those dealing with the more recent period. Ford and Beach point this out, moreover, with regard to the United States in the first half of the twentieth century: 'The attitude of our society toward feminine homosexuality might almost be characterized as one of disregard. The penal codes of many states provide severe penalties for men convicted of homosexual practices, but very few states have similar laws pertaining to women.'[7]

In her book on homosexuality in Europe, Florence Tamagne states that '[l]esbians, moreover, suffer from an awkward disparity in the sources; in every field (especially the legal) the evidence and documents concerning homosexuals are more abundant than those dealing with lesbians.'[8] The reason, as she herself observes, is that there was no legal repression of female homosexuality, and therefore no creation of judicial sources. And so, in a way, female homosexuality wasn't a theme. With regard to lesbianism, the attitude of societies has oscillated between denial and disinterest.

Let's look at one exception all the same: a study by Katherine Davis, cited by Beach and Ford, that concerns 2,200 American women and must date back to the 1920s.[9] She finds that couples of homosexual women have more 'emotional' relationships, in other words more oriented towards feelings. But G.W. Henry notes that homosexual intercourse allows women to reach orgasm more easily than heterosexual intercourse – in 91% of cases, much higher than the heterosexual average.[10] This is thanks to cunnilingus for the most part, because the use of fingers or objects for vaginal and, one assumes, anal penetration is very rare.

What is interesting here is the verification that, in the homosexual bond, the same-sex relationship is an asset in the search for pleasure. The comparative and quantitative study of homosexuality is, on the whole, difficult because if homosexuality is clearly a universal human possibility, its repression by various societies is variable, going theoretically, if one may say, from 0% in classical Athens to 100% in Nazi Germany after the Night of the Long Knives. The expression of their preference by the individuals concerned will be easy or impossible, and the comparison of the results will be, at the very least, really difficult. In any given society, if it is changing, the results will sometimes be ambiguous: does an increase in the number of declared homosexuals reveal an increase in preference or in its expression? In some cases, however, we can decide. Let's look at the example of France.

Around 1985, homosexuality tended to be associated with a high educational level, with the reservation that the educational level was then itself strongly correlated with age and might just correspond to a generational shift. Tragic and reliable statistical data verify that the polls refer to behaviour. The map of deaths due to AIDS reproduces the

231

map of high educational levels, of the Paris region, of the cities of the Mediterranean coast, and also of the whole of Occitania, an area of stem families remarkable at the time for its rates of obtaining the baccalaureate per cohort. The Nord-Pas-de-Calais region, more working-class and less educationally advanced, had the lowest rate of AIDS-related deaths.[11]

Let's fast-forward to 2014, almost 30 years later. A major IFOP survey on sexuality shows that those defining themselves as homo- or bisexual included 9% of craftsmen and small traders, 8% of executives and those in senior intellectual professions, 8% of employees and 8% of workers. The implicit educational gradient had clearly disappeared. But is this a change in behaviour, or a new freedom of expression in working-class circles that had briefly converted after the war, as we have said, to a petty-bourgeois puritanism?

My personal feeling is that we are dealing with a real liberation of behaviour, as such an evolution is absolutely parallel to that which we observed for experimentation with lifestyles in general in chapter 9, with a sexual revolution beginning among those with a higher education, then a re-solidification of marriage among them, accompanied by a diffusion of experimental behaviour downwards in society ending with an accumulation of single-parent families in the working-class and intermediate professions.

At this point we can note an important difference: the 'final' homosexual rates of socio-professional categories were, in 2014, very close to each other, which would confirm our initial observation of a universal homosexual human potential which escapes the determinations of class. Lovers of social diversity can be reassured, however, as the same 2014 poll shows very significant political diversity: 8% homo- or bisexuality among those who voted for François Hollande or Marine Le Pen, but only 4% among those who voted for François Bayrou.[12] I have no doubt that this variability is an opportunity for adaptability among the particular group of *Sapiens* that occupies France.

Mapping homophobia: the BBO axis yet again

There remains a general difficulty: a planetary mapping of the frequency of homosexual behaviour is impossible. Paradoxically, it is the repression of homosexuality, by law or by the attitudes of the various populations, that is easy to map. The planetary distribution of homophobia will bring us back to the BBO axis.

If we look at the current world, as it has emerged from the Western sexual revolution of the 1960s–2020s, we see low homophobia in societies with a high status of women, and a resistant homophobia in societies with patrilineal traditions.

Map 14.1 should not disorient the reader of this book too much. We find here the same overall contrasts as in many of the maps in the previous chapters. The BBO axis appears clearly, as do the great patrilineal cultures it crosses: China, India, Africa, Russia and even Vietnam. A number of Muslim countries appear as undefined because no survey was possible there, which of course suggests a high level of homophobia.

There are, all the same, a few quirks in this map. While Japan's intermediate level may reflect a certain reality, that of Thailand can only be wrong. This country is one of the least sexually repressive in the world. Similarly, the fact that Indonesia is shown as strongly homophobic attributes too much importance to Islam, and overstates, from what I have read, the homophobia of the region. I have some doubts about Germany, ranked among the most gay-friendly countries. Germany's relationship to homosexuality throughout its history is complex. The Bundestag voted for marriage for all only in 2017. Admittedly, even before the 1914 war and under the Weimar Republic, Germany was a pioneering nation in the struggle for the liberation of homosexuals. All of this, however, ended with the homosexual eccentricities of Röhm's SA, which led to the Night of the Long Knives and the sending of homosexuals to concentration camps. So much so that, in the second phase of Nazism, the best option for a homosexual seeking shelter was to enlist in the Wehrmacht, which prohibited the practice but did not want to disrupt its divisions by seeking out and persecuting homosexuals.

Bilateral cultures, which tend initially to be rather feminist, are those where it is the easiest, nowadays, to live one's homosexuality. This fully justifies the examination of homosexuality in this book, and it is valid not only for the most advanced societies. It applies to the most developed part of the Western world, but also to Argentina, Brazil and Spain, despite the Catholic influence. The moderately liberal situation of Mexico, Ecuador, Peru and Bolivia appears, quite subtly, intermediate. These are Latin American countries where significant Indian peasant populations have survived. Whether on the central Mexican plateau, speaking Nahua, or in the Andes, speaking Quechua or Aymara, these peasants had very patrilineal systems, which appeared, as I said above, after Spanish colonization.

In 2006, Western Europe had a rate of acceptance of homosexuality lying in general between 86% and 94%.[13] Italy was a little lower, at 75% – this marks the trace of a patrilineal culture in central Italy. But Germany, France and the UK were at 86%. Sweden, of course, was a beacon of light, at 94% – the leader of feminism could hardly fail to shine. The Netherlands, the first country to legalize same-sex marriage, was at 92%, Spain at 89%, Canada at 85%, Australia at 81%; Japan was at 68%, Mexico at 69%, Brazil and Argentina at 67%. The United States, at only 49%, and Israel at 47%, were far behind Western

Percentage who consider they live in a tolerant environment for gays and lesbians

0–20%
20–40%
40–60%
60–80%
80–100%

Map 14.1 Homophobia
Source: Richard Florida, 'The Global Map of Homophobia', Bloomberg City Lab, 7 February 2014, based on data from Gallup's World Poll

Europe, demonstrating the effects of particular religious influences. The acceptance of homosexuality in the United States rose sharply to 72% in 2020. This evolution was linked to the final collapse of religion in North America.

With Eastern Europe, acceptance drops to 46%. People generally attribute this contrast to the legacy of communism, but we will see that it is also a religious effect, albeit of another type, and a matter of socio-economic structuring.

One important anomaly needs to be explained: Russia. It is certainly patrilineal, but the status of women there is high. However, it appears today as a region of very high levels of intolerance to homosexuality, which was criminalized by Stalin in 1934 and decriminalized in 1993 following the collapse of communism. But its level of acceptance by the regime and the population, unlike what we have seen in most other countries with a high status for women, has dropped further, falling, between 2013 and 2019, from 16% to 14%.[14] The 1993 liberalization was followed by a 'gay offensive' perceived by a rather patriotic population as Western interference. The conversion of homosexuality as a sexual practice into homosexuality as a social identity, and, moreover, as the spearhead of new Western thinking, seems to have led to this tension.[15] It is not impossible to interpret Russian homophobia as to some degree a reaction of dissociative negative acculturation: 'Ah, you Westerners define the gay phenomenon positively. Well, we Russians think that homosexuality is not a value to be promoted and we are proud to be homophobic.'

Homophobia: a male business

As I said above, homophobia actually targets male homosexuality alone. Let's go further: in general, homophobia is a repressive passion of men who persecute men. Women are not involved, either as victims or as oppressors. The OECD confirms this in its report on 'how to better include sexual and gender minorities?' previously quoted: 'Acceptance of homosexuality is greater among women, younger adults, the better educated and people living in urban areas [. . .]. The finding that women are more open to homosexuality than men is explained by the more negative attitudes of men toward gay men [. . .]. In fact, men's acceptance of lesbians is similar to women's acceptance of both lesbians and gay men.'[16] The greater tolerance of women towards homosexuality is confirmed, across France, by an IFOP poll of October 2012.[17] In 1986, 54% of people agreed with the proposition that homosexuality was 'a way like any other to experience one's sexuality'. In 1996, the figures were 67%, and 87% in 2012. But on this last date, the survey shows a difference between men and women: 83% expressing acceptance for the former, 91% for the latter. This was, it should be noted, just before the vote in favour of marriage for all.

Women in most countries, bilateral or patrilineal, accept homosexuality more easily than men, with gaps that range from fourteen to five points – in descending order, in Korea, Japan, Canada, Poland, Argentina, the UK, South Africa, Australia, Germany, Spain, Sweden and the Netherlands.

Homophobia, dominant or not, is indeed a male affair, a repression that some men impose on other men, or possibly on themselves: in other words, a constraint that the male sex imposes on itself. If homophobia is not a problem for women, it is logical that it should cease to be the problem of a society that is shifting into ideological matridominance. A society that emancipates women also emancipates homosexuals because the habits of male self-repression lose their importance.

However, we have seen a paradox emerge when examining the data country by country. Not all variations of homophobia could be explained by the status of women, or by the bilateral or patrilineal character of the kinship system. In the United States, religion has intervened as a powerful factor of homophobia, to the point that its resistance and then its collapse could explain the difference and then the rapprochement between the United States and Europe. A high level of religiosity maintains a high level of homophobia and, conversely, the decline in belief leads to a decline in homophobia. But religion, as we saw in chapter 8, was largely a women's affair in Christian countries. We must therefore solve one last problem: to understand how the dissolution of religious belief, which kept Western societies fairly largely in a state of homophobia, has liberated first women, and then male homosexuals.

— 15 —

WOMEN, BETWEEN CHRISTIANITY AND BISEXUALITY

Talking about the West often amounts to talking about the Christianity that was at the heart of its culture, and more specifically about Latin Christianity, subdivided by history into Protestant and Catholic branches. Religion and homophobia are closely linked. In 2020, at the level of states, the correlation coefficient was +0.78.[1]

The fundamental peculiarity of Christianity, which distinguishes it from all other religious systems, is not so much a tendency to asceticism and a somewhat unfavourable view of sexuality, a distrust common to most universalist religions with the exception of Tibetan Buddhism, but rather a rejection of sexuality that is so intense as to have been rarely achieved in human history. It was expressed as early as Saint Paul, then with the first Fathers of the Church, but at that stage remained rather experimental.[2] The Christian rejection of sexuality did not really shape society until the Reformation and the Counter-Reformation, in the sixteenth and seventeenth centuries. It was at this time that the age of marriage and the celibacy rate rose in the population as a whole. There was a drop in the number of illegitimate children and, in general, a sexual disciplining of Western Europe.

Simple Protestant homophobia and Catholic ambivalence

The Protestant crisis, which sought to transform men into priests, in the words of Pierre Chaunu, was the driving phenomenon here, and yet again we will need, in this chapter, to rid ourselves of the recent and misleading vision of a liberal Protestantism, open by nature to the idea of tolerance. Luther and Calvin were as hostile to homosexuality as they were to women. Let us not be fooled by the recent innovations of female pastors and homosexual pastors. Judaism, early Christianity, Protestantism and Counter-Reform Catholicism were homophobic, ready to see the act of sodomy as committed under the influence of Satan. Sodom appears in the Bible and, as the old joke has it, one always wonders what people got up to in Gomorrah. One could even, at first glance, assume that close attention to the Bible evokes a superior homophobia, something that would bring Judaism and Protestantism into the camp of maximum repressiveness. The low rates of acceptance of homosexuality noted for Israel and the United States around 2006 would be a first verification of this.

But let's go further and envisage a certain complacency of Catholicism towards homosexuality, albeit a homosexuality which must not be physically realized through an act of the flesh. I said above, following Eileen Power, that convents (closed by the Protestants) allowed certain women of the nobility to escape marriage and men. We can speculate that the much more numerous male monasteries and the Catholic secular priesthood allowed men to escape from marriage and women. It is not impossible to describe the Catholic Church as a vast monosexual institution. The Church's active hostility to sodomy should not conceal the main thing: this institution was, down the centuries, a place of development for exclusive male friendships and, secondarily, for exclusive female friendships. Pushing what is perhaps not actually a paradox, we must note that the cassock, like the homespun robe, could dissociate the clergy from the male population by a disguise that evoked female clothing. Let's rest content, however, with a vision of the Church that accepts the structural ambivalence of this institution concerning homosexuality.

Again, we must note the homophobic simplicity of Protestantism, which closed down monasteries, required priests to get married (to women!), and effectively suppressed most spaces for homosexual living in the West. The married man forced into a parallel homosexual life existed in France, but it is a cultural commonplace only in the Protestant Anglo-American world. I would point out again that the homosexuality of the religious that I am talking about here is sentimental rather than physical.

Continuing the logic of the interpretation, we can see in women's affection for priests, which politically frightened the radicals of the Third Republic so much, the same type of affection, described elsewhere, as their liking for male homosexuals: these were men who, like priests, did not threaten them with seduction or rape.

This rapid examination makes classical Protestantism, which has removed all these ambiguities, the epicentre of modern Christian homophobia. The indifference of French legal codes to male as well as female homosexuality ever since Napoleon could thus be interpreted not only as republican in nature but also as Catholic in tradition.

Let us not idealize either the Church or the Republic, but rather content ourselves for the moment with a homophobic Christian religion, absolute in the case of original Protestantism, but concentrated in the case of Catholicism on the act of flesh – sodomy in particular.

The collapse of religious sentiment and homophobia

We will end this statistical review by returning to the decisive evidence from the United States. We have seen that acceptance of homosexuality there was only 49% in 2006. If it rose to 72% in 2020, it is because one of the major phenomena in recent American history has been the collapse of residual Protestant religious feeling. Attendance at Sunday services was still 45% for the generation that reached adulthood in 1940 or 1950; it fell to 20% for those who reached adulthood in 2000. And serious studies show that you have to halve all the figures, which means that religious practice has fallen from 22.5 to 10%.[3] The United States is becoming non-religious. No wonder homophobia is collapsing there.

The final downfall of religion in the Western world is a sociological commonplace, and I myself, with many others, have underlined the importance of the terminal collapse of Catholicism on the periphery of France for understanding the evolution of French society since 1965. We have seen the Socialist Party invade the bastions of the conservative right, anchored until then in a religious practice that remained regionally significant; we have seen the subsequent fall, in a kind of domino effect, of communism, the double negative of the Church, implanted in regions which had been dechristianized from the middle of the eighteenth century onwards, on the Laon–Bordeaux axis and on the Mediterranean facade. We have observed a strong educational drive in the areas evacuated by the Church, filled with the dynamic 'zombie Catholics' studied in *Le Mystère français*.[4] On the map of demonstrations of support for Charlie in *Who Is Charlie?*, I noted a Catholic zombie outburst, only to note five years later in *Les Luttes de classes en France au XXIe siècle* (*Class Struggles in Twenty-First-Century France*) the probable extinction of this final flame.[5] I underlined the role of the development of higher education since 1950 in the dissolution of the collective beliefs inherited from the years 1789–1950, whether political or religious. But what I had not perceived, as a typical androcentric historian, was the historically crucial impetus provided by the educational ascent of women in this general movement. We have seen that, from 1968 onwards, the number of female baccalaureate holders exceeded that of male baccalaureate holders and that, through a few quick stages, women prevailed over men in higher education. I had missed the essential point: if, until 1950, women had remained the strongest support of religion, it was their educational emancipation which brought about the final collapse of Catholicism, and activated the whole ideological mechanism of the years 1965–2020. In other words, women, more than men, have made the general history of the last half-century, and not just their own. In this history, there is not only the decline of the Church, of communism and nationalism, but also the decline of homophobia. I can't believe I have been blind for so long to the decisive role of women in this historic process.

I mentioned above the Church's fight against sodomy. The collapse of Christianity was accompanied by the collapse of the taboo concerning what was considered – absurdly given the possibilities of pleasure it gave the species – as an act against nature. The 2014 IFOP survey, which I discussed with Jérôme Fourquet in *Marianne*, showed that anal penetration had become, if not a daily practice, at least a majority experience in French society. It has become rather commonplace for a majority of heterosexual couples, with relatively few differences according to socio-professional category.[6] Among the higher socio-professional categories, 61% of men and 50% of women said they had already practised it. Among people whose level of education was below the baccalaureate, the proportions respectively were 60% and 42%. The survey revealed that even those women who voted for François Bayrou, with the lowest rate, had already, by a small majority, experienced sodomy.

It is easy to see that in a world where the majority of women have experienced anal penetration, the denunciation by the Church of sodomite homosexuals no longer makes much sense.

Are gays zombie Christians?

One of the most interesting changes observed in Western countries was the transition, between 1980 and 2000 (see the curve in figure 14.2 in chapter 14), from homosexuality defined as a particular sexual practice to homosexuality as defining membership in a gay community. Making sexual preference a primary social identity obviously implies the broadest possible view of sexuality.

I am convinced that a thing and its opposite are always close, in a certain dimension that needs to be found. In absolute values, 1 and −1 are identical. We can call this always open possibility the 'Principle of the Equivalence of Opposites' (PEO). Basically, the PEO is behind the conceptual proximity of matrilineality and patrilineality, of hard exogamy and quadrilateral endogamy, of totally rejected co-residence and definitive co-residence, of strict monogamy and mass polygyny, of equality and inequality – all those binary oppositions by which human communities have emerged from their original indifference. The Christian West has been negatively obsessed with sex for two millennia. But if we turn sexual orientation into the central element of a personal identity, isn't that still

240

maintaining an obsession with sexuality? For centuries, the Christian West considered sexuality the worst evil for the soul. Now it posits it as the essence of the soul.

Let's note the strange, inverted similarity of attitudes, at the time of the Fathers of the Church and during the sexual revolution. Let's first recall the reason why sexuality was rejected by Saint Augustine (who, unlike theoretical liberators like Freud, had considerable practical experience in this area): sexuality dominates us; it expresses our animal nature and is as such an obstacle to human freedom. To get rid of sex is to access a higher degree of freedom. Sexuality was therefore condemned by Christianity for the same reason that it is glorified today: in the name of freedom. Far from being unstable, the Western world has a constant obsession, negative then positive: sexuality – always in the name of freedom.

Hence the question raised by the emergence of gay identity, a social identity based on sexuality: might it not simply be a legacy of Christianity, that religion which has made the West a world inhabited by sexuality? We would thus be dealing, in the sexual domain, with a 'zombie Christianity', a concept that, as I have just remarked, I have used in several books to account for the permanence of latent Christian attitudes, in people or populations who have lost their faith.[7]

The fact that gay identity has failed to take off in countries like Japan or Thailand outside the Christian tradition suggests that this hypothesis deserves to be explored.[8] Thailand follows the Buddhist tradition of the Small Vehicle, its kinship system is bilateral and its family type is clearly matrilocal. The status of women there is high. Japan combines, on the religious level, the Buddhism of the Great Vehicle with an animist Shinto cult exploited by nationalism from the Meiji era onwards; its kinship system remains bilateral but the family there is of the patrilocal stem type (according to my classification, the result of a level 1 patrilineal emergence). The status of women is lower there than in the western Atlantic world or in Thailand, but not as low as in China.

In Japan as in Thailand, two cultures analysed from this point of view by very competent gay men from the Anglosphere, male homosexuality exists as a sexual preference and practice but it has not been able to mutate into a gay identity. In Thailand the cultural code defines as masculine any man who is not a transvestite, and offers him the possibility of heterosexual or homosexual relations according to his taste. In Japan, the fundamental order is familial rather than sexual, as a reading of novelists like Kawabata or Tanizaki reveals. In his discussion of the methodological problems of his Japanese survey, Mark J. McLelland tells us that one of his difficulties in interviewing homosexuals resulted from their strong investment in their work, which left them with little time. I suddenly find myself wondering if identity at work is not more important in Japan than sexual identity.

These cultural systems, endowed with their own logic and dynamics, probably do not resort to a gay identity if this is only a positive reversal of the Christian obsession with a sexuality that was once persecuted and is now supposed to structure social life. Moreover, and perhaps above all, Buddhism questions the idea of a unified self, which probably makes it – long before psychoanalysis – the most intelligent of religious systems. It is difficult to see how a plural ego could support a social identity entirely condensed in sexuality.

It should be noted that these two countries, which share the fact that they have never been invaded militarily by the West, nevertheless had to confront, successively, in the nineteenth century the puritan militancy of the Victorian West, and since 1990 the gay militancy of the same West. I think Japan has been affected the most, as a result of its desire to compete with the great powers in all things: in that country, sexual propriety seems to be a logical complement to the economic catch-up. On the other hand, one has the impression that the Puritan wave and the gay movement have slipped over Thai culture like water off a duck's back.

A question therefore arises at this stage of the analysis: is Christianity a necessary and sufficient condition for the emergence of gay identity at the current stage of historical evolution?

The objection of Eastern Europe

One objection immediately comes to mind. Gay identity has not taken hold in Russia and Eastern Europe, which are nevertheless regions of Christian tradition and, of course, of patrilineality, albeit of a moderate kind outside Serbia. Poland is frankly bilateral, and yet homophobic. We can, however, narrow the scope of our new 'law' associating gay identity with zombie Christianity. Age at marriage and the celibacy rate have remained low in the East. In a still celebrated article from 1965, John Hajnal first highlighted the pattern of late marriage and the importance of permanent celibacy west of a Saint Petersburg–Trieste line after 1650.[9]

Europe east of this line did not experience the great sexual mutation. Yet it is precisely in this Eastern Europe that we find today a reserved, if not frankly hostile, attitude to gay identity. This hostility has perhaps been too quickly attributed to the legacy of communism. It also draws on a more distant and deeper history. A conventional religious description of the European sexual duality gets things wrong: among the homophobic countries and/or those that are hermetically sealed against gay identity, we find many Orthodox countries, such as Russia, Bulgaria, Romania and Serbia, but also countries with a Catholic tradition, such as Poland, Hungary (with a strong Calvinist component) and Slovakia.

Gay identity, born in Protestant countries, only became ideologically hegemonic in the middle classes of Protestant or Catholic countries, which had, moreover, experienced the great mental transformation of the years 1550–1650, representing a shift in sexual mores on the scale of entire societies. This narrower definition effectively excludes Poland, Slovakia and Hungary. But I offer researchers the hypothesis of gay identity as a manifestation of zombie Christianity, and perhaps even of zombie Protestantism.

Marriage for all men and all women

Homosexuality exists as a general concept. But there are two sexes (I must here insist on the conservative definition that I gave in the introduction: the female sex can bear a child and the male sex cannot). There are, therefore, in the sensible reality of the world, two homosexualities: between man and man, between woman and woman. However, as I said above, beyond tactical alliances, homosexuality is about men and women separating out. Accepting homosexuality means liberating two concrete homosexualities and opening up the possibility of a new divergence between men and women.

We notice this divergence first of all in the type of sexual life. Martin King Whyte noted that, in just 18% of pre-industrial societies, men were thought to have more sexual needs than women. French society is a post-Christian society, and one which therefore takes sexuality quite seriously; it seems to fall into this category of a supposedly more active male sexuality, with a fairly good agreement on the subject between men and women, one deplored, moreover, by the researchers who report it: 'images of female sexuality and male sexuality continue to diverge sharply: in 2006, more than 60% of men and 75% of women thought that "by nature men have more sexual needs than women"'.[10] This mismatch of sexual needs must logically lead to negotiation and/or conflict within the couple.

If this is accepted for our society, and perhaps for the whole world within the Christian tradition, what if we separate the two sexes, with men having sex with men and women having sex with women? Natural frequencies by sex can be established. What one can imagine, in the case of lesbian couples, is a lower frequency of intercourse. We also noted above, according to American data from the interwar period, very satisfactory orgasm rates in lesbian couples. Among men, we can also postulate the emergence of an ideal-typical male sexuality, of opposite intensity, unchecked by the more measured desire of women. This phenomenon could be gauged at the start of the AIDS epidemic: frequency of intercourse, multiple partners, backrooms, etc., resulting in the rapid

243

spread of the virus within the male homosexual world.[11] This period of crisis marked the emergence of the gay identity, and we witnessed the shift from a vision of the homosexual as effeminate to the homosexual as hypervirile.

Let's pursue the idea that there is not one homosexuality, but two, and that they are different in their consequences, not simply sexually but matrimonially speaking. The divergence manifests itself in same-sex marriage. On the eve of the vote on same-sex marriage, the IFOP poll quoted above showed greater activism among women: 'Do you think that society is not tolerant enough towards the homosexual community?' This time, only 39% of men felt that society was not yet tolerant enough, but 50% of women (and, among those under the age of 35, 63%) thought this was true. There was therefore, in a context, let me repeat, of a general acceptance of homosexuality, a difference between the sexes when it came to the continuation of the programme, with men who thought that the results obtained were sufficient and women who thought that it was necessary to go further. This 'further' was here represented by the 2013 law on marriage for all. Behind this latest advance, we can sense the female element of the electorate, a manifestation of ideological matridominance.

Statistical analysis will reveal significant differences between gay and lesbian marriages.

The age structure is not the same: the average age gap between men who get married is high, at 7.3 years, while the average age gap between women is only 4.9 years, close to the national average for heterosexual couples of 4.3 years.[12] To properly measure what this 7.3-year gap represents within male homosexual couples, it should be noted that it is very similar to the age gaps between spouses in the Arab–Muslim world of the 1980s, between Egypt (then at 6.6 years) and Bangladesh (7.7 years, the highest gap at the time). Although this figure concerns male couples, it points to a 'patriarchal' situation, while female couples are relatively egalitarian. American studies confirm the existence of greater educational and economic inequalities in gay couples than in lesbian couples.

The evolution in the number of male and female same-sex marriages is not the same, either. Initially, there were only 41.5% female same-sex marriages. Between 2013 and 2017, their proportion rose to 49.7%. This relative increase in the place of women was the result not only of an absolute increase (3,060 marriages between women in 2013, 3,607 such marriages in 2017) but also of a drop in the number of marriages between men (from 4,307 in 2013 to 3,637 in 2017).

I now come to the essential aspect of this contrast between marriage for all women and marriage for all men. The reproductive potential of homosexual female couples is theoretically double that of heterosexual couples; that of gay couples is zero. I leave aside male homosexual adoption here, and surrogate motherhood, because I note, as a demographer, that both refer to births outside the couple. For lesbian couples, everything is quite simple. In fact, the women of same-sex couples who wanted children, even before the legalization of medically assisted procreation, could have them, either by borrowing a little sperm, or by artificial insemination – by going to Denmark, for example. Reading Maupassant also reminds us that, long before artificial insemination, a woman could compensate for the sterility of her husband by resorting to an occasional male partner. The excellent bisexual capacity of women, with which I will conclude this chapter, suggests that, for a lesbian couple, the direct use of a man for fertilization is in many cases a reasonable option.

The marriage of homosexual women, by its age differences or its potential demographic results, therefore seems very close to the heterosexual norm. With one difference, perhaps: since women have more demands than men with regard to the emotional quality of their life as a couple, lesbian couples seem to have a higher probability of breaking up by divorce than heterosexual couples. The potential fragility of the lesbian couple would, however, simply produce an increase in single-parent families, that is to say a completely commonplace social form. Distinguishing a single-parent family headed by a homosexual woman from a single-parent family headed by a heterosexual woman seems a somewhat vain conceptual exercise.

Gay marriage essentially recognizes the economic and fiscal solidarity of the couple and it protects the spouse in the event of death. This is an important achievement for those who have not forgotten the essential economic dimension of marriage. Gay marriage is therefore for all, in these times of economic difficulties, a salutary reminder. Lesbian marriage, unlike gay marriage, is overall comparable to heterosexual marriage in terms of reproductive capacity. It is easier to understand the higher degree of activism among women when marriage for all was about to become a reality.

The rise of female bisexuality

As we have said, homophobia is easier to analyse than homosexual behaviour. We must, however, go beyond the figures of same-sex marriages, which reflect only part of the reality, and try to measure the significance of the two homosexualities and their evolution in society as a whole.

A properly grounded international comparativism is, as I have said, an impossibility. A recent article has attempted to correlate, at the level of different countries, sexual orientation with a series of variables: equality between the sexes (the authors say 'genders'), economic development and the level of individualism.[13] With remarkable honesty, the authors acknowledge that no correlation appears significant. The OECD agrees: it refuses to classify countries according to the frequency of homosexuality, the data being, according to this institution that specializes in international comparison, not comparable. We will have to content ourselves with internal developments in each country. One certainty already emerges from the data that I have been able to consult on France, the United States and other Western countries, a certainty that I have mentioned above for France: sexual behaviour now varies little according to social class and educational level.

The 2014 IFOP study, cited above for a few socio-professional categories, indicated an overall rate of homosexuality in the French population of 4% and a rate of bisexuality of 3%. Another study by IFOP, from 2019, indicates 3.2% homosexuality and 4.8% bisexuality. The data are difficult to compare because the definitions have changed: the second study distinguishes people who 'assume' their sexuality from those who 'do not assume' it. There is nevertheless a stagnation, if not a decrease, in the number of people who declare themselves to be homosexual and an increase in those who identify as bisexual. However, bisexuality isn't a matter for just anyone.

'To bi or not to bi',[14] an excellent study carried out by François Kraus for IFOP, shows us that the proportion of women who have had a homosexual experience is increasing sharply: it rose from 2% in 1970 to 4% in 2006, then 6% in 2012 and 10% in 2016. What is increasing is female bisexuality.

This general trend of a stagnation of homosexuality in general and of male homosexuality in particular, but of a sharp rise in female bisexuality, as a practice and an identification, is found in other Western countries.

For the United States, we have countless studies. One of them, carried out by the Gallup Institute, tells us that the proportion of Americans who identify as LGBT rose from 3.5% in 2012 to 4.5% in 2017.[15] This increase is basically due to the younger generations and, more particularly, young women. The study finds a growing divergence between the sexes in terms of identification with the LGBT group: 'Gender gap in LGBT identification expands', we read.[16] The proportion of men who identify as LGBT is almost stagnant, from 3.4% in 2012 to 3.9% in 2017; the same proportion among women rose sharply: from 3.5% to 5.1% during the same period. And, as in France, this increase mainly reflects an increase in bisexuality.

In the United Kingdom, the Office for National Statistics gives rather low LGBT rates: 1.6% in 2014 and 2.2% in 2018 for the population as a whole, with no reversal of the male–female balance of power, since in 2018, 2.5% of men declared themselves LGBT compared to 2% of women.[17] On the other hand, 1.1% of women declare themselves to be bisexual and 0.6% of men. Even if the data are not entirely comparable,

I doubt that there could be such a difference between the British and the Americans, and that it would be so detrimental to the British. The male homosexuality rate of 1.9% in 2018 for the United Kingdom would put the French homosexuality rate at 210% of the British rate, which certainly poses a problem of interpretation of the data but does have the merit of casting doubt on certain archaic national stereotypes.

Sweden, finally, also seems to be part of this trend. I refer to a study with the evocative title 'Young Swedish Women More Likely to Have Sex with Each Other.'[18] What seems to be emerging in societies with a post-Christian bilateral tradition is the combination of male homosexuality, now stabilized at its natural level, with a rapidly increasing bisexuality in the female population. It comes down to a difference between men and women.

Quantitative studies suggest that male bisexuality, while possible, is much less common in the West than its female equivalent. The statistical trend among men is towards exclusive homosexuality. Women seem more able to navigate between homosexuality and heterosexuality. Because this divergence contradicts the dominant ideology, it has raised controversy in the United States. Militant sexologists have endeavoured to measure the physiological reactions of this or that category of men to the sight of men and men, or of men and women, making love, in order to find out whether the men were truly capable of bisexuality.[19]

I do not pretend to pronounce definitively on these questions. I am simply suggesting that the prevalence of exclusive male homosexuality is specific to the Christian West. Thai men seem quite capable of a fairly broad bisexuality. It is not even certain that the whole Christian world is concerned. In Mexico, a country whose Catholicism was more affected by Aztec traditions than by the Counter-Reformation, male bisexuality seems quite widespread.[20] And we must not forget Brazil.

Let's summarize the evolution experienced by the countries of the West as narrowly understood, Anglo-American, Scandinavian and French, at the beginning of the third millennium. Within the LGBT group, we went from a situation of strong G and weak L and B to a situation of a G weakened compared to L but especially compared to a B that is in rapid expansion. Let's just go ahead and say it: within sexual minorities, women are taking power. They are doing so through bisexuality rather than homosexuality. The rainbow flag should not hide from us the fact that the historic LGBT bloc has passed into matridominance.

— 16 —

THE SOCIAL CONSTRUCTION OF TRANSGENDER

Comparative anthropology tells us that the existence of men who take on feminine social roles and, more rarely, of women who take on masculine social roles, is a frequent phenomenon in the history of societies – it may even be universal perhaps, like homosexuality. It can above all be identified at the very source of human history. Transvestism is an old and recurrent mythological theme, and in many peoples we can find specific ritualized institutions. Thailand, a very feminist society on a general level, has its *kathoey*. As far as twentieth-century Europe is concerned, cross-dressing was, along with homosexuality, a major concern in the Berlin of the Weimar Republic, a society in which the status of women had been lowered by level 1 patrilineality.

These two examples, with opposite meanings in terms of family and sexual context, immediately suggest that a systematic study would reveal, depending on the society, different meanings of attraction for the opposite sexual role: the expression of an innate tendency in certain individuals, the elevated position of the other sex, the flight from a too painful role of one's own sex. I would not dare to speculate too much on the multiplicity of motivations or explanations.

Nor will I engage in a patient search for possible precursors of the transgender issue as it currently stands: Peter Gabriel, decking himself out in his wife's red dress and covering his face with a fox mask before going on stage; or the appearance of 'Brazilians' in the Bois de Boulogne at the very end of the 1970s.

The aim of this chapter – as of those on homosexuality – is not to develop a general theory, but, in a limited way, to consider a relationship between the liberation of women and the irruption of the transgender question at the heart of Western ideology. This restriction of the subject will not prevent us from diving into the most distant past by revisiting the case of the berdaches, men who played the roles of women in pre-European North America, or remembering their geographically very close equivalents in northeast Siberia, across the Bering Strait. Throughout this book, the Indians of the far west of the United States have – once we have eliminated the competing hypothesis of the Australian Aborigines – played the role of the best representatives of early humanity; today transgender ideology assigns berdaches (or 'two-spirits') a theoretical importance. It would be a shame not to take advantage of this conjunction of interests between fundamental anthropology and contemporary ideology.

If the transgender question, as it is currently posed, with a clear epicentre in the Anglosphere, cannot be detached from past models, it nevertheless leads us beyond the examples provided by primitive societies. Always and everywhere, men endowed with a genetic heritage and therefore with a masculine physiology have sometimes experienced sexual dysphoria, an unhappiness at being men. The same goes for women. But today, for social or technological reasons, it will not always be enough for the individuals concerned to step out of the male or female social role and accept their own biology. It will also involve transforming nature and attempting a physiological change of sex. Cross-dressing or adopting one of the traditional occupations of the opposite sex are no more than preparatory and, as it were, weak elements in a sexual reclassification that can lead first to a physical transformation by hormonal treatment in order to acquire some of the secondary sexual characteristics of the opposite sex, then by surgical treatment to the fitting of an artificial vagina to obtain a transgender woman or the fitting of an artificial penis to create a transgender man.

Let me remind you of the definitions: a transgender woman is a biological man by conception who thinks of himself as, and 'becomes', a woman; a transgender man is a biological woman by conception who thinks of herself as, and 'becomes', a man. We have seen above that no hormonal or surgical treatment can change the reality that, at the current stage, only those who are biologically women at conception can bear children. Only transgender men can thus in practice possibly bear children. There are therefore no transsexuals in the strict sense and I would tend to say that the term 'gender' is in this case appropriate. It points to something that can go beyond cross-dressing but does not fundamentally alter the original sexed nature. If transgender ideology had not achieved a dominant status in the zombie Christian West, we would no doubt have the right to speak of hormone or surgical treatment as an organic disguise. Despite the simplicity of the criteria (clothing, hormones, surgery), the levels of transformation are in practice poorly measured in the literature because an ideological struggle is underway to maximize the number of transgender people in society, a struggle that usually entails combining the three levels to obtain a significant overall quantity. We therefore observe, with regard to the transgender category, the same type of compaction already observed for the LGBT category, but in a statistical zone of less than 1%.

There is in fact a fourth level of transformation, quite different technically, socially and morally: that of children who have shown dysphoric behaviour and whose parents have deemed it appropriate, with the agreement and participation of doctors, to block puberty by hormonal treatment to give them time to decide on their 'gender'. The state of the adolescent thus treated is a developmental arrest, an entry into a sort of purgatory leading later either to the return to a normal maturation of the gonadotropic axis, or to entry into a treatment leading to 'gender' transition. I will let my readers decide for themselves what heaven and hell are here. What is certain is that the question of human freedom and its insertion into the social structure arises differently for the transgender adult and for the dysphoric child whose puberty is arrested by his or her parents. The case of England, where the GIDS (Gender Identity Development Service, a section of the National Health Service) carried out this kind of arrested puberty, prohibited by a court decision of 1 December 2020, is particularly interesting. In April 2021, Sweden followed England in this ban.

I hope the reader will have sensed my moral indifference to all the sexual questions discussed so far. It extends to the case of transgender adults, who are human beings like myself, and with whom I am in solidarity. Their persecution is as abominable as that of homosexuals. On all these points, I am faithful to the education I received from a liberal family: 'All tastes are natural'. My moral neutrality stops at the case of children. I think that intervening in the physical development of a child with hormonal treatment is immoral. I am not writing these lines in a militant state of mind, but so that the reader can precisely locate the exact limit between my subjectivity and the scientific objectivity deployed in this book.

Now that these definitions and this limit have been established, we will be able to compare with serenity the transgender phenomenon of our modern society to the berdache phenomenon of original humanity.

The case of the berdaches

In the view of some transgender activists, the case of the Indian berdaches, or 'two-spirit', justifies their quest for a humanity that blurs the differences between the sexes. This quest, they claim, is no more than the return to an original human nature, pre-industrial, pre-Christian, pre-agricultural. The berdaches were discussed in the left-wing liberal mainstream press, *The Guardian* in England and *Libération* in France:

In the First Nations of Canada and the United States, the male–female binary only arrived with colonization. Today, activists claim to be 'two-spirit' and focus on the history of fluid identities in indigenous populations.[1]

The comparison is indeed useful. The study of berdaches makes it possible to situate the modern transgender question in a broad anthropological perspective. It frames the problem conceptually.

In their article 'The North American Berdache', Charles Callender and Lee M. Kochems provide us with a very complete picture of the facts about and interpretations of those societies which offered people born men the possibility of adopting a female adult role.[2] The article is followed by a long discussion with other researchers. It contains a list of 113 Indian peoples among whom it is certain that the institution existed, and a list of the 30 peoples where the institution was reversed, that is to say berdaches who had been born women and then adopted male social roles. Let us immediately say that these latter can all, with the exception of one – a gap in the sources, no doubt – also be found in the list of the 113 ordinary cases in which a man takes on the role of a woman. The woman who becomes a man is here, when she exists, merely the reflection of the man who becomes a woman.

I propose a cartography of these Indian groups which does not content itself with placing them in the North American space, but situates them within Murdock's sample.[3] The cross-referencing of the two sets certainly means that we are leaving out some cases which are not in the *Atlas*, but it allows us to measure the *frequency* of the institution by region, mode of subsistence or family system. It somewhat increases the number of peoples in the sample by subdividing certain groups from California and the Rocky Mountains. I have added the Iroquois, for whom Callender and Kochems do not note the existence of berdaches, but for whom Signorini gives a reference in the discussion following the article (see map 16.1).

Let us first recall the universal meaning of Native American berdaches. I gave above the reasons why I think that the right model for approaching the initial state of humanity is not that of the Australian Aborigines but the set of hunter-gatherers of America far removed from the Mexican and Andean agricultural hubs. North America admittedly contained peoples to the east and south who possessed low-intensity agriculture, and some low-intensity unilineal kinship systems as well, including the curious group of patrilineal hunter-gatherers of southern California, close to farmers in the American Southwest, which will somewhat disturb our results here and whose case I will re-examine in volume II of *L'Origine des systèmes familiaux* (*The Origin of Family Systems*). But the North American peoples as a whole provide us with the finest sample of hunter-gatherers with undifferentiated kinships in the entire world. They clearly

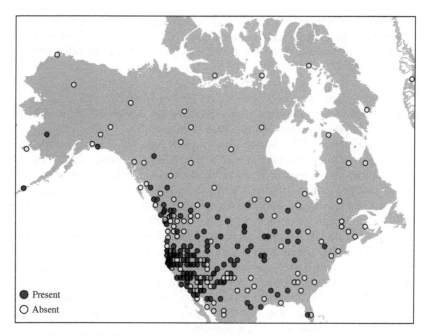

Map 16.1 Berdaches in North America

show a close similarity with our West, in the restricted sense, including the Anglo-American world, Scandinavia and France, and possibly Spain and Portugal. It is this proximity of kinship systems that validates the comparison at first sight.

The ideologues of the third sex frequently cite the case of the Siberian berdaches. They too were mainly found in bilateral societies, the so-called Palaeo-Siberian societies, the Chukchi, Koryak and Kamchadal peoples in particular.[4]

Let us summarize the main features of the institution of berdaches. Identification with a sex other than that defined by biology sometimes begins in childhood and is then manifested by an interest in the activities of the opposite sex. The sexual division of labour therefore seems more important than sexual relations when it comes to identifying with the other sex, which nonetheless most often leads to physical relations or marriage with an individual of one's own sex. This priority of transgression in the field of work has prompted a majority of authors to reject the hypothesis of an explanation by homosexuality – but not all authors, since the explanation by sexual orientation remains the second major interpretation.

Even more often than an attraction for feminine activities, manifested from childhood, what reveals the vocation of the berdaches is a personal vision in adolescence. This vision fits well with the highly individualistic dimension of the Native American culture which, in my opinion, stems, as in the West, from the nuclear family.

Berdaches are often prestigious in their society, most often doing exceptionally well in their feminine craft, whether it be basket-making, pottery or gathering. It is true that they are physically stronger than women. But the women who had become berdaches and adopted male roles hunted (in the groups where they existed), and also had the reputation of being competent.

Berdaches frequently have important ritual functions which derive from their special status as human beings combining male and female characteristics within themselves. The berdache occupies a place in the social group which some authors view as indispensable and which therefore sometimes requires, in certain peoples, the quest for a child who will have to perform this function. Callender and Kochems try to give an estimate of the number of individuals involved. They find the figures proposed by anthropologists a little low when compared to the testimonies of explorers of the seventeenth and eighteenth centuries. But the 1% given by Kroeber for the Yuroks, the 6% for the Gros-Ventres, the 5% for the Tetons-Dakota, the 4% for the Flatheads, the 2% for the Nez-Percés and the 1% for the Shoshones reported by Holder in 1889 represent frequencies that are already higher than those of current transgender people.[5]

Callender and Kochems insist that the Indians in no way believe that berdaches have actually become women. This is not gender-crossing, but gender-mixing. They are a third sex which unites in itself certain characteristics of both sexes – hence, I repeat, their possible supernatural functions. Callender and Kochems reject both the homosexuality interpretation and the most frequently adopted interpretation: an authorized escape from a male condition marked by a high risk of death in war after being tortured.

The two authors observe that there is no correlation between the intensity of war and the presence of berdaches. A detailed examination of the groups in the interior basin of the Rocky Mountains does indeed reveal an omnipresence of berdaches and an absence of warfare. The fact remains that the groups of the Great Plain to the north, which after the acquisition of the horse produced one of the most violent cultures in North America, all have the institution of berdaches: in their case, it is likely that certain men were not able to assume the socially required hysterical masculine role.

As shown in map 16.1, the first fundamental dimension of the berdache phenomenon in North America is its quasi-universality. Only the Great North has no berdaches, but the predominance of hunting in that region makes absolute the sexual division of labour. All men are essential to the acquisition of food resources. Berdaches are found somewhat less frequently among the eastern farmers, but there may be a bias in the data because these groups first came into contact with English Protestants who were uninterested in their customs. The first ethnological evidence comes from Spanish or French explorers who were Catholics, and whose penetration was carried out further west, either from the south or from the north down the Mississippi. The mass of ethnographed peoples in the far west is partly the result of late contact with Europeans, at a time when ethnological interest shown by the latter was already more marked.

Still, the second lesson of the map, after universality, is a relative over-representation among the gathering peoples, especially in the far west (see table 16.1). The institution has been identified in 75% of them, an estimate resulting from the matching of the sample of Callender and Kochems and the *Atlas* of Murdock. Fifty-seven per cent of fishers and 53% of hunters are familiar with berdaches, and the figures for extensive farmers and intensive farmers are 50% and 46%, respectively. If we remember that absence of proof is not proof of absence, and that all these percentages are therefore minima, we can affirm that the majority

Table 16.1 The berdache phenomenon in North America

	With berdaches		
	Percentage	Absolute number	Total number of peoples
By mode of subsistence			
Gatherers	76%	57	75
Fishers	57%	32	56
Hunters	53%	32	60
Extensive agriculture	50%	7	14
Intensive agriculture	46%	11	24
By place of residence of spouses			
Patrilocal	71%	20	28
Uxorilocal	66%	12	18
Ambilocal	66%	73	110
Matrilocal	61%	13	21
Virilocal	46%	16	35
Avunculocal	25%	1	4
Neolocal	8%	1	12
Not specified	50%	3	6
By kinship system			
Patrilineal	72%	29	40
Bilateral	58%	93	161
Matrilineal	52%	17	33

of peoples, whatever their dominant mode of subsistence, had berdaches. These latter were, however, even more frequent among peoples whose main activity was gathering, in which men often participated. In these societies, the sexual division of labour was in fact less rigid than among hunters and fishermen. The greater initial proximity of masculine and feminine roles undoubtedly facilitated the transition from men's to women's roles.

The association with bilaterality and bilocality is less clear, but this is mainly because of the anomaly of southern Californian pickers: 57% of peoples with bilateral kinship systems had berdaches and 72% of patrilineal peoples; we find the same apparent inflection, albeit weaker, for the residence of spouses at marriage, with berdaches in 66% of cases of bilocality as against 71% for patrilocality. There remains the central fact for a planetary comparison: 60% of American peoples with berdaches are bilocal and 65% bilateral. It is the dominant trait of the continent that these figures above all express, and this dominant trait was inherited from the initial groups that populated it. The alignment of berdache peoples along the Pacific coast, as far as the Aleutian Islands, which leads to Palaeo-Siberian berdaches on the other side of the Pacific, confirms that the institution was by its nature at the 'source'. If we accept the hypothesis that North America, rather than Australia, was a repository of the most archaic forms of male social life, we must admit that the possibility of some males being able to become socially female is part of the general human potential.

Note that the peoples who had the opposite institution of berdaches who were 'women turning into men' were concentrated along the west coast, with again a predominance of gathering as their main activity. Thus, it seems that the berdache phenomenon does not involve any particularly unbearable form of the masculine condition, but a high proximity of men and women in societies that are rather egalitarian as far as their relations are concerned, although they are patridominant. This quick survey therefore confirms the thesis of current ideologists of the transgender phenomenon who consider berdaches as relevant points of comparison for our Western societies where the social roles of women and men are close.

Berdaches and transgender people

What are the similarities and differences between berdache people and transgender people today? In both cases, our context is that of a bilateral family system where there are (moderate) inequalities between men and women and where the transition from one status to another is conceivable. A first piece of proof of this proposition, in the negative, is given to us by Germany, which is less comfortable than other OECD countries with transgender people. It is true that it was in Germany that the first sex 'change' operation took place, in 1922, but this was in the context of a society that was adrift. *Society at a Glance 2019*, our favourite OECD publication at the minute, puts the proportion of people who express 'comfort with transgender people' at around 30% in Germany, 50% in France, 65% in England and 80% in Sweden.[6] Germany had reached level 1 patrilineality and the male and female roles are more distant there than in the Western world strictly speaking.

Now let's move on to the differences between berdaches and current transgender people. In the case of berdaches, no radical physical change is envisaged. A radical spiritual change, perhaps, but the body, in its reality, does not need to be affected. The sexual relations of berdaches remain unproblematic. Their role change often leads to a sexuality that can be interpreted as transvestite or homosexual, but the pleasure principle is not altered. The berdaches often have a high status, even if some groups look at them with indifference. They tend to be rich, either by their professional qualities, or as an effect of their religious specialization.

In the case of current adult transgender people, I have distinguished three levels of transformation. Let's focus on the surgery. If I can trust my readings, the pleasure principle is, at least, weakened, and the objective of a harmonious sexuality is not the desired goal. Moreover, despite the ideological centrality of the transgender question for the middle classes, if not in the Western world, at least in Anglo-American countries – or perhaps among Protestant zombies – the transgender state, at the present stage, leads if anything to poverty. There are certainly prestigious transgender people such as the Wachowski brothers, who made the film *The Matrix*, then became the Wachowski sisters. But these are rare and their social success generally precedes their change of 'gender'. There are, however, in France and elsewhere, transgender people belonging to the middle classes: it would be interesting to know if they are more numerous in the public sector or the private sector. Any important social phenomenon in the advanced world must be situated in relation to the state because the latter mobilizes between a third and a half of economic and social resources.

The general social context of the transgender phenomenon is different from that of berdaches: Western societies are not, like American Indian societies, economically stationary and ideologically patridominated. They are engaged in rapid economic transformation, although some of the changes are regressive, with large areas of impoverishment and even increases in mortality. As we saw in chapters 9 and 11, they are now ideologically matridominated in their middle classes, even if a certain political-economic patridominance remains in the upper middle classes.

256

One important difference was mentioned above: transgender people are proportionally much less numerous than berdaches. But the main difference seems to me to relate to the question of psychological well-being or suffering. Western transgender people do not seem to correspond to the traditional representation of berdaches, who tend to lead rather contented lives.

'My new vagina won't make me happy'

A text that appeared in the *New York Times* in November 2018 is striking in its intellectual quality and allows us to get straight to the heart of transgender issues: 'My New Vagina Won't Make Me Happy'. Its subtitle is important: 'And It Shouldn't Have To'. Andrea Long Chu, a transgender woman, born male, is about to have an artificial vagina inserted; she introduces us to the pain of her transgender condition in the period of transition, after hormonal treatment and on the eve of a surgical transformation. Here are the key passages:

Next Thursday, I will get a vagina. The procedure will last around six hours, and I will be in recovery for at least three months. Until the day I die, my body will regard the vagina as a wound; as a result, it will require regular, painful attention to maintain. This is what I want, but there is no guarantee it will make me happier. In fact, I don't expect it to. That shouldn't disqualify me from getting it.

I like to say that being trans is the second-worst thing that ever happened to me. (The worst was being born a boy.) Dysphoria is notoriously difficult to describe to those who haven't experienced it, like a flavor. Its official definition – the distress some transgender people feel at the incongruence between the gender they express and the gender they've been socially assigned – does little justice to the feeling. But in my experience, at least: Dysphoria feels like being unable to get warm, no matter how many layers you put on. It feels like hunger without appetite. It feels like getting on an airplane to fly home, only to realize mid-flight that this is it: You're going to spend the rest of your life on an airplane. [. . .]

I feel demonstrably worse since I started on hormones. One reason is that, absent the levees of the closet, years of repressed longing for the girlhood I never had have flooded my consciousness. I am a marshland of regret. Another reason is that I take estrogen – effectively, delayed-release sadness, a little aquamarine pill that more or less guarantees a good weep within six to eight hours.

Like many of my trans friends, I've watched my dysphoria balloon since I began transition. [. . .]

I was not suicidal before hormones. Now I often am. [. . .]

As long as transgender medicine retains the alleviation of pain as its benchmark of success, it will reserve for itself, with a dictator's benevolence, the right to withhold care from those who want it. Transgender people have been forced, for decades, to rely for care on a medical establishment that regards them with both suspicion and condescension. And yet as things stand today, there is still only one way to obtain hormones and surgery: to pretend that these treatments will make the pain go away. [. . .]

I [. . .] believe that surgery's only prerequisite should be a simple demonstration of want. Beyond this, no amount of pain, anticipated or continuing, justifies its withholding.[7]

This moving text denies doctors the right to decide on the operation, based on the old principle that the doctor is there to do good for his patients. For Andrea Long Chu, an adult subject decides for him- or herself. I find the argument convincing, if the transgender concerned is an adult. I note only one error, which results from the use of the term 'gender', which here makes it possible to make society responsible for the assignment of gender. If we keep the word 'sex', we see that it is chance that governed the assignment of sex, and that it is on the contrary society that authorizes – with the conditions which Andrea Long Chu disputes – the change of 'gender'. Nature is blind and society is emancipatory.

My feeling is that this type of open debate can take place only in a Protestant country, where, before the transgender question, there was a tradition of transformation of the body rejected by Catholicism. Eugenic sterilizations between the wars took place in Protestant countries. Male sterilization by vasectomy is now common in the Anglo-American world. Here we are brought back, with the transgender phenomenon, to the hypothesis of a zombie Protestantism.

What is striking when you read this article is the disappearance of the pleasure principle. Sexual life is no longer the issue. The issue is identity and, in this case, identity in its purest form since it relates to one of the most obvious elements of the human condition: its division into men and women.

This article tells us something else: it was published by the *New York Times*, one of the great newspapers where Anglo-American social thought is expressed. It is symptomatic of a preoccupation of the years 2015–20, within the Anglosphere, in its more highly educated classes.

Ideological centrality . . .

To take the measure of this ideological centrality, let's take another look at the OECD social report, *Society at a Glance 2019*, published ten years after the start of the Great Recession and on the eve of the Covid-19 epidemic.[8] The special topic of the year was the LGBT issue.

> This edition of *Society at a Glance* puts the spotlight on lesbians, gay men, bisexuals and transgender (LGBT) individuals, as they still suffer from various forms of discrimination. Indeed, there is still a long way to go before LGBT people meet full-fledged acceptance in OECD countries. Only half of OECD countries have legalised same-sex marriage throughout their national territory, and less than a third allow for a change of gender on official documents to match gender identity without forcing the transgender person to undergo sterilisation, sex-reassignment surgery, hormonal therapy or a psychiatric diagnosis. Steps backward have also been witnessed. Yet, discrimination is not only ethically unacceptable, it also entails substantial economic and social costs. The inclusion of sexual and gender minorities should therefore become a top policy priority for OECD governments.[9]

We can see that the OECD is here proposing the broadest definition of the transgender category: it considers as having changed sex any person who declares they have done so. Words could not be granted more power.

... but statistical weakness

If we want to progress in our historical and sociological understanding of the transgender question, we must at this stage consider its ideological centrality and its low quantitative importance. Figures without much value are in circulation: 0.3% of transgender people in the adult population in the United States and 0.7% among young people.[10] When we study behaviour such as male or female homosexuality, or bisexuality, we remain in a statistical universe accessible to opinion polls. If it is a question of measuring rates of 2%, 3% or 5%, a sample of around 10,000 people will suffice. With transgender, we are looking at a phenomenon that goes beyond the capacity of the microscope to capture. The figures we are offered are most often the result of samples biased by an element of voluntary self-designation by the subjects.

Conversely, the study conducted in the United States by Benjamin Cerf-Harris, of the Census Bureau, represents decisive progress in the quantification of the transgender phenomenon. Cerf-Harris has cross-referenced the American social security files that have existed since Roosevelt with the 2010 census in order to count changes of first name, from male to female or from female to male (with a coefficient of uncertainty, since some names can be both male and female), as well as changes in self-designation by sex.[11] It resulted for the United States in 2010 in a

259

PART II. OUR REVOLUTION

maximum of 89,000 transgender people, which would represent not 0.3% of the adult population, but 5 per 10,000, that is to say six times fewer.

The article notes an increase in the years 2000–10, but it minimizes this by rectifying the figures by way of a technique that does not convince me. One of the reasons why I am not sure that the raw figures (before adjustment) are so overestimated is the existence of a Swedish study which gives higher rates.[12] Of course, it does not constitute proof in itself. Nothing a priori would prevent the phenomenon from being statistically less significant in the United States than in Sweden. Still, it would be a statistical error to refuse to see that, even if the American data, like the Swedish data, indicate very low levels, they also reveal an increase in the 2000s, within the generation of 'millennials', that is to say people who reached adulthood in the 2000s (whom we have already seen, in the previous chapter, to be at the forefront of the question of bisexuality). Something is happening: a new fluidity is developing that associates an increase in the number of bisexual women with an increase, at a level one hundred times lower (say, by modelling, 5 per 10,000 as against 5 per 100), of transgender reassignments.

This change can also be observed in England with the increase in requests to arrest puberty by parents of children with symptoms of sexual dysphoria.[13] In the case of England, I mentioned at the beginning of this chapter the GIDS (Gender Identity Development Service), which carried out these arrests of puberty. For the whole of the United Kingdom, it registered, during the financial year 2009–10, 109 requests for reassignment. During the year 2018–19, after a steady increase, the figure was 2,364, twenty-two times the initial number. Since then, as I said, these arrests of puberty by hormonal treatment have been prohibited by a court decision, against which the GIDS has lodged an appeal.

What is really intriguing, for anyone interested in the dynamics of societies, is that the increase in the number of cases of reassignment came after the increase in the use of the term 'transgender'. Figure 16.1, on the evolution of the frequency of use of the words '*transgenre*' and 'transgender', shows that it took off as early as 1990, whereas we have just observed an increase in reassignments or requests for reassignment dating from 2000 at the earliest. We observe a priority of the ideological evolution compared to the statistical evolution of the cases. This is confirmed by Susan Stryker, herself a transgender woman and specialist in this field, in her excellent book.[14] I am therefore impressed by the prescience of Judith Butler's classic, *Gender Trouble*, published in 1990, which seems to have foreseen and even perhaps 'made' history.[15] The obscurity of her text adds to the feeling that I am dealing with a new Delphic Oracle.

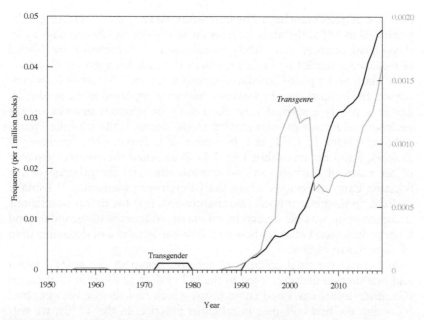

Figure 16.1 Evolution of the frequency of use of the terms 'transgender' (scale on the left) and *'transgenre'* (scale on the right)
Source: Google Ngram Viewer

Women and identity

So we face a series of factors: an initial statistical insignificance, an ideological interest, an increase in the number of cases in the last generations that does not turn transgender people into a majority phenomenon but is occurring against a backdrop of increasing bisexuality, particularly among women. How are we to make sense of these disparate elements? We must, to begin with, define an overall historical sequence that dynamically poses the question of identity. Identity is not the individual, but rather the individual who places him- or herself within a group. The expression 'collective identity' is a pleonasm. The transgender phenomenon, the epicentre and culmination of the questioning of sexual differences, results from a generalized identity disorder.

As early as 1981, at a time when the Left was interested in the nationalization of the means of production, Régis Debray drew attention in his *Critique of Political Reason* to the religious matrix of our political and social life.[16] The disappearance of collective religious belief seems indeed to be the source of all the disintegrating identities that followed. One could speak of a relative consensus on this point. We can cite, for example, Marcel Gauchet's *The Disenchantment of the World*, originally published in 1985; the author rather curiously deems Christianity, by its theological essence, more likely to disappear.[17] *Submission* by Michel Houellebecq, published in 2015, traces the link between an obsession with Islam and a post-Christian religious vacuum.[18] As far as I am concerned, the importance of religious structuring appeared to me gradually, and in a purely empirical way: the ebbing of religious practice on the periphery of France gave its rhythm to the decomposition of the French political system. In 1981, in *L'Invention de la France* (*The Invention of France*), I and my co-author Hervé Le Bras noted the complementarity of the maps of Catholicism and communism, and the progress of the Socialist Party in regions where the Church was weakening.[19] I finally realized, in the present book (see chapter 15), that the motor of religious decomposition was the accession, en masse, of *women* to secondary and higher education. Let us try here to follow the sequence of decomposition of identities to its end.

In France, the final collapse of religion began in the years 1960–5 and, within two decades, it led to the fall of derived identities – national (Gaullist, in this case) and communist, which had themselves appeared following the first collapses in religious practice. In the 1970s, we witnessed the flowering of replacement identities, regionalist identities for example: people became Basques or Bretons, or at least they tried to. The collapse of the socialist ideal under Mitterrand even led some to imagine themselves as Europeans.

In the United States, the ultimate collapse of religious identity did not occur until the turn of the millennium, but the 1980s had seen the fall of class identities. Class and religion are closely connected in the United States and their declines are intertwined. I would tend to postulate a collapse of these identities which accelerated under the Reagan presidency, and which led, as they classically do in the US, to a re-emergence of racial identities. Being non-Black is becoming important again in the United States, just as, in France, being non-Muslim will be important.

In chapter 14, I mentioned the emergence of gay identity during the 1980s and I linked it to the religious matrix by showing the filiation between the traditional Christian sexual obsession and a social identity based on sexuality. The driving role of women's liberation in male homosexual liberation was highlighted. I am here adding a connection with the collapse of class identities. But, once again, the irruption of women into the active tertiary population, and the decline of industry and of the working-class world, put the modification of the sexual order back at the heart of the general historical evolution.

The transgender emergence, on both sides of the Atlantic, occurred ten years later in ideological terms, twenty years later in terms of the statistical occurrence of cases. Would it not be 'common sense' not only to integrate it into this general movement of dilution of identities, but perhaps also to make it the culmination of a continuous process of erosion of identities, of all identities: of religion, class, nation, political ideology and region?

The general engine of this mechanism of dissolution of identities seems to me to be women's liberation, a hypothesis already proposed in chapter 10, albeit in a more restricted way. Hunter-gatherer men bore the collective, the identity of the group first and foremost, symbolized by the sharing of the products of the hunt. On this occasion, I mentioned the parodic character of residual masculine power, and therefore of the residual collective. I will repeat in the conclusion of this book why such an interpretation of the differences between men and women is not based on biological data. I am describing here a phenomenon of transition, not a stable structure, and there is nothing to stop us from thinking that the women of the future will develop a new type of capacity for feeling and taking collective action.

The fact remains that after more than half a century of decomposition of identities, if we see 1965 as a kind of starting point for the final fall of religion, accompanied by the emergence of replacement identities that were soon worn out, we can sense the quest for identity mutating between 2000 and 2020 into an active self-destruction of all identity, of everything that could integrate the individual into any group. Here, I readily admit, I am explaining nothing. But I feel *a dynamic of the erosion of identities* which is becoming socially autonomous and leading to a *generalized identity disorder*, the culmination of which is vagueness and a diffuse, nihilistic ideology that tries to abolish the fundamental category: the opposition between men and women. The rapprochement of male and female conditions actually observed nevertheless provides a factual basis for this attempt to go beyond it. Women, being less securely anchored in the collective to begin with, seem to be the driving force behind this ultimate dilution of identities. I repeat that I am not proving anything. But I am suggesting a path, a scenario for researchers, and especially those of the younger generations who are experiencing this consummation. The word 'nihilism', moreover, is fully relevant only when associated with a qualifier specifying that this nihilism, destroying concepts, categories and logical thought, presents itself as benevolent, and even fulfilling for the individual, finally released into his or her multiple potentialities. It is therefore perhaps appropriate to evoke a soft nihilism, as I spoke of a soft anomie.

The concept of *generalized identity disorder* mixes without prejudice religious, sexual, national, class and regional identities, without looking too closely into what differentiates them. It postulates that identification with a group, of whatever kind, was one of the aptitudes of the species *Homo sapiens* (this is Aristotle's man as social animal). I must admit that it came to me in a rather unexpected and trivial way, while reflecting on the case of Judith Butler: true, she is the author of *Gender Trouble*, but is also Jewish and was criticized for taking anti-Israeli and pro-Arab positions, and thus showing solidarity with countries where the status of women is among the lowest in the world. One could perhaps speak in her case of ethno-religious dysphoria. Her identity crisis is multidimensional.

A final thought comes to me on rereading this paragraph which presents the opposition between men and women as being the most elementary opposition for *Sapiens*. It's correct internally speaking. However, the opposition between human beings and animals is even more fundamental. But we can see this too weakening with more and more men and women worrying about the survival of bears and wolves or the consumption of meat. I don't know if the activists who attack slaughterhouses identify with the animals sacrificed for human consumption. But, decidedly, *self-destruction of identity* may be the right concept.

The omnipotence of mothers

Certain elements suggest a direct role for women in the transgender phenomenon. I mentioned those English dysphoric children whose parents, with the agreement of the doctors, delayed puberty. But these 'parents' are mothers. The fathers go along with it all but, as certain articles boast, mothers are the driving forces.[20] I come back to what I said about the authority of women in chapter 12. A man is not sure enough of the intrinsic value of his paternity to intervene in the biological development of his child in this way. Only a mother, who has made her child's body in her own body, can feel legitimate enough to make such a decision.

To point to the specific role played by certain women in decisions that are, in my opinion, morally reprehensible is not to demonize women. Rather, it is, once again, part of an attempt to identify their now major contribution to current historical developments, good or bad. It was also a *woman* judge who banned the practice of hormonal blockages in England.

There is another new element: probably two-thirds of adult transgender people are born male, but the direction of the flows is changing. According to GIDS statistics, while in 2009–10 there were indeed seventy-seven boys compared to thirty-two girls for whom an arrest of puberty was requested, in 2018–19 the number of requests for boys had assuredly risen to 624, but requests for girls had now hit 1,740. This inversion of the sex ratio was also observed in the United States and Canada.[21] It is the status of woman that is now most often shunned, a sign that women have accessed an anxiety previously reserved for men. We still need to understand the psychological, family and social mechanisms by which little girls, assisted by their mothers, reject a feminine identity or acquire a masculine identity.

Let's accept, as a postulate, in the case of Native American berdaches as for the Western transgender people of the past few years, that identification with the opposite sex results, at least partly, from a masculine role that did indeed imply more power, but also for some people too many responsibilities. A patridominated society, even if its kinship system is bilateral and if the participation of both sexes in the acquisition of resources is quite egalitarian, offers more anxiety-provoking male roles. The flow of gender reassignments will therefore consist more of men aspiring to a feminine status. But if a society switches to matridominance, female roles become more anxiety-provoking, an inversion that will lead to more people born as girls who want to become men. If the flow of individuals who want to escape the feminine condition outweighs those fleeing the masculine condition, this may simply mean that the feminine condition is now more anxiety-provoking than the masculine condition.

However, let's not lose sight of the statistical values, which are here very small. But the idea of a feminine condition that freedom is rendering harder than the masculine condition seems to me a strong hypothesis that cannot be rejected out of hand.

Does society think through individuals?

We saw above that the word 'transgender' took off at the beginning of the 1990s, whereas the number of cases increased from the 2000s. The transgender ideology therefore predates the statistical emergence of the phenomenon, a temporal sequence that leads to the fundamental sociological question of the influence of society on individuals who identify as transgender.

Durkheim describes a society thinking through individuals in the conclusion of *The Elementary Forms of Religious Life*.[22] He suggests – and even better, he manages to convey the feeling – that the concepts with which we reason do not depend on us but result from social interactions and are imposed on us. We are dealing not only with religious ideas, provided by society to individuals and not the other way around, but also with logical categories that are imposed by the force of the collective. Could we not see, following Durkheim, the sequence which leads from the fall of religion to transgender ideology as an example of a social phenomenon whereby the decomposition of collective beliefs produces a generalized identity disorder which, having become an ideology of the self-destruction of identities, imposes itself on certain individuals more predisposed than others not to 'belong to their sex'? I am convinced by the existence of the berdaches, and I believe that identification with a sex other than that defined by biology is a universal human possibility. But we still have to understand *the increase in frequency, in the West today*, of the number of transgender people. In short, why now? Insofar as their proportion, until very recently, was much lower than that observed in the past in American Indian populations, we could certainly imagine that what we are measuring today is a return to a kind of 'natural' rate, that of American hunter-gatherers, the 1% found by Kroeber for the Yuroks for example. But why now?

It seems to me that the Western transgender phenomenon has emerged in a very specific society, and results from an equally specific logic: we are experiencing the end of male domination, the dissolution of collective identities. Transgenderism is manifested by its centrality, finding its place in a review of the very consensual OECD. I believe that society is acting on the young people of our time in a way that offers them an uncertain relationship to sexual identity. An overall sociological analysis must underline that the mass adherents of the ideology, readers of *The New York Times* or *The Guardian*, tend themselves to be rather committed, as we saw in chapter 9, to the return to a stable heterosexual marriage. These bourgeois couples over the age of thirty-five leave single-parent families to working-class backgrounds and sex changes to young people. Again, I am trying to open up avenues of research and I will not try to pass off an intuition as a solidly demonstrated conclusion.

To sum up: sexual dysphoria does exist, and has always existed, but the way it has managed to occupy a central place in the mental system of Western societies seems to be the result of a recent ideological dynamic completely external to the individuals concerned. The use of a Durkheimian approach allows us here to grasp society thinking through individuals. We must then face the ultimate paradox: that of the middle classes who have set their sights on a stable life as a couple but who are passionate about sex changes.

The Christian taste for extraordinary sexuality

Christianity has succumbed, but I have already suggested, in connection with gay identity, that some of its values have survived it, including its obsession, negative and then positive, with sexuality. It is not impossible that the transgender phenomenon also represents a late mutation of the Christian heritage. Our societies' fascination with transgender people is a fascination with pain. The fine text by Andrea Long Chu presents the transgender condition as an unhappy one. The OECD report fights discrimination: the transgender person is not someone who has succeeded but a victim of the world. We are a long way from those berdaches who, in their pre-Christian societies, led happy lives.

266

This pain is consubstantially linked to the quest for something impossible: a change of sex, involving information inscribed in almost all of the tens of thousands of millions of cells of each individual. We are approaching a Christian problem. In *The Body and Society*, Peter Brown does not content himself with dissecting the Christian obsession with sexuality.[23] He shows that the early Christians had to justify their claim to offer eternal life. Their solution was to accomplish, here below, extraordinary actions, proof of their belonging to a superhuman order: they rejected wealth and loved the poor first. The poor person, for a Greek or a Roman, was abject. Christianity suggests that you wash a poor person's feet. For the Greco-Romans, sexuality was reasonably good. Christians say it is bad.

With transgender people, aren't we still in this good old Christianity that promises us the overcoming of our earthly humanity? The fascination with transgender people is perhaps just a revisiting of the old Christian dream of overcoming the human condition. If eternal life seems excluded, a sex change would remain a possibility. Again, the rereading of this text leads me, as in the case of animal identification, a step further, since transhumanism, contemporary with transgenderism, is again dreaming of eternal life, which went out by the door only to come back in through the window. Having spent too much time in completely irreligious Japan, I never really believed in Marcel Gauchet's idea of Christianity as a 'religion of leaving religion'.[24] My recent work would lead me, rather, to see this hypersexual Christianity as the religion one can never get out of. I specify that this remark emphasizes, to my mind, the quality of the work of Gauchet, who, by arriving at the opposite of the truth, has, according to the Principle of the Equivalence of Opposites (PEO) approached it very closely.

With the idea of a post-Christian transgenderism we can resolve our last paradox: the fascination of the middle classes who have become sexually sober again, particularly in the American world, where, as we have seen, the last bits of Christian belief are in the process of collapsing. The transgender phenomenon would then, perhaps, be like the apotheosis of zombie Protestantism. The role of women in the spread of the belief would replicate their role in the spread of early Christianity.

— 17 —

ECONOMIC GLOBALIZATION AND THE DEVIATION OF ANTHROPOLOGICAL TRAJECTORIES

In the introduction to this book, I stated that, to describe the history of women's liberation, I would stick to my usual 'levels': the political and economic conscious, the educational subconscious and the anthropological and sometimes religious unconscious. However, I specified that I would stop considering a priori that the unconscious was the most important. This horizontalization of fields makes it possible to define nuanced historical and causal sequences in which anthropology, religion, education, economics and politics alternate or, better, co-evolve. The anthropological can thus determine the economic, and the economic the anthropological. I also emphasized that women's liberation and the development of the tertiary sector together defined a historical movement.

I will add here a second principle, that of a competition that is more collective than individual and which favours the scale of the group. For the historian, what is obvious, over the last 10,000 years, is the competition between societies. They interact, and we cannot content ourselves with asking the question of their 'internal' viability, so to speak. One can very well imagine that a very original anthropological system, on some Pacific island, in some inner basin in the Chinese mountains, or even a dominant system on an American continent isolated until the sixteenth century or an Australian continent isolated until the eighteenth century, may be perfectly viable on its own. The fact remains that, brought into contact with a more efficient system, economically, educationally or militarily, or all three together, this system, viable in itself, will collapse, annihilated by the greater force of the opposing system. I beg those tender souls who think, no doubt with some reason, that morally speaking all systems are equal, to forgive me. But the point is to understand history and not to judge it.

Of course, the human species is also distinguished as a whole through rationality and individual capacity for action. But let's bear in mind that today the group is the right scale if we want to really understand the consequences of women's liberation. In the West, as regards the status of women, the essential competition does not fundamentally bring the individuals within the group into opposition with each other, but groups of individuals into opposition with other rival groups, today as yesterday. Human groups today are no longer small peoples of hunter-gatherers, LBK agricultural settlers or nomads from the steppe, but modern nations. The renunciation of war does not liberate them from competition. In truth, economic globalization has set against each other nations which, in the aftermath of the two world wars, seemed to have given themselves time for a break. Note, all the same, that between 1945 and 1990 the competition between capitalism, rooted in the nuclear family structures of the Anglosphere, and communism, based on the communitarian family structures of Russia and China, had continued; it led to the fall of communism, though the anthropological background that supported it did not disappear. The considerable demographic mass of the rival systems today a priori excludes the possibility that the peoples will die.

If the question of the ultimate victory of this or that system is still an issue in the long term, what we can already observe, above all, is that the economic complementarity and ideological rivalry have produced, at the current stage, in each of the major countries, an accentuation of its underlying anthropological tendency – either feminist or patrilineal of level 1, 2 or 3 – and maybe even a deviation. Because economic globalization affects all systems, it produces anthropological distortions in all of them, going in opposite directions, but most often leading to internal imbalances of a new kind.

So far, we have discussed various nations and cultures: the United States, England, France and Sweden, which are feminist; Thailand, which is close to them in terms of individualism and relations between the sexes, though without having to struggle, in terms of sexual life, with the weight of zombie Christianity. We have also mentioned Russia, China, Germany and Japan, all patrilineal in their various ways. The aim was to study and compare the economic, social, family and sexual structures of these societies. We have as yet to grasp the interactions between these societies. The time has come to move on from the internal dynamics of nations to their interaction in the global space.

Globalization and the tertiarization of the economy

Let us re-examine, from the perspective of globalization, the functional relationship between women's liberation and the development of the tertiary sector.

269

From the point of view of individuals, who are born, grow up, go to school and college, and then gain access to a profession (or unemployment), education comes before the economy. The development of higher education has clearly had its share of autonomy in relation to the economy, and this autonomy has produced a cultural aspiration to tertiarization. As women are making faster progress in education, we can conclude that they have been the main bearers of this aspiration. Aspiration is not the same as achievement. For mass tertiarization to take place, and because it has required an accelerated drop in the industrial workforce, it needed large parts of the secondary sector to be transferred to other societies. Economic globalization, by carrying out this transfer, has enabled the mass entry of women from certain countries into an overdeveloped tertiary sector. In practice, globalization has therefore contributed to the tertiary liberation of women, at least in the countries where there was originally quite a strong feminist tradition, in nuclear and bilateral family cultures.

For 21 OECD countries, the coefficient of correlation between, on the one hand, the proportion of women who have completed higher education and the proportion of the labour force employed in industry is negative, at −0.56: highly significant. The more women have advanced, the more industry has shrunk. But logically, we must expect industrial employment to have been promoted in other countries and the liberation of women through the tertiary sector hampered. And, of course, we will rediscover the patrilineality associated with the maintenance of, or even the increase in, the industrial workforce.

Economic or anthropological specialization?

We have become accustomed in this book to mapping phenomena on a planetary scale. Map 17.1 therefore indicates the proportion of industrial jobs in the labour force. To begin with, let's rid ourselves of the idea that automation alone enabled the deindustrialization and tertiarization of advanced societies. Globally, the proportion of the working population in industry rose from 20.3% in 2003 to 23.1% in 2020. Indeed, it is relocations that have enabled the accelerated evolution towards the tertiary sectors of Western economies. Our computers, our smartphones, our washing machines, our cars, our children's toys, our condoms, our anti-Covid masks and our paracetamol are still made by workers. They live elsewhere, and they are paid less, but they are still workers.

Let's take sub-Saharan Africa out of the analysis, as it has not yet been fully integrated into the process of globalization, which assumes a workforce that has been literate for some time and the creation of minimal infrastructures. But Africa is the last continent to have become literate.

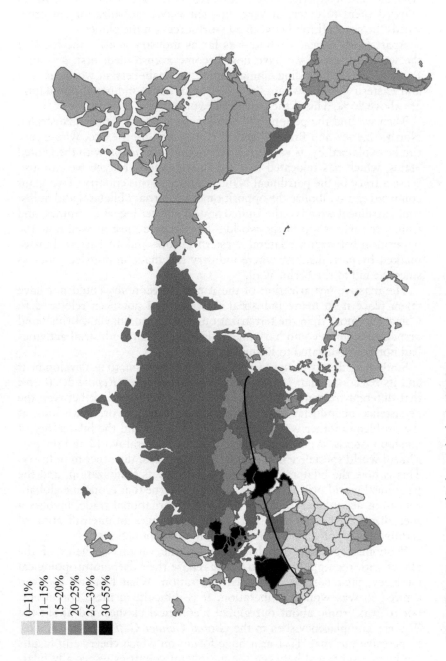

Map 17.1 Proportion of industrial jobs in 2019

0–11%
11–15%
15–20%
20–25%
25–30%
30–55%

Asia and South America were literate from the start of the 1980s, which allowed them to enter, in very different ways, globalization, in other words the competition between all workforces on the planet.

Apart from Africa, we find – as far as industry goes! – the form of the world to which we have now become accustomed: first, a central Eurasian block, including China, India, the Arab–Persian world, Russia and Eastern Europe, where the levels of an active industrial population are above 25%. This is the patrilineal world.

Then we find the periphery: Scandinavia, England, France, Australia, North America and Brazil. There is one exception: Mexico, whose case can be explained by its very strong economic interaction with the United States, which has relocated many industries there. Maybe we can also sense a trace of the patrilineal Nahua culture in this country. Two giant countries can symbolize the opposition of the tertiary bilateral and industrial patrilineal worlds – the United States, an ever bigger consumer, and China, the workshop of the world – but we could just as well note the opposition between a bilateral Western Europe and an Eastern Europe marked by patrilineality, where industry has made impressive progress since the fall of the Berlin Wall.

The massive tertiarization of the American economy could not have taken place if so many industrial activities had not been relocated to China. No more than the tertiarization of the Scandinavian, British and French economies could have taken place if so many industrial activities had not been relocated to Eastern Europe.

Studying industry brings us back again to feminism, to its development and its rejection. Map 1.3 of the *Global Gender Gap Report 2020* isn't that different from map 17.1. What we have here is a link between the persistence of industry and the patrilineal principle, or, if we look at the problem another way, between tertiarization and the bilaterality of kinship systems. We need to realize that the bilateral world and the patrilineal world specialize in tandem: one in services, the other in industry. This is how the bilateral world can accelerate its feminization, and the patrilineal world protect its masculinity. It is true that economic globalization, in accordance with the theory of international trade, favours a specialization of economies, but it also encourages an intensification of certain anthropological features found in different nations.

Economic specialization has provided the various societies of the planet with the opportunity to better realize their deep anthropological tendency, their current ideological aspiration. What bilateral societies aspired to was women's liberation. It is difficult, in these conditions, not to wax ironic about our global ideological clashes and about the Western complacency seen in the *Global Gender Gap Report*. Let's try to perceive our map 17.1 as a huge forum on which cheers and insults are being exchanged between the peripheral countries (especially bilateral) and the central countries (especially patrilineal). The peripheral countries are proud of their feminism, proud of the collapse of their homophobia – a collapse that feminism has made possible – proud of their brand-new bisexuality, and proud of their fight for transgender rights. They demand that the central countries promote more feminism, more freedom for homosexuals and an increased acceptance of transgender people. However, they do not seem aware that their own, quite radical evolution towards feminism was made possible by their specialization in tertiary activities and by the complementary industrial specialization of their retrograde ideological adversaries – let's just call them 'homophobic' so as not to have to trot out the entire list of significant traits – namely the Chinese, Russians, Iranians, Indians and Eastern Europeans. Their industrial counter-specialization has of course favoured the maintenance among these adversaries of the oldest sexual division of labour, and of patricentric societies. Let's gauge the full absurdity of the situation: the 'advanced' Western societies blame their ideological adversaries for their archaic character in matters of mores, even though it is the specialization of these adversaries in male economic activities that has enabled 'advanced' societies to fully realize their own feminist tendency!

The worker nations of Eastern Europe

The preponderant proportion of China in industrial production is well known. We may be surprised to see, on map 17.1, countries such as Algeria and Iran with a proportion of their active populations in industry at above 30%. We are dealing here with economies that are not very globalized, partially socialized, archaic and dependent on oil revenue, or even, in the case of Iran, subject to sanctions. This is, I recognize, one of the limits of a map of industrialization showing the percentage of industrial jobs in the labour force, which mixes together in the same category the production of clogs by a craftsman and the output of a large car-manufacturing company. The level of the secondary sector in countries such as Turkey, Egypt, India and Pakistan is, without a doubt, significant. My anti-Covid mask was made in Turkey, even though my television set, manufactured I don't know where, is getting het up about Erdoğan's ideological intrusion in Strasbourg where a mosque under Turkish control is being built. To take just one other example from countless I could mention: Renault is assembling the latest generation of Clio cars in Turkey and Slovenia.

One of the great lessons of this map is the staggering proportion of the industrial labour force in Eastern European countries. To gauge this fully, I will note the active industrial population in countries labelled feminist: United States, 20%; Great Britain, 18%; France, 20%; Sweden, 18%.

Within the most developed zone, Japan is at 24%, Italy at 26% and Germany at 27%. But these are countries where patrilineality is at level 1. Let's compare them with the Baltic republics: Latvia 24%, Lithuania 26%, Estonia 29%. These latter are close, geographically and industrially, to Russia which is at 27% and Ukraine at 25%.

In the old 'people's democracies', the importance of industry is continuing to rise: Romania 30%, Bulgaria 30%, Poland 32%, Slovenia 33%, Hungary 33%, Slovakia 36%, the Czech Republic 37%.

David Cayla has described in striking terms this hyperspecialization of Eastern Europe:

> In the manufacturing industry, executives and engineers tend to conglomerate in Germany while the industrial army of low-skilled workers from the continent converges in Poland and the Czech Republic. This reorganisation of the European economy does not bring solidarity or more cordial understanding among countries, but rather strengthens competition and rivalries among people, sometimes generating a type of implicit class struggle.[1]

Cayla calls these societies worker nations. In *Lineages of Modernity*, I talked of an 'inner China' within the European Union, but China has an active industrial population of only 28%, even if it remains true that 28%, related to a population of 1.4 billion inhabitants, constitutes a mass more considerable than 34.5%, related to a total population of 92 million inhabitants in the former popular democracies cited.[2] But all the same, Slovakia and the Czech Republic, with 36% and 37%, today represent a sort of industrial 'roof of the world'. These countries, as Cayla rightly notes, are integrated into the German space. It was almost inevitable that Germany, faced with its demographic problems, should turn towards this workforce, which has been well educated by communism. But, with the exception of individualist Poland, an interpretation in terms of proximity does not contradict the influence of patrilineality on industrialization.

The level 1 patrilineal character of most of Eastern Europe would have led all by itself to a resistance on the part of industry, since industry is, as we have seen, a world of men – of workers, but also of engineers and technicians. The Czech Republic has the stem family, Slovakia the communitarian family, Hungary a mixture of the two, Slovenia the stem family, Romania a nuclear family but with a peasant bias of transmission to the younger son, and thus patrilineal, Bulgaria the communitarian family. Only Poland is dominated by a nuclear family without a patrilineal inflection. For Poland, the decisive factor is very clearly an absolute proximity to Germany. The western arc of its territory was German until 1945.

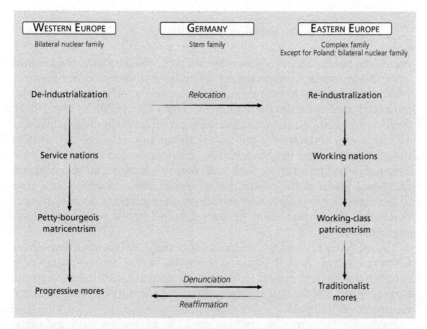

Figure 17.1 East/West dialectic of relocation/denunciation–reaffirmation

Economic and anthropological approaches help to explain the internal cultural divergence of Europe, better in any case than the incessant denunciations by *Le Monde* or *The Guardian* of the politics of Viktor Orbán in Hungary or of the Law and Justice Party in Poland. Eastern Europe is experiencing the internal distortion noted above: the European single market has ensured this area specializes in industry and has strengthened its patrilineal anthropological component. But who set this specialization in place, if not us, in the west of the continent? By specializing in the tertiary sector, we have better emancipated our women, and they have emancipated our homosexuals, but by transferring male industrial tasks and perhaps, basically, with the factories, by shifting our reactionary masculine impulses to the countries east of Germany. If we add to this interpretation the hypothesis that the East is reacting defensively to our insults, we can include the additional element of a dissociative negative acculturation, according to Devereux's concept: an identity-based reaction that is taking Eastern Europe beyond its natural masculinist conservatism (see figure 17.1).

Sweden, yet again . . .

Again, the borderline case of Sweden deserves consideration. The feminist 'roof of the world' is experiencing an industrial decline commensurate with its feminism, which in this case threatens one of the most powerful industrial traditions on the continent. From the 1970s to the 1990s, Sweden was distinguished by the excellence of its technologies. Around 1975 it was a country of 8 million inhabitants (it has nearly 10 million today), smaller than the Netherlands. This nation had two well-known automobile manufacturers, Saab and Volvo; it manufactured warplanes and was a leader in the production of special steels. Sweden was a kind of Germany in miniature and enjoyed, on an international scale, an aura that went far beyond what its demographic significance would have suggested.

Today, Saab no longer produces cars, while Volvo has come under Chinese control. And if Ericsson seems to be the western equipment supplier that is least behind in 5G, the group was crushed on the phone market in the 2000s, and is now a dwarf in comparison with Samsung Electronics or Huawei.

David Cayla notes the collapse of 21% of the Swedish industrial working population between 2000 and 2019. There are admittedly worse cases (UK, 32%; Portugal, 30%; Finland, 29%; France, 27%). This drop in the Swedish labour force employed in industry may be producing a disappearance of the commercial surplus. Between 1960 and 1984, the Swedish trade was more or less balanced. At the crucial moment of globalization and economic specialization, between 1984 and 2008, it entered a period of heavy surplus, following the example of Germany. In 2008, Sweden had a 6% GDP surplus. Since then, a steady decline has been evident. The latest figures showed a surplus corresponding to 2% of GDP.

It should be noted that Sweden's main trading partner is Germany, patrilineal and still industrial. The question that now arises is that of maintaining Swedish efficiency.

The cost of rejecting liberation

Women's liberation has thus come at a cost: the fall in productive activities, and the dependence on the outside world, a dependence of which Covid-19 has shown the dangers. During the first wave, death rates were aligned with the presence or absence of an industrial system. Among the countries which resisted the best were China (albeit using totalitarian methods), Japan, Germany and Korea. England, the United States,

France and even Sweden have been forced to face their vulnerability.[3] Is feminism dangerous for our societies? The rejection of a full and complete liberation of women actually leads to problems even more serious than the collapse of the industrial apparatus. In order to survive, a society must ensure the renewal of the generations. Reproduction comes before production. This is blindingly obvious, but it is an obviousness often forgotten by the defenders of the 'German model'.

Advanced countries that have remained industrial such as Germany, Japan or Korea, where women's liberation has, through education, reached a certain level, have been faced with a demographic dilemma. Their patrilineal trait has meant that women – statistically – have chosen between career and children, particularly if they have completed a higher education. The result of this 'choice' has been a very low fertility rate for Germany and Japan (1.5 or 1.4 children per woman), and the ultra-low rate for South Korea (1.1).[4] Feminist Western societies have long maintained much more reasonable indicators of fertility, between 1.8 and 2.0.

Between 2000 and 2015, there were two contrasting hubs when it came to demography. On the one hand, there were countries with a high status for women (the United States, the United Kingdom, France and Sweden), approaching a birth rate of two children per woman, an almost adequate reproduction of the population. On the other hand, there were patrilineal countries such as Germany and Japan, in which every generation lacked a third of the children needed to reproduce their population. Germany decided to appeal massively to immigration to maintain its economic power, while annexing the labour force of Eastern Europe; Japan has long preferred the reduction of its population and its power to massive immigration, while relocating a great deal of its production to China. The drop in its working population in certain economic sectors is becoming unbearable, and so Japan, silently, is starting to accept immigration. Its net migration, in absolute numbers, suggests that twice as many immigrants settle there each year than in France (per capita, the levels must be comparable).

We said above that the coefficient of correlation between the level of higher education of women and industry was –0.56. The coefficient linking women's higher education with fertility was +0.51 in 2015. What we are obliged to see, in rough terms (a coefficient of correlation of 0.5 explains only a quarter of the variations), is a contrast between, on the one hand, a high level of women's liberation that allows fertility to be maintained but devastates industry, and, on the other hand, an unfinished liberation that preserves industry but devastates fertility.

The future is still open. The coefficient of correlation between women's higher education and fertility, which was +0.51 in 2015, fell to +0.36 as early as 2018. Faced with declines in the standard of living and even in life expectancy in the case of the United States, feminist bilateral societies are also now registering declines in fertility.

It is important to realize that the demographic weakness of patrilineal societies, for nearly forty years, could not have persisted without economic globalization. The concentration on industrial export objectives has hindered women's liberation and, in these nations, it has aggravated the tension between profession and procreation. The masculinization of societies that have remained industrial is not an autonomous trajectory, no more than is the feminization by tertiarization that has led to a deviation in the anthropological trajectory of Western nations. Bilateral and patrilineal societies seem fully engaged in a process of mutual repulsion and deviation from their natural anthropological trajectories. If the result is, for some, a drop in the standard of living and, for others, a decline in the reproduction of life, we can describe this as a lose–lose mechanism.

CONCLUSION: HAS HUMANITY COME OF AGE?

Ideology is not reality and, as we come to the conclusion of this book, it is time to return to the reality of the world. Researchers in the humanities talk to us about 'gender'. We have seen that these researchers, 85% of whom are women, deplore the enslavement of women in a world which is actually experiencing a tension between ideological matridominance and economic–bureaucratic patridominance. Books are being published that describe the rise of antagonism between the sexes. We have located, in Gramscian terms, the social epicentre of this ideology: the 'executives and higher intellectual professions' of teaching and journalism. This epicentre contains researchers who, in France, can be economically located as executives of the public sector. Ordinary people, of which I am one (despite being a researcher), do not as yet support this ideology which veils rather than transforms the reality of the world. A study by INSEE reveals this world to us and deplores it.[1] It presents a description of the 'social roles of women and men' and their perception by the population; this text passes a judgement on the general attitude of the population.

To determine the opinion of the French on the intellectual capacities and professional skills of women, the text examines the positive or negative reaction of men and women to a series of statements: 76% of women and 75% of men think that 'a man does not naturally have more authority than a woman'; 76% of women and 80% of men think that 'men don't have a brain more competent in mathematical reasoning than women'; 93% of women and 96% of men would 'trust a female airline pilot as much as a male pilot'; 88% of women and 76% of men would 'trust a man as much as a woman to take care of children in a crèche'. It also appears that both men and women believe that the differences that still exist are of social rather than biological origin. So here we have citizens who are unable to think in terms of sexual inequality.

But ... 'If there is a pre-school child in the family, more than eight respondents out of ten are in favour of a division of tasks which implies

279

a limitation of the remunerated activity of women.' We therefore observe in the population the predominance of a belief in a particular relationship between the mother and . . . motherhood. Or, to put it differently, a belief in some difference between the sexes in their relationship with young children. The researcher – is he really aware that a child can be breastfed by its mother? – expresses his worries: 'The persistence of significant support for the sexual division of work may seem contradictory with statements that point out that skills are not determined by the sex of individuals.' One could, indeed, imagine the woman bearing a child for nine months within her then, after childbirth, detaching herself from the child *instantly*, so that her relationship with the newborn would be identical to that of the father with his child. For such an ideal to work, we would have to live in a world without the psychological principle of inertia: a world of robots. The attitude of the population seems to me to be of a pragmatic egalitarian type, expressing a commonplace and healthy belief in the complementarity of the sexes rather than antagonism. It assumes that the human being who biologically produced the child will retain a special bond with that child that extends somewhat beyond the delivery room.

This opinion poll exempts us from thinking about the fantasmatic risk of a world that would abolish the difference between men and women. Margaret Mead noted, in the conclusion of *Male and Female*, that all societies had used the difference between men and women to organize themselves.[2] They will continue, and the transgender horizon will therefore remain, like any horizon, a line which recedes as one moves towards it. The return of the Anglo-American middle classes to matrimonial stability is their reality; transgender advocacy is their dream. The model of double-wage couples, at the beginning of the third millennium, is the solidarity of the Shoshone hunter-gatherer couples, not their berdaches . . . Let us never forget that gender ideology, far from being fomented by a revolutionary class, is supported by a hypogamous petty bourgeoisie, on both sides of the Atlantic. Transgender people suffer, but society will not be destabilized by transgender ideology.

As for the war of the sexes, it does less harm to the hypogamous men of the middle classes than to single mothers from the bottom of the social structure, who indeed played a very large part in the Yellow Vests movement. One could contrast two ideal-types, in the sense of Weber, and put them face to face: the female academic who, armed with the concepts of gender and patriarchy, worries about the oppression of women in general but mainly denounces successful men from the upper middle classes; and the woman supporter of the Yellow Vests who, armed with the concept of poverty, fights against an unreasonable increase in taxes on gasoline levied by the state.

But once again, I must emphasize my refusal to hierarchize the variables of sex and class. The set of hypotheses deployed in this book would

Table C.1   The National Front vote by sex

	Men (%)	Women (%)	Sex ratio
1988	18	11	164
1995	19	12	158
2002	20	14	143
2012	20	17	118
2017	22	21	104
Intentions 2021	25	25	100

also lead to an explanation of the exceptional atomization of the Yellow Vests movement in terms of its strong female component and the lack of a sense of the collective that this implies.

One notch lower in the social structure, the evolution of the women's vote for the National Front, which has now become the National Rally, shows the power of the class vote within the female sex. In an IFOP note of April 2021 on the evolution of the National Front since 1988, Jérôme Fourquet measured the strengthening of the vote according to educational and class stratification, and the ongoing disappearance of the difference between men and women in support for the National Front. The sex ratio of 164 in favour of men in 1988 dropped steadily, reaching parity at 100 in the forecasts for 2022 given by Fourquet at the time he was writing (see table C.1).[3] Once Marine Le Pen had taken over the party, she could accelerate a process that was actually already underway in her father's time.

The generalized intersectional reflex impels us to set these data within the context of a weakening of the sex divide in relation to the class divide. Contrary to first- and second-wave feminism, antagonistic feminism is indeed a class phenomenon rooted in the petty bourgeoisie. Women from working-class backgrounds are, potentially at least, the class adversaries of the women academics who support gender theory. However absurd, the ban on abortion in some American states must be interpreted in terms of a new class conflict rather than of a lowering of the status of women. Indeed, just like the Yellow Vests movement, the pro-life movement, as explained in chapter 9, presupposes a division of women into two opposed social classes. I guess that the American example of a new class conflict within the female sex is even more significant than the French. 'Class conflict' is after all a traditional and boring piece of French discourse. But the waning explanatory power, here, of religion and race, both so important in American history, is something new. We can now see directly a class effect on a map of American states. The supreme irony of antagonistic feminism would be to lead, in the US, to the birth of a new perception of class antagonism.

* * *

This book has examined in detail the persistence of many differences in behaviour and social trajectories between women and men, and, in terms of sex equivalence, it clearly lags behind the INSEE opinion poll discussed above which points to a very egalitarian French people, except when it comes to the bond with children after their birth. I have pointed out the persistence of a strong sexual division of labour, even in Sweden, *the* country of feminism. I explained the collapse of the capacity for collective action by a lesser ability of women to take charge of a group, whether local or national. The hypothesis of a weak relationship between women and the collective leads to several satisfactory proposals for my system of values, on the weakening of racism, for example, and to others that are unfavourable to my values, on the ebbing of the economic action of nations in particular. This is, it seems to me, a guarantee of axiological neutrality.

This book has underlined the existence of a specific way in which women exercise authority. It has suggested that the collapse of economic equality and the slump in industrial potential and the standard of living have something to do with women's liberation. All of this assumes the existence of statistical differences in behaviour between men and women. But it would be absurd to deduce from this that some unsurpassable, biologically innate characteristic explains these differences. The first part of this book has schematically described the *Homo sapiens* couple over, say, its first 300,000 or 100,000 years of existence. Its second part described our anthropological revolution of the last seventy years. It would be totally implausible that 300 millennia of habits can die out in seventy years. I appeal again to the principle of inertia. But the change will continue.

Historical anthropology of the very long duration (*très longue durée*) also warns us that certain insignificant evolutions on the scale of a lifetime can, by the accumulation of generations, go very far and have regressive long-term consequences, even if their short-term effect seems promising. Chapter 5 showed how the invention of the patrilineal principle, which was considered as an achievement of modernity, ended up crippling the central part of Eurasia by enclosing women, and men, in infantilizing groups. This could be a lesson for us, leading to a new application of the principle of caution. The marginalization of one sex has brought humanity to a standstill. The inferiorization, three to five millennia later, of the opposite sex might not be a good idea.

I presented the residues of male power as fragile, going so far as to describe the persistent grip of men on the networks of power as a parody, incapable in any case of maintaining the structures of collective thought and action that human groups need. The sole masculine excellence that I have underlined is ultimately, in the purest tradition of Margaret Mead, that which stems from the fragility of men, from their inability to bear

282

a child, which frees them from an existential choice: professional self-realization remains for them the only possible option, even if excellence is achieved by withdrawing from the world into a meditation of the religious kind. There is nothing new under the sun of the masculine.

If the existential goals of men, ultimately, have hardly evolved, those of women have been profoundly shaken. The central theme of this book is that women's options have become more numerous than those of men, and that their life choices have become potentially more anxiety-provoking. I return to the original concept of Durkheimian anomie, in the transitional version of a 'soft anomie': the individual, in a constantly changing society, no longer knows what to expect from life. But for a man, the choice is simply a choice of job. For a woman, now there is the possibility of a job, but procreation remains an option. Let's be concrete and come back to those higher studies that continue to age 25; if fertility declines at age 35, that leaves a range of ten years during which to produce, without too much uncertainty, one or more children, in a context of family–work negotiation which is becoming insanely difficult. Men have nothing to do with it and there is no need to demonize them to understand this problem. Zabou Breitman puts it nicely in *Cuisine et dépendences* (*Kitchen with Apartment*), written by Jaoui and Bacri: 'Life is a delicate situation', and I would add: 'for women now perhaps more than for men'.

Ideology, which has succeeded religion, often bolsters the idea that our problems are not the result of the human condition, but of clashes between men or, now, between men and women. The right approach would be to understand that the difficulty of the human condition (the relationship to death and all that sort of thing) has, through women's liberation, split into a difficulty in the male human condition and a difficulty in the female human condition.

Let me summarize. There is an inertia in the differentiation of male and female social roles, together with a restriction that has nothing to do with intellectual or social abilities differing according to sex but with the differentiation between paternity and maternity; this sustains some men at least in a particular effort to transcend their condition, while many women have to negotiate with themselves, as much as with their partners, over the choice between profession and procreation. One to two years of gestation are sufficient to establish a gap between men and women professionally. My argument is always statistical, and I never exclude the possibility of many exceptions: men who are happy not to succeed socially and women who are capable of excelling simultaneously in work and procreation. This is the dilemma of Western societies that are very advanced in feminism.

I suggested in the last chapter of this book that the problem would not be solved purely internally for each society: the path chosen defines its effectiveness vis-à-vis other societies. The choice of patrilineality throughout the heart of Eurasia allowed the rise to power of the Western world over the last 1,000 years. But is the trajectory of Western societies still today, in a moderate and collective evolutionary sense, competitive?

I expressed the respective weaknesses of the opposing systems and the mechanism of mutual distortion they are engaged in: relatively satisfactory fertility and industrial decline on the one hand, the maintenance of industrial production and very insufficient fertility on the other. In the West the dilemma of women – work/reproduction – has led to an exaggerated tertiary orientation in the various societies. The rise in American mortality, and the Covid epidemic, warn us of the dangers of abandoning male industrial and technological occupations. But the real question is a much larger one, and brings us back to Margaret Mead's hypothesis on the deep motivation of men: compensating for their inability to have children by resorting to action. If a society wants to progress, can it really deprive itself of the extra creativity and intensity in the work men can produce thanks to their inability to manufacture children?

There remains the ultimate question about the future: the new anxiety among women, which should lead them to a creativity that we cannot even imagine. But, to end with, let's concentrate our concerns on the near future. We don't need those petty-bourgeois women who tirelessly denounce, in the name of 'gender', the oppression of one sex by another, and demonize men who have worked a bit too hard. What we need right now is women who take their part in social struggles and the organization of the collective.

284

NOTES

Notes to Preface

1 Emmanuel Todd, *La chute finale: Essai sur la décomposition de la sphère soviétique* (Paris: Robert Laffont, 1976); English translation: *The Final Fall: An Essay on the Decomposition of the Soviet Sphere*, translated by John Waggoner (New York: Katz Publishers, 1979).
2 Emmanuel Todd, *Lineages of Modernity: A History of Humanity from the Stone Age to Homo Americanus*, translated by Andrew Brown (Cambridge: Polity, 2019).
3 Emmanuel Todd, *Le Fou et le prolétaire* (Paris: Éditions Robert Laffont, 1978).

Notes to Introduction

1 #BalanceTonPorc (literally 'denounce/expose your pig') is the French equivalent of the #MeToo movement. (Translator's note.)
2 National (French) study on violent deaths within couples for the years 2018 and 2019.
3 Cédric Mathiot, 'Le nombre de fémicides augmente-t-il vraiment?', *Libération*, 20 November 2019. This article contains a very good discussion of the concepts involved.
4 OECD, *Education at a Glance 2020*, table A1.2, 'Trends in educational attainment of 25–34-year-olds, by gender (2009 and 2019)', p. 51. Available at: https://www.oecd-ilibrary.org/docserver/69096873-en.pdf?expires=1651 056088&id=id&accname=guest&checksum=7EA10D75C18744A1BC057 BA8A0B2A692.
5 Mona Chollet, *In Defence of Witches: Why Women Are Still on Trial*, translated by Sophie R. Lewis (London: Pan Macmillan, 2022).
6 Emmanuel Todd, *L'Origine des systèmes familiaux*, vol. 1, *L'Eurasie* (Paris: Gallimard, 2011).
7 Emmanuel Todd, *The Explanation of Ideology: Family Structures and Social Systems*, translated by David Garrioch (Oxford: Basil Blackwell, 1985).

8 Emmanuel Todd, *The Causes of Progress: Culture, Authority and Change*, translated by Richard Boulind (Oxford: Blackwell, 1987).
9 Emmanuel Todd, *Les Luttes de classes en France au XXIe siècle* (Paris: Seuil, 2020).
10 The first published version seems to have been *The History of Human Marriage* (London: MacMillan & Co, 1891). The Finnish version dates from 1932. The French translation was published between 1934 and 1945.
11 Kathryn R. Kirby, Russell D. Gray, Simon J. Greenhill, Fiona M. Jordan, Stephanie Gomes-Ng, Hans-Jörg Bibiko et al., 'D-PLACE: A Global Database of Cultural, Linguistic and Environmental Diversity', *PLOS One*, 11 (7), 2016, doi: 10.1371/journal.pone.0158391. The project is available at: d-pla ce.org.
12 https://le-seuil.shinyapps.io/ose2022.
13 Todd, *Lineages of Modernity*.
14 The pill is obviously not the only modern contraceptive method, but it has had an unparalleled symbolic and effective weight, despite differences from one country to the next. In France, it is a more important means of contraception than elsewhere. In Japan, on the contrary, it was rejected for a long time.
15 This law is known by the name of Simone Veil, the Minister of Health under whom it was passed. (Translator's note.)
16 Judith Butler, *Gender Trouble* (New York: Routledge, 1990).
17 On the appearance of the concepts of patridominance and matridominance, see below, p. 42.
18 This representation reached its final form in my *Lineages of Modernity*. See Introduction, pp. 9–15.
19 Mirra Komarovsky, *The Unemployed Man and His Family: The Effect of Unemployment upon the Status of the Man in Fifty-Nine Families* (New York: Dryden Press, 1940).
20 Michael Young and Peter Willmott, *Family and Kinship in East London* (London: Routledge & Kegan Paul, 1957).
21 Olivier Schwartz, *Le monde privé des ouvriers: Hommes et femmes du Nord* (Paris: PUF, 1990).
22 Hanna Rosin, *The End of Men: And the Rise of Women* (New York: Riverhead Book, 2012).
23 See, on the Na of China, Cai Hua, *Une Société sans père ni mari: Les Na de Chine* (Paris: PUF, 1997); and, on the Nambudiri Brahmins of Kerala, the article by Joan P. Mencher and Helen Goldberg, 'Kinship and Marriage Regulations among the Namboodiri Brahmans of Kerala', *MAN*, new series, 2 (1), 1967, pp. 87–106.
24 See, for example, Harold E. Driver and William C. Massey, *Comparative Studies of North American Indians* (Philadelphia, PA: American Philosophical Society, 1957); Julian H. Steward, *Basin–Plateau Aboriginal Sociopolitical Groups* (Washington, DC: Smithsonian Institution, Bureau of American Ethnology, Bulletin 120, 1938); Alfred Kroeber, *Cultural and Natural Areas of Native North America* (Berkeley and Los Angeles, CA: University of California Press, 1939).
25 Available at: https://le-seuil.shinyapps.io/ose2022.

Notes to Chapter 1

1 The French word '*patriarcat*' covers both English 'patriarchy' and 'patriarchate' – something that Todd discusses in the next sentence. (Translator's note.)

2 The French word '*genre*' can mean, for example, 'type' as well as 'gender'. (Translator's note.)

3 Auke Rijpma and Sarah G. Carmichael, 'Testing Todd and Matching Murdock: Global Data on Historical Family Characteristics', *Economic History of Developing Regions*, 31 (1), January 2016, pp. 10–46. Rijpma and Carmichael also note the weakness of my description of Africa in my first book, *The Explanation of Ideology*. I had indeed grouped all family types into one category: see Emmanuel Todd, *The Explanation of Ideology: Family Structures and Social Systems*, translated by David Garrioch (Oxford: Basil Blackwell, 1985). Murdock, on the other hand, is strong on Africa, to which he has also devoted a complete book: *Africa: Its Peoples and Their Culture History* (New York: McGraw-Hill, 1959). The article by Rijpma and Carmichael, however, verifies that there is a good general agreement between the two samples.

4 For a summary presentation of the data codified from the Yale HRAFs, see George Peter Murdock, 'Ethnographic *Atlas*: A Summary', *Ethnology*, 6 (2), 1967, pp. 109–235.

5 The D-PLACE project offers a visualization of the 'raw' data of the *Atlas*, useful as a first approach but not always very user-friendly due to its choice of colours, its failure to group certain categories together, etc. This is why we have built our own visualization tool, available at https://le-seuil.shinyapps.io/ose2022.

6 The weakness of the *Atlas* on Europe was noted above.

7 For China, see Margery Wolf, 'Women and Suicide in China', in Margery Wolf, Roxane Witke and Emily Martin, *Women in Chinese Society* (Stanford, CA: Stanford University Press, 1975). In Taiwan in 1905, the suicide rate per 100,000 population was 19.5 for women, 13.5 for men (ibid., p. 117). For Russia, see figures 9.1–9.3 in the present work.

8 The database is presented in Paola Giuliano and Nathan Nunn, 'Ancestral Characteristics of Modern Populations', *Economic History of Developing Regions*, 33 (1), 2018, pp. 1–17. It is available at: https://scholar.harvard.edu/nunn/publications/ancestral-characteristics-modern-populations.

9 They write: 'We link the ancestral characteristics from the ethnographic samples to current population distributions using the sixteenth edition of the *Ethnologue: Languages of the World* (Gordon 2009), a data source that maps the current geographic distribution of over 7,000 different languages and dialects, each of which we manually matched to one of the ethnic groups from the ethnographic data sources.'

10 Johann Jakob Bachofen, *Mother Right: A Study of the Religious and Juridical Aspects of Gynecocracy in the Ancient World*, 5 vols, translated by David Partenheimer (Lewiston, NY: Edwin Mellen, 2003–8). Originally published as: *Das Mutterrecht: Eine Untersuchung über die Gynaikokratie der alten Welt nach ihrer religiösen und rechtlichen Natur* (Stuttgart: Verlag von Krais & Hoffmann, 1861).

11 Marija Gimbutas, *The Goddesses and Gods of Old Europe. 6500–3500 BC* (Berkeley, CA: University of California Press, 1982).
12 Sandrine Teixido, Héloïse Lhérété and Martine Fournier, 'Les *Gender studies* pour les nul(le)s', *Sciences humaines*, no. 157, February 2005.
13 'Études de genre', [French] Wikipédia, accessed 29 January 2021.
14 Jacques Derrida, 'Qu'est-ce que la déconstruction?', *Commentaire*, 2004/4, no. 108: 'During an unpublished interview recorded on 30 June 1992, Jacques Derrida gave this long oral response: "This term 'deconstruction' should be understood not in the sense of dissolving or destroying, but of analyzing the sedimented structures that form the discursive element, the philosophical discursivity in which we think. It involves language, Western culture, and the whole of what defines [*sic*] the way we belong to this history of philosophy. The word 'deconstruction' already existed in French, but its use was very rare. I first used it to translate words, one found in Heidegger, who spoke of 'destruction', the other in Freud, who spoke of 'dissociation'. But very soon, of course, I tried to demarcate how, under the same word, what I called deconstruction was not simply Heideggerian or Freudian. I have devoted quite a lot of my work to marking both a certain debt towards Freud, towards Heidegger, and a certain inflection of what I have called deconstruction."'
15 Butler, *Gender Trouble*.
16 I found these concepts in a 1971 anthropological paper, where they are used to summarize a measure of the respective shares of men and women in food production (Melvin Ember and Carol R. Ember, 'The Conditions Favoring Matrilocal versus Patrilocal Residence', *American Anthropologist*, 73 (3), June 1971). But this article refers to an earlier use by Driver and Massey (Harold E. Driver and William C. Massey, *Comparative Studies of North American Indians*, Philadelphia, PA: American Philosophical Society, 1957), which associates the matridominance of women in obtaining food resources with the tendency to matrilocality in North America. (Matrilocality, just to remind the reader, is the tendency of young couples to settle with the wife's family. It produces a local aggregation centred on kinship between women.)
17 Kimberlé Crenshaw, 'Demarginalizing the Intersection of Race and Sex: A Black Feminist Critique of Antidiscrimination Doctrine, Feminist Theory and Antiracist Politics', *University of Chicago Legal Forum*, 140, 1989, pp. 139–67.
18 By using the terms 'harmonic' and 'disharmonic' I am parodying the vocabulary of anthropology which considers, for example, a patrilocal patrilineal system to be harmonic and a patrilocal matrilineal system to be disharmonic although there is no real relationship between intersectional analysis and anthropology.
19 Sonya Faure, 'Intersectionnalité [nom]: concept visant à révéler la pluralité des discriminations de classe, de sexe et de race', *Libération*, July 2015.
20 See Hervé Le Bras and Emmanuel Todd, *Le Mystère français* (Paris: Seuil, 2013), pp. 224–5. The exogamy rate among men from the Sahel is even higher (59%).

Notes to Chapter 2

1 Ruth Benedict, *Patterns of Culture* (Boston, MA: Mariner Books, 1934).
2 Recent ethnicist claims have led to the replacement of the term 'Kwakiutl' by

'Kwakwaka'wakw', but I will stick to the name traditionally used by anthropology to designate this people famous for its custom of the potlatch, a competitive exchange of gifts in a highly hierarchical society. The D-PLACE project has unfortunately adopted some of these new designations, causing us to waste hours of work comparing the data of the *Ethnographic Atlas* of Murdock with those of Charles Callender and Lee M. Kochems on berdaches (see chap. 16).

3 Margaret Mead, *Male and Female: A Study of the Sexes in a Changing World* (New York: William Morrow & Company, 1949).
4 Audrey Richards, 'Some Types of Family Structure among the Central Bantu', in A.R. Radcliffe-Brown and D. Forde (eds.), *African Systems of Kinship and Marriage* (London: Oxford University Press, 1950).
5 Lucy Mair, *Marriage* (Harmondsworth: Penguin, 1971), and *African Societies* (London: Cambridge University Press, 1974).
6 Irawati Karve, *Kinship Organization in India* (Pune: Deccan College, 1953).
7 Germaine Tillion, *Le Harem et les cousins* (Paris: Seuil, 1966).
8 June Helm, 'Bilaterality in the Socio-territorial Organization of the Arctic Drainage Dene', *Ethnology*, 4 (4), 1965. For Australia, see, from eight years later, Warren Shapiro, 'Residential Grouping in Northeast Arnhem Land', *Man*, 8 (8), 1973, pp. 365–83.
9 Chie Nakane, *Kinship and Economic Organization in Rural Japan* (London: Athlone Press, 1967).
10 Phyllis M. Kaberry, *Aboriginal Woman: Sacred and Profane* (London: George Routledge & Sons, 1939).
11 Hildred Geertz, *The Javanese Family: A Study of Kinship and Socialization* (New York: Free Press of Glencoe, 1961).
12 Margery Wolf, *Women and the Family in Taiwan* (Stanford, CA: Stanford University Press, 1972).
13 Nancy E. Levine, *The Dynamics of Polyandry: Kinship, Domesticity and Population on the Tibetan Border* (Chicago, IL: University of Chicago Press, 1988).
14 Richard B. Lee and Irven DeVore (eds.), *Man the Hunter: The First Intensive Survey of a Single, Crucial Stage of Human Development. Man's Once Universal Hunting Way of Life* (Chicago, IL: Aldine, 1968).
15 Carol Ember, 'Myths about Hunter Gatherers', *Ethnology*, 17 (4), 1978, pp. 439–48.
16 Julian H. Steward, *Basin–Plateau Aboriginal Sociopolitical Groups* (Washington, DC: Smithsonian Institution, Bureau of American Ethnology, Bulletin 120, 1938), reprint (Salt Lake City, UT: University of Utah Press, 1997), p. 242.
17 Martin King Whyte, *The Status of Women in Preindustrial Societies* (Princeton, NJ: Princeton University Press, 1978).
18 Ibid., pp. 167–8.
19 Henrietta Moore, *Feminism and Anthropology* (Minneapolis, MN: University of Minnesota Press, 1988).
20 Ibid., p. 1.
21 Marilyn G. Gelber, *Gender and Society in the New Guinea Highlands: An Anthropological Perspective on Antagonism toward Women* (New York: Avalon Publishing, 1986).
22 Ibid., p. 154.

23 Janet Carsten, *After Kinship* (Cambridge: Cambridge University Press, 2003).
24 Ibid., p. 59.
25 See, for example, Hugh D.R. Baker, *Chinese Family and Kinship* (London: Macmillan, 1979), p. 47.
26 John E. Williams, Susan M. Bennett and Deborah L. Best, 'Awareness and Expression of Sex Stereotypes in Young Children', *Developmental Psychology*, 11 (5), 1975, pp. 635–42.
27 https://decasia.org/academic_culture/2009/09/12/gender#-imbalance-in-anthropology/.
28 https://www.amacad.org/humanities-indicators/higher-education/gender#-distributiondegrees-history.
29 Peter Laslett (ed.), with the assistance of Richard Wall, *Household and Family in Past Time* (Cambridge: Cambridge University Press, 1972).
30 Paul Kirchhoff, 'Kinship Organization: A Study of Terminology', *Africa*, 5 (2), 1932, pp. 184–91.
31 Brian P. Levack (ed.), *The Oxford Handbook of Witchcraft in Early Modern Europe and Colonial America* (Oxford: Oxford University Press, 2013).
32 Ibid., pp. 449–67.
33 I disregard the possibility of transgender individuals among contributors, the distribution of which could modify the meaning of the analysis. This remark, of little importance here, no doubt, is a methodological one. The sex ratio of the authors cannot here be substantially amended. When we come to the analysis of works that study the transgender phenomenon, this precaution will not be absurd. I am constrained by my definition of women as being able to bear children, and men as unable to do so. Only transgender men (women having opted for the male gender) can potentially bear a child.

Notes to Chapter 3

1 For the emergence of the concept of 'the developmental cycle in domestic groups' in anthropology, see Jack Goody (ed.), *The Developmental Cycle in Domestic Groups* (Cambridge: Cambridge University Press, 1958).
2 Bae Wo, 'Sex Ratio at Birth in Korea', *Bogeon sahoe nonjib*, 11 (2), 1991, pp. 114–31, https://pubmed.ncbi.nlm.nih.gov/12179748/ and Statistics Korea, http://kostat.go.kr/portal/eng/pressReleases/8/10/index.board?bmode=read&aSeq=273490&pageNo=4&rowNum=10&amSeq=&sTarget=title&sTxt.
3 Orvar Löfgren, 'Family and Household among Scandinavian Peasants: An Exploratory Essay', *Ethnologia Scandinavica*, 1974, pp. 17–52.
4 Todd, *L'Origine des systèmes familiaux*.
5 Chie Nakane, *Garo and Khasi: A Comparative Study in Matrilineal Systems* (Paris and The Hague: Mouton, 'Cahiers de l'homme', 1967).
6 Peter Czap, '"A Large Family: the Peasant's Greatest Wealth": Serf Households in Mishino, Russia, 1814–1858', in Richard Wall (ed.), *Family Forms in Historic Europe* (Cambridge: Cambridge University Press, 1983), pp. 105–51.
7 N.J. Coulson, *Succession in the Muslim Family* (Cambridge: Cambridge University Press, 1971).

8 Divya Leducq, 'The Spatial Diffusion of IT in India', *EchoGéo*, no. 10, September 2009. Mumbai used to be Bombay, and Chennai was Madras. Maharashtra, the state of which Mumbai is the capital, speaks an Indo-European language, but its marriage system is of the Dravidian type, which means it practises cross-cousin marriage.

Notes to Chapter 4

1 Frédéric Le Play, *L'Organisation de la famille selon le vrai modèle signale par l'histoire de toutes les races et de tous les temps* (Paris: Téqui, 1871), chap. 1, p. 16 of the second edition (1875).
2 Edward Westermarck, *The History of Human Marriage*, 3 vols, 5th edn (London: Macmillan and Co., 1921).
3 Claude Lévi-Strauss, 'The Family', in Harry L. Shapiro, *Man, Culture and Society* (Oxford: Oxford University Press, 1956), pp. 261–85.
4 Robert Harry Lowie, *Primitive Society* (New York: Liveright Publishing Society, 1919); George Peter Murdock, *Social Structure* (London: Collier-Macmillan, 1949).
5 Also known as the San. (Translator's note.)
6 Whyte, *The Status of Women in Preindustrial Societies*, p. 172.
7 Laurent Sagart and Emmanuel Todd, 'Une Hypothèse sur l'origine du système familial communautaire', *Diogène*, no. 160, 1992, pp. 145–75.
8 As a reminder, Robert Lowie's classic, which dates from 1919, was called *Primitive Society*. As for Murdock, though he may have included in his sample, in low doses and often with errors, various modern peoples (the Irish, the Russians, and so on) and added various historical peoples such as the ancient Romans, we still find in him the usual inability of anthropology to fully include modern Western peoples into his field of analysis. What allowed me to escape this limitation was my anthropological training at Cambridge, where I studied the history of the family in Europe's past.
9 I am using the types as they are defined in *L'Origine des systèmes familiaux*, but the existence of a tempered, rather than pure, nuclear family in Spain is quite possible.
10 I would have liked to extend the patrilineal axis of the Old World as far as Dakar, in homage to the rally of the same name, but this would have entailed an unacceptable lack of precision. The epicentre of the patrilineal principle is located inside West Africa, as is the hub of agricultural innovation. When we get closer to the Atlantic coast, family and kinship systems become more bilateral. Thus, the Wolofs, who dominate Senegal, show a gradient leading from patrilineality to bilaterality when we go from the interior to the coast. But the same can be said of the Yorubas of Nigeria. In Ghana and in Côte d'Ivoire, on the contact front of the patrilineal advance, we encounter the Ashanti matrilineal systems.
11 Todd, *Lineages of Modernity*, chap. 2.
12 In *L'Origine des systèmes familiaux*, I use the term 'patrilocal' rather than 'virilocal' to describe the tempered nuclear family, in the case of marriage on the husband's side, and the term 'matrilocal' rather than 'uxorilocal' in the case of marriage on the wife's side. Here, I reserve the term 'patrilocal' or 'matrilocal' for stable complex family types (stem or communitarian

families), to bring me as close as possible to the categories of the *Ethnographic Atlas*.

13 Laurent Barry, *La Parenté* (Paris: Gallimard, 2008).
14 See Todd, *L'Origine des systèmes familiaux*, chap. 8, 'Europe patrilinéaire', pp. 313–75, in particular the map on p. 315.
15 Kirchhoff, 'Kinship Organization'.
16 Murdock's complex family types are harder to use and I will not map them here. The *Atlas*'s categories for family organization are not always up to date. This is not too much of a problem for nuclear family systems, insofar as, by definition, they are simple. In contrast, the map of complex family systems as described by Murdock doesn't work for the whole planet. The problem doesn't come from what Murdock calls 'minimal extended', which corresponds to the stem family: it is found placed, correctly, in Ireland, in the north of the Iberian peninsula, in Germany, in Japan and in Korea (and, erroneously, this time, in Russia). The problem lies with everything else. Murdock mixes very stable, very compact, patrilineal family systems, which I call communitarian, that do indeed dominate Eurasia and West Africa, and complex family systems which, although they are extensive, are based on a principle of bilocality, and can correspond, for example, to fluid associations of brothers and sisters mixed together. The limited or broad extended families that we distinguish in America corresponds to this – in other words, to bilateral kinship systems.
17 Typical cases: sororal polygyny in which the co-wives co-reside or non-sororal polygyny in which the co-wives have separate living quarters. Atypical cases: sororal polygyny in which co-wives are not reported as co-residing, and non-sororal polygyny in which wives are not reported as having separate residences.

Notes to Chapter 5

1 See, for example, his *What Happened in History* (London: Penguin Books, 1942).
2 Murdock, in his *Africa: Its Peoples and Their Culture History*, plumps for the independence of this zone, while others such as Peter Bellwood are dubious, and yet others think the complete opposite.
3 As in the translation of Emmanuel Todd's *Lineages of Modernity* (Cambridge: Polity Press, 2019), I here follow the author in using the term 'Indian' and 'American Indian' for the Indigenous peoples of North America; the nomenclature is vexed, and no term ('Indigenous', 'Native American', 'Amerindian' etc.) has met with complete approval. (Translator's note.)
4 See p. 291, n. 12.
5 R. Alexander Bentley, Penny Bickle, Linda Fibiger, Geoff M. Nowell, Christopher W. Dale, Robert E.M. Hedges, et al., 'Community Differentiation and Kinship among Europe's First Farmers', *PNAS*, 109 (24), 2012, pp. 9326–30. For the colonization effect moving west, see Marek Zvelebil and Paul Pettitt, 'Biosocial Archeology of the Early Neolithic: Synthetic Analyses of a Human Skeletal Population from the LBK Cemetery in Vedrovice, Czech Republic', *Journal of Anthropological Archaeology*, 32 (3), 2013, pp. 313–29.

6 R. Alexander Bentley, Michael Pietrusewsky, Michele Toomay Douglas and Tim C. Atkinson, 'Matrilocality during Prehistoric Transition to Agriculture in Thailand?', *Antiquity*, 79 (306), 2005, pp. 1–17.

7 Lyle W. Konigsberg and Susan R. Frankenberg, 'Postmarital Residence Analysis', in Marin A. Pilloud and Joseph T. Hefner (eds.), *Biological Distance Analysis* (Amsterdam: Elsevier, 2016), pp. 335–47.

8 Penny Bickle and Alasdair Whittle (eds.), *The First Farmers of Central Europe: Diversity in LBK Lifeways* (Oxford: Oxbow Books, 2013).

9 Todd, *L'Origine des systèmes familiaux*, p. 117.

10 Childe, *What Happened in History*.

11 Todd, *L'Origine des systèmes familiaux*, p. 258.

12 Alfred Kroeber, *Cultural and Natural Areas of Native North America* (Berkeley and Los Angeles, CA: University of California Press, 1939), map between pp. 134 and 135.

13 Ibid., p. 220.

14 See above, p. 34.

15 This phenomenon was noted by William Goode in *World Revolution and Family Patterns* (New York: Free Press of Glencoe, 1963).

16 Emmanuel Todd, 'Mobilité géographique et cycle de vie en Artois et en Toscane au XVIIIe siècle', *Annales ESC*, 30 (4), 1975, pp. 726–44, and 'Seven Peasant Communities in Pre-industrial Europe', typewritten PhD dissertation, University of Cambridge, 1975.

17 Alain Gabet, 'Structures familiales et comportements collectifs en Haut-Poitou au xviiie siècle', typewritten PhD dissertation, University of Poitiers, 2004; Jean-Claude Peyronnet, 'Famille élargie ou famille nucléaire? L'exemple du Limousin au début du xixe siècle', *Revue d'histoire moderne et contemporaine*, XXII (4), 1975, pp. 568–82.

18 The manufacture of bronze, an alloy of copper and tin, needs these two metals to be brought together and would not have been possible without the trading organization of the cities of Mesopotamia. The Bronze Age defined a space extending from the mines of the Urals to the consumer zone of Denmark.

19 Emmanuel Todd, *The Causes of Progress: Culture, Authority and Change*, translated by Richard Boulind (Oxford: Blackwell, 1987).

20 Whyte, *The Status of Women in Preindustrial Societies*, table 8, p. 133.

Notes to Chapter 6

1 Shapiro, 'Residential Grouping in Northeast Arnhem Land'.

2 A.P. Elkin, *The Australian Aborigines* (New York: Doubleday in collaboration with the American Museum of Natural History, 1964).

3 Alain Testart, *Avant l'histoire: L'évolution des sociétés, de Lascaux à Carnac* (Paris: Gallimard, 2012), see chaps 5 and 6 and in particular his diagram of evolution (p. 323).

4 Alfred L. Kroeber, *Cultural and Natural Areas of Native North America* (Berkeley and Los Angeles, CA: University of California Press, 1939). In Kroeber's view, there is no original Great Plains culture because the presence of horses allowed the late entry of groups from all regions outside the zone.

5 Bronisław Malinowski, *The Family among the Australian Aborigines:*

A Sociological Study (London: University of London Press, 1913). This book is not a field study but a particularly systematic and rigorous synthesis of all previous monographic studies.

6 Elkin, *The Australian Aborigines*.

7 Phyllis M. Kaberry, *Aboriginal Woman: Sacred and Profane* (London: George Routledge & Sons, 1939).

8 H.C. Brookfield, 'The Highland Peoples of New Guinea: A Study of Distribution and Localization', *The Geographical Journal*, 127 (4), 1961, pp. 436–48.

9 Peter Bellwood, *First Farmers* (Malden, MA: Blackwell, 2005), p. 144. On agricultural innovations, see also Marcel Mazoyer and Laurence Roudart, *Histoire des agricultures du monde* (Paris: Seuil, 1997), map on p. 69.

10 See above, chapter 2.

11 We find this combination in the matrilineal system of the Trobriand Islands so well described by Malinowski.

12 Peter Gluckman, Alan Beedle and Mark Hanson, *Principles of Evolutionary Medicine* (Oxford: Oxford University Press, 2009), p. 141.

Notes to Chapter 7

1 George P. Murdock and Caterina Provost, 'Factors in the Division of Labour by Sex: A Cross-Cultural Analysis', *Ethnology*, 12 (2), 1973, pp. 203–35. Alain Testart, *Essai sur les fondements de la division du travail chez les chasseurs-cueilleurs* (Paris: Éditions de l'École des hautes études en sciences sociales, 'Cahiers de l'homme', 1986).

2 Robert Kelly settles the question of female Agta hunters as the exception that confirms the rule, in *The Lifeways of Hunter-Gatherers: The Foraging Spectrum* (Cambridge: Cambridge University Press, 2013), pp. 219–20.

3 Testart, *Essai sur les fondements*.

4 Randall Haas, James Watson, Tammy Buonasera, John Southon, Jennifer C. Chen, Sarah Noe, et al., 'Female Hunters of the Early Americas', *Science Advances*, 6 (45), 4 November 2020.

5 Paola Tabet, 'Les mains, les outils, les armes', *L'Homme*, no. 3–4, special issue: *Les Catégories de sexe en anthropologie sociale*, 1979, pp. 5–61.

6 Currently, prehistorians are themselves trying to reproduce the tools and other artefacts of our distant ancestors so as to gain a better understanding of them. One talented prehistorian, interviewed about this, told me something that I really must share: 'It's funny: in our groups, it's always the men who want to carve flints and the women who want to make pottery.'

7 Frank Marlowe, 'Paternal Investment and the Human Mating System', *Behavioural Processes*, 51 (1–3), 2000, pp. 45–61.

8 Kaberry, *Aboriginal Woman*.

9 There is an excellent (and unintentionally amusing) presentation of the terms of the debate in Kenneth Ames, 'On the Evolution of the Human Capacity for Inequality and/or Egalitarianism', in T. Douglas Price and Gary M. Feinman (eds.), *Pathways to Power: New Perspectives on the Emergence of Social Inequality* (New York: Springer, 2012), pp. 15–44.

10 Todd, *Lineages of Modernity*.

11 The transition from the pragmatic equality of hunter-gatherers to the

inequality of Neolithic societies is an insoluble problem for methodological individualism, for two reasons, which come down in fact to just one.

(1) The first *Homo sapiens* groups did not think in terms of equality or inequality, two concepts that would be born together as antagonists. Hunter-gatherers are undifferentiated, that is to say not conceptually polarized, on this point as on many others: they are neither egalitarian nor inegalitarian, neither patrilineal nor matrilineal, neither patrilocal nor matrilocal; they are basically exogamous but tolerate some marriages between cousins, they are nuclear but practise temporary co-residence, they are rather monogamous but can have up to 15% polygyny or polyandry, etc.

(2) They exist as groups and never only as individuals. It is inside the group – this is actually a tautology – that the strict notions of inequality and equality develop, in that order it seems to me, as far as the family is concerned, which is a stem family before it is a communitarian family. What we need to try and conceptualize is a group that differentiates itself according to an inegalitarian or egalitarian mode. The rise of some fiercely inegalitarian Neolithic societies – with human sacrifice, cannibalism, etc. – cannot be thought of without reference to a group which 'holds together' because it pre-exists differentiation. The hypothesis of an inequality that emerges as the free expression of a tendency of the 'individual' is unrealistic at first glance, and above all logically impossible if we think for just a minute for two reasons: there is no rich man without the poor man, no master without slaves, no 'superior' individual without reference to a group. It is the collective that allows inequality, not the individual.

Notes to Chapter 8

1 See Todd, *Lineages of Modernity*, chap. 9: 'The English Matrix of Globalization', pp. 153–73.

2 Ibid. I analysed this process in detail, in chapter 6 for the Europe of Latin Christianity as a whole, and in chapter 9 for England specifically.

3 Rachel Guillas, 'Le silence des penseurs ecclésiastiques du Moyen Âge sur la question de la primogéniture', a paper given at the seminar 'L'émergence du droit d'aînesse: Où en sommes-nous? Sur l'origine de la primogéniture en Occident (IXe–XIIIe siecles)', Université Panthéon-Assas, Paris-II, 17 April 2019.

4 Ibid.

5 Joshua R. Goldstein, 'A Secular Trend toward Earlier Male Sexual Maturity: Evidence from Shifting Ages of Male Young Adult Mortality', *PLOS One*, 6 (8), 17 August 2011.

6 Hector Gutierrez and Jacques Houdaille, 'La mortalité maternelle en France au XVIIIe siècle', *Population*, 38 (6), 1983, pp. 975–94.

7 I have been trying for at least forty years to understand the Protestant personality, which is, after all, at the heart of the ascent of the West. So: we can distinguish in Protestantism an egalitarian earthly component and an inegalitarian metaphysical component. Predestination is in fact only the metaphysical, inegalitarian dimension of Protestantism, as I defined it in *L'Invention de l'Europe*: see Emmanuel Todd, *L'Invention de l'Europe* (Paris: Seuil, 1990). The demand for direct access for all people to the reading of the holy

texts constitutes Protestantism's earthly and egalitarian component. I noted at the time the contradiction between these two components, and I felt that it enabled me to grasp the dynamic element in Protestantism. But there was an even deeper contradiction that I failed to grasp. There is a paradox in the Protestant personality, whether Lutheran or Calvinist, structured by a belief in predestination which *ought* to lead to passivity but instead seems to lead to the opposite, to a constant educational, economic and social activity – hence the success of Protestant societies. There is an apparent contradiction here: if every man is called to death or to eternal life by a decree of God which preceded his birth, why should he be so restless? Why not wait, in a state of inactivity, for the revelation of God's choice for him – saved or damned? Earthly success on earth is indeed closely observed, anxiously awaited as the indication, coming from outside, of God's choice. But one could say that the passivity of the Protestant man is only superficial. It seems to me that the only way to resolve the contradiction is to bring in the concept of the unconscious. The Protestant individual is driven to action by his or her unconscious; the unconscious guides Protestants in their efforts towards intellectual or social success, and their success here below will then be interpreted as a mark of divine election. The Protestant unconscious gets around God's power; without the believer realizing, the unconscious replaces God. If the anguish born of predestination were not so strong, we could detect a comic element in this mechanism, since God's merciless decree, to death or to life, comes in fact from the depths of the human being. What we have here is a mental system that, through literacy, combines a heightened awareness of the self with an intensified unconscious action.

8 Steven Ozment, *When Fathers Ruled: Family Life in Reformation Europe* (Cambridge, MA: Harvard University Press, 1983).
9 Janine Garrisson-Estèbe, *L'homme protestant* (Paris: Hachette, 1980).
10 Eileen Power, *Mediaeval Women* (Cambridge: Cambridge University Press, 1997). This work was published posthumously, as Power died in 1940.
11 Ozment, *When Fathers Ruled*, pp. 25–49.
12 Erich Fromm, 'The Theory of Mother Right and Social Psychology', in *The Crisis of Psychoanalysis: Essays on Freud, Marx and Social Psychology* (London: Jonathan Cape, 1971), pp. 106–34, especially p. 131.
13 Lawrence Stone, *The Family, Sex and Marriage in England 1500–1800* (Harmondsworth: Penguin Books, 1979), p. 111.
14 Brian P. Levack, *The Witch-Hunt in Early Modern Europe* (London: Routledge, 2016), p. 129. See also Brian P. Levack (ed.) *The Oxford Handbook of Witchcraft in Early Modern Europe and Colonial America* (Oxford: Oxford University Press, 2013).
15 Peter Brown, *The Body and Society: Men, Women and Sexual Renunciation in Early Christianity* (New York: Columbia University Press, 1988).

Notes to Chapter 9

1 Michael Young and Peter Willmott, *Family and Kinship in East London* (London: Routledge & Kegan Paul, 1957).
2 Olivier Schwartz, *Le Monde privé des ouvriers: Hommes et femmes du Nord* (Paris: PUF, 1990).

3 Guy Desplanques and Michel de Saboulin, 'Première naissance et mariage de 1950 à nos jours', *Espace populations sociétés*, 2, 1986, pp. 47–56.
4 Florence Tamagne, *A History of Homosexuality in Europe: Berlin, London, Paris 1919–1939*, vols 1 and 2 combined (New York: Algora, 2006).
5 Clellan S. Ford and Frank A. Beach, *Patterns of Sexual Behavior* (New York: Harper, 1951), p. 41.
6 Jean-Claude Chesnais, 'La population des bacheliers en France: Estimation et projection jusqu'en 1995', *Population*, 30 (3), 1975, pp. 527–50.
7 See Desplanques and de Saboulin, 'Première naissance et mariage de 1950 à nos jours'.
8 Alfred Nizard, 'La population active selon les recensements depuis 1946', *Population*, 26 (1), 1971, pp. 9–61.
9 INSEE is the Institut national de la statistique et des études économiques, i.e. the (French) National Institute of Statistics and Economic Studies; it regularly publishes surveys on 'Emplois', i.e. the employment situation in France. (Translator's note.)
10 Milan Bouchet-Valat, 'Plus diplômées, moins célibataires: L'inversion de l'hypergamie féminine au fil des cohortes en France', *Population*, 70 (4), 2015, pp. 705–30.
11 These are all qualifications obtained in French secondary schools. (Translator's note.)
12 Christine R. Schwartz and Robert D. Mare, 'Trends in Assortative Mating from 1940 to 2003', *Demography*, 42 (4), 2005, pp. 621–46; Milan Bouchet-Valat, 'Les évolutions de l'homogamie de diplôme, de classe et d'origine sociales en France (1969–2011): Ouverture d'ensemble et repli des élites', *Revue française de sociologie*, 55 (3), 2014, pp. 459–505; Milan Bouchet-Valat, 'Hypergamie et célibat selon le statut social en France depuis 1969: Une convergence entre femmes et hommes?', *Revue de l'OFCE*, no. 160, 2018, pp. 6–44.
13 This is roughly equivalent to a master's degree in the UK or the US: it means a degree obtained five years after the baccalaureate, which is usually taken at age 18 or so. (Translator's note.)
14 Wilfried Rault and Arnaud Régnier-Loilier, *Étude des parcours individuels et conjugaux* (Épic), 2013–2014, Ined.
15 Marie-Carmen Garcia, *Amours clandestines: Sociologie de l'extraconjugalité durable* (Lyon: Presses universitaires de Lyon, 2016).
16 Sara McLanahan 'Diverging Destinies: How Children Are Faring under the Second Demographic Transition', *Demography*, 41 (4), 2004, pp. 607–27.
17 Young-hwan Byun, 'Middle-Class Single Parents', in Rense Nieuwenhuis and Laurie C. Maldonado (eds.), *The Triple Bind of Single-Parent Families* (Bristol: Policy Press, 2018).
18 Robert D. Putnam and David E. Campbell, *American Grace* (New York: Simon and Schuster, 2012), p. 105.
19 Anne Case and Angus Deaton, *Deaths of Despair and the Future of Capitalism* (Princeton, NJ: Princeton University Press, 2020).
20 Ibid., p. 66.
21 Todd, *Les luttes de classes en France au XXIème siècle*.
22 Gary Becker, *A Treatise on the Family* (Cambridge, MA: Harvard University Press, 1981).
23 Marc Collet and Émilie Pénicaud, 'En 40 ans, la mobilité sociale des femmes

a progressé, celle des hommes est restée quasi stable', *INSEE Première*, no. 1739, February 2019.

24 Émile Durkheim, *Suicide: A Study in Sociology*, translated by John A. Spaulding and George Simpson, edited by George Simpson (London: Routledge, 2002), p. 214.

25 Todd, *Les Luttes de classes en France au XXIe siècle*, pp. 141–7.

26 Personal communication. See also Thierry Jobard, *Contre le développement personnel* (Paris: Rue de l'Échiquier, 2021).

Notes to Chapter 10

1 Vanessa Di Paola, Arnaud Dupray, Dominique Epiphane and Stéphanie Moullet, 'Accès des femmes et des hommes aux positions de cadres en début de vie active: Une convergence en marche?', *INSEE Références*, 2017, pp. 31–47.

2 *Le Quotidien du médecin*, 25 November 2017.

3 UNESCO, 'Women in Science', *Fact sheet*, no. 43, March 2017.

4 French Ministry of Higher Education and Research, 'Égalité entre les femmes et les hommes: Les chiffres clés de la parité dans l'enseignement supérieur et la recherche.'

5 Thomas Piketty, *Capital in the Twenty-First Century*, translated by Arthur Goldhammer (Cambridge, MA: Harvard University Press, 2014).

6 A *normalien* is a graduate of the elite École normale supérieure, which has traditionally supplied France with many of its high-school and university teachers. (Translator's note.)

7 See Olivier Bouchara, 'Qui est Françoise Bettencourt-Meyers, la nouvelle femme la plus riche du monde?', capital.fr, 24 September 2011.

8 See his page on French Wikipedia.

9 These are both highly selective *grandes écoles* with a general bent towards the sciences and the more technological aspects of business and government; the École centrale (now CentraleSupélec, part of the University of Paris-Saclay) tended to produce high-flying engineers and entrepreneurs, while the École polytechnique, traditionally more prestigious, has produced a wide range of technocrats, civil servants and politicians. (Translator's note.)

10 Although there is considerable overlap, the former school has tended to focus on the humanities, the latter on science and technology. (Translator's note.)

11 Louis Chauvel, *La Spirale du déclassement: Essai sur la société des illusions* (Paris: Seuil, 2016), p. 117.

12 Piketty, *Capital in the Twenty-First Century*, p. 287.

13 Carole Bonnet, Bertrand Garbinti and Anne Solaz, 'Les conditions de vie des enfants après le divorce', *INSEE Première*, no. 1536, February 2015.

14 Élisabeth Algava, Sandrine Penant and Leslie Yarikan, 'En 2016, 400,000 enfants alternent entre les deux domiciles de leurs parents séparés', *INSEE Première*, no. 1728, January 2019.

15 The Heckscher–Ohlin theorem, a strong point in the theory of international trade, tells us that, in a situation of openness to trade, the relatively scarcest factor of production will be disadvantaged in a given country, and the abundant factor will be favoured. In Western countries, the young are the

scarce factor and the old the abundant factor. The binary opposition between young and old here overlaps with that of labour and capital.

16 Lionel Tiger, *Men in Groups* (New York: Random House, 1969).

17 Since the book dates from 1969, a time when, on the surface at least, male domination did not seem to be really threatened, and since the evolution of American society seemed to have proved him wrong, thirty years later, in 1999, Tiger published another book, *The Decline of Males* (New York: St. Martin's Press, 1999), which seems to correct the previous one. We can of course salute Tiger's ability, not so widespread among researchers, to admit his mistakes. But while *Men in Groups*, whether true or false, is a good, focused book, *The Decline of Males* is neither.

18 Nadine Cattan and Stéphane Leroy, *Atlas mondial des sexualités: Liberté, plaisirs et interdits* (Paris: Autrement, 2016), pp. 82–7.

19 The Marais district in Paris, on the right bank of the Seine, was from at least the 1980s known as an area popular with gay men. (Translator's note.)

20 The ENA was the École nationale d'administration, an elite training school for French bureaucrats and politicians. Since the beginning of 2022 it has been replaced by the Institut national du service public. (Translator's note.)

21 On this point, see my *Les Luttes de classes en France au XXIe siècle*, pp. 344–6.

22 Ibid., pp. 134–7.

23 Agata Zielinski, 'L'éthique du *care*: Une nouvelle façon de prendre soin', *Études*, 2010/12, vol. 413. I quote: 'The notion of care emerged in the public arena in France following a statement made by Martine Aubry [leader of the French Socialist Party, 2008–12]: "We have to move from an individualistic society to a society of 'care', according to the English word that we could translate as '*le soin mutuel*' (mutual care)." This statement was immediately followed by a very French controversy, but we can nevertheless hope that a debate will emerge from it. Care may seem like a new idea in Europe, but the philosophy or philosophies of care already have a rich history in the Anglo-Saxon world, particularly in the United States. France is not to be outdone: here, an increasing number of studies are fostering the encounter between philosophy, sociology and medicine. If the English term "care" is not always translated into French, this is because its semantic richness is not exhausted by a single French equivalent: to take care, to pay attention, to show solicitude ... Between care and solicitude, the notion of care invites reflection on its mode of acquisition. Where does caring come from? Where does the ability to care about others come from? And the behaviour that consists in acting to meet the expectations of the latter?'

Notes to Chapter 11

1 Pierre Rosanvallon, *Le Sacre du citoyen* (Paris: Gallimard, 'Folio', 2001; first edn, 1992), pp. 522–3.

2 But on the basis of an inadequate description of the middle and upper classes, which led me to describe matridominated intermediary classes and a CPIS [*Cadres et professions intellectuelles supérieures*, i.e. executives and higher intellectual professions] petty bourgeoisie that was still somewhat patridominated. I admit that I am here shifting my standpoint somewhat;

I now distinguish between patridominated upper middle classes and a matri-dominated petty bourgeoisie.

3 See note 2.

4 Todd, *Les Luttes de classes en France au XXIe siècle*, pp. 260–4.

5 Managed by the Agence bibliographique de l'enseignement supérieur (ABES), it can be accessed online at https://theses.fr/.

6 Data downloaded on 25 March 2021.

7 Data downloaded on 25 March 2021. Available online at https://www.insee.fr/fr/statistiques/2540004?sommaire=4767262.

8 The procedure is successful for about 92% of doctoral students. The remaining 8%, whose first name was not found in the First Names File, are by definition people whose first name is not (or is very rarely) given to children born in France. In other words, they are in the overwhelming majority of cases born abroad and it doesn't seem problematic to work on the remaining 92%.

9 It suffices for any arbitrarily defined group to sum the probabilities for each member of being a woman or a man. Thus, since the Alices are 99.98% women and the Bernards are 0.01% women, we estimate that the proportion of women in a group of two Alices and one Bernard is $(99.98 \times 2 + 0.01 \times 1)/3 = 66.66\%$. The disciplines listed in theses.fr are sometimes vast ('Mathematics'), sometimes narrower ('Political Psychology'). We group disciplines on the basis of the presence of character sequences: thus 'math' identifies mathematics (thus grouping together 'Pure mathematics', 'Mathematics and mathematical interactions', etc.), 'socio' or 'social' identifies sociology, etc.

10 For this analysis, doctoral students whose probability of being a woman is greater than 50% are considered to be women, which may lead to some classification errors. These errors could only lead to a slight underestimation of the effect of sex on the variables studied (mention of gender, etc.).

11 Aurélie Djavadi, 'Les journalistes en France en 2018: Moins nombreux, plus de femmes et plus précaires', *The Conversation*, 15 March 2018.

12 Available at: https://www.oecd.org/social/society-at-a-glance-19991290.htm.

13 INED is the Institut national d'études démographiques (the National Institute for Demographic Studies). (Translator's note.)

14 Graduates of the École polytechnique (see above, chap. 10, n. 9). (Translator's note.)

15 Elizabeth Brown, Alice Debauche, Christelle Hamel and Magali Mazuy (eds.), 'Violences et rapports de genre: Enquête sur les violences de genre en France', Ined, 2021.

16 Cécile Charlap, *La Fabrique de la ménopause* (Paris: CNRS Éditions, 2019).

17 Maki Hirayama, 'Why and How Modern Contraceptive Methods Have Not Spread in Japan', *Meiji University Journal of Psycho-sociology*, 14, 2019, pp. 43–62.

18 'L'Âge de la puberté chez les garçons', Ined, 2020.

19 Priscille Touraille, *Hommes grands, femmes petites: Une évolution coûteuse* (Paris: Éditions de la Maison des sciences de l'homme, 2008).

Notes to Chapter 12

1 Tim Malloy and Doug Schwartz, '68% Say Discrimination against Black Americans a "Serious Problem"', Quinnipiac University, 17 June 2020.
2 'Immigration: Le regard des Francais', IFOP, poll conducted on 4 December 2018. (IFOP is the Institut français d'opinion publique, the French national institute for polling and marketing research (Translator's note).)
3 'Les Français et le COVID-19: Confiance dans le gouvernement et intention de se faire vacciner', IFOP for the *Journal du dimanche*, November 2020.
4 Ruth Lidz and Theodore Lidz, 'The Family Environment of Schizophrenic Patients', *American Journal of Psychiatry*, 106 (5), 1949, pp. 332–45; Suzanne Reichard and Carl Tillman, 'Patterns of Parent–Child Relationships in Schizophrenia', *Psychiatry*, 13 (2), 1950, pp. 247–57; J.C. Mark, 'Attitudes of Mothers of Male Schizophrenics toward Child Behavior', *Journal of Abnormal and Social Psychology*, 48 (2), 1953, pp. 185–9; C.W. Wahl, 'Some Antecedent Factors in the Family Histories of 568 Male Schizophrenics of the United States Navy', *American Journal of Psychiatry*, 113, 1956, pp. 201–10; Melvin Kohn and John Clausen, 'Parental Authority Behavior and Schizophrenia', *American Journal of Orthopsychiatry*, 26 (2), 1956, pp. 297–313.
5 Geoffrey Gorer, *The American People: A Study in National Character* (New York: Norton, 1948; revised edn, 1964).
6 See Claudia Goldin and Lawrence F. Katz, *The Race between Education and Technology* (Cambridge, MA: Belknap Press of Harvard University Press, 2008). The figure on p. 231 shows women getting ahead in secondary education from 1910 to 1950.
7 Erich Fromm, 'The Oedipus Complex: Comments on the Case of Little Hans', in *The Crisis of Psychoanalysis: Essays on Freud, Marx and Social Psychology* (London: Jonathan Cape, 1971), pp. 88–99, especially p. 92.
8 Todd, *The Explanation of Ideology*.
9 David Gaunt, 'Pre-industrial Economy and Population Structure: The Elements of Variance in Early Modern Sweden', *Scandinavian Journal of History*, 2 (1–4), 1977, pp. 183–210, especially p. 98.
10 See Christer Lundh, Emiko Ochiai and Yoshiro Ono, 'Institutional Arrangements and Demographic Behavior in Japan and Sweden 1650–1900: A Life-Event Approach to Household Composition and Family Lines in Comparative Perspective', Chicago: EurAsian Project on Population and Family History, November 1995.
11 Janken Myrdal and Mats Morell (eds.), *The Agrarian History of Sweden* (Lund: Nordic Academic Press, 2011), p. 143.
12 Gaunt, 'Pre-industrial Economy and Population Structure', p. 202.
13 Jonas Lindström, *Distribution and Differences: Stratification and the System of Reproduction in a Swedish Peasant Community 1620–1820* (Uppsala: Uppsala Universitet, 'Studia Historica Upsaliensia', no. 235, 2008, p. 146).
14 Mark Magnuson, 'Regional Variations in Farming Household Structure for the Swedish Elderly, 1890–1908', *Journal of Family History*, 41 (4), 2016, pp. 378–401, maps on p. 394.
15 Lindström, *Distribution and Differences*, p. 146.
16 Todd, *L'Origine des systèmes familiaux*, pp. 394–6.

17 John F. Embree, 'Thailand – A Loosely Structured Social System', *American Anthropologist*, 52 (2), 1950, pp. 181–93.

18 Philippe Carrer, *Le matriarcat psychologique des bretons* (Paris: Payot, 1983); Agnès Audibert, *Le matriarcat breton* (Paris: PUF, 1984).

19 *Infostat* Justice, no. 161, April 2018.

20 The *Gilets jaunes* protesters wore hi-visibility yellow vests to show their solidarity with industrial workers and others. They were demonstrating their opposition to the fuel tax increases which President Macron sought to introduce, as well as to many other policies pursued by his government that they felt were socially unjust. Police repression was harsh. (Translator's note.)

Notes to Chapter 13

1 See also Gøsta Esping-Andersen, *The Incomplete Revolution: Adapting to Women's New Roles* (Cambridge: Polity, 2009).

2 Janken Myrdal, 'Farming and Feudalism, 1000–1700', in Janken Myrdal and Mats Morell (eds.), *Agrarian History of Sweden*, pp. 72–117, especially p. 115.

3 Whether this was an original matriarchy or one associated with primitive agriculture is of little importance for our purpose. Let's just say: very long ago.

4 Gimbutas, *The Goddesses and Gods of Old Europe*.

5 Original French version: Émile Benveniste, *Vocabulaire des institutions indo-européennes* (Paris: Éditions de Minuit, 1969); English version, *Dictionary of Indo-European Concepts and Society*, translated by Elizabeth Palmer (Chicago, IL: Hau Books, 2016).

6 David W. Anthony, 'Nazi and Eco-feminist Prehistories: Ideology and Empiricism in Indo-European Archaeology', in Philip L. Kohl and Clare Fawcett, *Nationalism, Politics and the Practice of Archaeology* (Cambridge: Cambridge University Press, 1995), pp. 82–96; David W. Anthony, *The Horse, the Wheel and Language: How Bronze-Age Riders from the Steppes Shaped the Modern World* (Princeton, NJ: Princeton University Press, 2007), p. 329. The author notes that among the Scythians and the Sarmatians, and among the Yamnaya 2,000 years earlier, 20% of the women were dressed as warriors in the tombs; Philip L. Kohl, *The Making of Bronze Age Eurasia* (Cambridge: Cambridge University Press, 2007).

7 Bentley et al., 'Community Differentiation and Kinship among Europe's First Farmers'; Bickle and Whittle (eds.), *The First Farmers of Central Europe*.

8 Stig Welinder, 'Early Farming Households, 3900–800 BC', in Myrdal and Morell (eds.), *The Agrarian History of Sweden*, pp. 18–45, especially p. 21. See also the excellent synthesis by T. Douglas Price, *Ancient Scandinavia: An Archaeological History from the First Humans to the Vikings* (Oxford: Oxford University Press, 2015).

9 Price, *Ancient Scandinavia*.

10 The estimate I use is for Danish women. See Price, *Ancient Scandinavia*, p. 353.

11 Charlotte Hedenstierna-Jonson and Anna Kjellström, 'A Female Viking Warrior Confirmed by Genomics', *American Journal of Physical Anthropology*, 164 (4), 2017, pp. 853–60.

NOTES TO PP. 215–19

12 In actual fact, the case of this burial is still controversial in a region where signs of 'cosmopolitanism' are frequently found (as we know, the Vikings travelled quite a bit), and the individual in question may possibly be of foreign origin.

13 Lotta Fernstal, 'Female Boat Graves in Sweden: Aspects of Elite and Cosmopolitanism during the Late Iron Age', in Dieter Quast (ed.), Weibliche Eliten in der Frühgeschichte (Mainz: Verlag des Römisch-Germanischen Zentralmuseums, 2011), pp. 111–19.

14 Margrethe Watt, 'Images of the Female Elite? Gold Foil Figures Guldgubbar from the 6th and 7th Century Scandinavia', in ibid., pp. 229–50.

15 This was an alphabet inspired by, but absolutely distinct from, the Latin alphabet.

16 Birgit Sawyer, The Viking-Age Rune-Stones: Custom and Commemoration in Early Medieval Scandinavia (Oxford: Oxford University Press, 2000), relationship chart p. 169, appendix 3.

17 See, for example, Snorri Sturluson, Egil's Saga, translated by Bernard Scudder (Harmondsworth: Penguin Classics, 1976) and King Harald's Saga, translated by Magnus Magnusson and Hermann Pálsson (Harmondsworth: Penguin Classics, 1966), as well as the Laxdaela Saga, translated by Magnus Magnusson and Hermann Pálsson (Harmondsworth: Penguin Classics, 1969).

18 French Islamophobes apparently take the Qur'an more seriously than do Muslims when they denounce Qur'anic law as incompatible with French republican law. Muslim practice always gives precedence to the civil law of the country in which Muslims live.

19 Maria Ågren, Domestic Secrets: Women and Property in Sweden, 1600–1857 (Chapel Hill, NC: University of Carolina Press, 2009).

20 Lindström, Distribution and Difference, p. 151.

21 Ibid., pp. 161–2.

22 Egil Johansson, 'The History of Literacy in Sweden', in Harvey J. Graff, Alison Mackinnon, Bengt Sandin and Ian Winchester (eds.), Understanding Literacy in Its Historical Contexts: Socio-cultural History and the Legacy of Egil Johansson (Lund: Nordic Academic Press, 2009), pp. 28–59, especially p. 49.

23 Ian Winchester, 'The Role of Literacy from the Vikings to the Seventeenth Century', in ibid., pp. 120–3.

24 Ingrid Markussen, 'The Development of Writing Ability in the Nordic Countries in the Eighteenth and Nineteenth Centuries', Scandinavian Journal of History, 15 (1–2), 2008, pp. 37–63.

25 Ågren, Domestic Secrets, p. 23.

26 This interpretation in terms of dissociative negative acculturation may possibly be applicable to several of the far western European cultures mentioned in the previous chapter which present an authoritarian feminine deviation: Brittany and Ireland remained Catholic – to put it mildly! – but the Bretons had to face the intrusion of the nobility and maritime trade, and the Irish had to face the Protestant British conquest, which in both cases brought stem and/or patrilineal values. Their 'matriarchies' could also be dissociative negative acculturation reactions. Stem family forms tend, in both cases, to be geographically located on the coasts. The case of Poher, that inshore region of the Breton peninsula which presented a strong rural communist vote and

303

highly original matrilocal forms of fluid primogeniture, demonstrates that this family form is not an ancient characteristic. Indeed, when we go back further in Breton history, as shown by Vincent Prudor's outstanding work on the seventeenth century, we can see that, in the seventeenth century, this central part of Brittany was bilocal and in no way matrilocal. See Vincent Prudor, *Structure et organisation de la propriété foncière de la paroisse de Duault d'après la réformation du terrier royal de Bretagne (1678–1685)*, a dissertation directed by Albane Cogné (2013), and *Les Familles de Duault selon le recensement de 1856* (personal communication). For the nineteenth century, see also Éric Le Penven, 'La Famille étendue en Basse-Bretagne, Plounévez-Quintin au XIXe siècle' (unpublished). Matrilocality thus emerged between the seventeenth and the middle of the nineteenth century. In Ireland, no one has ever spoken of matrilocality and what exists in terms of inheritance tends to suggest a preference for sons.

27 Jan Lindegren, *Utskrivning och utsugning: Produktion och reproduktion i Bygdeå, 1620–1640* (Stockholm-Uppsala: Almqvist and Wiksell, Acta Universitatis Upsaliensis. Studia Historica Upsaliensia, 1980).

28 Paul Douglas Lockhart, *Sweden in the Seventeenth Century* (Basingstoke: Palgrave Macmillan, 2004), p. 84.

29 Tina Askanius and Jannie Møller Hartley, 'Framing Gender Justice: A Comparative Analysis of the Media Coverage of #Metoo [sic] in Denmark and Sweden', *Nordicom Review*, 40 (2), March 2019, pp. 19–36. I would like to thank Pierre Salvadori, a specialist in sixteenth- and seventeenth-century Scandinavia, for bringing this article to my attention.

30 Ibid., p. 20.

31 Ibid.

32 Ibid., p. 31.

33 Todd, *L'Invention de l'Europe*, pp. 286–94 for Sweden, pp. 409–20 for Denmark.

Notes to Chapter 14

1 Guy Hocquenghem, *Homosexual Desire*, translated by Daniella Dangoor (Durham, NC: Duke University Press, 1993); first published in French as *Le désir homosexual* (Paris: PUF, 1972).

2 Peter Gluckman, Alan Beedle and Mark Hanson, *Principles of Evolutionary Medicine* (Oxford: Oxford University Press, 2009), p. 159.

3 Edward Westermarck, *The Origin and Development of the Moral Ideas*, vols 1 and 2 (London: Macmillan & Co., 1906 and 1908). See, in this case, chap. 43, vol. 2.

4 Ford and Beach, *Patterns of Sexual Behavior*; see chap. 7, 'Homosexual Behaviour'.

5 In his definitive biography, *John Maynard Keynes, 1883–1946: Economist, Philosopher, Statesman* (London: McMillan, 2003), Robert Skidelsky indicates that Keynes married Lydia in 1925, whom he had been seeing since 1921 (see chap. 22, 'Gold and Marriage', pp. 339–63). But it was exactly during this period that he began to express heterodox opinions. As early as 1923, in his *Tract on Monetary Reform* (pp. 329–35), he considered that of the two evils of inflation and deflation, the worst was deflation. Then, in

1924, he distanced himself from economic laissez-faire. Finally, his articles, destined to become *The Economics of Mr Churchill*, which castigated the return to the gold standard, as this could only aggravate unemployment, appeared on 22, 23 and 24 July 1925, while his wedding took place on 4 August.

6 Ford and Beach, *Patterns of Sexual Behavior*, chap. 7, 'Homosexual Behavior'.
7 Ibid., p. 126.
8 Tamagne, *A History of Homosexuality in Europe*, p. 8.
9 Ford and Beach, *Patterns of Sexual Behavior*, chap. 7, 'Homosexual Behavior', p. 126.
10 Ibid.
11 Le Bras and Todd, *Le Mystère français*, p. 130.
12 Jérôme Fourquet and Emmanuel Todd, 'Les Français, le sexe et la politique', *Marianne*, 23–29 May 2014.
13 For all the figures, see Jacob Poushter and Nicholas Kent, 'The Global Divide on Homosexuality Persists', Pew Research Center, 25 June 2020.
14 Ibid.
15 Brian James Baer, *Other Russias: Homosexuality and the Crisis of Post-Soviet Identity* (Basingstoke: Palgrave Macmillan, 2009).
16 OECD, *Society at a Glance 2019: OECD Social Indicators*, chap. 1, 'The LGBT Challenge: How to Better Include Sexual and Gender Minorities?', p. 23. Available at: https://www.oecd-ilibrary.org/social-issues-migration-he alth/society-at-a-glance-2019_soc_glance-2019-en.
17 IFOP, 'Les Français et la perception de l'homosexualité', 15 December 2012.

Notes to Chapter 15

1 Poushter and Kent, 'The Global Divide on Homosexuality Persists'. All religions are combined. A coefficient of maximum correlation would be +1.
2 Brown, *The Body and Society*.
3 See Robert D. Putnam and David E. Campbell, *American Grace: How Religion Divides and Unites Us* (New York: Simon and Schuster, 2010), p. 74.
4 Le Bras and Todd, *Le Mystère français*.
5 Emmanuel Todd, *Who Is Charlie? Xenophobia and the New Middle Class*, translated by Andrew Brown (Cambridge: Polity Press, 2016); Todd, *Les Luttes de classes en France au XXIe siècle*.
6 Fourquet and Todd, 'Les Français, le sexe et la politique'.
7 See Le Bras and Todd, *Le Mystère français*, pp. 70–2.
8 On Thailand, see Peter A. Jackson, *Dear Uncle Go: Male Homosexuality in Thailand* (Bangkok: Bua Luang Books, 1995). On Japan, see Mark J. McLelland, *Male Homosexuality in Modern Japan: Cultural Myths and Social Realities* (Richmond: Routledge Curzon, 2000).
9 John Hajnal, 'European Marriage Patterns in Perspective', in David V. Glass and David E.C. Eversley (eds.), *Population in History: Essays in Historical Demography* (London: Edward Arnold, 1965), pp. 101–43.
10 Christelle Hamel and Wilfried Rault, 'Les inégalités de genre sous l'oeil des démographes', *Population et sociétés*, no. 517, December 2014.

11 Michael Pollack, *Les Homosexuels et le Sida: Sociologie d'une épidémie* (Paris: Métailié, 1988).

12 INSEE, 'Les mariages en 2017: En 2017, dans deux tiers des mariages entre personnes de sexe différent, la femme est plus jeune que son mari', *INSEE Focus*, no. 146, 2019, figure 1.

13 Oazi Rahman, Yin Xu, Richard A. Lippa and Paul L. Vasey, 'Prevalence of Sexual Orientation across 28 Nations and Its Association with Gender Equality, Economic Development and Individualism', *Archives of Sexual Behavior*, 49, 2020, pp. 595–606.

14 IFOP, 'To bi or not to bi? Enquête sur l'attirance sexuelle entre femmes', 1 February 2017.

15 Frank Newport, 'In US, Estimates of LGBT Population Rises to 4.5%', Gallup, 22 May 2018.

16 Ibid.

17 Office for National Statistics, *Sexual Orientation*, United Kingdom, 2018.

18 This study was conducted by Kristian Daneback and Sven-Axel Månsson at the University of Malmö.

19 Michael Castleman, 'The Continuing Controversy over Bisexuality', *Psychology Today*, 15 March 2016; Jeremy Jabbour, Luke Holmes, David Sylva, Kevin J. Hsu, Theodore L. Semon, A.M. Rosenthal, et al., 'Robust Evidence for Bisexual Orientation among Men', *PNAS*, 117 (31), 2020, pp. 18369–77.

20 Rob A.P. Tielman, Manuel Carballo and Aart C. Hendriks (eds.), *Bisexuality and HIV/AIDS* (Buffalo, NY: Prometheus Books, 1991).

Notes to Chapter 16

1 Eva-Luna Tholance, '"Two-spirit": Les autochtones canadiens décolonisent le genre', *Libération*, 1 March 2020. For *The Guardian*, see, for example, Walter L. Williams, 'The "Two-Spirit" People of Indigenous North Americans', *The Guardian*, 11 October 2010.

2 Charles Callender and Lee M. Kochems, 'The North American Berdache', *Current Anthropology*, 24 (4), 1983, pp. 443–70. See also, for a discussion mostly of concepts, Henry Angelino and Charles T. Shedd, 'A Note on Berdache', *American Anthropologist*, 57 (1), 1955, pp. 121–6.

3 I have established a correspondence between the list given by Callender and Kochems of the peoples where berdaches are found and the whole set of peoples in Murdock's *Atlas* to study the distribution of this trait in North America (map 16.1). The establishment of this correspondence required a thorough examination of the sources used by Callender and Kochems, mainly the 'Culture Element Distributions' published in the University of California Anthropological Records from 1937 onwards.

4 Waldemar Bogoras, 'The Chukchee', *Memoirs of the American Museum of Natural History*, 11, 1909, and 'The Chukchi of Northeastern Asia', *American Anthropologist*, 3 (1), 1901, pp. 80–108; Vladimir Jochelson, 'The Mythology of the Koryaks', *American Anthropologist*, 6, 1904, pp. 13–25.

5 Callender and Kochems, 'The North American Berdache', p. 446.

6 OECD, *Society at a Glance 2019*, figure 1.10, p. 27.

7 Andrea Long Chu, 'My New Vagina Won't Make Me Happy', *New York*

NOTES TO PP. 259–67

Times, 24 November 2018. Available at: https://www.nytimes.com/2018/11/24/opinion/sunday/vaginoplasty-transgender-medicine.html.

8 OECD, *Society at a Glance 2019. OECD Social Indicators.*

9 Ibid., p. 3.

10 Susan Stryker, *Transgender History: The Roots of Today's Revolution* (New York: Seal Press, 2008; revised edn, 2017).

11 Benjamin Cerf Harris, 'Likely Transgender Individuals in U.S. Federal Administrative Records and the 2010 Census', United Stated Census Bureau, May 2015. Harris counts between 43,547 and 89,667 name changes (depending on the requirement of probability) and among these, 11,028–14,338 reported sex changes. If we take the maximum total, 89,667, for 207 million people aged over 16, we get 4.4 per 10,000. I round this up to 5. The 'official' figure of 0.3% corresponds to 30 per 10,000, which is six times too many.

12 Cecilia Dhejne, Katarina Öberg, Stefan Arver and Mikael Landén, 'An Analysis of All Applications for Sex Reassignment Surgery in Sweden, 1960–2010: Prevalence, Incidence, and Regrets', *Archives of Sexual Behavior*, 43 (8), 2014, pp. 1535–45.

13 For the United States, see C.M.D. Lopez, S. Solomon, R.A. Boulware, D.E. Cowles, D.H. Ozgediz, M.G. Stitelman, et al., 'Trends in the Use of Puberty Blockers among Transgender Children in the United States', *Journal of Pediatric Endocrinology*, 31 (6), 2018, pp. 665–70.

14 Stryker, *Transgender History*, p. 153.

15 Butler, *Gender Trouble*.

16 Régis Debray, *Critique of Political Reason*, translated by David Macey (London: Verso and New Left Books, 1983). (This is an abridged version of the French original: *Critique de la raison politique ou l'inconscient religieux* (Paris: Gallimard, 1981). Translator's note.)

17 Marcel Gauchet, *The Disenchantment of the World: A Political History of Religion*, translated by Oscar Burge (Princeton, NJ: Princeton University Press, 1999).

18 Michel Houellebecq, *Submission*, translated by Lorin Stein (London: Vintage, 2015).

19 Hervé Le Bras and Emmanuel Todd, *L'Invention de la France: Atlas anthropologique et politique* (Paris: Gallimard, 1981; new edn, 2012).

20 See Diana Tourjée, 'How the Mothers of Transgender Children Are Changing the World', *Vice*, 23 August 2016.

21 Madison Aitken, Thomas D. Steensma, Ray Blanchard, Doug P. VanderLaan, Hayley Wood, Amanda Fuentes, et al., 'Evidence for an Altered Sex-Ratio in Clinic-Referred Adolescents with Gender Dysphoria', *Journal of Sexual Medicine*, 12 (3), 2015, pp. 756–63.

22 Émile Durkheim, *The Elementary Forms of Religious Life*, translated by Karen E. Fields (New York: The Free Press, 1995).

23 Brown, *The Body and Society*.

24 Gauchet, *The Disenchantment of the World*.

Notes to Chapter 17

1 David Cayla, *Populism and Neoliberalism* (London and New York: Routledge, 2021), p. 31.
2 Todd, *Lineages of Modernity*, p. 312.
3 Subsequently, regardless of the level of discipline and access to masks, respiratory machines and hospital beds, no one was safe from Covid – for example, Germany was soon as badly affected as other countries. But that is only to be expected. A certain type of social organization can resist colds and flu better at first. To my knowledge, no anthropological system can escape these ailments for all eternity.
4 The fall in Chinese fertility, contrary to popular belief, is not linked to the one-child policy. Moreover, since this one-child policy has been relaxed, fertility has not risen: it is still around 1.7 children per woman and seems to have fallen recently to 1.3. I write 'seems' because Chinese demographic data are not reliable.

Notes to Conclusion

1 Adrien Papuchon, 'Rôles sociaux des femmes et des hommes: L'idée persistante d'une vocation maternelle des femmes malgré le déclin de l'adhésion aux stéréotypes de genre', *INSEE Références*, 2017, pp. 81–96.
2 Mead, *Male and Female*.
3 IFOP note and quantitative data kindly provided by Jérôme Fourquet.

INDEX

Page numbers in *italics* refer to figures and tables.

abortion 12, 145, 146
  sex-selective 30, 34, 65
  US 153–6
Africa 72, 76–7, 87, 95, 112, 270
  see also Beijing–Baghdad–
    Ouagadougou (BBO) axis
age difference between spouses:
  hunter-gatherers 109, *111*, 112
ageing population 198
agriculture 88–98, 100–1, 112–13
  Sweden (1960) *204*
AIDS 39, 231–2, 243–4
ambilocality 80, *82*
Americas
  kinship systems and residence of
    spouses 116–17
  North American model of original
    family 9–10
  see also berdaches (North American
    Indians)
anger as general social phenomenon
  184–5
Anglo-American world and France
  179–82
anomie 184
  profession vs procreation 172
  risk of 157–9
  soft 159–64, 283
antagonistic feminism 2–3, 18–20
anxiety 265
  see also anomie
Arab family system 68, 69, 103,

  205–8
Australian Aborigines
  debate 108–12
  role of New Guinea 112–16
  vs North American model of
    original family 9–10
authority 196
  constructed and natural 210–12
  ideological anomalies and family
    types 200–1
  and masculine collective 198
  mother at centre of family 209–10
  paternal and maternal 206–9
  racism 196–8
  riddle of authoritarian feminism
    206
  Swedish family types 201–5
  and US Prohibition 198–200
avunculocality 80

Bachofen, Jakob 34–6, 214
Barry, Laurent 78
Becker, Gary 157
Beijing–Baghdad–Ouagadougou
  (BBO) axis 30, 32, 34, 76, 79,
  80
  cross-cousin marriages 86
  homophobia 232–5
Bem, Sandra 57
Benedict, Ruth 48
berdaches (North American Indians)
  9, 18, 118

berdaches (North American Indians)
(*cont.*)
  case of 250–5
  and transgender people, compared
    255–7, 265–6
Bernstein, Eduard 2–3, 5
bilateral kinship systems 29–30, 64,
  79, 86–7, 115, 116–17, 255
bilocality 255
  communitarian family 68–9
  temporary co-residence 62
Binford, Lewis R. 9
  database *89*, 109, *110*, *111*
birth control 12, 145, 181
  see also abortion; contraceptive
    pill
bisexuality
  female, rise of 245–7
  use of term 227–8
Black Americans 154, 155–6, 196–7
  and intersectionality 43–6, 185
  use of term 41
boat building: sexual division of
  labour *123*
Bouchet-Valat, Milan 149–50, 151,
  152, 170
Breitman, Z. 283
Brown, Peter 139–40, 267
Buddhism 50, 241, 242
  Tibetan 50, 63, 237
Butler, Judith 12, 40, 54, 260, 264

Callender, Charles and Kochems, Lee
  M. 251, 253
Calvin, Jean 137, 180, 237
cancel culture 212
care/mutual care 176, 177
Carsten, Janet 56–7, 70, 163
Catholicism
  Counter-Reformation 133
  France 179, 180, 181, 239–40
  Ireland 201
  and Protestantism, attitudes to
    homosexuality 237–9
  zombie 16, 239
Cattan, Nadine and Leroy, Stéphane
  174
Cayla, David 274, 276
Cerf-Harris, Benjamin 259–60
Charlap, Cécile 193

Chaunu, Pierre 237
child-birth/child-rearing
  economic rationality vs sentiment
    157
  maternal risk 136
  'natural' maternal authority
    210–11
  see also procreation
children
  custody following divorce 172–3
  gender dysphoria, UK 250, 260,
    264–5
chimpanzees 130
China 68, 98, 100, 104, 269
  see also Beijing–Baghdad–
    Ouagadougou (BBO) axis
Chollet, Mona 5–6
Christianity 132–4
  early 134–5
  premarital sex 145
  sexual security 135–6
  see also Catholicism; Protestantism
Christianity and homosexuality 237
  collapse of religious sentiment and
    homophobia 239–40
  Eastern Europe 242–3
  gays as zombie Christians 240–2
  Protestant vs Catholic attitudes
    237–9
  rise of female bisexuality 245–7
  same-sex couples/marriage 243–5
Christianity and transgender people
  266–7
citizenship phase of feminism 11–12
clans 98, 100
Clark, Colin 148
classical anthropology
  original family 71–4
  sexual equality in hunter-gatherer
    societies 51–2
collectivism *see* masculine collectivism
communism 200–1
  and homophobia 235
communitarian family 66–9
  Arab world 205–8
  and communism 200–1
confinement of women 68, 208
  nomads and history of family
    98–100
  patrilineal impasse 103–6

patrilineality and social
stratification 100–3
see also agriculture
conscious, subconscious and
unconscious layers of influence
15–17
conservatism of peripheral zones
(PCPZ) 74–7
constructed and natural authority
210–12
contraceptive pill 12, 145, 146, 172
birth control methods prior to 145,
181
and homosexuality, frequency of
use of terms 225, 226–7
cousin/cross-cousin marriages 68,
69–70, 80, 83–6, 103, 112
Crenshaw, Kimberlé 43

D-PLACE project 9, 29, 50, 78
Dahlerup, Drude 221
Darwin, Charles 72
Davis, Katherine 231
Debray, Régis 261
decomposition 56–7
deconstruction 39–40
degendering anthropology
classical and feminist perspectives
51–7
insufficiently feminist history 58–60
tribute to female anthropologists
48–51
Denmark and Sweden 215–16, 218,
220–2
Derrida, Jacques 40
Desplanques, Guy and de Saboulin,
Michel 144
Devereux, George 115, 219, 275
Di Paola, Vanessa et al. 167
Dick, Philip K. 44
dissociative negative acculturation
115, 219, 235, 275
divorce 172–3
doctorates 58, 186–9, *190*
Durkheim, Emile 158, 163, *265*

Eastern Europe
gay identity 242–3
workers nation of 273–5
economic crisis (1929) 16–17

economic globalization and
anthropological trajectories
268–9
cost of rejecting liberation 276–8
economic vs anthropological
specialization 270–3
Sweden 276
tertiarization of economy 269–70
worker nations of Eastern Europe
273–5
economic rationality vs sentiment 157
economics and anthropology 15–18
education
homosexuality 231–2
pro-life attitudes, US 155–6
secondary, US 199, 212
subconscious layer of influence 15
see also higher education;
hypergamy to hypogamy; literacy
egalitarianism, France 179–81, 183–4
Elkin, Adolphus Peter 108, 109
Ember, Carol 50
employment *see* economic
globalization and anthropological
trajectories; sexual division of
labour
ENA, France 175
endogamy and exogamy 83–6, 208
equality issue 51–2, 130–1
patrilineal principle and
Protestantism 137
Ethnographic Atlas 9, 27–32, 34, 52,
217
agriculture 91, 93–8
Australia and New Guinea 113–15
berdaches 251, *252*
homosexuality 229
sexual division of labour 118–26
structuralist approach to original
family 78–86
executive positions 166, 167, 174
and higher intellectual professions
182–3
and social mobility 158
extra-marital affairs 152

family structures
and Christianity 132–4
ideological anomalies 200–1
and patriarchy 26–7

family structures (*cont.*)
  unconscious layer of influence
    16–17
  see also kinship systems; original
    family; *specific structures*
father's role in procreation, rejection
  of 108, 115
Faure, Sonya 46
female bisexuality, rise of 245–7
female homicide 3, *4*
female homosexuality 230–1
  'lesbian', use of term 227–8
female infanticide *see* infanticide
feminism
  antagonistic 2–3, 18–20
  phases of 11–13, 195
  third-wave ideology vs research
    9–10
  see also degendering anthropology
fishing: sexual division of labour 119,
  122
Ford, Clellan S. and Beach, Frank A.
  144, 229, 230, 231
Fourastié, Jean 148
Freud, Sigmund 199
Fromm, Erich 138, 199

Garcia, Marie-Carmen 152
Garrisson-Estèbe, Janine 137
gathering
  sexual division of labour 119, *121*
  see also hunter-gatherer societies
Gauchet, Marcel 262, 267
Gaunt, David 202
'gay', frequency of use 226, 227–8
Geertz, Hildred 49
Gelber, Marilyn G. 55–6
gender
  emergence of concept of 36–40
  in research publications 192, 194
  and sex, in doctorate theses 188–9,
    190
  as useless and ideologized
    duplication 41–2
  see also degendering anthropology;
    intersectionality
generalized identity disorder 261,
  263–4
generalized intersectionality 42–6,
  150–2, 192, 281

Germany 64, 67–8, 76, 103
  and Eastern Europe 274, 275
  homosexuality 233
  Protestantism 137, 138, 139
  and Sweden 201, 218, 219, 220,
    276
  transgender peoples 255–6
gerontocracy 109, 198
Gimbutas, Marija 34–6, 214
Giuliano, Paola and Nunn, Nathan
  34
Global Gender Gap Report (2020)
  32, *33*, 42, 166, 272
Gorer, Geoffrey 199, 212
government ministers 166

Helm, June 49
Henry, G.W. 231
higher education 5
  decline in homophobia 239–40
  doctorates 58, 186–9, *190*
  and intersectionality 46–7
  matridominance (2000–2020)
    148–9
  profession vs procreation 172
  science and technology 168–9
  and sexual revolution (1965–2000)
    145–6
  tertiarization of economy 270
  top 4%: residual patridominance
    169–70
historical anthropology 6
  tools of 61–70
Hocquenghem, Guy 227
homicide, female 3, *4*
homosexuality and homophobia 223
  Anglo-American world vs France
    181
  and contraceptive pill, frequency of
    use of terms 225, 226–7
  female 230–1
  'gay', use of term 226, 227–8
  LGBT groups 191, 205, 224–5,
    246–7
  male 174, 235–6
  mapping: BBO axis 232–5
  natural human behaviour 228–32
  orders of magnitude and causal
    sequences 223–4
  and social class 144

see also Christianity and
homosexuality
Houellebecq, Michel 262
house building: sexual division of
labour 119, *125*
hunter-gatherer societies
and male collective 174, 175, 176
patriarchy 27
see also Australian Aborigines;
berdaches (North American
Indians); original family; sexual
division of labour
hunting: sexual division of labour
118–19, *120*, 127–8, 129
hypergamy to hypogamy 149–50,
151–2, 170, 171, 184

'identity' phase of feminism 12–13
ideological issues
authority 200–1
sexual division of labour 127–9
vs reality 127–8, 193–4
vs research 9–10
IFOP surveys 197–8, 281
homosexuality 232, 235–6, 240,
244, 246
immigration issue, France 197
industrial employment 270–2
Eastern Europe 273–5
and service sector/tertiarization
147–8, 269–70
Sweden 276
INED surveys 151, 192
infanticide 30
and abandoned newborns 69
and confinement of women 68
India 149
inheritance
capital vs income from labour 171
Sweden 201–2
see also primogeniture
INSEE surveys 148–9, 279–80
female executive positions 167
social mobility of women 157–8
socio-professional categories 182–3
intersectionality 185
French 46–7
generalized 42–6, 150–2, 192, 281
intimacy 70
Ireland: Catholicism 201

Islam
France 197
see also Arab family system

Japan 64, 65, 66, 76, 101–2, 193
homosexuality 233, 241–2
journalism 190–1
Judaism 56–7, 237–8
judicial system 211–12

Kaberry, Phyllis M. 49, 109–12, 129
Karve, Irawati 49
Keynes, John Maynard 230
kinship systems
Americas 116–17
Australia and New Guinea 113–16
before urbanization 27–9, 79
bilateral 29–30, 64, 79, 86–7, 115,
116–17, 255
Kirchhoff, Paul 58, 80
Komarovsky, Mirra 17
Korea 65
Kraus, François 246
Kroeber, Alfred 78, 101, 212

Laforgue, Philippe 21
Laslett, Peter 58–9, 66, 202
Latin America: homosexuality 233
Le Bras, Hervé and Todd, Emmanuel
262
Le Play, Frédéric 16, 27, 66, 72
leather work: sexual division of
labour *126*
'lesbian'
female homosexuality 230–1
use of term 227–8
Lévi-Strauss, Claude 72, 73, 78, 80
Levine, Nancy 50
LGBT groups 191, 205, 224–5, 246–7
see also bisexuality; Christianity
and homosexuality;
homosexuality and homophobia;
'lesbian'; transgender people
liberation 143
1950–1965: height of petty-
bourgeois conformism 143–5
1965–2000: educational and sexual
revolution 145–6
antagonism between (or abolition
of) sexes 18–20

liberation (*cont.*)
  cost of rejecting 276–8
  educational matridominance
    (2000–2020) 148–9
  hypergamy to hypogamy 149–50,
    151–2, 170, 171, 184
  middle class in survival mode 156–7
  poverty and single-parent families
    152–3
  service sector/tertiarization 147–8,
    269–70
  social class differences 150–2
  see also anomie
Lindegren, Jan 219
Lindström, Jonas 202
linear pottery culture (LBK) 91–2,
  101, 214–15
literacy 4–5, 138
  17th and 18th centuries, Sweden
    218–20
local group and marriage 69–70
Löfgren, Orvar 65, 201–2
Long Chu, Andrea 257–8
Lowie, Robert H. 72
Lundh, Christer 202
Luther, Martin/Lutheranism 137, 138,
  180, 199, 219, 237

McLanahan, Sara 153
McLelland, Mark J. 241
Magnuson, Mark 202
Mair, Lucy 49
Malinowski, Bronisław 109
Man the Hunter (collective work) 50
marriage 69–70
  age difference between spouses 109,
    111, 112
  Christianity 134–5
    and other religions 63
    Protestant Reformation 137–9
  hypergamy to hypogamy 149–50,
    151–2, 170, 171, 184
  residence of spouses after *81*, *82*
  same-sex 243–5
Marx/Marxists 2, 128, 185, 193
masculine collectivism
  disintegration/weakening of 173–7,
    198
  hunter-gatherer societies 174, 175,
    176

  vs female individualism 129–30,
    176, 268–9
masculine investment in work 172–3
masculine violence 3, 26, 53, 192
  matrilineal/matrilocal societies 101
  warfare 219–20, 253
mathematics 168–9
Mathiot, Cédric 3
matriarchy 34–6
  myth of 214–15
matridominance
  agriculture 93–5
  higher education (2000–2020)
    148–9
  OECD and INED 190–2
  and persistent patridominance 194
matrilineality 29–30, 79, 101, 105–6,
  113–15
matrilocality
  communitarian family 68–9
  and matrilineality 101, 105–6
  and patrilocality *see* patrilocality
  stem family 66
Mead, Margaret 49, 172, 199, 280,
  282–3, 284
medical profession 168
'menopause' 193
#MeToo movement 220–2
Middle East *see* Arab family system;
  Beijing–Baghdad–Ouagadougou
  (BBO) axis
Milton, John 139
monogamy 7, 8
Moore, Henrietta 54–5
mothers
  at centre of family 209–10
  and transgender identity 264–5
Murdock, George Peter 9, 27, 72
  see also Ethnographic Atlas

Nakane, Chie 49, 66
natural and constructed authority
  210–12
neoliberalism 38–9, 130, 175–6, 177
neolocality 80, *82*
Neuwirth law 12, 146
new geography of world 86–7
New Guinea 55–6, 91, 112–16
nihilism and generalized identity
  disorder 263

Nizan, Paul and Henriette 227
nomads 98–100
nuclear family
  and Christianity 132–3
  types of 61–3, 83, *84*, 132
  see also original family

OECD
  higher education 5
  and labour force participation
    270
  homosexuality 235, 246
  journalism and politics 190–1
  transgender/LGBT groups 191, 256,
    258–9
original family 7–8, 9–10, 71
  block in anthropology 74
  classical anthropology and 71–4
  conservatism of peripheral zones
    74–7
  critique of Murdock's structuralism
    (*Ethnographic Atlas*) 78–86
  new geography of world 86–7
Ozment, Steven 137

patriarchy, fog of 25–36
patridominance
  persistent 194
  residual 169–70
patrilineality 34, *35*
  confinement of women 103–6
  higher education and fertility
    277–8
  and matrilineality 29–30, 79,
    113–16
  and Protestantism 137, 138, 199
  and social stratification 100–3
  stages of 77
  see also communitarian family;
    stem family
patrilocality 98–100
  and matrilocality 80, 90, 91–2,
    93–8, 100–1, 113–16
  Sweden 217–18
  and virilocality 83, 87
Pew Research Center, US 153–5
Piketty, Thomas 169, 171
political male dominance 8, 53–4
politicians 191
polygyny 77, 83, *110*, 112

Australian Aborigines 109, 112
  and polyandry 8, 50, 51, 52, 63
population density and patrilocality/
    patrilinearity 101
pottery
  linear pottery culture (LBK) 91–2,
    101, 214–15
  sexual division of labour *124*, 128
poverty
  family disorganization and pro-life
    attitudes, US 153–6
  single-parent families 152–3, 154
power *see* authority; status of women
Power, Eileen 137–8, 238
premarital sex/conception 144–5, 146
primogeniture 50, 63, 66, 103
  and ultimogeniture 64–5, 66
'Principle of the Equivalence of
    Opposites' (PEO) 240–1
procreation
  choice 172, 283
  higher education and fertility in
    patrilineal countries 277–8
  rejection of role of father 108, 115
  roles of parents 53
  same-sex couples 244–5
  see also child-birth/child-rearing
Protestantism 180
  and Catholicism, attitudes to
    homosexuality 237–9
  patricentrism 10, 136–40, 181
  Reformation 133–4, 137–8
  zombie 16, 137, 243, 258
psychoanalytic perspective 199–200
public and private sector executive
    positions 166, 167, 174
pure nuclear family 61–2
  and tempered nuclear family 75,
    132

racism 196–7
religion
  collapse of religious identity
    239–40, 262–3, 265–7
  and family 10
  and homophobia 236
  and marriage 63
  subconscious and unconscious
    layers of influence 15–16
  see also specific religions

reproductive roles *see* child-birth/
  child-rearing; procreation
research vs ideology 9–10
Richards, Audrey 49
risk
  male and female 135–6
  premarital sex 145
Rosanvallon, Pierre 181
Rosin, Hanna 17–18
Rowlands, Alison 59
Russia 32, 67–8, 269
  homophobia 235
  and Sweden 214

same-sex couples/marriage 243–5
Sawyer, Birgit 216
Schwartz, Christine and Mare, Robert
  151
Schwartz, Oliver 17, 144
science and technology: sexual
  division of labour 168–9
service sector/tertiarization 147–8,
  269–70
sex ratio 30–2
  child gender dysphoria 264–5
  doctorates 187–8
  higher education 148–9
  INED 192
  sex-selective abortions 30, 34, 65
  suicide rates *161*
sex roles, traditional 57
sex/gender distinction 12–13, 41
sexual division of labour 8, 118–27
  berdaches 252–5
  collectivist men vs individualist
    women 129–30
  equality issue 130–1
  ideology against itself 128–9
  ideology vs reality 127–8
  mathematics 168–9
  medical profession 168
  persistent 166–7
  public and private sector 166, 167,
    174
  services and industry 147–8
sexuality
  male vs female needs 53, 243–4
  phase of feminism 12
single-parent families 152–3, 154
social class 17–18, 182–5, 280–1

1950–1965 143–5
1960s–1970s 146
child custody following divorce 173
liberation (1950–2020) 150–2
middle class in survival mode 156–7
sex-based social structure 171–2
see also poverty
social constructionism 193–4
social democracy 201, *205*
social mobility 157–8
social stratification and patrilineality
  100–3
society, influence on transgender
  identity 265–6
sociology theses 188–9, *190*
sodomy/anal penetration 230, 237–9,
  240
soft anomie 159–64, 283
Stark, Rodney 135–6
state
  and Christian Church 133, 134
  and complex social organization
    132
  public sector executive positions
    166, 167, 174
status of women, current 1–6, 10–15,
  33
stem family 63–6
  Protestant Reformation 137
  Sweden 65, 201–2, *203*, 205
Steward, Julian 51–2, 63, 109
Stone, Lawrence 138–9
strontium isotope analysis 90, 91–2
Stryker, Susan 260
suffrage movement 11–12
suicide 158–9, 160, 163
  sex-ratio and life expectancies
    161–2
Sweden 213–14
  14th to 21st century 213–14
  against myth of original matriarchy
    214–15
  birth of 'Swedish woman': literacy
    in 17th and 18th centuries
    218–20
  and Denmark 215–16, 218, 220–2
  family types 201–5
  female bisexuality 247
  industrial decline 276
  interpreting runic steles 216–17

316

peasant patrilocality from 17th to
    20th century 217–18
persistent sexual division of labour
    166–7
pre-Christian age 215–16
stem family 65, 201–2, *203*, 205

Tabet, Paola 128
Tamagne, Florence 144, 231
tempered nuclear family 62, 63, 80
    and pure nuclear family 75, 132
temporary co-residence 62, 63
tertiarization/service sector 147–8,
    269–70
Testart, Alain 108, 116, 127
Thailand
    family type and political ideology
        205
    homosexuality 233, 241–2
third sex, berdaches as 252, 253
Tibetan Buddhism 50, 63, 237
Tiger, Lionel 174
Tillion, Germaine 49
Todd, Dorothy 230
Todd, Nicolas 21
Todd, Oliver 227
tool manufacture: sexual division of
    labour 128
totemism/totemic groups 108, 115
Touraille, Priscille 194
Touverey, Baptiste 21
transgender people 248–50
    collapse of religious identity and
        262–3, 265–7
    ideological centrality 258–9
    omnipotence of mothers 264–5
    society thinking through individuals
        265–6
    statistical weakness 259–60
    transition 257–8
    use of term 228, 260, *261*
    women and identity 261–4
    see also berdaches (North American
        Indians)
Trevor-Roper, Hugh 59
'two-spirit' people 250–1
    see also berdaches (North American
        Indians)

ultimogeniture 64–5, 66
United Kingdom (UK)
    Gender Identity Development
        Service (GIDS) 250, 260,
        264–5
    LGBT identification 246–7
United States (US)
    collapse of religious sentiment
        and homophobia 239
    'gender', use of term 41
    historical matriarchism 214
    LGBT identification 246–7
    presidential election (2020) and
        intersectionality 45–6
    pro-life attitudes 153–6
    sexual behaviour (1950s)
        144–5
    transgender people 259–60
    see also Americas; berdaches
        (North American Indians);
        Black Americans
'unstable family' 72
uxorilocal marriage 62, 80

Veil law 12, 146
virilocality 62, 80
    and patrilocality 83, 87

Wall, Richard 66
warfare 219–20, 253
Westermarck, Edward 7, 8, 72, 73,
    74, 83, 229
Whyte, Martin King 52–4, 73, 100,
    243
Williams, John E, et al. 57
Willmott, Peter 17, 144
witch hunts 59, 139, 220
Wolf, Margery 49
World Health Organization (WHO):
    parent–child communication
    209–10

Young, Michael 17, 144

zombie Christians 240–2
    Catholic 16, 239
    Protestants 16, 137, 243, 258
Zwingli, Ulrich 137